Steve Endean
Vicki L. Eaklor, PhD, Editor

Bringing Lesbian
and Gay Rights
Into the Mainstream
Twenty Years of Progress

Pre-publication
REVIEWS,
COMMENTARIES,
EVALUATIONS . . .

"**F**or anyone who wants to understand where the gay civil rights movement is and where it is going, *Bringing Lesbian and Gay Rights Into the Mainstream* is an essential read. Steve Endean's memoir gives a detailed blow-by-blow description of the growing of this civil rights movement. It is filled with detailed descriptions of the exhilarating wins and heartbreaking losses that activists have faced over the past two decades in moving the gay rights agenda forward. Readers' only regret will be that they never got to meet Steve personally—a man who died well before his time but left a lasting legacy in the fight for fairness and equality for gay people."

Senator Cheryl A. Jacques
Former State Senator, Massachusetts;
Former President,
The Human Rights Campaign;
Fellow, Kennedy School of Government,
Harvard University

"**T**he GLBT community would not be the same if it were not for the work of Steve Endean. Steve wonderfully tells the story of his fight to bring our movement into the American cultural middle by teaching the rest of us how to lobby our government to change the archaic laws that existed in the early days of our movement.

Steve Endean's *Bringing Lesbian and Gay Rights Into the Mainstream* was written by him before his death. This is the story of a man who understood how politics work and what it took for the GLBT community to change the laws of this nation. He tells his stories of all of the early politicos in our community: good, bad, indifferent, and even hostile. He tells his story of his encounters with each of us while helping to change America."

Reverend Troy D. Perry
Founder and Moderator,
Metropoliotcan Community Churches

"Steve Endean's memoir of the extremely important role he played in the development of the gay and lesbian rights movement in America is both invaluable and poignant: poignant because it reminds those of us who had the privilege and pleasure of working with him of how great our loss was when he died far too young of AIDS; invaluable because this fight, in which we have made so much progress and still have a long way to go, has been inadequately chronicled, and a better understanding of our history to date is an important element in our formulation of a strategy to continue the work.

Steve Endean was an early proponent of what was once an inadequately appreciated strategy, namely that of using the political process in the United States as the main goal for fighting against discrimination based on sexual identification and gender identity. This resulted from both his intellectual understanding of how America works and his own personal predilection for politics—a happy combination. He also, of course, was one of the first to realize the importance of being honest about our sexuality. His unique contribution early in the movement was the importance of combining these insights. Steve was among the very first gay or lesbian leaders to come out and simultaneously engage with the political mainstream.

As his book demonstrates, he paid an unfairly heavy price for this, especially from those gay and lesbian leaders who mistakenly saw his commitment to the political fight as some sort of compromise with the goal of ending discrimination. What Steve Endean understood—and what he demonstrates in this history—is the importance of combining a zealous idealism with a hardheaded pragmatism if we are to make significant progress.

Much of what Steve worked for early on—and was then controversial—is now accepted within the gay and lesbian mainstream, but some people in the community have not yet reached the understanding that Steve had thirty years ago of the importance of using every aspect of the American political system to the fullest to achieve the equality we seek.

For this reason, *Bringing Lesbian and Gay Rights Into the Mainstream* is both a fascinating and much-needed contribution to the inadequate stock of gay and lesbian histories, and an extremely relevant document as we focus on what remains to be done."

Barney Frank
United States Representative,
4th Congressional District,
Massachusetts

More pre-publication
REVIEWS, COMMENTARIES, EVALUATIONS . . .

"This book is essential. We badly need to know all we can about the early development of what is now the GLBT civil rights movement, and Steve Endean was by all accounts a major player in that development. His political memoir provides unique insights into the politics of the time, both within the movement and without. Endean has done us a major favor by leaving this book for us to learn from, and Vicki Eaklor has done us a major favor by editing it for publication. Eaklor edits with a deft touch, adding essential information but allowing Endean's personality to show through. Endean was not afraid to point out the flaws of others, but neither did he try to hide his own.

The GLBT civil rights movement is remarkable for many reasons. One of the most important is the speed with which it transformed from its early, radical days in the Gay Liberation Front through the increasing respectability and professionalization of the National Gay (and Lesbian) Task Force and the Human Rights Campaign Fund. As the title suggests, Endean strove to promote both respectability and professionalization at HRCF and Gay Rights National Lobby, with con-

sequences that continue to shape the movement. He initiated the annual fund-raising dinners that continue as the controversial centerpiece of HRC's highly successful fund-raising machine. He lobbied astutely to win admission for lesbian/gay civil rights groups into the Leadership Conference on Civil Rights, thus ensuring almost automatically a level of credibility for lesbian/gay civil rights issues that they had lacked before.

Endean's life as a lobbyist and his struggles with David Goodstein, owner of *The Advocate* at the time, illustrate the conundrums that face many GLBT activists—'bringing . . . into the mainstream' suggests the liminal position of one who is at once respectable by dint of birth and disreputable by dint of sexual orientation. Endean's book, and Eaklor's editing, make required reading for anyone who wants to understand both the institutional and the personal politics of GLBT civil rights advocacy."

William B. Turner, PhD
Author, *A Genealogy of Queer Theory*
Co-editor, *Creating Change: Sexuality,*
Public Policy, and Civil Rights;

HPP

Harrington Park Press®
An Imprint of The Haworth Press, Inc.
New York • London • Oxford

Bringing Lesbian and Gay Rights Into the Mainstream
Twenty Years of Progress

HARRINGTON PARK PRESS®
Sexual Minorities in Historical Context
Vern L. Bullough, PhD, RN
Editor

Bringing Lesbian and Gay Rights Into the Mainstream: Twenty Years of Progress edited by Vicki L. Eaklor

Titles of Related Interest

Before Stonewall: Activists for Gay and Lesbian Rights in Historical Context edited by Vern L. Bullough

From Hate Crimes to Human Rights: A Tribute to Matthew Shepard edited by Mary E. Swigonski, Robin S. Mama, and Kelly Ward

Gay and Lesbian Rights Organizing: Community-Based Strategies edited by Yolanda C. Padilla

Gay Ethics: Controversies in Outing, Civil Rights, and Sexual Science edited by Timothy F. Murphy

Homosexuality and the Law edited by Donald C. Knutson

Sexual Minorities: Discrimination, Challenges, and Development in America edited by Michael K. Sullivan

Sexuality and Human Rights: A Global Overview edited by Phillip Tahmindjis and Helmut Graupner

Speaking for Our Lives: Historic Speeches and Rhetoric for Gay and Lesbian Rights (1892-2000) edited by Robert B. Ridinger

Bringing Lesbian and Gay Rights Into the Mainstream
Twenty Years of Progress

Steve Endean

Edited by
Vicki L. Eaklor, PhD

HPP

Harrington Park Press®
An Imprint of The Haworth Press, Inc.
New York • London • Oxford

For more information on this book or to order, visit
http://www.haworthpress.com/store/product.asp?sku=5207

or call 1-800-HAWORTH (800-429-6784) in the United States and Canada
or (607) 722-5857 outside the United States and Canada

or contact orders@HaworthPress.com

Published by

Harrington Park Press®, an imprint of The Haworth Press, Inc., 10 Alice Street, Binghamton, NY 13904-1580.

PUBLISHER'S NOTE
The development, preparation, and publication of this work has been undertaken with great care. However, the Publisher, employees, editors, and agents of The Haworth Press are not responsible for any errors contained herein or for consequences that may ensue from use of materials or information contained in this work. The Haworth Press is committed to the dissemination of ideas and information according to the highest standards of intellectual freedom and the free exchange of ideas. Statements made and opinions expressed in this publication do not necessarily reflect the views of the Publisher, Directors, management, or staff of The Haworth Press, Inc., or an endorsement by them.

Cover design by Kerry E. Mack.

Line drawing of Steve Endean on back cover by John Yanson.

Library of Congress Cataloging-in-Publication Data

Endean, Steve.
    Bringing lesbian and gay rights into the mainstream : twenty years of progress / Steve Endean ; edited by Vicki L. Eaklor.
        p. cm.
    Includes bibliographical references and index.
    ISBN-13: 978-1-56023-525-5 (hc. : alk. paper)
    ISBN-10: 1-56023-525-X (hc. : alk. paper)
    ISBN-13: 978-1-56023-526-2 (pbk. : alk. paper)
    ISBN-10: 1-56023-526-8 (pbk. : alk. paper)
    1. Gay liberation movement—United States. I. Eaklor, Vicki Lynn. II. Title.

HQ76.8.U5E53 2005
306.76'6'0973—dc22

2005015865

CONTENTS

To my parents, who taught me the values that have sustained me through these twenty-three years of full-time activism in the lesbian and gay community, and who particularly taught me the importance of fairness and persistence. Even in the earliest years, they practiced what they preached. Their constant love and support helped more than they could ever know.

And to the Good Lord, who has not only blessed me in more ways than I could possibly mention but who guided me through both the good and the bad times. And no acknowledgment of God's role in my life could be complete without personally acknowledging the Metropolitan Community Churches and most particularly my pastor, the Reverend Larry Urhig, and the Reverend Elder Troy D. Perry, the founder and moderator of the Universal Fellowship of Metropolitan Community Churches. Both are good friends who have patiently nurtured me along when the roads were bumpy and my faith failing.

Finally, to the Human Rights Campaign Fund, to the HRCF staff who worked for or with me, and particularly to the grassroots organizing staff who were like a family to me, along with a board of directors who often demonstrated a shared vision of bringing our movement into the mainstream. I'm particularly indebted to the two executive directors who came after my initial involvement, Vic Basile and Tim McFeeley, for taking a dream and continuing to build upon it. While I recognize I was sometimes tough to manage and often fought on behalf of our grassroots programs, they both led the organization with pride, integrity, and incredible dedication.

Steve Endean

Editor's Foreword

Fate has a funny way of bringing people together. Steve Endean and I were born only six years apart, both baby boomers turned GLBT* activists and both raised far from the coastal areas commonly considered "America." Apparently at least once we even were both at the same place at the same time, the 1993 March on Washington, but we never met. This is not that unusual in my profession of history, of course, since I never got to meet my subjects from the nineteenth century and earlier that so absorbed me before my professional and personal lives merged. However, reading and editing Steve's memoirs—I feel I now know him well enough to call him "Steve"— has been especially poignant, perhaps because this is all so recent. It is one thing to read archival documents of those long gone, but it has been quite another to decipher the word-processing files of a virtual contemporary. It has made me appreciate both him and historical work all the more.

My work on this book is the result of a series of fortunate events. I began research on the history of the Human Rights Campaign in the summer of 1999 and very soon discovered not only Steve Endean, but that he had completed a book manuscript before his death from AIDS in 1993. A few phone calls led me to the executor of his political papers, Bob Meek, and by December my partner and I were driving to Minnesota so I could meet Bob. Although I doubt I'll choose to experience Minnesota in December again (it was 54 below the night we arrived), Bob was and is among the most generous and kind people I've met; I left our conversation with a box of disks and a complete hard copy of the book.

Next was deciding how to proceed. If fate had brought me to Steve, and to Bob because of him, it was still smiling: Steve, like me, had been a Macintosh user, and I was eventually able to open all the files. (I'm old enough to have written my dissertation by hand, typing the final copy on a typewriter, but the thought of reorganizing and editing a 400-plus-page manuscript without those files available was enough to make me quit before I'd begun.) Here I discovered, even before a careful reading, how alike Steve and I were: he saved everything. Good for him, bad for me. Hard copy

---

*I use GLBT when speaking with my own voice and referring to contemporary times, but use "gay and lesbian" when referring to the 1970s and 1980s and/or Endean's concepts, in an effort to be historically accurate.

by my side, I began the project of sorting out not only the most recent version of each chapter but, when there were discrepancies with the hard copy, determining which was the "best." Then the real task of the editor was before me.

As any editor will understand, Steve's wishes and Steve's "voice" were always my primary considerations. At the same time, I had to face that an author isn't always the best judge of his own work. For example, he stated in his original Introduction that *Bringing Gay and Lesbian Rights Into the Mainstream* is neither an "autobiography" nor a "how-to" book. In many ways it is both, though, and in fact is a masterful interweaving of the two forms. Perhaps "political memoirs" with "reflections" on what was done better captures what he was after.

It was not genre but organization that provided the greatest challenge. Upon the third reading or so, I finally had to admit that this would be no cursory spell-and-grammar-check project, but a fundamental rethinking of the book and its potential audience. As Steve put it in his original Introduction, his twenty-two chapters, ranging in length from five to fifty-seven pages, were organized "by broad subject or aspects of an effective lobbying campaign, rather than a chronological timeline"; a plan adopted, he admitted, "despite the recommendations of friends." His friends were right, I'm afraid. Despite the time line he provided, the book as he wrote it seemed written for friends, or at least for those well acquainted with the people and issues of the political world in Minnesota and Washington, DC, in the twenty-plus years prior to his death. My task, as I saw it, was to make a fascinating story accessible to those not already "in the know" by creating more of a chronological narrative and eliminating a great deal of repetition.

To do this, I reorganized the information into two sections. In *Part I: The Roller Coaster* material was adapted from throughout the book to construct a more-or-less chronological narrative of his political career. It begins with his activities in Minnesota and takes us, in Chapter 2, through the state level to his arrival in Washington, DC, in 1978 to become executive director of the Gay Rights National Lobby, an important organization too often overlooked in movement history. Chapter 3, "Money Talks," traces the founding and early years of the Human Rights Campaign (Fund), while the following chapter recounts his painful removal from both HRC(F) and GRNL by the end of 1983. The two concluding chapters of Part I recount his return to HRC(F) as he built a remarkable initiative for constituent pressure (using mailgrams in those pre-e-mail days), Speak Out. By the mid-1980s all three components of what Steve envisioned as necessary to the effective mainstreaming of gay and lesbian rights on the national level—a lobby, a PAC, and grassroots organizing—were in place.

Part II: Reflections of an Old, Tired Activist is just that: his commentary on such issues as ways to mount successful lobbying and hearing efforts, mistakes he and others made along the way, and some elaboration on topics or incidents mentioned in Part I. An interested activist could very well read only this section and it would make sense, especially in conjunction with the time line Steve kindly provided. In this section, more of his original chapters could stand nearly unchanged, while for Part I many of his chapters were combined to construct a narrative flow. Overall I have tried to be as unobtrusive as possible, though. I added only a few subtitles and notes for clarification, and I left intact quotes from primary materials such as pamphlets or letters.

It is in these latter eight chapters especially that Steve airs the views for which he was controversial, while remaining (perhaps surprisingly to friends and foes alike) self-effacing. The idea of "mainstreaming" gay and lesbian rights seemed to many who came of age as 1970s activists to be "selling out" to the power of conformity and accommodation over truly radical goals. Indeed, Steve reports being called an "Uncle Tom" on occasion, an epithet significant given the way in which the GLBT movements have paralleled and even been modeled, to some degree, on African-American movements, whether for rights, liberation, power, and/or pride. It seems an unfortunate side effect of all our movements for social and political justice that there will be conflicts over goals, means, and tactics, and those conflicts usually follow the same general patterns. Steve Endean's conviction that equal rights for gay and lesbian Americans would come only from working with and within established political institutions led him to the activities described in this book, and especially to his determination to get a national lesbian gay civil rights bill passed. Whether one agrees with the objectives or not, his is an impressive record.

As I write this, debates over strategy are strangely relevant, but perhaps they always are. Although the word his friends use most consistently to describe him is "visionary," I feel safe in saying that not even Steve Endean would have predicted how quickly same-sex marriage would come to the forefront of national politics. At the same time, I doubt that the cynical attempt to mobilize antigay bigotry in the political process in order to win an election would have surprised him at all, nor would the ongoing internal debates over the wisdom of championing this most mainstream of goals now or ever. If I had to guess, I'd imagine that Steve would be nervous about promoting same-sex marriage as an issue even now, since he believed in incremental steps toward full civil rights. However, he also believed in facing the situations one is handed, and the "right time" may not always be that which is carefully planned. Through it all he had tremendous optimism, always believing in people's ultimate goodness and desire for fairness. Whether a prophet or a "dinosaur," Steve Endean felt that Americans' concern for justice had repeatedly triumphed over our prejudices and would continue to do so. This faith alone makes his story inspiring, while the record of achievements of twenty years are instructive and encouraging, to say the least.

I never met Steve Endean, but I wish I had. We would not always have agreed, but I'm glad to know he was working for our side.

I have many people to thank for bringing this book to light more than ten years after its completion. Foremost is Bob Meek, who has been generous in every sense of the term. He not only gave me the full manuscript and accompanying disks but also offered me a free hand in the editing process, demonstrating a rare confidence in someone he barely knew. I am also indebted to him for an extremely careful reading of the final draft, with helpful suggestions and corrections, and for writing a wonderful tribute to Steve. I also thank Allan Spear for writing a beautiful remembrance of Steve, and on short notice, and for corrections in the chronology. On the winding road that brought me to this, present and former staff of the Human Rights Campaign, and Education Director Kim Mills in particular, provided important information as I have sought to understand the organization's history. I am grateful to all those I interviewed as I researched HRC history, all of whom freely gave time they probably could not spare; for insight into Steve and/or related matters I especially thank Phil Attey, Vic Basile, Terry Bean, Elizabeth Birch, Larry Bye, Joe Cantor, Barbara Gittings, Tim McFeeley, Jean Tretter, and Michael Weeks.

I am grateful to The Haworth Press for taking this on and making it available at last. Anissa Harper, Jillian Mason-Possemato, and Robert Owen were very helpful along the way, and Vern Bullough's faith in this work made it possible. John Yanson generously provided his drawing of Steve. Alfred University provided time and funding at various stages, through the NEH Steering Committee and by honoring me with the Margaret and Barbara Hagar Chair in Humanities from 2000 to 2003. Macintosh technician Dennis Adams-Smith, a kind and patient man, located the program to open all of Steve's files. Finally, I am most grateful to my partner, Pat O'Brien, for her patience and for bearing the burden of the home care, food provision, and dog and cat care (we are lesbians after all) through the year I was unavailable for too many nights and weekends.

Preface

Bringing Lesbian and Gay Rights Into the Mainstream is not an "autobiography." It is a first-person account of the lesbian and gay movement's early progress in the 1970s and the 1980s, particularly the legislative and political struggles I have lived through. I've put off writing this book, long after friends started harassing me to do so, because it always seemed like there was so much to do and there wasn't the time to look back. I was exhausted from more than twenty-two years of full-time advocacy for lesbian and gay civil rights, and I was also beginning to feel the early effects of AIDS. And I confess I didn't want to do a memoir per se, let alone some of the recent "get even books" I had seen in other movements.

Moreover, when friends and associates first urged me to write a book I was flattered but felt it could well come off as an ego trip. Yet I felt there was a sad lack of solid, accurate information on how we had made much of our national political and legislative progress. Too often I've heard others describe early developments that were very different from my firsthand knowledge of the way the events unfolded. I realized that although I no longer had the energy to work full-time, let alone the normal sixty to eighty hours a week many of us worked, I thought I could still make a contribution by sharing how we won some of these important victories and describing some of the serious mistakes we made along the way.

People kept pointing out that I'd been blessed to have been able to play a small role in many critical developments as the gay movement has emerged as a political force: Launching the first successful adoption of a lesbian and gay civil rights plank in the Democratic Party's national platform; admittance into the civil rights coalition; initiating the AFL-CIO's shift from opposition to gay rights to active support; introduction of the first lesbian and gay civil rights bill in the Senate; and securing record (at the time) co-sponsorship in the House all helped transform the movement's political stature during my "tour of duty."

I've been deeply concerned at the failure of the lesbian and gay movement to record its history and therefore too often to repeat the same mistakes. My hope is that this book and some of the others now beginning to come out will help stop us from reinventing the wheel again and again. With AIDS causing the lesbian and gay civil rights movement to lose some of its best and brightest, the need is more compelling than ever before to chronicle what efforts have led to this stage of development in the quest for civil rights, human dignity, and equal justice for lesbian and gay Americans.

The death of countless friends from AIDS, and the fact that I'm now combating AIDS myself, convinced me to move forward. Long-term activists, who had contributed enormously and had told me wonderful stories of their efforts, too often failed to share those stories in such books. *Bringing Lesbian and Gay Rights Into the Mainstream* tells of my encounters with many extraordinary activists as well as my involvement in many historic developments.

I have tried to be as candid as possible about my remembrances. As I've written, I have reviewed a massive amount of background materials collected over the years and have talked with other players in virtually every effort or story told. Those who deny the reality of the role internal strife and personal movement conflicts has played will be left with those dry histories that I personally perceive as utterly unrevealing and unsatisfying. Further, my own experience is that many of those writing such "histories" carry their own prejudices and opinions into their works but are simply more subtle about whose ox is being gored and how. I know that's the case in a number of instances where I had firsthand knowledge, only to see it badly misrepresented by the so-called objective historians.

Many books that have purported to tell the history of the national gay and lesbian civil rights movement have actually focused on specific localities, such as San Francisco or New York. As a proud Midwesterner, I've always resented such representations. Although my views about some activists and events may seem harsh to some, it's important to remember this book isn't a dry, abstract history, but rather a first-person account—and it clearly represents the perspective of an opinionated activist.

When I began in the gay movement, I sought information on activists' experiences. Almost nothing had been written, and what little I could find was abstract, theoretical, generally far to the left, and utterly impractical. The tendency of too many activists to act as if the movement began the day they walked in the door is extremely frustrating to me. Such an approach is not only arrogant and ignorant, but it costs our movement for fairness dearly. I've tried to benefit from other people's experiences. Through the years I've tried to avoid the pitfalls of other activists and movements, and I've "borrowed" liberally.

Although we still have a long way to go in our quest for civil rights, human dignity, and equal justice for lesbian and gay Americans, incredible progress has been made in the past twenty years. It's very irritating to hear people who think such progress has somehow "just happened," without recognizing the efforts of dedicated movement activists who gave up tremendous amounts in their personal and professional lives to advance our quest.

Bringing Lesbian and Gay Rights Into the Mainstream isn't a how-to book, as I have little patience for abstract ideological tracts, which bear minimal relationship to real-world politics or to the lives of lesbians and gay men. Also, my national legislative and political efforts for lesbian and gay rights have been based substantially on my experiences in Minnesota. Therefore, I can't easily, or properly, eliminate references to those efforts. So readers will occasionally begin a new chapter only to find themselves back in Minnesota. With the exception of the tough winters, you could face far worse fates.

I've faced many challenges over the years of full-time activism and, ironically, now one of my greatest remaining challenges is learning how to "let go and let God." It isn't easy for a control freak like myself to watch others ignore our previous experiences and make the same or worse mistakes. So perhaps this is one final opportunity to offer my perspectives on past efforts and on some of the future developments that our movement is likely to face.

Both my critics and my friends would quickly acknowledge that I am a highly opinionated activist. I hope you will find the experiences I share to be interesting, instructive, or both.

July 1993

Acknowledgments

It was my hope that *Bringing Lesbian and Gay Rights Into the Mainstream* would be only one of many books to come from the activists of the 1970s, 1980s, and early 1990s. Tragically, far too many individuals who played a vital role in the progress of that period, which far too many today take for granted, have passed on without recording their experiences in print. A number of people assisted, both with advice and with encouragement, in the preparation of this book.

First and foremost, Bob Meek, an astute political strategist, public relations wizard, and a good friend, deserves my deep thanks. After I initially convinced Bob of how critical it was to produce a book about the substantial progress we've made over the past twenty years, I realized what a formidable task it would be. So I put it off in favor of other activist projects. Bob's patient prodding and ability to endure working closely with a high-strung control freak who was increasingly losing control and facing the horrors of AIDS, as well as the affection which he's shown, had much to do with making this book a reality.

Several other friends and fellow activists have made helpful suggestions on either the style or content of this book. In addition to Bob Meek, both Gregory King and Ralph White assisted significantly with feedback and editing suggestions. I especially would like to thank longtime friends Jerry Weller, Kerry Woodward, Charles Stewart, Tom Bastow, Denis Wadley, Terry Bean, Joe Cantor, Allan Spear, and Lee Bush, who's now passed on.

And I want to acknowledge my lover and dear friend, George Norris, who has lovingly and patiently pushed me on to complete the project. I've never known an individual who was as thoughtful and considerate, and I've leaned on him a great deal as I've faced completion of the book while I've also faced the challenges and uncertainty associated with AIDS.

Finally, I owe so much to the countless dedicated activists—both those cited within these pages and those who go unnamed—because without their extraordinary commitment and dedication, even in the face of extremely difficult odds and despite the then-far-too-common apathy within the gay community itself, there simply wouldn't be a story to tell.

Abbreviations

ACLU	American Civil Liberties Union
ACS	area canvass supervisor
ADA	Americans for Democratic Action
AFL-CIO	American Federation of Labor–Congress of Industrial Organizations
AFSCME	American Federation of State, County, and Municipal Employees
APA	American Psychiatric Association
BWMT	Black and White Men Together
COPE	(AFL-CIO) Committee on Political Education
DFL	Democratic-Farmer-Labor Party
GMHC	Gay Men's Health Crisis
GRLC	Gay Rights Legislative Committee
GRNL	Gay Rights National Lobby
HRCF	Human Rights Campaign Fund
IGA	International Gay Association (International Lesbian and Gay Association [ILGA] as of 1986)
JRLC	Joint Religious Legislative Coalition
LCCR	Leadership Conference on Civil Rights
LFOC	Lesbian Feminist Organizing Committee
MCGR	Minnesota Committee for Gay Rights
MECLA	Municipal Elections Committee of Los Angeles
MHAM	Mental Health Association of Minnesota
MOHR	Michigan Organization for Human Rights
NAACP	National Association for the Advancement of Colored People
NARAL	National Abortion and Reproductive Rights Action League
NCBLG	National Coalition of Black Lesbians and Gays
NCC	National Council of Churches
NCEC	National Committee for an Effective Congress
NEA	National Endowment for the Arts
NEC	National Endorsement Campaign

This list of abbreviations was compiled by the editor to assist the reader.

NGTF	National Gay Task Force (National Gay and Lesbian Task Force, as of 1986)
NORA	National Organizations Responding to AIDS
NOW	National Organization for Women
PAC	political action committee
PFLAG	Parents, Families and Friends of Lesbians and Gays
SEIU	Service Employees International Union
SIR	Society for Individual Rights
SWP	Socialist Workers Party
UFCW	United Food and Commercial Workers
UFMCC	Universal Fellowship of Metropolitan Community Churches
YAF	Young Americans for Freedom

Introduction

Rules of the Road

I'm not a political theoretician. I have generally seen myself as a pragmatist, a political operative and strategist who has been committed to winning. But, as I've looked back at my career to prepare this book, I realized
that in fact I have generally operated on some unstated principles or "rules
of the road" which have guided me through the years. It is not necessary for
the reader to share these views, but it's fair to know some of my guiding
principles.

1. We will win by capturing the middle and taking the "political center" from our moralistic opponents. Strategies and issues that take us
   back to the fringe can only be counterproductive.
2. We must never, ever give up. We must understand that we will win
   the war even if we lose battle after battle.
3. There is nothing unique about movement activists and leaders, except their willingness to make a difference. God has given each of us
   talents and gifts which we can either choose to utilize in the fight for
   fairness or not.
4. There is a massive gap between our movement's rhetoric about
   "grass roots" and our movement's genuine capacity to generate constituent mail. That goes for other forms of grassroots pressure we
   profess to care about as well. Even those who claim to care most
   about grass roots are seldom willing to commit the staff and resources necessary to turn their rhetoric into reality. Despite the vast
   improvements we've made in the past few years, it's our moralistic
   opponents who can still swamp Congress with mail and pressure,
   distorting legislators' views of public opinion. We saw this in the
   early years of the Clinton administration, when followers of Pat
   Robertson and Rush Limbaugh were able to shut down the Capitol
   switchboard. While these zealots have several built-in advantages,
   they've also been successful because they put their money and staff
   into the nitty-gritty grunt work of grassroots organizing.

5. "Inclusiveness" means not only including racial minorities (although we've done a disgraceful job here, really only giving lip service to the matter), women, and the economically disadvantaged, but also involving people of means. However, too many activists, who constantly spout "isms," also exclude people. It is a form of "blue-denim elitism," which is counterproductive in terms of both human and financial resources. Since ours is a political fight, which depends on not only person power but also financial resources, elitism—which seems based on resentment—is very destructive if we are going to win.

6. People don't have to become "activists" to make things happen. Most people—gay and nongay alike—aren't very "political" and don't want to be "activists." "Empowerment" occurs by helping people take incremental and relatively painless steps; this allows them to make a difference and may result in additional involvement.

7. Defeat is sometimes necessary (for instance, to help us clarify the votes on a city council or state legislature) but is never romantic. Sometimes it seems there's a small minority actually afraid to win because victory would remove their excuses and "victimhood" and they'd have to accept responsibility for their lives.

8. Talk is cheap. There are too many talkers and spokespersons looking for the limelight and far too few "doers." Further, there's no work that any of us, regardless of our movement seniority, should be too good to do.

9. There's a need for a wide range of strategies, including strong militant direct-action approaches. Too often, though, some of these actions seem to be based more on self-indulgence than their political or strategic advantages. Also, better communication, based on respect, between those involved in direct action and those into "establishment approaches" would benefit the broader community.

10. Activists are only a small portion of the broader lesbian and gay community, and it's our obligation not only to lead the community but also to represent it as accurately and effectively as possible.

Steve Endean. Photography by Jim Marks.

Part I:
The Roller Coaster

Election day in early November 1982 was one of the longest but one of the most satisfying days I could remember since entering the gay and lesbian civil rights movement more than twelve years earlier. I was both the executive director and lobbyist for lesbian and gay civil rights on Capitol Hill and the founder and treasurer of our new political action committee, the Human Rights Campaign Fund (HRCF), which I'd hoped would play a key role in winning both respect and votes from members of Congress.

In that context, we'd stumbled onto an almost ideal political year. Just a short time earlier, Reaganomics had swept the country, leaving the Democratic Party leadership in serious retreat and confusion. But as the 1982 elections approached, the nation was in the midst of a serious recession and it seemed likely to be a good Democratic year.

We'd successfully launched our PAC (political action committee), the Campaign Fund, in well under a year. We'd raised more than $650,000 in just eight months. Although that might not seem like much by today's standards, this was before the AIDS crisis had mobilized the gay and lesbian community and transformed the community's willingness to contribute. We had an early success in a spring primary, where we were the biggest donors to help a cosponsor of the gay and lesbian civil rights bill defeat a cosponsor of the so-called Family Protection Act (redistricting had thrown the two Democrats into the same district); also, a videotape by *M*A*S*H* star Mike Farrell and an unprecedented direct mail letter by noted playwright Tennessee Williams contributed to our credibility. We'd become solid, respected political players within the political power structure—so essential to effectively moving a political and legislative agenda—by building close working relations with other progressive political action committees, a range of political operatives, and the candidates themselves. We probably knew more about the candidates (and in some cases, even the lay of the land) than many of the other, better-established political action committees.

Now it all culminated on election night of 1982, and we all held our breath. Nothing breeds success like success. People want to go with a winner, and the results of the evening would help define just how successful, from a purely political point of view, the Human Rights Campaign Fund would become.

Both the Human Rights Campaign Fund and the Gay Rights National Lobby (GRNL) were housed across from a rundown, somewhat dangerous housing project (which has since been boarded up). I was dead tired from trying to prove I could indeed run both organizations for several months, but I was on cloud nine in anticipation of our expected victories. There was a small party at our offices, but I couldn't get the information I wanted about House races. I went over to the election headquarters of the National Committee for an Effective Congress (NCEC), the "granddaddy" of all liberal PACs, to try to get the results.

As the evening turned into the early morning, I finally decided I had about all the information I'd be able to get that night. I returned to the new apartment that my lover, Will, and I had rented several months earlier. Will, who wasn't particularly politically active or even out, had long since gone to bed, but he understood completely how important this night was to me. I got home just a few moments before 6:00 a.m. I was exhausted but far too hyper to just go to bed, so I calculated and recalculated the results we had thus far. It appeared that, despite losing several heartbreakingly close races, we'd won over 80 percent of the races we'd entered. The Human Rights Campaign Fund had proven itself to be a truly major player in the top forty to fifty races we got into, with an average contribution of more than $4,000. And, with the crucial help of GRNL's constituent lobbying of candidates, we'd elected sixteen new cosponsors of the national lesbian and gay civil rights legislation prohibiting discrimination in jobs and housing.

As I sprawled in front of the fireplace of our English basement with several yellow legal pads, I allowed myself to really enjoy the experience and feel the incredible satisfaction. Although this might seem natural to most, I tended to always be impatient, demanding, and wanting more, particularly from myself. But this time we'd really proven we could be big-league players and I'd shown people I could supervise both groups. Some people had been dubious about one person running both operations, but I believed the lobbying effort and PAC contributions absolutely had to stay tied together, even if it was exhausting or killing me. Because I'd been personally in charge of the candidate disbursement process, I'd shown people the political savvy to spend those resources well. It was, at that point, the culmination of a twelve-year gay movement career.

Our 1982 successes were the result of the efforts of many people, but as the treasurer and one of the spokespersons, the gay media—including *The*

Advocate—gave me lots of positive coverage. Such praise was particularly appreciated given that I grew up with a significant inferiority complex and worked 90 to 100 hours a week throughout the campaign season (from May on) to try to keep GRNL functioning while we launched the Campaign Fund. I hadn't yet discovered how quickly it all could turn around.

Little did I know on that early November night that within two months I would be under full-scale assault by several of the most powerful figures in the lesbian and gay civil rights movement, including the then-publisher of the only national gay paper, *The Advocate*. In hindsight, there had been signals: my conflict with fund-raising consultant Jim Foster and the spring meeting when *Advocate* publisher David Goodstein asked me if I had a strong personal support system. At the time I was so swamped with work and later was riding high and full of myself over our success that I didn't focus on it much, but now I think Goodstein had already decided I didn't fit the profile he thought appropriate for our lobbyist or PAC director.

Given all the positive feedback heaped on me until that point from so many sources and the success we'd just achieved, the attacks took me totally by surprise. Unfortunately, it played into plenty of personal insecurity and more than a little political paranoia. Even once the attacks began, I didn't initially understand their real purpose was to oust me from both the Campaign Fund and from the Gay Rights National Lobby.

So as I lay in front of the fire on election night, I couldn't imagine being forced out of both the GRNL and HRCF by the following October. Although I had almost unanimous support on both boards, it eventually became clear that only my leaving could save the groups from the withering assault. The national movement was still very, very young and the attacks alone could seriously distort reality. The appearance of so much "smoke" led many across the country, activists and major donors alike (who depend on the gay media, at least in part, for their information), to conclude there had to be fire.

One of the key players attacking me wrote columns for several important local gay papers. Although he had a right to his opinion, his columns gave the impression that it was news rather than the opinions of only one bright but vicious and unethical person. Unfortunately, Washington, DC's gay paper, the *Blade,* which had a reputation as one of the best local gay papers in the country, had begun bending over backward to prove their objectivity and independence. Other local papers—the *Philadelphia Gay News (PGN),* the *Gay News Telegraph* out of St. Louis, and *Update* from San Diego come to mind—thought I was getting a raw deal.

At least as painful as what I was about to go through politically, my two-year relationship with Will, an attractive, stable, and loving black man, seemed to be crumbling in the process, in part because of the extraordinary pressure. He was extremely loyal and stood by me every step of the way, but my increasingly insecure behavior, which sometimes played out in promiscuous sex, made it difficult for him to hang in there. After the battle was lost, I'd left the gay movement, and Will was sure I could take the next trauma without falling completely apart, he ended our relationship. We remained roommates as we tried to sell the home we'd bought only a year and a half earlier. Just a few months after our biggest success to date, I'd lost not only the career in the movement I loved so much but also the love of the man of my life for long after our relationship ended and, in fact, until recently.

As I've watched the 1992 elections and the vital role the lesbian and gay community played, particularly in the presidential race, I remember what a breakthrough we thought we'd made back in 1982. On reflection, I think both developments were critical, although I suspect we still have some distance to go before we get to the "final breakthrough," whatever that might be.

Chapter 1

My Minnesota Roots

I began working full time for the lesbian and gay civil rights movement in 1970, just a year after the Stonewall riots, which mark for some the beginning of the modern gay and lesbian movement.[1] I ended up spending my entire adult life working on gay rights and cannot imagine anything that could ever be so satisfying.

It was my early Minnesota experience that led me to becoming involved nationally. I joined the first national board of the National Gay Task Force (NGTF) and eventually became board cochair. Later, I was hired as the first executive director and lobbyist for the Gay Rights National Lobby, founded the Human Rights Campaign Fund, and, years (and serious internal battle scars) later, launched the Fairness Fund to generate grassroots mail and pressure on Congress.

Because I focused much of my movement attention on the newly emerging national arena so early, my experience may have been unique. Most such politicos either opted for involvement at the local or state level, where they had a chance of quicker success or, more likely, they wisely chose involvement in nongay politics.

Growing Up and Putting Politics
and Gay Rights Together

When I became aware of my sexual orientation at age twenty-one or so, more than twenty years ago, homosexuality just was not a widely discussed subject. I'd grown up a good Catholic, even considered joining the priesthood, and sensed that my apparent same-sex orientation wouldn't be approved by the Church. At about the same time I struggled with my orientation, I discovered my other true love, politics, spending the summer of 1970 as a full-time aide for the Anderson for Governor campaign, probably in part because the candidate was a handsome former Olympic hockey star. I had always been interested in politics but hadn't figured out where to fit in. I vividly recall carefully following the struggles of the civil rights movement, but I was just a little young to get involved myself. Moreover, Minnesota was a 98 percent white state, so black civil rights seemed distant and remote.

My experience in the campaign had been very satisfying (when I wasn't assisting in the campaign manager's office I was Wendell Anderson's alternate driver), but with the 1970 governor's race coming down to a dead heat, I worried that my sexual orientation could hurt my candidate, totally misjudging the damage a single gay volunteer could have on the race. I had loved being so centrally involved, but I reluctantly left the campaign without even explaining my decision.

When Anderson won, I helped on the Governor's Inaugural Committee. The inaugural was a big deal because the Democratic-Farmer-Labor (DFL) Party hadn't won either the governor's seat or the legislature in years. Later, I served briefly as an intern to two DFL state legislators. Several people associated with the campaign, always on the lookout for potential candidates, suggested I consider running for the state legislature at some point. Although Minnesota has since elected several openly gay and lesbian officials, that was considerably later, so at the time it never occurred to me to be a genuine possibility.

I realized even then that many elected officials were probably gay and just hid the fact, but I also knew it wouldn't work for me. "Discretion" and I have never had much in common. If I really was gay, trying to pretend I was straight would be very, very tough. In my heart I knew I'd never be heterosexual, but I thought I *could* just stop being gay. After months of extraordinary effort, as I abstained from sex and tried to stop being gay, I realized that being gay wasn't about whether I did anything about it or not. I was gay. This was a quite painful period, but two developments made my coming to grips with my sexual orientation easier.

The first was my discovery of the book *The Homosexual in America* by Donald Webster Cory. Everything I'd seen before had described homosexuals as sick, sinners, or criminals. His book would hardly qualify for "enlightenment" today, but back then it gave me my first glimmers of hope. With the knowledge this book provided, I began to try to find someone involved in the gay movement so I could learn more.

I'd heard of a group called Mattachine, so I called directory assistance to get a number. A key advantage of such a call would be that the operator probably wouldn't know what kind of group it was. But there was no Mattachine in Minneapolis. I swallowed hard and asked for number for any groups with "gay" or "homosexual" in their name. There was a group called Gay House, which I later learned was one of the first gay drop-in centers in the country. It took weeks of driving past Gay House before I mustered the courage to go in.

Having grown up in the suburbs of Minneapolis, I was straitlaced and was somewhat taken aback by the "early Salvation Army" look of the drop-in center. Inside, I met several outrageous counterculture queens who seemed to personify every stereotype I'd heard about. But since it was basically clear that my sexuality wasn't just a phase but a reality, I was incredibly anxious to meet people that might assist in helping me develop a positive self-image as a gay man

One man I met at Gay House, Mike McConnell, seemed different from most of those involved—he was warm, stable, friendly, and sensitive. As I later discovered, Mike was a well-known gay activist who had been fired from his job at the University of Minnesota Library because of his sexual orientation. The common response in those days was to slink off into the night and hope you could find another job somehow, but Mike fought back and sued the university.

Mike's case got a great deal of media attention, and I think his case was the first time I had ever thought of the issue as a matter of simple fairness. Until then I guess I would have thought such discrimination was unjust but had assumed that the Constitution protected him. His lover, Jack Baker, wasn't nearly as warm or nice, but he had a brilliant capacity for public relations and had successfully run for student body president at the University of Minnesota as an openly gay man. Even then, they had already been on the cover of *Life* magazine.[2]

Mike nurtured and guided me through the process of coming out to my parents and into activism in this period. With his help, I became the board chair of Gay House and began to associate with the very small group of Twin Cities gay activists. I did not anticipate becoming a gay activist, let alone a lobbyist for lesbian and gay rights. I just wanted to figure out how to reconcile my apparent homosexuality with the rest of my life.

I'd been chunky most of my life, but that summer I ran several miles a day, lifted weights, and drove a truck for a beer company, hauling kegs and beer cases. So I was in the best shape I had ever been in and got lots of attention when I came to Gay House. One particular dinner still sticks out in my memory. I casually asked whether anyone wanted to go get something to eat. An obese, outrageous queen named Dahl who was very interested in me immediately said, "Yes, darling, I'd love to go dinner with a hunk like you anytime." I was still trying to reach a comfort level about being gay and felt a little awkward even being seen in public with this character, but I decided I just had to bear with it. I had casually put my hand on the table when the waitress came over to take our orders. When she asked whether it would be one check or two, Dahl, in his most outrageous "high queen" manner, put his fat little hand on top of mine, said, "My husband always pays." My movement career almost ended then and there as I just about keeled over.

These were the protest days for most of the social issue causes. Jack's spice-and-vinegar, splashy public relations style served the gay movement extremely well at that time. While I eagerly joined in a range of protests and zaps at that time, it was not a style I was completely comfortable with. Looking back, it's probably true, if a bit uncharitable, to say that most of those who were involved in those early days tended to have little to lose. One of my concerns, which suddenly seems far too relevant again, was protest activities that too often seemed to have more to do with acting out activists' frustrations and need for instant gratification than anything based on strategic movement plans.

The term used then was "gay," not "gay and lesbian," which can be explained only by sexism, since many of the strong, dynamic leaders within our small band of activists were indeed women. Also, the term in those early days was "gay liberation," but I worked to shift it to "gay civil rights" because I thought the term "liberation" seemed foreign to most people. Without much conscious analysis, I sensed our victories would come in direct relationship to how well we were able to move the issue of lesbian and gay civil rights into the mainstream; I opted for "gay civil rights," because I thought it more effectively conveyed our mission of securing nondiscrimination. Could we reach the broad middle ground of people who probably weren't ready for gay marriage and gay adoption, let alone cross-dressing? Even in the early 1970s, I believed most Americans believed in fairness and agreed someone doing a good job shouldn't be fired from their jobs or evicted from their apartments because of their sexual orientation.

Looking back, getting involved in gay politics became my alternative to a more traditional political/electoral career. It became the logical way to combine my gay lifestyle with my commitment to politics, allowing me to try to make a difference. Although I would have enjoyed serving in the state legislature, in hindsight I can see I'm where I was called to be. Becoming a gay civil rights lobbyist was both appropriate and somewhat ironic, as it allowed me to combine my lifestyle with pursuit of my father's longtime ambition for me to become a salesman. It took Dad some getting used to the issue, but he eventually thought it was amusing that I had rejected "sales" only to go on to sell a pretty tough issue.

Coming from Hubert Humphrey's Minnesota, my involvement also grew from my commitment to politics and government as a means to improve people's lives. In addition, there's a real dose of Catholic guilt and I didn't want future generations of gay men and lesbians to suffer from discrimination or, more important, from the same feelings of guilt, inferiority, and loneliness I went through.

Although I didn't really identify with much of the radical nature of the movement, I did always enjoy shocking people. Most people who know me well think I'm fairly assertive. For instance, I often walked from my apartment near downtown to the gay bars wearing gay rights T-shirts. As one might imagine in the early 1970s, such T-shirts provoked lots of hostility and response, but as a stocky, muscular guy, when I was confronted I'd just turn around to face the bigots and yell back, defying them to start something. Thank God they never took me up on it, as I'm not much of a boxer.

Over time, it became clear that a within-the-system lobbying initiative was essential to continued progress, certainly in terms of the enactment of the nondiscrimination laws that obsessed me. We needed a full-time lobbying presence at the state capitol, and I felt I could do an effective job, though I hardly anticipated such lobbying would become my life's work. I hadn't lobbied before but thought I had the political savvy I needed. I knew I had a lot to learn, but on-the-job training seemed reasonable because it appeared likely that repeal of the sodomy laws and extension of the civil rights laws to protect lesbians and gay men from discrimination in jobs and housing would be a long-term task.

Even in those early "radical" years, I slowly gravitated to a group of more like-minded and fairly middle-class folks like myself—Jean Nicholas Tretter, Steve Badeau, Mike Garrett, Rick Davis, and others—that in 1972 became the base for a largely paper group, the Gay Rights Legislative Committee (GRLC). Somewhere in this period, it was my good fortune to meet the lobbyist for the liberal Americans for Democratic Action (ADA), Denis Wadley. His support, guidance, and nurturing were extraordinarily valuable as I learned the ropes of lobbying the legislature. Unlike the Minnesota Civil Liberties Union, which seemed to care more about both press and about being right than winning, ADA was committed to practical, effective advocacy on behalf of their causes.

Denis's first love was teaching and, in many respects, he seemed to be the perfect role model for the character Robin Williams played in *Dead Poets Society*—a bit iconoclastic but determined to stand on principle. He spent countless hours with me going over the details of legislators' positions on other ADA issues, provided important insights on lobbying tactics, and agreed to lobby directly a certain number of legislators himself. Just as important, he helped demystify the entire process, convincing me I had the political skills to undertake this difficult task. He also provided the friendly ear over lunch quite often, which meant a lot since there generally wasn't much of a demand for the gay lobbyist to take legislators to lunch. Denis probably did more to "train" me to lobby than anyone else and often faced the unpleasant task of picking me up, dusting me off, and shoving me back out there against the lions. I owe him a great deal, far more than I can ever repay.

Another source of encouragement was the small band of extraordinary feminist lobbyists who were pushing ERA ratification and pro-choice positions through the legislature.[3] I formed fast friendships with the leaders of the then newly created DFL Feminist Caucus, Koryne Horbal, Cynthia Kitlinski, Jeri Rasmussen, and Peggy Specktor. They recognized a wayward soul and took me under their wings. Their help ranged from putting in good words with the many legislators (a number which shrank, unfortunately, as the focus shifted from the ERA to choice), to Cynthia helping train our volunteer lobbyists, to taking me for an ice cream cone and good advice in the dingy cafeteria that served the legislature, to including me in their weekly "Therapy Session," the Wednesday-night gathering of progressive lobbyists and legislators over drinks.

During much of this period, 1973 to 1975, I worked five to seven nights a week at the most popular gay bar in town, Sutton's, checking coats. (There were actually two popular bars in town, the Gay '90s, which catered to an older crowd and usually had too many drunks in it for me, and Sutton's.) A long, narrow establishment dominated by an oblong bar in the middle, Sutton's had mirrors on all the walls. On weekends it was packed to the rafters with young, good-looking men in T-shirts and tight blue jeans. In the earliest years, the song "Ain't No Mountain High Enough" by Diana Ross blared from the jukebox and practically knocked you off the tiny dance floor in the back. (Ironically, as I write this section, "Ain't No Mountain" has just come on the radio and, to this day, I identify it as my coming out song.) In later years, they expanded and had a DJ, great music, and a much larger dance floor; the song that sticks out from this period was "Love's Theme" by Barry White. On relatively quiet weeknights, I would sneak out of my coat check and get in a dance or two, but I still had a long way to go before I got to that point.

Much, much earlier, when I was just coming out and trying hard to get comfortable, I had wandered into Sutton's on a very slow weeknight. Sitting on a ledge near the back, I practically fell on the floor when a guy came up and asked me to dance. It was early, the bar was fairly empty, and no one else was dancing. In fact, I'd never seen or even thought of two men dancing together before. I politely declined, explaining I could not approve of two men dancing together. He looked at me awfully strangely, and I think he thought I was pulling his leg, but he didn't give up and, I think, actually convinced me to dance.

Sutton's was not only my favorite social center—probably because the men did not act like the screaming queens I had been taught gay people were—but also a source of critical financial support for a struggling activist trying to make ends meet. I did not get paid a salary, but I got all the money (at 25 cents a coat) from the charge per coat. Coupled with the small salary I got from the GRLC and later from the Minnesota Committee for Gay

Rights (MCGR), I was able to get by financially, even if it meant I was working all the time.

The coat check gave me a little spare, badly needed funds but, more important, "Well-Hung Coats by WeeBee" (my nickname for years) served the critical function as a "constituent service" center. Weekends were usually too busy for more than a "hi, how are you" or a little cruising, but on the calmer weeknights, I stayed behind the Dutch door of the coat check and talked with nonactivists about what they thought. I wanted them to know what and why we were doing what we were and, likewise, I wanted to know where the community really was.

For as long as I could remember, I wanted to help make Minnesota the first state in the nation to enact a lesbian and gay civil rights bill. The so-called political experts told us we'd never get either the consenting adults legislation (repeal of sodomy, fornication, and adultery laws) and the non-discrimination bills out of committee, but we proved them wrong. The excellent job done by our chief sponsor in the state senate, Majority Leader Nick Coleman (who died of cancer some years ago), almost helped us actually pass the nondiscrimination bill in 1973. However, with our opponents focusing on the gay teacher issue, and with the potential political danger of voting for gay rights lingering in the background, we lost by a handful of votes.

After the defeat of the gay civil rights bill in the state senate, which took place very late in the session, which is known as the "crunch," I flew off to the national ADA convention, where I'd just been elected to the national board. But I had not realized that Nick had not officially killed the bill when we lost but simply "progressed" it, meaning he could amend it, try to twist some arms, and try once more. To my dismay, with several of us off at the ADA convention, Nick deleted the job category of gay and lesbian teachers. Although I believe in compromise (as in our decision to delete "public accommodations" and "public services" from the bill in 1975) and have prided myself on being politically pragmatic, Nick's action, while well-intentioned, was nonetheless a grievous mistake: unlike deleting categories such as public accommodations—and most protected classes aren't covered in all categories in the beginning—a specific exemption by job would write actual discrimination into law and set a truly horrible precedent. Nick was and is a political hero of mine and I still have a picture of him on my wall, but I'm just thankful his misguided effort narrowly failed. During the next session both Nick and Allan Spear agreed we would never delete specific occupations such as teachers.

From the beginning Allan Spear was central to our state efforts. A truly brilliant history professor and an antiwar leader at the University of Minnesota, Allan was elected to the state senate in 1972 and often described himself as one of the few people in the country to get elected in part on George McGovern's coattails. Not "out" as a gay man when he was first elected, Spear was very politically astute, but he was a predictable liberal from the university area. More important, he was a freshman, so he didn't serve as our chief sponsor during the 1973 session. Nonetheless, he spent countless hours working with me and we became very close friends. I am proud I was there with and for him when he later came out publicly on the front page of the Minneapolis papers. Even fourteen years after I left Minnesota, we remain close friends (although he almost failed to forgive me for dragging him into internal national gay politics when I convinced him to become cochair of GRNL as I was going through my personal hell at the hands of the press).

People Who Love Sausage . . .

There is an old and far too accurate phrase that goes something like, "People who love sausage or respect the law should never see either made." Although legislative bodies have hit new lows for political gutlessness and a sometimes shocking stupidity and bigotry on countless instances, here we're talking about the truly unbelievable. And since lobbyists usually work with staff rather than the members of Congress themselves, most of my best examples seem to come from the state legislative level in Minnesota.

I vividly remember most of the floor debates, when the most outrageous, unbelievable things were said about gays. The fact that so many of these statements were made by men of mediocrity (okay, so I'm being generous—many were downright stupid) somehow wasn't as consoling as you might think. (I say "men" because the Minnesota legislature, like most, was overwhelmingly male and most women legislators were on our side.) Neither I nor any other lesbian or gay man should even care what these idiots thought—nor did I—but it was still painful to listen to those debates.

Usually, I watched the debates with our other lobbyists from the galleries. The dedication and amazing capacity of our lobbyists, particularly people such as Doug Elwood (who used his experience as a therapist to good advantage in his one-on-one lobbying with his assigned legislators), was another silver lining. But, despite these small consolations, I almost always slipped away after the debate to be alone in a remote corner of the marble halls of the state capitol and cry my eyes out after we'd lost yet again. Usually, within a half an hour of private tears and pain, I was able to rejoin Allan, Marcia and Lee Greenfield (two of Allan's oldest friends who, though not gay themselves, became central to every lesbian and gay rights effort), and our lobbyists and we'd go out to dinner.

I now realize that only laughter at our legislative opponents could keep me from becoming too bitter to continue lobbying. As my buddy Cynthia and I told each other, there were days when their stupidity, complete lack of political courage, and/or commitment to fairness made us just as soon want to kick them as lobby them; on such days I did avoid lobbying and instead focused on the necessary behind-the-scenes work.

Probably at the top of the list has to be a representative who spoke out frequently against the lesbian and gay rights bill. During the floor debate the representative fell into his all-too-common tendency to malapropisms, suggesting that gay people should be sent to "leopard" colonies (he presumably meant "leper" colonies). His fellow legislators, who had to have a sense of humor in order to serve in the Minnesota House anyway, weren't too surprised by his comment.

But at least "Representative Malaprop" was on the floor to vote. When the consenting adults bill, repealing the sodomy and fornication laws, came up the previous session, the practice of letting your seatmates vote for you was still prevalent. Rep. Jim Adams, a moderately liberal legislator from Minneapolis, voted for his seatmate. Adams, who drew considerable criticism by more progressive activists in his district, was anxious to win favor with these activists, who controlled his renomination. So Adams not only voted in for our bill, which was probably consistent with sentiment in his liberal district, but also cast a vote on behalf of his seatmate. The catch was that his seatmate was a conservative and quite irascible Irish Catholic from St. Paul's more conservative part of town.

Just a day after the vote, which unfortunately we still lost, I got on the elevator to discover that this representative was the only other passenger. Although I knew what had really happened, I couldn't resist and proceeded to heap praise on him for his courageous vote on sodomy repeal. It worked out pretty much just the way I thought it would. What can you say when someone's praising you like that, except to say thank you? When he got off the elevator, I doubled over with laughter. There are so many depressing things about these guys, you have to get your fun where you can.

One of the low points came when the state senate was debating the lesbian and gay civil rights bill. One conservative Republican stood up and talked about how he didn't want his son being taught by a gay teacher. What I could not tell him is that his son would benefit from the bill this ignorant legislator was opposing. Another leading opponent had a gay brother who'd always been a pillar of the community. Then there was the Republican senator from the Minneapolis suburbs who was actually a decent man and not a right-wing bigot, so I'd hoped we could win his vote. To my dismay, when he spoke it was to point out that he knew many gay people and said, "They don't have job problems" so he saw no need for the bill. Of course, the fact that most people from his class level owned their own companies or simply didn't need to work seemed to escape him.

I also remember a particularly ignorant state senator from south Minneapolis and his unbelievably bigoted comments. My friend and fellow lobbyist Jean Tretter, who had served his country in the military for several years, leaned over and told Denis and me it was the first time he had ever been told he wasn't a human being. Listening to the ignorant and really hateful things said about lesbians and gay men during these floor debates was often almost more than one could take.

Also early in my state lobbying career, I ran into a situation that didn't demonstrate the bizarre nature of the legislative process as much as it pointed to some unique aspects of gay rights lobbying. As I prepared for the 1973 legislative session, I consulted a range of politicos to try to figure out who my best targets should be. Among those I met with was Allan Spear, who was not yet "out," and as the evening progressed and more and more wine was consumed, Allan shifted from the 1 to 5 rating scale to marking "cute" next to the names of a couple of freshmen legislators.

A short time later I met with Rep. Tom Berg, the progressive DFL legislator representing the gayest district in Minneapolis, who was liberal but pretty straitlaced. Recently he had been unsuccessfully (and unfairly, I thought) challenged for DFL endorsement by an openly gay lawyer, partly because people said he didn't do enough about gay rights. I was just beginning my lobbying career and, needing the help, support, and cooperation of such a well-respected liberal legislator, I hoped our review of the "targeting" would not only give me insights but cement a valuable relationship to advance our goals. I wanted him to know we were serious, mainstream, and respectable, and I wanted him to think of gays in general and me in particular as more than just "sexual" beings. As we went through page after page of ratings, we suddenly came to page with a large "CUTE" written next to the name of a freshman legislator from Rochester. When we flipped to that page, Berg and I both saw the "CUTE!" at the same moment and I could sense Berg freeze up. However, because Allan Spear wasn't publicly out yet, I couldn't explain that it was him who had written it, so I just swallowed hard and realized that I'd have to redouble my efforts to get Berg's assistance.

One of the real classic moments took place when the Minnesota legislature was revising its sexual assault laws. The lead sponsor, Rep. Linda Berglin, took the opportunity to include the repeal of the sodomy and fornication statutes as they pertain to noncommercial sex in private (adultery laws would not be repealed because some contended that there was indeed a victim in that instance). She didn't want us to lobby for her bill and we agreed to just see if it could slide through (I'm not often comfortable with this approach). The bill moved uneventfully through the subcommittee and committee process and we held our breath. Although twenty-five states now have gotten rid of these archaic laws, only one—California—did so outside of either a general revision of their criminal codes (which had already been completed in Minnesota some time ago) or through revision of these sexual assault laws.[4] When Berglin's bill hit the floor, Rep. Arnold Kempe, from South St. Paul, moved to reinsert the penalties for fornication.

I recently listened to a tape of that debate and realize just how superb Berglin was, often responding to questions with what must have been purposely obscure answers. After a debate that was, for once, almost satisfying, the good guys were nonetheless defeated by three or four votes. Then Speaker of the House Martin Olav Sabo (now an extremely effective member of Congress), realizing that the morality zealots had blown it by not reinserting (such a nice word in this context, don't you think?) sodomy prohibitions on their earlier amendment, followed the normal procedure of asking, "Any further amendments?"

Although he could see Ray Kempe, Arnold's older brother, practically jumping on top of his seat to get the Speaker's attention, Speaker Sabo carefully did a half circle with his eyes, somehow not looking in Kempe's direction and asking, "Any further amendments?" After repeating the inquiry three times, he stated something to the effect of, "Hearing no request for further amendments, we'll move to a vote on H.R. ____," which passed overwhelmingly. Of course, both the Kempe brothers were fit to be tied while Marty feigned innocence. As a result, had the state senate not wrecked the fun, the Speaker's ploy during the consenting adults debate would have resulted in a bill stating that sex outside of marriage in Minnesota would be legal—but only if it was with the "anus or the mouth."

With the leadership of Allan Spear and Larry Bye, and the help of Marcia and Lee Greenfield, we held a founding conference of a new group, the Minnesota Committee for Gay Rights, a far better-developed and broader-based organization with a statewide board of directors. The keynote speaker for the conference was Phyllis Lyon, co-author (with her longtime lover, Del Martin) of *Lesbian/Woman*. Del and Phyllis were two of the genuine pioneers of our movement, starting the Daughters of Bilitis years earlier. Phyllis was a perfect speaker, even if she gave us holy hell for our sexism.

Her influence helped press us to balance the MCGR board, although it took longer for us to get up to speed on the name of the organization.

At that time I developed close friendships with Kerry Woodward, the woman who served as MCGR's cochair, and Brad Kohnert, who was on MCGR's board along with his then lover, Jimmy Sorenson, who often drove me around running errands. I have remained very close to them in the seventeen years that have passed since then.

Although there was a clear consensus within MCGR about working within the system, lobbying, and an electoral approach to the movement, there was far less agreement about the issue of staffing. I argued that groups such as the Urban Coalition, the Urban League, the NAACP, and countless other social change groups had long since understood the need for full-time staff, if only to help coordinate volunteers, but Allan's recent antiwar experience led to his wanting everything to be based on volunteers. When we finally agreed to hire a staffperson, Allan and a majority of the board insisted on the title "coordinator" while I thought it should be "executive director." Probably the bigger issue for me was that the staffer be me. Because of my experience in the previous legislative session working more than seventy hours a week to just barely keep up—and because it was a number of my social friends and associates who were likely to provide much of the funding—the issue was settled. I was hired as MCGR's coordinator.

Our 1975 legislative efforts were far more difficult and confused by internal gay movement battles. A small handful of activists, who'd never lobbied for the legislation or had any appreciation for the political realities associated with such an effort, demanded that the state bill include transvestites and that "public accommodations" and "public services" include gay marriage and gay adoption. When MCGR, which had always lobbied the bills, refused to go along with their demands, they staged a range of protests (in fact, along with my widely reported battles with *The Advocate's* David Goodstein, this is the only other internal conflict I treat in detail in Chapter 4, "We've Met the Enemy . . ."). By the end, we'd refocused the battle on the continuing homophobia of the legislature.

After we had all recovered from the losses of 1975, and moreover the internal brawls, we simply redoubled our efforts to build an unstoppable machine to enact the state bill in 1977. When the 1977 session began, our lobbying team of eleven trained, able volunteer lobbyists did extremely well and it appeared that we were finally on track to finally pass the bill. Shortly before the vote, however, we faced an unimagined right-wing mobilization and literally hundreds of constituent phone calls and letters opposing our bill from virtually every district in the state; this was in a nonfundamentalist state where polls showed 77 percent supporting the bill, every statewide elected official on record for the bill, and a well-respected, openly gay state senator. Despite excellent floor leadership by Allan Spear and a head count showing a surplus of at least eleven votes, we won narrowly on the preliminary "General Orders" vote but came up two votes short for a final passage victory.

State Senator Skip Humphrey, who'd led us on a merry chase for his vote, stuck with us, but among those we lost because the fundamentalists outorganized us and generated floods of mail and calls was a liberal Republican who had been one of three cosponsors for three years. Senator Tim Penney, who's since moved on to Congress, voted with us on General Orders but pleaded with Allan to not make him vote on "Final Passage" unless his vote would make the difference. Since moving to Congress, Penney's been either hostile or gutless or both on gay and lesbian issues and even AIDS. To say we were devastated seriously understates it.

Unfortunately, before we could come back for the next session, fundamentalists in St. Paul moved to follow Anita Bryant's lead and seek repeal of St. Paul's ordinance. Lobbying the ordinance in the first place, I joined with my close friends Kerry Woodward and Larry Bye to run the campaign against repeal. (Again, I ran into a strong subcurrent of internal conflict—with most of the attacks coming from a brand-new person named Carla—which diverted far too much time and attention. If Kerry had not fought vigorously on my behalf, the women/men split would have led to my ouster.) Despite polls showing us winning and broad community support, we were crushed by a wide margin.[5]

It was at that point when I finally gave up the dream of enacting statewide lesbian and gay civil rights legislation in Minnesota and instead agreed to accept the challenge of becoming the community's first lobbyist at Congress as the executive director of the Gay Rights National Lobby. For years, my obsession had been passage of the state bill, but given my exclusive attraction to black men, I had not only had to endure the bitter cold of Minnesota winters but had also done so without the attention and affection I sought in very, very white Minnesota. If my dream was no longer possible, Washington, DC's obsession with politics—and a 70 percent black population—seemed enticing, to say the very least.

Mainstreaming the Issue

I have long thought the key to our success was to be seen not as a fringe, bizarre issue but as one that is respectable and mainstream. Our task was to get average nongay citizens to think of "gay rights" as nothing more than simple fairness for a segment of American citizens. But in my earliest movement involvement most activists were anything but mainstream. Many of them came out of the antiwar movements, full of rebellion and a bit oriented to anarchy. The last thing many wanted to do was "to buy a piece of a rotten pie." While movement involvement in those days required courage and conviction—or perhaps simple foolishness—for many activists victory didn't appear to be one of the goals. In fact, some seemed to be afraid of victories, perhaps because for some their group victimhood helped them avoid taking personal responsibility. Many of them either had little to lose by their movement involvement or at least thought so, and most of the hundreds of thousands who've gotten involved in recent years, because of the AIDS crisis, were still deeply in their closets and not available to the gay movement in the 1970s.

Especially in these early years, rightly or wrongly, I often felt out of step and a bit like a duck out of water. Movement work was far too difficult to undertake with any intention other than to win. I know that some, maybe many, thought I was just a political hack, but I wanted to be practical. I was prepared to take half a loaf rather than holding out grandly for the whole loaf. This was politics and politics is the art of the possible. Compromise was hardly a dirty word to me.

Our job as gay rights advocates was, and is, to create the right "we/they" in the public mind. As long as our opponents incorrectly try to portray our efforts as an attempt by the homosexual perverts to undermine traditional values, we have to continue to help demonstrate to nongay people in the heartland that our struggle is completely consistent with the traditional American value of fairness, as well as the now-well-established tradition of civil rights. We needed to create a "we" which includes lesbians and gay men as part of the majority, those who believe in the American value of fairness, versus the small group of narrow-minded bigots who want both to discriminate and to impose their morality on the rest of us. This view goes far to explaining why I so completely abhor the term "queer" and will never use it: I don't believe nongay people can identify with the term, nor should they.

Although some gay activists recoiled from all the talk about "selling the issue" and "family values," the American people must understand lesbians and gay men are part of the family structure. As I write this, it seems quite obvious, but early in my movement career many activists thought we had to overturn traditional values and reject institutions such as the family. I learned a long time ago, however, that most useful efforts don't grow from abstract theory but from the small, practical necessities of life. In the early 1970s we were struggling mightily to get society to take our efforts for fairness seriously; to far too many, this new issue was very bizarre.

To address the problem we sought to embrace the well-tested strategy of building endorsement lists. However, that was easier said than done in those early days, since very few community leaders initially were willing to even consider supporting lesbian and gay rights. In the beginning we turned to leaders of liberal groups such as the Americans for Democratic Action, the American Civil Liberties Union (ACLU), the National Organization for Women (NOW), and so on. Unitarian-Universalist ministers sometimes provided religious support. The problem with this is that those willing to endorse, though often wonderful people, were often perceived as being on the liberal fringe. So the idea of "mainstreaming" was quite a relative thing.

One of the first to help us in Minnesota in the early 1970s was the state human rights commissioner, Conrad Balfour (he soon became the former commissioner, in part because of the guts he showed in speaking out against antigay discrimination). Another early endorser was Harry Davis, president of the Minneapolis Board of Education, executive director of the Urban Coalition, and a major leader in Minneapolis's small black community. I'd gotten to know Harry as his scheduling coordinator and driver when he ran as the Democratic-Farmer-Labor Party candidate for mayor, and his commitment to fairness was well established. Although he'd been defeated by a wide margin in his mayoral race, his endorsement was nonetheless a major breakthrough at that point.

It was no accident that both Balfour and Davis were black. Although no segment of society is immune from society's ignorance and bigotry about gay people (and some actually contend that the African-American community is more homophobic than the general public), civil rights leaders generally understand that discrimination based on an irrelevant factor in gay people's private lives is wrong. Although the black community in the Twin Cities is very small, their support was particularly important. There are some differences in the way the discrimination occurs, but in many respects discrimination against gay people is similar to discrimination against racial minorities in that it's based on judging people by so-called group characteristics, otherwise known as stereotypes. And, like discrimination against others, discrimination against gay people can have a devastating impact.

On the other hand, had black community leaders opposed gay civil rights initiatives and contended that such issues were substantively different it would have made things far more difficult. Some black community leaders, particularly among the clergy, do make that contention, but the vast majority of civil rights leaders have stood solidly with the effort for gay civil rights for years (see Appendix C). Securing the support of black community leaders continued to be a high priority when I assumed leadership of the national lobby.

Aiming for the broadest possible support, we carefully focused our battles and our endorsement efforts around ending discrimination in jobs, housing, and public accommodations rather than proving "gay is good." Within a fairly modest period of time, we were able to move from the lists of usual suspects from the liberal edge and into the mainstream of Minnesota thought: we got the endorsements of the former mayor of Minneapolis and from business leaders such as the presidents of General Mills and the Judson Bemis corporation. By the time of the first St. Paul referendum on the lesbian and gay civil rights ordinance in 1978, we were able to secure the endorsements of a virtual "who's who" of the community. The city's five most recent mayors, at least one of whom was to the right of Ghengis Khan, endorsed our position. The city's newspaper, the *St. Paul Pioneer Press and Dispatch,* which had opposed the ordinance when it first passed three years earlier, endorsed our position in an earthy manner that blue-collar St. Paulites could identify with.

Because of spectacular efforts of our religious organizers, Leo Treadway and Craig Anderson, we had the support of the bishops of virtually every major denomination. Even Catholic Archbishop Roach, who'd opposed gay rights during previous legislative sessions, issued a statement deploring discrimination against gay people. Although his statement was couched in the standard disclaimer of disapproval of the lifestyle, it was widely and correctly interpreted as supportive of the gay rights ordinance. In part because the ordinance wasn't designed as a "Good Housekeeping Stamp of Approval" but as a prohibition from discrimination, Leo and Craig were able to secure three times as many endorsements from ministers, priests, and rabbis as our opposition (and we had twice as many sermons the Sunday before the referenda as the opponents). Especially in the context of that 1978 battle, the endorsements still stand as a monument to the dedication and ability of our religious coordinators.

When I think about St. Paul one individual endorsement stands out. In 1975 I lobbied the new city council president, Ron Maddox, who was a conservative Democrat and didn't automatically embrace "crazy" issues such as gay rights. When he agreed to meet with me, it wasn't at the council offices but at the downtown topless bar he owned. After half an hour of trying to respond calmly to some fairly insulting comments, Ron decided my answers had been pretty good. Years later I was told he was still talking about how surprised he was to find a "homo" who could drink and talk football. When the repeal effort came up Ron was solidly with us.

I've always thought that the lesson of the lobbying of Ron Maddox is that we should try to not respond with anger and hostility to bigoted comments or questions. Maybe those that are working from the outside can and should be the voices of anger and rage over bigoted, ignorant statements, but it's critical for lesbian and gay rights lobbyists to try to establish and maintain honest communication with legislators. If we respond with anger and make people wrong for expressing their honest opinions, they will just remain silent and we will never really learn what their reservations and barriers are or how to turn them around.

Our Minnesota endorsement efforts didn't focus exclusively on individuals but also on key statewide organizations. One of the first groups we went after was the Minnesota League of Human Rights Commissions, which had member commissions across the state. It not only seemed logical, but we also thought it would give us a base for grassroots mail to legislators statewide—such constituent mail was particularly important since the gay and lesbian community was concentrated in the Twin Cities. In addition, the league's endorsement would play a constructive role in helping legislators understand that antigay discrimination was as destructive and invidious as discrimination based on race or gender.

In addition, we secured the support of the Mental Health Association of Minnesota and the League of Women Voters (LWV). The backing of the MHAM was more important at that time than I think it would be today because of the prevailing notions at that time about gay people being sick. The League of Women Voters had a reputation for studying issues to death before taking a position on them and seemed to personify the mainstream of Minnesota. I discovered, however, that they had a national policy opposing discrimination against all people, so eventually we were able to convince them to lend their support.

The LWV state president had agreed to testify at an upcoming Judiciary Committee hearing in 1975 but, at the last minute, canceled because she was fearful that her appearance might cause too much controversy within the outstate leagues. With so little time and so much to do, I had little choice but to accept her position for the moment, but prior to their state convention that summer I demanded that they either come out for nondiscrimination legislation or modify their policy position to indicate they opposed discrimination for everyone but gay people. They responded affirmatively and lent their support. Like the leagues in countless other states, their support has proven invaluable over the years because of their legitimacy and ability to deliver grassroots pressure. League members are among the few liberals, along with Common Cause members, who actually are willing to write to their legislators.

One group whose support we failed to win was the Joint Religious Legislative Coalition (JRLC), the ecumenical lobbying group for the religious community at the state capitol. When I first began lobbying, securing the support of JRLC was my first and top priority—even before the 1973 legislative session. We had the protestant Council of Churches and the Jewish Community Relations Council on board, but the third key partner—the Minnesota Catholic Conference—had veto power and exercised it. A key opponent helping to block the archdiocese's support was their lobbyist, John Marquart.

Making Support for Gay Rights an "Article of Faith" for Minnesota's Dominant Political Party

Although the Democratic Party at times looks a bit chaotic and inept, when I began lobbying gay civil rights in the early 1970s in Minnesota the Democratic-Farmer-Labor Party had just captured both houses of the legislature by solid margins. Securing DFL support was not just desirable but essential. Also, as I interpreted the national struggle for black civil rights, the Democratic Party's leadership, since Hubert Humphrey's historic battle for a strong civil rights plank in the party platform, had been a central foundation for many civil rights bills, most particularly the 1964 Civil Rights Act banning discrimination in jobs, housing, and public accommodations.

We still sought Republican support—we'd have to gain a small number of GOP legislators to complement the vast majority of Democratic votes—but experience was already suggesting that conservatives who were increasingly dominating the GOP party were far less open to potential support. As fundamentalists increasingly took over the Republican Party across the country, that situation only accelerated.

There were two major breakthroughs in winning the support of the DFL in the early 1970s: the first platform plank in 1972 and the second and more important one in 1974. Although the first plank would normally be the milestone, the whole 1972 state convention and platform was widely seen as tainted and unrepresentative because of the influx of "McGovern crazies." Also, the fact that the plank called not only for nondiscrimination but also for gay marriage and gay adoption contributed to the perception that it was far outside the mainstream. Although the idea of domestic partner legislation has now secured popular support in cities across the country, the plank didn't call for domestic partners laws but gay marriage—and it was 1972. Political observers and longtime DFL activists alike tended to be critical of the plank at the least and some dismissed it out of hand; DFL candidates quickly disassociated themselves from the gay rights plank.

While the DFL took control of both houses of the legislature in the 1972 election despite the "radical platform," party regulars remained unconvinced and set out to change the rules so such crazy platform planks as gay rights couldn't pass in the future (I remember that leading political figure Walter Mondale was among those critical of the plank). The 1972 platform planks required only 50 percent plus one of the delegates for adoption, but they were amended to require a full 60 percent at future conventions.

Minnesota's parties operate by a caucus system of neighborhood and town meetings both to elect delegates to higher levels and to adopt resolutions on issues. Party leaders, no matter how liberal, might have opted for avoidance as the safest approach to such emerging issues, but caucus attenders were far more open to inclusion. Nationally, I think that's been part of the difficulty in advancing gay rights: liberal political consultants, like their comparable state party leaders, advocate that their candidates avoid the issue like the plague and, in the face of bigotry and ignorance, this has contributed to serious discrimination in jobs and housing.

Minnesota's participatory caucus democracy allowed us to prove the presence of genuine grassroots support, though, and win the necessary support for this generational issue. Faced with the new 60 percent requirement and without the insurgency of the McGovern campaign, we could anticipate a tough time securing even a moderate lesbian and gay rights plank that focused on the twin goals of protecting lesbians and gay men from job and housing discrimination and repealing repressive sex laws. Such laws included not only the sodomy laws that many interpreted as aimed at gay people, but fornication and adultery laws as well. The term we used was "consenting adults" legislation. With politics as the art of the possible, we eliminated any reference to gay marriage or gay adoption without a second thought. Once we had a strong "vehicle" our next priority was to get resolutions adopted at as many of the precinct caucuses as possible, and hopefully from diverse geographic areas. The strategy from there was to get the resolutions passed by the next level of party apparatus, at the state senate district, congressional district, and, finally, the state convention.

On a parallel track, we tried to get the majority of the state DFL Platform Committee, which was preparing the draft platform for convention review, to include the moderate lesbian/gay civil rights plank and thereby avoid a floor fight, but this turned out to be unrealistic. We benefited enormously from the advice and insight of the leaders of the liberal Americans for Democratic Action, whose executive director, Denis Wadley, had become a friend and mentor during the previous legislative session.

If Denis provided much of the sage advice as we sought the platform plank, it was the relatively new DFL Feminist Caucus that helped provide the grassroots muscle. It was founded on the principles of support for women's rights in general and for the ERA and abortion rights specifically. The caucus' founding "mothers" were women within the DFL who were tired of making coffee and not policy. They were determined that the DFL party they loved and had worked so hard for would show courage on women's rights and, happily, they were deeply committed to lesbian and gay civil rights as well. Since they were fighting for a pro-choice plank themselves, and were facing an increasingly well organized anti-abortion movement, they were already organizing across the state.

Because we were willing to settle for a moderate plank our grassroots effort to get resolutions passed was quite successful, with at least 70 to 100 precincts passing resolutions. It also passed in countless state senate district conventions, which was the next step up the process. The three congressional district conventions that make up Minneapolis, St. Paul, and the suburbs overwhelmingly passed the forwarded resolutions. We went into the platform committee with a full head of steam.

The final piece of our strategy called for the election of at least one openly gay person to the state DFL Platform Committee and quizzing all the potential candidates for the committee positions from other conventions about their support of gay rights. An openly gay person on the committee would enable us essentially to trade votes with more neutral committee members who felt strongly about other issues, such as family farming. With that preparation, we'd lobby the entire platform committee once it was selected. I was elected to the state platform committee from the 5th district and Kerry was elected an alternate. Kerry, who has since come out as a lesbian, became a lifelong friend and played key roles in most of my movement endeavors, including being an early regional staffperson for the Gay Rights National Lobby and the first cochair of the Human Rights Campaign Fund.

When it came time to bring the issue to a vote, to our surprise there was very little debate on the platform committee. We quickly included a gay rights plank in the draft platform, but this smooth sailing did not continue when we got to the 1974 State DFL Convention. The gay rights buttons our DFL Gay Rights Caucus passed out became the most popular button of the convention, but the moralists' challenge to our plank, led mostly by anti-abortion forces, led to a brief but very intense debate. Along with a number of other gay and lesbian delegates and alternates, I worked the convention floor to try to gather enough votes.

Just before the vote, it seemed like we had an outside chance of upsetting the odds and the conservative DFL forces' predictions that we would get creamed. Among these "moderate, status quo" forces was Governor Wendell Anderson and his people, for whom I had unwisely worked my heart out in 1970. The vote took place by a standing division of the room. The DFL Feminist Caucus forces delivered big-time, working hard on our behalf. I particularly remember watching Peggy Specktor work the suburban 3rd district delegation. Peggy, who had become a good friend from our legislative lobbying in the previous session, begged, cajoled, and, when all else failed, literally threw delegates from their seats to stand up for gay rights.

We held our breath as the vote was tallied. Had we needed only the 50 percent of the last convention, we would have been very safe, but could we actually get to 60 percent? After a very, very long pause, the convention secretary announced that the gay rights plank had prevailed with 63 percent of the vote! Some of the old-time regulars looked completely shocked as our supporters cheered wildly.

The debate and the long time it had taken to tally the vote meant our people then scattered to the bathrooms, and, to our shock, the opposition moved to reconsider the previous vote. We scrambled frantically to regroup our supporters. The Minneapolis delegation was virtually 100 percent. St. Paul, where gay activist Dennis Miller was a fixture in every DFL-endorsed campaign, was almost as strong, but we had to get as many others as possible to get to that 60 percent again.

Again, Peggy literally kicked ass over in the 3rd. Koryne Horbal and Cynthia Kitlinski dragged their friends from their seats in the Anoka part of the 8th congressional district delegation. Over at the 7th district, which is one of the outstate districts in the northwest part of the state, Ray Anderson was standing and trying to convince fellow delegates to do likewise. Ray was an elderly farmer who had served on the platform committee and had turned around on the issue during the deliberations of the state platform committee. He was very well respected among his delegates.

We waited for word. And waited. What was taking so long? Finally we found out that we had held on to win again! With the state legislature controlled by DFLers and a DFL governor, support for lesbian and gay rights was again in the platform and on its way to becoming an article of faith for the party. Capping months of hard work, it was a very emotional moment, with much crying and hugging—and expressions of deepest thanks to our buddies from the feminist caucus. The convention ended and State Senator Allan Spear and I went to a gay bar in downtown Minneapolis to celebrate (Spear had come out publicly the previous year, making him the second openly gay elected official in the country). The television news made much of our upset victory, but the crowd at Sutton's seemed completely oblivious to what I thought was the importance of our victory.

Since we never wanted the issue of lesbian and gay civil rights to become a partisan one, we did a mailing to every delegate and alternate to the State Republican Convention as well. We understood what a slim chance we had of winning their support, and so we focused on consenting adults legislation, which had had a Republican chief sponsor in the previous session. The mailing was paid for by the Playboy Foundation.

Jean Nicholas Tretter of the Gay Rights Legislative Committee, a nominal Republican at the time, signed a cover letter in the mailing to GOP delegates and alternates. The mailing also included a letter from Jim Newman of

the Young Americans for Freedom. Despite these efforts, the gay rights issue was ignored, which is better than what has happened at GOP conventions since that time. The lesbian and gay civil rights issue has to be bipartisan, and we've supported Republicans when their positions justified it. It is
great that a group of gay people who are active within the GOP is emerging,
but, at present, the fundamentalists seem to have extraordinary power within the Republican Party.

We must continue to press both parties and it is important to have lesbian
and gay activists within both parties, but I am tired of some of them acting
like apologists for a party where silence seems to be the best we can hope
for. Too often, gay Republicans take "crumbs off the plate" and defend the
party and any Republican no matter how bad they are, while it seems they'll
easily denounce anyone who doesn't support every plausible Republican,
even if his or her opponent's record or commitments are far stronger.

Funds: The Mother's Milk of Politics

Getting "land legs" in the gay movement in the early 1970s and translat-
ing political experience into a young, somewhat rebellious movement, I
also had to learn how to raise funds. Gay rights work is just like an extended
political campaign—and campaigns are quite expensive—so we needed
strong financial backing.

It quickly became obvious where we couldn't get it: the Twin Cities' gay
bars of the time. The largest gay bar in town, the Gay '90s, was then owned
by a nongay family whose level of community consciousness was revealed
by their unwillingness even to have gay rights materials available on top of
their cigarette machines. Sutton's started out in a similar mode but they improved and ended up helping pay for some of my movement trips.

But if we couldn't raise the money from gay bars, maybe we could from
their patrons—people directly impacted by our efforts—right? Wrong!
From 1970 until 1974, when we tried to get support from the people in the
bars, whether it was fund-raising or just trying to inform them of something,
we met total rejection.

A good 40 percent of the flyers we handed out outside Sutton's, a bar frequented by hundreds of young, attractive men, ended up crumpled up. More
than a few were thrown in our faces by angry men screaming at us about
"rocking the boat." It was very painful, to say the least. Although I wouldn't
admit it until a good deal later and did not let people see me at the time,
there were more than a few nights when I went home in tears. I tried hard to
not become bitter with my brothers and sisters, but it seems safe to say the
consciousness was amazingly low. By then, we had formed the Gay Rights

Legislative Committee to lobby the state legislature on lesbian and gay rights and sodomy repeal. It was clear (if only to me) that lobbying gay rights was a full-time job. And there were countless other expenses as well.

One of the first and worst fund-raisers I have ever been a part of was an event aimed at gay and nongay people alike. As it turned out that it could be used to teach classic lessons on how not to do it. It was jointly sponsored by the Americans for Democratic Action and held at the home of prominent liberals, Nancy and Ellis Olkon.

I knew very little about putting on fund-raisers, which soon became obvious. Invitations were sent to a number of gay people, but the primary invitation list was the ADA membership. We failed to set up a committee, put out good publicity, assign coordinators, or do phone follow-up, and we assumed, without any evidence, that nongay liberals would support the cause financially.

When we got there it became clear just how little we knew. Only ten people showed up, including the hosts. Nongay people, even the most supportive, didn't exactly place gay rights at the top of their priority list in 1973, but instead somewhere below garbage collection. Talk about an issue whose time had not come! It demonstrated clearly how limited GRLC was as an organization and it forced me to acknowledge we really had very little support and participation from the gay and lesbian community. The best things about that fund-raiser were the lessons we learned. We had nowhere to go but up.

In the meantime, our lobbying efforts were beginning to pay off with the passage of the Minneapolis lesbian and gay civil rights ordinance in 1974. Suddenly some of my friends from the bars, who had largely ignored my political work earlier, indicated a willingness to help raise funds. Two people particularly helped: Tom Weiser and Walt Nelson; together with several others they hosted parties for affluent gay people in the Twin Cities gay party circuit. Finally, with their help, it actually became fashionable to go to these events. Usually they were held in one of their nice homes, which in Tom's case almost always meant a newly restored house he'd just finished, with a lavish spread. Instead of a cover charge at the door we depended on a pitch and lots of peer pressure. After a buffet dinner, one of the key social players briefly spoke about the effort's importance and introduced me.

I was not a great speaker but I got by, focusing on the importance of the legislation, and how it helped change attitudes, and was adequate. As we began to run into conflict with activists who took a more extreme, confrontational approach, my pitch shifted to letting the assembled group know they had a choice. If they wanted these more confrontational gay activists— who were leading "drag queen parades" and generally being as outrageous as possible—to be their spokespersons "then we can all go home, because their efforts don't cost anything." If they wanted a within-the-system, suit-and-tie, moderate lobbying approach they could be proud of, however, then we had to have their help. Then several people from the audience, who had already agreed to lend their support, pledged their support: "I'll give $250, Steve" which got the snowball rolling, and we'd usually do pretty well. But two stories of these parties, which probably totaled seven or eight over the years, come to mind.

The very first time, at Tom's home in Wayzata, as discussion focused on the need to repeal the sodomy statute, a very drunken man went off on a tirade about how "we're all faggots who don't deserve any rights and these laws are just for society's protection." It was very unsettling and I was unsure how to handle it, but before I had a chance to speak a somewhat older gentleman (who has since supported virtually every gay political effort I have led both locally and nationally) took control and set the proper tone by demanding the drunk sit down. This distinguished gentleman, who turned out to be a retired lawyer, cited the other guy's self-hate as a good example of why the effort was needed so badly.

On another occasion I arrived early and one of our hosts asked to inspect our pledge cards. In those days, many of those who contributed made out their checks to the hosts, who in turn wrote checks to the organization. I'd just had the pledge cards printed and had carefully avoided spelling out the full name of the organization. Part of my sales pitch included the fact that they could make out their checks with just the committee's initials and they'd be endorsed the same way at the bank.

Instead, our host this afternoon insisted the tops of the pledge cards, with identifying letters only, be cut off so there was not only no name but also not even initials of the group on the forms. Most of those who contributed in those early days actually didn't make out their checks to even the initials, let alone the full name; they wrote their checks to Tom or Walt, who would add in their own contributions and write out their checks to "MCGR." It was hardly liberation at its finest and I found it upsetting, but we needed the funds and I believed in whatever worked.

Happily it unfolded the way I hoped and, over the years, there was extraordinary movement, growth, and a positive sense of gay identity by many of these people. They moved from writing their checks to their friends to writing them out to a group's initials to writing them out to the full name of the organization. Eventually many of these people, who thought they were risking their careers by even attending the fund-raisers, actually marched in gay Pride parades. But back then we were at the beginning.

Despite this relative success—which allowed our state lobbying effort to have an annual budget of more than $40,000 way back in 1975—we were never able to get to the biggest potential givers or get the attendees to give the kind of gifts they should have. For instance, one of the top executives of one of the largest department stores in the Twin Cities, who had a six-figure income almost twenty years ago, refused to attend. This was despite the fact that he often showed up at the hosts' homes for regular parties and I often bumped into him at the local gay baths. Some time later, I learned this man's "secret" didn't save him from facing the horrors of AIDS.

A constant challenge, then and now, is to be able to continue to press for support while avoiding becoming bitter with those who have such great resources but refuse to contribute. I have always felt such bitterness, although natural, was both personally destructive and quite unproductive. Fighting back this bitterness was hardest for me in two periods. The first was in these earliest years in Minnesota, when the collective gay and lesbian consciousness was still remarkably low. Given that I knew the strength of our lobbying and organizing depended on our ability to raise adequate funds, it was hard to watch people blow $25 to $30 a night on drinks but refuse to contribute "because they couldn't afford it." I can now look back with satisfaction at finding the patience which is normally so foreign to me, though; when a current leader, who I really had not known well, received an award he held me up as one of his role models as he and a whole new generation of middle-class and affluent donors became involved in lesbian and gay rights.

More recently, when I went back to Minnesota to receive an award from the Human Rights Campaign Fund Twin Cities dinner committee, an individual I had known marginally during my earliest years in Minnesota activism approached me. I knew he'd subsequently moved to San Francisco and had heard he'd become a part of the more reform-oriented portion of the community there. Al was clean-cut, good-looking, and came off as a typical Yuppie—precisely the sort of individual we were unable to attract to the movement in the early years, as either a foot soldier or a check writer. Al came up to me and told me what I already knew: that he'd thought I was crazy for my activism when he'd first known me. He went on to explain that as his consciousness expanded he'd come to respect me. He thanked me over and over again for being out there, visible, and relatively mainstream, and therefore giving him a role model. That conversation was as important to me as the beautiful award I received the following evening. I raise all this not to blow my own horn but to point out how critical it was to be patient with people who aren't willing to get involved. In fact, one of my central fund-raising principles—aside from simple harassment and persistence—was making it safe for people to give to us. So we had to be patient and forgiving as we got people to that point.

Even before the passage of the Minneapolis lesbian and gay civil rights ordinance, getting the funds together for a lobbying effort at the state legislature was a major priority. We did not have a real fund-raising plan when I agreed to meet a new friend at Sutton's one night. Mike Garrett was very nice but I was a little concerned, as I'd never heard him refer to what he did for a living. I asked him if I could help him get a job, which he found sweet and amusing.

Instead, Mike, who'd listened to my daydreaming about the need for a state lobbying effort, called me a few days later and asked me to meet him at Sutton's, and there he gave me an envelope to open when I got home. Still not aware of his strong financial position, I was shocked when I discovered a check for $500, which would give us a foundation to launch our state lobbying campaign. Mike later directly helped in lobbying, although he hated that part, and Mike's been a friend for years.

As time went on, and GRLC was replaced by the Minnesota Committee for Gay Rights, which had a real board and quickly established a membership of more than 250 people, we finally had a real base of operations. Most of our fund-raisers, often held at State Senator Allan Spear's home, cost $5 or $10 a person, but some were "quite expensive": $25 a person. I vividly remember MCGR successfully getting a couple, Dan and Keith, involved because until about that time we just could not get middle-class people involved in the lesbian and gay civil rights movement.

We were growing out of the period when most considered the gay movement an embarrassment, and were able to develop a solid base of middle-class people, who had both the commitment and the resources to give. To capitalize, we created a monthly pledge club, and by our high-water mark in 1977 we had more than forty people pledging from $5 to $50 a month.

Another high-water mark in our Minnesota fundraising was when MCGR hosted a major gala for the upcoming state legislative battle and to lay a base for an anticipated referendum by the right wing to repeal the St. Paul gay rights ordinance. The gala was to take place at a wonderful old mansion, owned by an extraordinarily pretentious queen. Although he'd had many notorious parties there and most people had heard of his fabulous home, it's safe to say that most gay people had never been invited to them.

We charged the then-expensive price of $25 per person but set up a limo delivery from the bars to help turn out a crowd. We didn't know it, but we followed a later model of gay and lesbian fund-raisers with establishment of a core committee. Word spread that "An Autumn Evening" was "the event" of the season. We hoped for a good crowd but were literally overwhelmed by massive numbers, and raised almost $10,000.

We had laid a good fund-raising base, but the 1978 St. Paul battle marked a zenith. We had doubts whether we could raise the funds but set a budget of about $60,000—a lot of money in those days in a Midwestern city notoriously tight with a dollar. We did terrifically with direct mail to donors to the Dade County, Florida, campaign, although we got conned into sharing the proceeds with the referendum defenses in Eugene, Oregon, and Wichita, Kansas, despite the fact that we were the only ones with the list at that point. Small fund-raisers were held throughout the Twin Cities, money poured in to retain the ordinance, and, under the direction of Larry Bye, we set up a "boiler room" operation for bigger gifts.

Larry and I called potential big donors and asked for major gifts. Oftentimes people pause and say something like, "Okay, I'll contribute $100," and Larry or I would counter by saying, "Gee, we'd really hoped you could give $250." Sometimes such pushiness worked and sometimes it didn't, but what came next was often even more startling to them. With so little time before the election, if they agreed to send their check in, we would explain we knew how busy they were and asked whether it was okay to send someone by to pick up the check. While we knew that almost everyone planned to fulfill their pledges, by sending someone over we eliminated any gaps. Rev. Troy Perry, who could squeeze blood out of turnips, came to be our special guest at a terrific event at Mike Garrett's and successfully helped raise several thousand more near the end of the campaign. Before we'd finished, we raised over $110,000.

Two individual contributions come to my mind as examples of people's extraordinary commitment. One supporter, who had given to various gay rights groups and causes for years, had already contributed very generously to our St. Paul citizens' campaign when he came into our headquarters one Saturday and pressed his tax refund check for more than $600 into my hand. Another donor, who was a Catholic priest, called and took me out to lunch. During lunch, he passed $1,000 to me in hundred dollar bills under the luncheon table, leaving me almost speechless.

Despite the tremendous financial support from the community, we were badly beaten in the vote, and the community was devastated. Larry, Kerry, and most of the other staff, including myself, walked around in a fog for months. About that time, one of our single biggest donors and key fundraisers, Tom Weiser, met me for lunch. He suggested that it was going to be very difficult to make real headway on gay rights legislation in Minnesota for a while and I should consider moving to Washington, DC. He offered to help fund my efforts if I would take over the basically dysfunctional national lobby, the Gay Rights National Lobby. He agreed to give $25,000 to help me get going while I established a track record and fund-raising base. In 1977, I was still one of the very few full-time gay rights lobbyists at the state level in the country, so when GRNL—which had never had an executive director or lobbyist—considered the idea, they jumped at the opportunity. They had no funds or significant donor base, so I'd have my hands full, but the Minnesota legislation that had driven me just wasn't viable, and frigid, white Minnesota had long since lost its allure.

Although it didn't occur to me at the time, in years since I have sometimes thought about my meeting with Tom and his pledge. Was it a glorified "one-way ticket out of town"? But very recently I was finally able to track him down again and we had a wonderful conversation. Tom assures me that such an interpretation was not true at all and our conversation reminds me of how much I always cared for him and how much the gay community and I owe him. He often led with his heart and not with his head, which got him into trouble, but then so did I.

I packed my bags and a few boxes and flew off to work for the new, emerging national gay and lesbian movement. Although I thought I could handle anything, I had never lived away from my own hometown. Both the city and the job turned out to be far more challenging than I ever imagined. I contacted Michael Bedwell, a DC activist I had met while working against Anita Bryant's Dade County repeal in Miami, and he readily agreed that I could stay with him for two or three weeks while I got my feet on the ground.

When I arrived by cab from the airport to my friend's house, I learned it was not actually Michael's house at all but that of another activist, Mayo Lee. He was the president of the largest local gay group and was amazingly gracious, given that Michael did not even tell him I was coming. Their third roommate was Leonard Matlovich, who'd been on the cover of *Time* magazine during his lawsuit against the military for summarily dismissing him.[6] We'd become friends in Dade County during the Anita Bryant fight, and Lenny was down to earth. He wasn't particularly astute politically, but both his commitment to the best interests of the community and sweet innocence were very appealing.

I began to get a sense of what a challenge I had ahead when Mayo asked what brought me to DC. Exhausted from a long flight, coping with tons of luggage, and very nervous about such a big move, I mustered the energy to explain earnestly that I'd been hired to be the first director and lobbyist for the Gay Rights National Lobby. To my shock, this distinguished gentleman doubled up with laughter and, in his charming Southern drawl, told me the Gay Rights National Lobby was dead as a doornail. He went on to suggest if that is what really brought me to Washington, DC, I might not want to haul all those boxes upstairs and perhaps I should just pack up and catch a return flight to Minnesota.

That was my welcome to Washington, DC. Cold, white Minnesota never looked so appealing.

Chapter 2

Pushing the Pedals of Power: From Minnesota to the Gay Rights National Lobby

One of the most important lessons I have carried with me for more than twenty years came from my earliest days in Minnesota. At the Minnesota Committee for Gay Rights, with only one staff person and limited volunteer power, we quickly had to learn we could not be all things to all people. We could not take on every legitimate movement cause, and we had to find ways to avoid just putting out brush fires.

Establishing Boards, and Planning with Goals and Objectives

After accepting the executive director position with the Gay Rights National Lobby in 1978, I began to focus on the variety of approaches to creating a board of directors. These ranged from attempting a representational balance of the group's many constituents—what I call "the UN divergent views" strategy—to one focusing on a "give, get, or get off" board. In between are countless possibilities.

My experience with the boards of the Minnesota Committee for Gay Rights and the National Gay Task Force led me to conclude that the board at the Gay Rights National Lobby should not be made up of "yes-people," but instead should include members with a shared perspective and sense of mission. This had been the case with the MCGR board, and I felt it would be best for GRNL as well.

My first review of the minutes of the previous GRNL board meetings—something I should have done before accepting the job—sent chills down my spine. For more than two and a half years since its creation, the board had floundered. The minutes revealed that the board had not gotten past constant conflict and extensive discussions about inclusiveness. In essence, what they had done—after flying around the country for board meetings on GRNL's dime—was rearrange the chairs on the *Titanic*. This was a board with fundamentally different views about the organization's goals and mission, and the results were disastrous.

The different political views on the board were accentuated by the failure to raise funds and hire a strong executive director to offer leadership and develop a shared vision and strategies. I was confident I could raise the initial funds necessary to get the group going effectively, but the greater challenge was to get the board firmly behind me, which included sharing my sense of mission and vision.

Sadly, once the board met, I was convinced the incumbent male cochair, Ray Hartman, was not as politically savvy as would be necessary. With the Rev. Troy Perry, founder of the Universal Fellowship of Metropolitan Community Churches (MCC), we rounded up the votes to elect Jerry Weller, the most politically astute gay operative in Oregon, to replace Hartman. I was excited about having Jerry serve as cochair because I had already developed a good friendship via our frequent phone conversations. Also, I had already seen his effective follow-through and lobbying with Oregon politicians on lesbian and gay issues, including securing a new cosponsor for the national gay rights bill; Oregon, under Jerry's leadership, had become one of the strongest gay rights states in the nation.

Jerry's cochair was a dynamite lesbian from Maine, Kate McQueen, who told me early on that she didn't believe in "reform politics." Her admission normally would have scared the hell out of me, but she explained that she had come to believe in GRNL's methods and even supported my incrementalist lobbying approach. Like Jerry, Kate did a terrific job as cochair. The three of us got along very well, which enhanced the organization's effectiveness; when either of them disagreed with my assessments, I took their concerns seriously and moved cautiously.

In addition to the change in the cochair positions, I felt that changes in the board's membership were needed. This was painful because a couple of the people who I felt had to leave were also my friends. However, besides board members sharing a common vision and sense of purpose, I felt attendance at board meetings was absolutely essential, so I invoked GRNL's bylaws to have ten to fourteen of the thirty board members removed for nonattendance. The remaining members agreed to replace the outgoing members with people who could bring the group the solid political and legislative judgement—and stature—we so badly needed then. My focus was not on their fund-raising capacity, partly because that is not what I believed should be their sole responsibility and partly because we concluded that it would be difficult to attract affluent or fund-raising types to a group that, as yet, had no accomplishments.

Despite our attention to the composition of the GRNL board, it could meet only once or twice a year, because GRNL had to pay the costs of their travel to meetings from all over the country to Washington, DC. The executive committee, though, met four times a year; in addition to Jerry and Kate, it included Jean O'Leary, a longtime movement dynamo who was a former co-executive director of the Task Force and then of the National Gay Rights Advocates (NGRA); Meryl Friedman, a terrific former NGTF board member and teacher; Mary Hartman, a very articulate activist from Minnesota; and the Rev. Troy Perry.

McQueen, Friedman, and Hartman already spent a great amount of time together. Troy's schedule made it tough to get him to actually attend board and executive committee meetings (he'd previously had an attendance problem on the NGTF board), but I had an ace in the hole in the form of Jerry Weller. Troy and Jerry had known each other before they joined the GRNL board, and Jerry's mere presence dramatically increased our chances of getting Troy to find time in his busy schedule. One exception I recall was when the two of them had stayed up too late and, having had a particularly vigorous night, arrived pretty late for the meeting. Jerry, who was an able board cochair and lent terrific political judgment, represented GRNL at the Mr. International Leather contest, sponsored by GRNL board member Chuck Renslow each year on Memorial Day. Troy also usually attended and was often a judge.

I've since realized that my first year at GRNL was dedicated to establishing a track record and just surviving, as well as helping the group get its land legs. After our changes—and with time, effort, and persuasion—the GRNL board of directors included some of the most effective, impressive activists in the country, and truly shared a vision on strategy and mission. It included two of the gay and lesbian community's key spiritual leaders: not only Rev. Troy Perry but also Frank Scheuren of the national gay Catholic group Dignity. The board also included two of the true pioneers of the lesbian and gay movement, Barbara Gittings of Philadelphia and Frank Kameny of Washington, DC. Later, the board also included Dan Bradley, president of the Legal Services Corporation in President Carter's administration and the highest ranking government official in the country's history to come out and publicly acknowledge he was a gay man. His coming out got major attention in *The New York Times* and *The Washington Post,* among other papers.

Establishing goals and objectives has become my way of working, so I can today pull out the "Goals and Objectives" from each of the past five years. Overall, I think that it's been a good approach, but it has sometimes meant that I've failed to capitalize on timely political developments.

As a founding member of the Task Force's first national board of directors, I saw firsthand a natural, if regrettable, tendency to spend a disproportionate amount of time responding to crises rather than establishing a battle plan and sticking to it come hell or high water. In fact, the Task Force wasn't the exception but the rule. One of the many skill development seminars I attended taught me about strategies to avoid this pitfall. In particular, they showed me how to establish yearly goals and objectives, and because I'd always had the discipline to stick to such goals and objectives, this wouldn't be a problem.

Goals and objectives were especially essential not only because the board had few meetings but also because the Lobby had an extreme shortage of funds to do everything that needed to be done. The fact that the challenge before us was a long-term one only made it more critical to have measurable short-term goals and objectives. Since I thought it would take many years to pass a national lesbian and gay civil rights bill, we had to find some means to assess how we were doing accurately and fairly.

Prior to board meetings, I prepared goals and objectives for the coming year and asked the board to review them so they could be revised and approved. The goals and objectives were as concrete as I could possibly make them, and the objectives usually had timelines as well. Although I definitely played a strong executive director role, I wanted the collective judgement of the board and agreement with the direction we were going. Usually, the board made minor changes while generally sharing my views.

In addition to reviewing the progress on the previous year's goals and objectives and approving those of the coming year, I tried to give the board of directors and executive committee a general sense of how I thought we were doing. In my January 1982 executive director's report to the Gay Rights National Lobby board of directors, which followed fast on the heels of both Reagan's election and the Republicans taking control of the United States Senate, I stated:

> There was plenty of bad news in 1981. Another loss on a McDonald amendment to Legal Services, cosponsorship of H.R. 1454 (the lesbian/gay civil rights bill) reduced from previous highs, the stunning defeat of the D.C. Sexual Assault bill (with its repeal of the District's sodomy laws) are just a few of the bad memories. Further, with Members of Congress living in a state of political paranoia, it's clear that Moral Majority can pass almost any regressive bill or amendment they can get to the floor of both Houses.
>
> If these developments stood alone, I could better understand those who think I must be living in a constant state of mourning. Nothing could be further from the truth.
>
> Our most important battles are *not* the short-term ones but the battle for effective continued growth so we can lay the groundwork for eventual victory. In this context, with the hostile political climate, our

community in general and Gay Rights National Lobby in particular must be prepared in the short run to accept incremental progress.

When I accepted the position of Executive Director of GRNL a few years ago, I had a sense of what our growth, development, and progress should look like if we were to stay "on target." My sense is that we are actually somewhat ahead of that timeline, in my head.

As GRNL grew, I learned that in order for other staff to really buy into them it was essential for the goals and objectives to come as a result of a staff retreat where we all talked about them. I used the "goals and objectives" strategy throughout my time with the Gay Rights National Lobby, the Fairness Fund, and, eventually, when the Fairness Fund merged back into the Human Rights Campaign Fund as the Field Division. Too often when I've seen others use this process it stops there and the goals are put on a shelf somewhere, which undercuts their purpose. So we began to employ a process of sending out reports to the board of directors three or four times a year, letting the board know where we were on each point. On many of the points, I could happily report we had met our objective, but on others, such as when I first referenced the idea of a "National Endorsement Campaign" in 1980, my later responsibility was to explain why we hadn't yet accomplished the goal (most often because of a lack of either funds, staff, or both).

On a day-to-day basis, I lived by college binders containing "things to do this week" lists. As I accomplished each task, I'd check them off and carry over the remainder to the next week—or sometimes conclude it wasn't critical in the first place. Such a system might not work for everyone (although I think it might), but I know it helped make me far more effective. I saved these "tasks notebooks" and, if I had a few moments of relative calm, I'd review all my old "tasks books" to see if I'd forgotten key efforts or steps. In general, I found our efforts were pretty complete, but I would be lying if I didn't acknowledge discovering a range of tasks we just hadn't gotten around to.

Although it could require significant time commitments on the front end, this planning was, overall, very, very helpful to my movement functioning. However, it wasn't without its pitfalls. At times it led people to think I was inflexible, which was sometimes a valid criticism, and at times it kept us from seizing the moment and taking advantage of opportunities. Despite our attempt to adapt to the dramatically different circumstances presented by the then-mysterious and deadly disease AIDS, for example, I can't help but question now whether our approach and the inflexibility that sometimes went with it may have contributed to a slower response from GRNL than any of us might have wanted. On most occasions, though, I felt it served us well.

If You Got 'em . . .
Grassroots Organizing, Constituent Mobilization

In January 1990, I vented my anger at so many "talkers" and so few "doers" in a George Buse interview with me in *The Windy City Times:*

> For 10 years polls have shown that the majority of Americans favor civil rights for gays and lesbians. At the same time, our side has never been able to generate as much mail and constituent pressure as our opponents have. What that tells me is we have been out-organized and out-worked.
>
> I have found for a long time that gay and lesbian activists haven't done the unglamorous, nitty-gritty "grunt work" of enrolling constituent pressure from both gay and non-gay supporters. Frankly, I'm getting tired of listening to gay and lesbian activists bitch about those 400 opponents' letters (generated through the churches). We can't control what the right wingers do. But we *can* control what we do.
>
> We can expect fairness, but we're simply not going to get it without being heard.

"If you got 'em by the balls, their hearts and minds will follow" is a well-known axiom. The phrase may seem crude to some, but it successfully conveys the lesson that just having truth is often not enough to win on controversial political decisions. Without political clout countless elected officials—who are seldom known for their collective political backbone—will opt simply to duck the issue and support either the status quo or the position backed by the majority or the most powerful. Although some might associate the phrase with PAC contributions or other formalized political power, I've long felt that the most critical form of clout resided with the ability to mobilize constituent pressure and mail on your side.

Many of us in the lesbian and gay movement spend vast quantities of time and energy talking about "grass roots," but too often that's exactly what it is: talk. Too often, "grassroots activists" is a phrase that accurately describes people working at the local level. Too often, such activists are attracted exclusively to quick, sensational actions and protests but don't seem to want to do the nitty-gritty grunt work inevitably involved in the best grassroots organizing. Many others, including those most likely to have the resources necessary for solid constituent mobilization, are attracted to the "insider" lobbying approaches and often ignore grassroots organizing efforts. Often, these are businesspeople that know that inside lobbying works very well for many low-visibility business issues, but that it almost always fails in controversial social issues. Both types of activists, who think they have so little in common, have gravitated to an instant gratification approach.

Ironically, such gratification seldom takes place on an issue such as gay rights. At the same time, my experience suggests that, sadly, it is our anti-gay opponents who really put their faith, energy, and resources into mobilizing grassroots mail and pressure. I certainly don't pretend to be the best grassroots organizer around, or even one of them, but the sheer passage of time and some painful losses have taught me much about the vital role grassroots organizing must play if we're to win.

During the 1973 legislative session in Minnesota I was so busy learning the legislative process and how to lobby that we didn't really do much in terms of grassroots mobilization. By the end of my first legislative session, though, I was convinced that my friends in the DFL Feminist Caucus and Americans for Democratic Action were right—we had to build a statewide network to generate constituent mail before the 1975 session.

First we had a great chance to build momentum for the state bill by passing a citywide law in Minneapolis. We put in a lot of solid legwork leading up to the ordinance; it wasn't traditional mobilization of constituent mail but instead took the form of both demonstrating the need for the law and then volunteering in critical elections: we'd picketed daily for about a month at Northwestern Bell Telephone to protest their antigay discrimination, and we worked our butts off in eleven of the thirteen alderman campaigns, volunteering for council candidates who had pledged to support the ordinance. By doing so, we showed we could turn out volunteers, and it allowed the aldermen and their committees to get to know real, live gay men and lesbians and to get over their stereotypes about who we were. Once the council and mayor were elected, however, passing the Minneapolis gay rights ordinance wasn't that hard, nor did we have to generate constituent lobby visits or grassroots mail from our supporters. Our task was easier because our antigay opponents weren't well organized.

A short time later we turned our attention to the enactment of a similar gay and lesbian rights ordinance in our sister city of St. Paul. Again, we didn't have to undertake what would later become the traditional efforts to generate grassroots mail, etc. The critical grassroots organizing came around the DFL city caucuses leading up to the St. Paul elections. Activist Dennis Miller played the key role in this organizing, securing the support of party activists and the 4th Congressional district convention for a lesbian and gay rights ordinance. A low-visibility but thorough lobbying campaign of the mayor and council, which included an overwhelming majority of DFLers, helped answer their questions and solidify their supportive inclinations. In addition to providing basic info to offset stereotypes, we generally made sure DFL party activists communicated their support to the council and turned out enough supporters at the hearings to demonstrate broad-based support. This groundwork helped us withstand last-minute opposition by the St. Paul newspapers, misgivings by the labor movement (which was very socially conservative at that point) and a last-minute letter from the then-Catholic archbishop opposing the ordinance (who was egged on by the right-wing *Wanderer* magazine crowd).

Although we were able to pass the Minneapolis and St. Paul ordinances without the traditional grassroots mail campaigns, we certainly couldn't win statewide lesbian and gay civil rights legislation without such an effort. With most Minnesota lesbians and gay men living in a handful of Twin Cities districts, we faced a serious task: somehow we had to build a network to generate citizen mail and show outstate legislators that there were gay rights supporters in their districts. Even in the suburbs, we had trouble finding many gay people willing to write or call their legislators.

However, a reputable statewide Minnesota poll, sponsored by *The Minneapolis Star and Tribune,* showed overwhelming support for extending the state human rights law to protect gay people. With that in mind, we realized we should be able to secure the help of nongay supporters around the state, so our organizing had to reach beyond gay and lesbian voters. To build such a grassroots network, we planned a statewide mailing to liberals likely to support fairness for gays, explaining the need for lesbian and gay rights legislation, as well as the need to repeal the antiquated sodomy and fornication laws, and asking for their support.

The plan was to provide them with response cards and postage-paid envelopes, but finding the money to pay for such a mailing was a real challenge. The Playboy Foundation, which is deeply committed to sexual freedom in general and to lesbian and gay civil rights specifically, paid for the mailing. Given our support in the feminist community, we briefly pondered whether we should take money from Playboy, but we had few other funding options and a range of leading feminists convinced us that we should accept the support.

So we got the help of countless progressive groups to send out a 40,000-piece statewide mailing. More than 2,000 people returned cards indicating their support, which we sorted by state legislative districts. This fairly primitive constituent network served us pretty well. When legislators expressed doubt about support for the issue in their district, we'd use our network to find and mobilize supporters in that district. The next time I'd see the legislator, they'd ask me, "How in the hell did you find a gay rights supporter in Thunder Bay, Minnesota?" I don't know if we actually picked up many votes this way, but at least our network helped keep us from losing votes we'd won by conviction.

In hindsight, we could have done much more and identified many more logical lesbian and gay rights supporters. We should have gone to each of those who signed up to ask them to give us the names of five to ten other potential lesbian and gay rights supporters, but we were still building a lobby and I don't think any of us really understood the importance of such grassroots efforts yet. Also, we didn't understand what a formidable network of fundamentalist hate and distortion awaited us, nor did we have the resources, volunteer power, or knowledge to build the system that might have been necessary. Nonetheless, compared to the grassroots mail systems by other statewide gay rights lobbies, ours was well developed.

In some ways, I guess subconsciously we were bracing for the storm of anticipated antigay mail. We'd tried to maintain a relatively low profile for our lobbying effort but anticipated that we would eventually run into antigay opposition. However, throughout the entire 1973 session it failed to materialize. When we had to cope with the more bizarre elements of the gay movement in 1975, our lobbying campaign got much more visibility and we prepared for an antigay backlash, but again it failed to really materialize. It finally hit in the last month before the vote in the 1977 legislative session, and it was far more formidable than we, our allies, and the legislators themselves had ever anticipated. Minnesota was well-known as a progressive state, without any organized antigay groups to spearhead their efforts or any indication of a large fundamentalist constituency, and it was long before the advent of the so-called Moral Majority. Also, our lobbying team had a head count showing we had eleven votes more than necessary when local Assemblies of God congregations and other fundamentalists began to pour on the constituent pressure; almost every state legislator received more than 100 calls or letters from his or her constituents. Although anti-abortion and anti-gun control forces had always produced more constituent mail than any other issue, our opposition's mobilization quickly eclipsed that of either the NRA or right-to-life groups. We'd carefully made friends with secretaries and receptionists, and they privately confided to us how many calls or letters their legislators had gotten and how the legislator seemed to be withstanding the pressure.

Objective statewide polls, sponsored by the state's largest papers, showed 77 percent on our side, and every constitutional officer in the state, from the governor on down, supported the legislation. The two largest cities had local ordinances that had already worked well, bishops of virtually every denomination had endorsed the bill, and openly gay state senator Allan Spear was very well respected by his colleagues. The powerful senate majority leader, Nick Coleman, who controlled debate in the senate, was a brilliant and deeply committed supporter. Yet when our fundamentalist opponents unleashed their avalanche of antigay pressure, it was unbelievable, and our own constituent network was just no match for the combination of their network, numbers, and zeal. I sat in a state of shock with other members of our lobbying team.

One board member of our statewide lobby, based in St. Cloud—which was one of the most conservative Catholic parts of the state—didn't sit back passively. Ken Nielson, a popular hairdresser in that small town, prepared a petition supporting the statewide gay rights bill and took it door-to-door, collecting more than 500 signatures. In my twenty-one years in the lesbian and gay civil rights movement, Ken's petition drive stands out as one of the most courageous I've ever seen. Unlike the rest of us, he didn't play victim and sit around complaining about how the fundamentalists had a built-in advantage. He simply went out to show that the state polls were really correct. It would be nice to report that Ken's courageous St. Cloud petition drive resulted in winning the votes of the state senator and representatives from St. Cloud but, unfortunately, it still wasn't enough. Perhaps if we'd followed it up by trying to get each of the 500 petitioners to write or call, we could have won their legislators' votes.

In the face of our opponents' grassroots pressure, our legislative support evaporated. As our eleven-vote margin slipped away, we lost by a heartbreaking two votes. We actually won on the preliminary vote but had to have a "constitutional" or absolute majority vote of the senate, and then even one of our three cosponsors, who had been on the bill for three years, voted against it. If we had put as much time and energy into grassroots organizing as we did into training our lobbying team, the outcome probably might have been different, but we'd lost because the other side had outworked us in grassroots organizing. It is a lesson I've never forgotten and it has molded the rest of my movement career.

When I moved to Washington, DC, to lobby for gay rights at Congress, grassroots organizing was my top priority. In fact, GRNL's commitment to grassroots organizing was the focus of one of our earliest newsletters, where I stated,

> I will never be part of an effort again that is just out-organized. Any lobbying effort I'm a part of must find the funds necessary for an effective constituent network or it isn't worth doing the lobbying effort at all.

CAPITOL HILL

THE NEWSLETTER OF THE GAY RIGHTS NATIONAL LOBBY

VOL. 1, NO. 1   OCTOBER 1978

New Beginning for GRNL; Executive Director Appointed to Take Charge of Lobbying Efforts

The Gay Rights National Lobby has appointed Stephen Endean to the position of Executive Director of the organization. Steve's responsibilities will include the broad areas of legislative advocacy, fundraising and administration. His appointment is seen as a major step forward to resolve some of the organizational difficulties in the recent past and to establish the strong lobbying presence necessary for passage of national civil rights legislation for lesbians and gay men.

Although GRNL has had an Office Manager in the past, Steve Endean's appointment to the Executive Director's position marks the first time GRNL has employed an individual with broad authority and responsibility over the lobbying effort. GRNL's last Office Manager, Joe Totten, left the position last May and, because of extreme financial crisis, the position has remained vacant. This has, as members have seen, caused major problems in communications to members and organizational maintenance. Because of this financial crisis and lack of full-time staff, these problems have not been overcome despite the best efforts of the members of the Board of Directors. It is hoped that Steve's appointment will now resolve these problems.

Steve formerly was the Coordinator for the Minnesota Committee for Gay Rights and, in this capacity, he has considerable experience in fundraising and administration of a gay organization. But he is quick to point out that his primary strength is in the area of lobbying. In his position with the Minnesota group, he served as the chief lobbyist for civil rights for gay people at the Minnesota State Legislature. Although they did not pass the legislation in 1977 they came within two votes of passage. He also served as the lobbyist for successful passage of the Minneapolis and St. Paul gay rights ordinances. Steve has been involved in the gay movement since 1970 and some of

his past involvement includes having been a volunteer in the final weeks in Dade County, having served as the Assistant Campaign Manager in the campaign against repeal of the St. Paul ordinance, and having served as the past Co-Chairperson of the Board of Directors of National Gay Task Force (NGTF). His experience is not, however, limited to gay rights as he has also worked as a lobbyist for the Minnesota Chapter of Americans for Democratic Action (ADA) and for H.I.R.E.D., a Minnesota organization specializing in public interest employment legislation. He is a past member of the Minneapolis Human Rights Commission.

GRNL Priorities Discussed

When asked about his priorities for GRNL, Steve said "Our top priorities must be to build a strong lobbying presence on Capitol Hill and to provide for greater membership service and organizational maintenance.

Building a strong lobbying presence includes a wide variety of things such as the education of Congresspersons and their staffs on gay issues and concerns, demonstrating to them that support for

New Name for GRNL Newsletter

As you can see, the name of the Gay Rights National Lobby newsletter has changed from "On the Line" to "Capitol Hill." It was the feeling of the new GRNL Executive Director that the new name more accurately reflects the mission of the Gay Rights National Lobby. It is hoped that the new name will not be confused with the fine newsletter of UFMCC-Washington Office, "Gays on the Hill." We would appreciate any feedback that you have on the new name, format or content of Capitol Hill.

GRNL Executive Director, Steve Endean

the civil rights of lesbians and gay men is not equivalent to political suicide; building a strong and large constituent network; and gaining and increasing the support of progressive and public interest lobbies. In view of the recent referenda and the growing conservative trend, I am sure that we face an uphill battle. While passage of the legislation is certainly not likely in the next year or two, passage of controversial legislation never comes quickly. The building of an effective lobbying effort now will allow us to move swiftly for passage when the political climate once again improves.

"But in our effort to establish our lobbying presence, we must be aware of the absolute necessity of providing solid membership service and organizational maintenance. You cannot have a truly effective lobbying organization without

Continued on page 2

Example of Early Newsletter. Courtesy of HRC.

Executive Director Appointed

Continued from page 1

an informed and committed membership. Members, who are the primary source of contributions and fundraising, must be kept better informed about the organization's operation. This area will receive special attention in the months ahead."

Endean went on to say, "I am aware of and regret the problems Gay Rights National Lobby seems to have had in the past, but I believe that it is critical to the success of the organization and the national lobbying effort for civil rights for lesbians and gay men that we now focus our attention on the future."

Upon hearing of Steve's appointment, Ginny Apuzzo, former Co-Chairperson of the Board and current Board member said, "We're indeed fortunate to have one of the most experienced and qualified lobbyists in the area of gay rights. I'm thrilled at the appointment."

Adam DeBaugh, Social Action Director of the Universal Fellowship of Metropolitan Community Churches-Washington Office (that has done much lobbying on the Hill to date) and GRNL Board member said, "I'm delighted that Steve has been appointed and that GRNL will now be able to begin lobbying. We at UFMCC-Washington Office look forward to working closely with GRNL."

CAPITOL HILL
VOL. 1, NO. 1
OCTOBER 1978

Published by Gay Rights National Lobby

Adrienne Scott, Board Co-Chairperson

Raymond Hartman, Board Co-Chairperson

Steve Endean, Executive Director

GRNL, Suite 210, 110 Maryland Ave. N.E., Washington, D.C. 20002

Please notify us of any change in address.

Is Support For Gay Civil Rights Political Suicide?

With the repeal of gay rights ordinances in several cities across the country, one question is continually brought up on Capitol Hill, "Isn't it political suicide to support civil rights for gay people?" The overwhelming majority of information that is presently available indicates that it is not. However, we do not have very complete information at this point nor do we have much information on what is happening on this in these "post-Anita" times. Gay Rights National Lobby will be collecting this information from a variety of sources and compiling it for use in the upcoming Congressional Session.

We would like your help on this project. Do you know of pro-gay rights candidates in your area who have had or are having this issue used against them? (For example, those Congresspersons who voted against the anti-gay McDonald amendment to the Legal Services Corporation

Act could have anti-gay rights attacks used against them. We include, for your convenience, a list of those Congresspersons who took pro-human rights positions on an enclosed page.) Are there pro-gay rights office holders in your area that have *not* had this issue used against them?

If you are willing to help us with this project, you can obtain the information requested in a variety of ways, including calling the supportive office holder's office and simply inquiring. While we are particularly interested in Congressional races, the outcomes of city and state races could also demonstrate our point that support for the civil rights of gay people is not like a death wish. Please fill out the questionnaire below upon the completion of the election in question (Primary or General). Thank you very much for your help on this important project.

GAY RIGHTS NATIONAL LOBBY (GRNL) STUDY OF ELECTORAL OUTCOMES

YOUR NAME _____ TELEPHONE _____

ADDRESS _____

CITY _____ STATE _____ ZIP _____

   NAME OF SUPPORTIVE PUBLIC OFFICIAL _____

      Public Office Held _____

   NAME OF ANTI-GAY OPPONENT _____

   HOW WAS THE ISSUE USED? _____

   HOW MAJOR A ROLE DID THE ISSUE PLAY IN THE CAMPAIGN _____

   WHAT WAS THE OUTCOME OF THE ELECTION _____

      Pro-human rights candidate's total _____

      Anti-human rights candidate's total _____

   THERE WAS A PRO-GAY RIGHTS OFFICE HOLDER IN MY AREA, BUT THAT PERSON DID *NOT* HAVE THE GAY RIGHTS ISSUE USED AGAINST THEM _____

      S/he won re-election by a wide or narrow margin _____

      S/he lost re-election by a wide or narrow margin _____

      Name of Office-holder _____

Please fill out a similar form for each race that you are aware of and return to: Gay Rights National Lobby, Suite 210, 110 Maryland Ave. N.E., Washington 20002

Page two of Newsletter.

When I arrived, however, I discovered I had a more fundamental organizing task: to demonstrate to the community why they should care about national legislative efforts and a national bill that would clearly take a very long time to pass. A conversation with a nationally prominent lesbian activist showed the magnitude of my problem. When I told this person I'd been hired to run our lobbying effort, she questioned whether lesbian and gay rights really needed a lobbyist, saying, "After all, it isn't like the economy or something." I was shocked, but it helped prepare me for what I soon found. Happily, most activists, rather than questioning our need for lobbying, were just preoccupied with their own local efforts, though to the extent they thought about national efforts, they tended to doubt our chances of success. They probably thought we were just putting the cart before the horse.

My first task was to establish a solid record of accomplishment that would give people a sense of hope. For instance, I sought to increase dramatically the number of cosponsors of the lesbian and gay civil rights bill so people would understand our potential for progress. At that stage, our job wasn't so much to win legislative victories per se but instead to establish a strong track record, energize activists across the country, and, fundamentally, begin to put the pieces in place for our long-term victories.

Securing the visibility for the Lobby was challenging because we had virtually no resources for either publicity or travel, but eight months after I came on staff I traveled across the country to meet with key local gay and lesbian activists and did interviews with the gay press. To keep it economical, I took an Eastern Airlines "All You Can Fly or All You Can Stomach" trip, and for about $500 for one month I was able to fly anywhere Eastern flew. I crisscrossed the country to fifteen cities in twenty-one days—Atlanta, Boston, Provincetown, Bangor (ME), Seattle, Portland (OR), San Francisco, Milwaukee, Chicago, Houston, and Dallas—building support and interest in our efforts.

Initially, the Gay Rights National Lobby's finances were so modest it was difficult to even think about grassroots staff, but we still dreamed of a time when we could have a national field coordinator and eight regional field directors based across the country. Each of these full-time organizers would, in turn, work to recruit, train, and mobilize volunteer coordinators in each congressional district in the country. Hiring a national field coordinator first would have been most logical, but because I got sick with hepatitis and longtime friend Kerry Woodward came to my rescue, we ended up hiring Kerry first as our West Coast regional director in November 1980. Her position was designed not only to increase GRNL's visibility in the seven western states of California, Oregon, Washington, Idaho, Alaska, Nevada, and Hawaii, but, more directly, to generate constituent pressure on members of Congress from those states.

A short time later, we hired Susan Green, who had been coordinating GRNL's system of volunteer grassroots organizers as a "legislative assistant." One of her major responsibilities was to act as our unofficial national field coordinator, though, and she supervised Kerry; within a year we were able to pare back Susan's other efforts and changed her title to better reflect her responsibilities. After that we hired Tanyan Corman, a dynamic San Luis Opisbo organizer whose father had been a member of Congress (and cosponsor), to assist Kerry on the West Coast. She was particularly good with politically correct California activists.

Finally, in 1983 we hired another regional organizer, the Midwest field director. Midwestern activists, including myself when I lived in Minnesota, had long felt ignored by the national movement. Further, there were many marginal districts in the heart of the country where we could win legislators' votes, but only if we successfully generated the grassroots mail and pressure necessary to show legislators that there was popular support for our position. We hired Kathy Patrick, a longtime NOW activist who lived in Madison, Wisconsin, for the job. However, by that point we were already in sharp conflict with David Goodstein, Larry Bush, and *The Advocate* and I don't think our Midwestern field operation ever really got off the ground.

As our staffing and resulting network of organizers got established, we tried to implement the traditional "Congressional Action Alert" approach to mobilize local activists and groups across the country. GRNL's Action Alerts, which were in bright red, were mailed to GRNL donors, to gay and lesbian groups, and to people who had signed GRNL's petitions. The system's purpose was to generate immediate constituent pressure. At that point, though, technology didn't allow us to personalize the letters or to tell each participant who their members of Congress were and where to write. We put out about three or four Action Alerts, on issues ranging from the federal lesbian and gay civil rights bill to the McDonald amendment (which could have cut off taxpaying gay and lesbian citizen's access to the government's legal aid program).

When Ronald Reagan won in a landslide in 1980, many predicted that it marked the end of the effort for lesbian and gay rights. At the least, they reasoned, cosponsorship would go down dramatically. The Action Alert on the Weiss-Waxman nondiscrimination bill at the time stated,

> In politics the name of the game is momentum. If we do not maintain our high co-sponsorship, continue on our path to Congressional hearings, and generally continue to press vigorously our legislation to end discrimination, the Far Right's moralistic tide could easily erode or eliminate all of our progress to date.

The Congressional Action Alert on the McDonald amendment to the Legal Services Corporation bill stated,

> Christian Voice is exploiting the fact that it's easier to pass such amendments, usually offered without warning, than carrying an anti-gay bill through the long subcommittee-committee process.
>
> The upcoming floor vote in the United States Congress could be a significant turning point in our national struggle for justice. A loss will not only write into law the persecution of lesbians and gay men and encourage amendments to other bills, but will also help anti-gay forces such as "Christian Voice" to grow in power. Although the chances of victory may be long, we're convinced that we can beat the amendment with your help.

Too many of these legislative emergencies came up on short notice, however, making it difficult to get the mailing out quick enough, let alone for concerned constituents to write and get their mail back in time. In addition, we were never able to show that these mailings resulted in significant mail to members of Congress, and what little mail we did generate didn't seem to come from the local groups that we'd expected to be our foundation. Instead, it became clear that activists were overwhelmed with local priorities and often didn't have either the interest or capacity to take on national legislative battles as well.

If the Action Alert system didn't seem to work, its failure didn't faze us; we realized we were still struggling to find the right strategies. We met good success at establishing a national constituent network, mostly using petition drives. We had petitions circulating on just about every gay issue of the time—against the McDonald amendment, the Moral Majority, and the Family Protection Act (which was kind of a "wish list" of the radical right wing, including several antigay proposals) and in favor of the National Gay and Lesbian Civil Rights Bill—to identify supporters in each state and district. We collected more than 140,000 names and addresses, but people who would sign petitions weren't necessarily willing to sit down and write heartfelt letters—even on those few occasions when we had enough advance notice to make such efforts viable. However, we did discover that these petitions provided a terrific base for direct-mail fund-raising, which played a critical role in allowing the GRNL to grow substantially.

Another key organizing effort that worked well for the Lobby was the "Constituent Lobby Day" for the 1979 March on Washington. The Gay Rights National Lobby, National Gay Task Force, and other national groups had initially opposed the march, but march organizers understood they needed our involvement in the constituent lobbying that was to take place the Monday after the march. Our opposition was based on the expected expenses of the march (GRNL's budget was less than $100,000 at the time and the march was expected to cost at least twenty times that much) and the fact that we didn't think it would have much of an immediate legislative impact. But opposition by all the national groups failed to slow plans for the march, so the Gay Rights National Lobby and the others got on board and supported it. Looking back, it's clear the 1979 March on Washington, with more than 120,000 people present, played an extremely important galvanizing role in building interest in a national lobbying effort.

I'd been working more than 100 hours a week and was sick by the time the 1979 March came around. My doctor discovered I had hepatitis right after the march, so Kerry Woodward stepped in to coordinate our efforts for the on-the-Hill citizen lobbying. The National March Committee had a specific committee, chaired by Paul Boneberg and DeeDee Knight, working on the task. We were worried they were so overwhelmed there might not be enough outreach or a large enough turnout, so we pitched in by helping publicize the Day on the Hill and providing the written materials for the day. In fact, the march committee did a great job and cooperated terrifically.

More than 500 people showed up, and fifty senators and more than 150 house members were lobbied. Sometimes, people met with staff members rather than their congresspeople, and we were sometimes disappointed (California's Alan Cranston and Massachusetts's Ted Kennedy each resisted the pleas of large delegations to cosponsor the nondiscrimination bill).

But there were victories: the New York delegation got Senator Daniel Patrick Moynihan to fulfill his pledge to his dying friend, activist Robert Livingston, to cosponsor. Then State Representative Barney Frank, who was the chief sponsor of the statewide lesbian and gay rights legislation in Massachusetts at the time and presumably heterosexual, led a delegation meeting with Rep. Tip O'Neill. Tanyan Corman, who'd grown up as the daughter of a congressperson and a friend to a number of California legislators, met with a number of California congresspeople and convinced Rep. Leon Panetta to cosponsor.

Later, when we had a reception and informal debriefing session on the Hill, it quickly became clear that the day had been a tremendous success. "The Constituent Lobby Day proved the importance of individual and local involvement in lobbying U.S. Senators and Representatives," said Kerry Woodward. "Citizen lobbyists came back excited and confident of their impact on Congress. This kind of pressure must now be continued by constituents in all parts of the country." With the march over, we still had to figure out how to mobilize *ongoing* grassroots pressure. Groups such as NOW had organized by state and local chapters, but my experience suggested that such a route would not work well within the gay and lesbian community. However, if a chapter structure wouldn't work, we had to think of an approach that might.

As a board member and later cochair of the National Gay Task Force (later the National Gay and Lesbian Task Force), I'd been part of NGTF's exploration of setting up a chapter system. With hundreds of local gay and lesbian groups already in existence, resentment and resistance were sure to arise from a chapter system; it just wouldn't work. The challenge remained of figuring out how to get local groups to help our national efforts.

Field Associates

Most local groups had neither the staff nor volunteers to handle the overwhelming workload, so we had to create some strategy to ensure accountability for those that agreed to work with us and on behalf of the Gay Rights National Lobby. We established a system of local volunteer grassroots coordinators, which we called field associates. Field associates could and often were involved in local groups, but they would also be directly accountable to GRNL. Until I was able to convince Susan Green to become our volunteer grassroots coordinator, however, the field associate program was largely just an abstract idea.

When Susan actually came on staff, the program began to take real shape. She recruited field associates through the gay press, mail, and phone calls to activists. She brought her own sort of charm to the program, but her greatest strengths were her superb organization and her determination and perseverance. Sometimes local groups tried to convince us just to make their group our field associate, but Susan and I agreed that we wanted—and had to have—a specific individual who would respond directly to the Lobby. Once people agreed to serve as field associates, Susan called them once a month to review what was happening on Capitol Hill, discuss how their organizing and efforts had gone in the past month, and collaborate on possible in-district strategy for the coming month or two. Of course, Susan and Kerry continued to work directly with local organizations as well.

Also, groups such as the New Jersey Coalition for Gay and Lesbian Rights sometimes actually went out and found people to serve as GRNL field associates from each congressional district within their state. Although these field associates worked with the New Jersey Coalition, it worked fine for us because they also worked directly with Susan as well, so it fit our criteria of at least some accountability directly to Gay Rights National Lobby.

I'm pretty goal directed and am therefore not the best ongoing field organizer myself, but Susan fully understood how critical team building, empowerment, and nurturing were to her task. She worked patiently with people who were taking on their GRNL volunteer work in addition to their full-time jobs and whatever local activism they were doing. Yet we counted on them, so Susan had to blend in equal measures of taskmaster and nurturer. Almost every field associate became one of Susan's dear friends, and often she saw it as part of her job to protect them from my demands, both reasonable and unreasonable. She remembered what I often chose to forget: they were, after all, volunteers.

Hiring Kerry Woodward in 1980 was another key to the growing success of the field associate program, since she quickly recruited quite a number of congressional district coordinators. Kerry and Susan maintained almost constant phone contact with field associates to ensure the best operation of the system, less turnover, and more effective follow-through. In the final analysis, though, the system still had to depend on volunteers scattered across the country. As of 1981, they'd been able to find about 100 field associates in thirty states.

In September 1981, our grassroots program faced a severe challenge when Washington, DC, passed the D.C. Sexual Assault Reform Act, which both revised the city's rape laws and repealed laws against private, consensual sexual activity. Such rape reform wasn't controversial, but when the council took the opportunity to reform the city's sodomy and fornication statutes as well we knew we could face trouble. Because Congress has veto power over the District's actions, the question was whether we'd face a congressional fight to overturn the District of Columbia law. We quickly learned the answer was yes.

With Reagan in office, congressional Democrats in retreat, and the newly formed Moral Majority—led by Rev. Jerry Falwell—riding high, this would be a formidable battle. GRNL hired local activist Tom Chorlton for a two-month stint to lobby the Hill on the consenting-adults legislation. Susan, Kerry, and the rest of the GRNL staff and volunteers shifted into high gear to build national constituent pressure on our side. Susan recruited volunteers for a seven-day-a-week phone bank, drafted scripts, developed lists of people to be called in each targeted area, supervised the phoning, and coordinated the entire operation.

GRNL staff and volunteers directly contacted more than 1,500 lesbian and gay rights supporters nationwide who, in turn, agreed to contact others in their communities and to help generate thousands of calls, letters, and telegrams to Congress. Even though the issue was a Washington, DC, law, gay activists across the country really understood how much was at stake in this battle against the moral majoritarians.

Congress overturned the act by a wide margin, but our networking with activists across the country provided significant long-term benefits. Later in the fall of 1981, we set up a smaller phone bank to combat the antigay McDonald amendment to the Legal Services Appropriations bill. Our opponents backed off from their announced plan to pursue the amendment, but we couldn't tell what role our efforts had played in deterring them; what we did know was that we couldn't keep going to the same dedicated activists—who already had plenty to do locally—and expect them to drop everything and help us generate the grassroots heat we needed every time. To them, coming back again and again just seemed like emptying the ocean with a teacup. There had to be a better way.

Susan Green reported to the GRNL board on the National Constituent Lobby Month, a project that worked superbly. Lobby kits were prepared, realistic goals were set for each legislator, and, most of all, we successfully identified coordinators in all fifty states. These state coordinators, in turn, were responsible for recruiting a team in each congressional district to meet with the congressperson when he or she was home in the district or state. Frankly, I think my own overwhelming workload at the time meant that I failed to really grasp the incredible accomplishment Susan and Kerry had secured in actually finding fifty able, functioning state coordinators.

More than 300 lobby kits were sent out to constituent lobby teams across the country. Our top priority was to secure additional sponsors of the federal lesbian and gay civil rights bill, but with some congresspeople the realistic goal was to secure a commitment that they would oppose antigay bills and amendments. As Susan said at the time, "For many legislators, these meetings may be the first time that they are consciously in face-to-face meetings with gay and lesbian constituents, so there's great potential for education and consciousness-raising." Although my direct lobbying was often given credit for the increased cosponsorship of the lesbian and gay civil rights bill, the constituent lobbying our field operation had initiated many, and probably most, of the new cosponsors.

In early 1982, with the newly created Human Rights Campaign Fund getting off the ground and expecting to contribute more than $100,000 to supportive candidates, we added constituent lobbying of congressional candidates to the mix. Although such constituent lobbying hasn't really been a key component since that time, it made sense when candidates were looking for votes and money and were most anxious to please. Also, since I was in charge of candidate contributions at the time, GRNL's constituent lobbying of candidates was one of the key factors as we determined which candidates deserved our support—and which did not.

By the end of 1982, when Susan became our national field coordinator, we still suffered from major turnover of these volunteer organizers. Although most of the field associates that failed just were too busy to do the job and had to be replaced, in a handful of cases we found we'd selected people who didn't serve or represent the GRNL well. Without the funds for extensive travel or much direct contact, we were lucky this wasn't a bigger problem than it was.

Despite the Lobby being seriously underfunded, the program grew and matured: Susan, Kerry, and Tanyan successfully recruited more than 150 field associates in forty states. Without the AIDS crisis creating a sense of urgency and inspiring the massive contributions that it since has, we had almost no travel funds for field organizing. To cut expenses, more than once I had to impose serious limitations on our long-distance calls, such as setting arbitrary time limits and insisting that we make as many calls as possible after 5 p.m.

In part to keep our locally based field associates from making policy statements more appropriately left to the board and executive director, and in part to clarify what was expected of each field associate, Susan, Kerry, and I designed the "Letter of Agreement." It spelled out what we'd provide to each field associate (an initial organizing packet, press releases, legislative updates, field associate identification cards, lobbying support materials, etc.). Moreover, it outlined field associates' required projects (establishment of a telephone tree, coordination of constituent lobbying, responding to action alerts, and completion of regular bimonthly progress reports) and optional initiatives (collection of petition signatures, speaking at gay and nongay groups, staffing info tables at community events, etc.).

Susan would describe a high point of the field as the first national field associate meeting, which took place in November 1983. Although we couldn't pay for their trips into Washington, more than fifty field associates came in from across the country, including leading activists from Hawaii, California, Ohio, and Connecticut. The weekend opened with a reception hosted by Rep. Ted Weiss, the chief sponsor of the National Lesbian and Gay Civil Rights Bill. The weekend was a wonderful chance for associates to meet the people they'd been working with for months, or even years, and they were addressed by various key members of Congress as well. I marveled at the tremendous bonding our team had secured within such serious limitations. "I learned a lot which will help me in talking to lesbians and gay men in my area and to members of Congress and their staffs," commented Rhea Diamond, from Toledo, Ohio, "I really enjoyed getting to know the other field associates who are struggling with problems similar to the ones I'm facing. The trip was well worth the cost and more." All in all, the weekend marked an extremely successful and empowering beginning, and we all agreed the field associate meetings should become regular events.

(Left to right) Weiss and Steve Endean. © 1982 Leigh H. Mosley.

(Left to right) Weiss, Henry Waxman (of the Weiss-Waxman Bill), Steve Endean, and Rep. Phil Burton. © 1982 Leigh H. Mosley.

The Gay Rights National Lobby's field associate system was dependent on efforts and enthusiasm of volunteers across the country. One of the major motivations of many that get involved in volunteer political work is the social interaction with others that share their commitments. Unfortunately, such interaction was limited for our local organizers so, to offset this disadvantage, our field staff had to build really solid relationships, usually primarily by phone. Another major benefit, from the field associates' perspective, was the knowledge that they were part of an incredibly successful effort that was marching resolutely forward.

When the assaults on GRNL began by Larry Bush and *The Advocate,* one of the quickest and saddest results was the collapse of field associates' morale and, with it, the deterioration of the single most successful aspect of the Lobby. Susan, who'd thrown her heart and soul into the field program's development and success and knitted together a fragile network based in part on field associates' affection for her, just couldn't stand the internal community conflict. She couldn't understand the motivations of those attacking us and decided to leave the staff. Eventually, she got over her bitterness and went on to make extraordinary contributions to the movement in Michigan and Madison, Wisconsin. We remained very close and, in fact, she'd agreed to serve on the board of the Fairness Fund, a new group I was founding to mobilize grassroots mail by proxy, until her ill health made her reconsider. She passed away from liver cancer a short time later.

Winning the Endorsement
of the National Democratic Party

When I moved to Washington, DC, in 1978 to become the first full-time lobbyist on gay rights at Congress, I had our Minnesota efforts to expand coalition support planted firmly in my mind. The challenge was to figure out how we could pass a similar plank in the national Democratic platform. As director of the Gay Rights National Lobby, I had been working to increase cosponsorship of the lesbian and gay civil rights bill and combating antigay amendments. But how do we win these battles nationally? Realistically it was going to take years to enact federal lesbian and gay civil rights legislation, and the AIDS crisis had not yet made the national legislative arena significant to most. So we had a real challenge in convincing overextended local activists, who were often the key to grassroots constituent pressure and mail, and donors, who were the key to critical growth and increased professionalism, that they should focus donations on our efforts.

Although I was asked often whether it would take three or four years to pass the national bill, or would it be a longer fight—even ten years—I always thought that we were in for an even longer struggle. This meant that laying the groundwork was really my primary obligation, but if things went the way I envisioned they would eventually culminate in unimagined successes. Passing a lesbian and gay civil rights plank in the Democratic Party platform may have seemed a little farfetched to some, but I thought it was plausible. The grassroots work we would have to do would be beneficial whether we won it or not.

In 1972, when the national Democratic Party was taken over by the anti-war forces of the McGovern campaign, the lesbian and gay rights issue was still too young and emerging to successfully become a part of the agenda of even these progressive forces. McGovern's people had desperately sought gay and lesbian support in their make-or-break California primary against Hubert Humphrey—and got it big time—but they now had the nomination sewed up and had to appear to be moving back to the mainstream to face the general election against Nixon. Gay rights advocates, led by gay rights pioneer Jim Foster, had enough strength to get a minority report to the floor, but the McGovern forces pushed the floor vote to late into the night, at 2 to 3 a.m., to ensure minimal TV viewership and enforced discipline. The plank was rejected by a wide margin in 1972 and didn't get to the floor again until 1980. (In 1976, the national battle was even more uphill. Jean O'Leary and Ginny Apuzzo, who were representing the National Gay Task Force and the community in general, were literally locked out of the Democratic National Platform deliberations.)

Unless we took a significantly different approach, I thought we were likely to face a similar fate in 1980, and the difference I envisioned was to try to move from a position of strength by actually electing gay and lesbian delegates to the national convention. I hoped that with this strategy we could get them to include a plank not because it was right but because we had "the might." Larry Bye, a close friend and brilliant political consultant now based in San Francisco, prepared a proposal for the platform plank project at my request, and it served as a takeoff point and as a fund-raising device for the "National Convention Project." As with the later proposal for the launching of the Human Rights Campaign Fund, Larry got it to me very quickly.

A short time later, I flew in to meet with Larry, Jim Foster, and David Goodstein, the owner of *The Advocate*. Goodstein was bright and committed to gay rights but also sometimes appeared to me to be more singularly dedicated to getting his own way. Larry and I felt we needed his help in publicizing the project as well as his assistance in fund-raising. At that stage of the movement, there were no large groups of lesbians and gay men who gave $1,000 to $5,000 a year, and funding would be a problem.

I summed up the difference between the convention project and previous efforts to secure the Democratic Party support by stating, "While the Project will, of course, testify before the Platform Committee, election of gay and lesbian delegates will be the primary objective. It is a step from just depending on good will to turning to real political power." Everyone agreed that it was a critical initiative and could make a huge difference to the community if we were successful.

My direct Capitol Hill lobbying on gay rights precluded me from doing the organizing necessary to find and help elect delegates all across the country. Bye and I discussed whether Jim Foster should run the project. In addition to starting the nation's first gay Democratic club, Jim was also the political director for the largest local gay group in the country in the early 1970s, the Society for Individual Rights (SIR). He had an incredible Irish charm, a rare gift of gab, and was able to schmooze politicians more effectively than almost any gay activist I'd ever seen. Yet I doubted his willingness to do the kind of nitty-gritty grunt work I thought was necessary to elect delegates in places such as Des Moines, Minneapolis, Seattle, and so on. A short time later, when GRNL's treasurer, Paul Kuntzler, and I went to lunch together, he reinforced my doubts about Jim and instead urged me to appoint Tom Bastow. Tom was just ending a term as president of Washington, DC's Gertrude Stein Democratic Club but, since I was only modestly involved in local gay politics, I didn't know him.

Paul arranged lunch with him for us to discuss the project. I came away thinking Tom was quite bright, diligent, and committed, but he also seemed a bit sarcastic, cynical, and dry. I knew he would put in the necessary energy to elect delegates and would not focus all of his attention in trying to schmooze politicians, but it was hard to tell if he could inspire people effectively. However, since I was increasingly convinced that Jim Foster was not the right person for this job, I had few choices. Tom was hired. I could not know then how able Tom was or how critical a role he would play in virtually every subsequent movement activity in my life.

Later Mary Spottswood Pou, known as Spots, was hired as Tom's co-coordinator, and we asked the National Gay Task Force to cosponsor the project. Their major advantage was having a larger membership than GRNL that could be solicited for donations to the project, but the main reason we asked them to jointly sponsor centered around keeping them from starting a competing project of their own. I doubted that they cared enough to do much, but from an ego point of view they might have felt compelled to do so unless they joined us. I was concerned about their cosponsorship, too, since it seemed more likely the Task Force would just try to take credit for the work.

I had been working between 90 and 100 hours a week, was completely exhausted, and felt I could not get the community's lobby above water. The 1979 March on Washington was fast approaching, and I was fading just as quickly. Shortly after the march I learned I had hepatitis and was ordered to bed for three months. Kerry Woodward stayed on in Washington to open the mail, answer the calls, and keep GRNL going. As usual, she was a lifesaver. As the National Convention Project, or Gay Vote '80, as Tom and Spots preferred to call it, got off the ground, I was missing in action. Happily, they carried on wonderfully—maybe better—without me.

Governor Jerry Brown of California, who had run for president in 1976 and was considering doing so again in 1980, spoke to more than 700 people at the kickoff of the National Convention Project at one of DC's gay superbars. In return, we helped him raise the $5,000 he needed in DC to get his federal matching funds. His presence brought invaluable national media attention and real credibility within the lesbian and gay communities. Brown spoke of his underdog status: "My role is to drive the dialogue in my party on a number of issues—nuclear power, nuclear disarmament, the issue of rights for gay and lesbian people in society." Both President Carter and his leading challenger, Ted Kennedy, were also represented at the historic event. Carter's representative was booed because of his noncommittal statement, while Kennedy's person, Susan Estrich, got a better response. Kennedy's statement still stopped short of pledging his Senate cosponsorship of the fair employment bill, however.

Despite the efforts of Tom and his dynamic, energetic lover of the time, Mike Ziskind, who arranged a number of fund-raisers in homes throughout Washington, funds were as tight as they were for GRNL itself. Without money for salaries, Spots eventually had to leave staff for a time. Luckily for every gay man and lesbian in America, Tom hung in there and continued to put in incredible work to make the project a success, even when he didn't get paid for weeks at a time. No one in America did more to ensure that our nation's majority political party endorsed lesbian and gay civil rights.

Other factors, in addition to Tom's dedication, contributed to the success of Gay Vote '80. It provided a national project for local activists to plug into, while Tom and Spots were able to provide key technical assistance for those willing to run. Also, activists genuinely shared our vision of the project's potential and loved the glamour of getting elected as national delegates. As a result, more than seventy gay and lesbian national delegates and alternates were elected across the country—about the same size as the Colorado delegation.

As winter became spring, I recovered from both the hepatitis and exhaustion and was prepared to work on the project, which was moving into a key stage of the platform hearings and associated lobbying. Since one of the key objections raised by those opposing the plank was that it could be damaging for Democratic candidates, we had to figure out how to respond.

Working with the cosponsors of the Weiss-Waxman Gay and Lesbian Civil Rights bill, we arranged a "Dear Colleague" of sorts to all the platform committee members, signed by thirty members of Congress. Senator Paul Tsongas (D-MA), chief sponsor of the Senate bill, sent his own separate letter. We also distributed our study "Does Support for Gay Civil Rights Spell Political Suicide?" This seventy-page study, done by Joe Cantor, carefully examined what happened to city council, mayoral, state legislative, and congressional candidates who had supported civil rights for lesbian and gay Americans. Contrary to prevailing notions, even within the gay community, the evidence showed that support for gay civil rights was seldom used against candidates, and when it was, it had no impact. We convinced Rep. Martin Sabo (D-Minneapolis), Speaker of the State House of Representatives, to testify at the final platform hearings in Washington, DC. I had known Marty, who was very progressive yet had a well-deserved reputation as very mainstream, since my earliest days lobbying gay rights.

This brought us to the final stage of the platform committee's deliberations. Just as a couple of us had succeeded in getting elected to the platform committee years earlier in Minnesota, six lesbians and gay men from across the country had secured positions on the national platform committee from their states. As we gathered one pivotal spring weekend at the Mayflower Hotel in Washington, it was clear that we had made major progress and could come out of the nearly year-long endeavor with an actual victory!

We had gotten lucky. Had there been no challenge to President Carter by liberal Senator Ted Kennedy, it seemed unlikely that a sitting president would have taken the political risk of allowing a gay civil rights plank in the platform. However, given this challenge, Carter's forces had to at least consider those seventy delegates and alternates and the plank they demanded. As the national convention approached, President Carter's forces increasingly asserted their control. Yet Kennedy wasn't willing to fold his hand, and he was widely expected to extract platform concessions before lending his support to the president in the fall. The state platform committee in Minnesota had been organized around issues, but the presidential candidacies dominated every national convention committee, including the platform committee. Kennedy's forces, which were in the minority but nonetheless formidable, were willing to support a strong lesbian and gay civil rights plank. Their support could ensure a minority report and a debate on the convention floor—but no actual plank.

On the other hand, we heard that Carter's forces were willing to allow the inclusion of a single sentence indicating support for the inclusion of "sexual orientation" in human rights laws to prohibit discrimination in jobs, housing, etc. But with Carter increasingly certain of the nomination and beginning to focus on the fall campaign against Ronald Reagan, they would not accept anything more expansive on gay rights in the platform. Further, we were told that if we didn't accept their offer and went forward with a minority plank, the Carter forces were fully prepared not only to defeat it on the convention floor but to defeat the offered reference to "sexual orientation" as well. The message was that Carter's forces would play hardball and the nation would see that gay rights advocates had sought Democratic Party support but had been rejected. So the six lesbian and gay members of the national platform committee, Tom and Spots, Lucia Valeska of the National Gay Task Force, Jack Campbell, and I met in Jack's hotel suite before the final platform committee meeting.

Jack, who is the president of a national chain of men's baths, was a key donor to Gay Vote '80 as well as a national delegate, and he has served on the boards of virtually every major national gay and lesbian rights group in the country. His generosity, particularly in the early years before we'd been able to begin to reach people of means, often made the difference between a struggling group surviving and successfully undertaking vital work, on the one hand, or going under, on the other. He's contributed significantly to virtually every organization or project I've launched since I came on the national scene, and I've hated how it's become almost chic in recent years to disparage him and make light of his support. Many of those now looking down their noses at him wouldn't have had movement organizations if it hadn't been for his never-ending support in the beginning!

As we gathered that day in Jack's suite, we had a major decision before us. The argument of those wanting to take a minority report to the convention floor, despite the fact that defeat was almost guaranteed, was that we'd come too far to accept anything less. Further, by taking it to the floor, we could focus critical national attention on the issue. Predictably, those from San Francisco advocated this view. The argument on the other side, in which I believed very strongly, was that no one remembers the exact language of platform planks anyway, so the wording—after the vital inclusion of nondiscrimination based on "sexual orientation"—was frankly irrelevant. Accept Carter's deal, proclaim victory, and come out of the 1980 Democratic National Convention with a historic inclusion of a gay and lesbian civil rights plank. Being a simple Midwestern boy, I thought the choice was abundantly clear.

I and others passionately made this argument, but it was the gay and lesbian platform committee members who were going to determine the outcome. Virginia Apuzzo, who was closely associated with then–Lt. Governor Mario Cuomo and was a Carter delegate, spoke strongly for what I thought was the only realistic option. Although Ginny and I have never been particularly close, I've always seen her as a very impressive and charismatic leader within our movement. Tom Bastow, a hardheaded realist who'd given up a tremendous amount personally to help elect the delegates across the country which were our bargaining chip, remained virtually silent throughout the hotly contested debate in Jack's suite. I was amazed. On reflection, I saw that he simply felt it more appropriate to defer to those who had gone through the hard work of getting onto the national platform committee. But I was about as subtle as a ten-ton truck and wanted him to weigh in strongly. Finally, after hours of anguishing debate and serious hand wringing, the group agreed to accept Carter's deal of simple inclusion of a single sentence in the civil rights section and would forego a floor battle for a minority report.

The hour of truth was before us and, when the platform committee met that night, we'd have to let them know our decision. We decided that Bill Krause, a relatively young activist from San Francisco, who'd fought most vigorously for the minority report approach while in Jack's suite, would deliver our message. Bill, who has since died of AIDS, gave a brilliant and moving speech about the bigotry and discrimination against lesbians and gay men. The normally raucous room was absolutely hushed. When he concluded his stirring speech by announcing the withdrawal of the minority report, there was an audible gasp and cries of dismay from our nongay supporters throughout the room. Several gay men I've worked with closely, including GRNL treasurer Paul Kuntzler and his lover of many years Steve Miller, had not known of our deliberations earlier in the day or all that went into our thinking. They denounced us bitterly. Although I'd argued for and strongly believed in this option as the only realistic one available to us, after Bill's speech and the withdrawal to those horrified cries, I remember turning to a colleague and saying, "Gee, I hope we've made the right decision."

By the time the actual convention in New York arrived, the real drama was over. There was minor skirmishing within the gay and lesbian caucus over who would serve as cochairs and a real effort to raise the issue by placing the name of an openly gay black man, Mel Boozer, in nomination for vice president.

The caucus successfully collected enough signatures and Mel gave an excellent speech, but the media largely ignored that aspect of our efforts. On the platform plank, the gay community declared victory and the media correctly reported that, for the first time in history, the Democratic Party had endorsed lesbian and gay civil rights. Other agenda items included positional fights between Ginny Apuzzo and Jean O'Leary as well as between the East and West Coasts. Two years later the Democratic Midterm Convention strengthened the lesbian and gay rights plank as well as speaking out on AIDS. And, despite occasional grousing by a few about catering to so-called special interests and dealing with such "fringe issues," essentially it has become a nondebatable article of faith within the party. Unfortunately, the days of party discipline on Capitol Hill have long since passed and we haven't been able to fully translate that party support into passage of non-discrimination legislation. Too often even Democratic legislators still opt for silence when it comes to ending job and housing discrimination for lesbian and gay Americans.

I've never had the opportunity to discuss the battle over accepting half a loaf or nothing with those with whom I strongly disagreed at the time. I suspect they might look at the same event and conclude that we made a serious error by missing a golden opportunity to secure national attention to our struggle, yet I've always felt vindicated by our decision. I thought then, and feel time has proved us correct, that the time for publicity for its own sake had passed. What we needed desperately—both to push our movement into the mainstream and to empower our own community—were actual victories. Nothing succeeds like success.

Getting into the Civil Rights Coalition

In Minnesota in the early 1970s, a central focus—beyond just establishing visibility for an emerging community, demonstrating the need for non-discrimination laws, and finding some way to mobilize lesbians and gay men who viewed our efforts as rocking the boat—was on building coalitions. Because I believed that the black community could play a central role in either advancing or deterring our efforts, it was natural that we turned to groups such as the Minneapolis Urban Coalition. The coalition, directed by friend and mentor Harry Davis, included representatives from various civil rights groups, civic organizations, and major businesses in the area. Our eventual admission, which required behind-the-scenes lobbying, served to help legitimize the gay civil rights issue. However, all we sought initially was membership in the coalition rather than official endorsement of our legislation.

With my experience in Minnesota as a guidepost, it wasn't long after I arrived in Washington, DC, in 1978 that I began exploring the civil rights organizations and whether there was a coalition-type organization which it would make sense for Gay Rights National Lobby to join. I began by meeting with the national executive director of Americans for Democratic Action, Leon Shull. Leon was a well-established, well-respected figure in progressive circles, and he suggested I meet with Joseph Rauh, who—with the NAACP's Clarence Mitchell—had been one of the leading lobbyists for the 1964 Civil Rights Act.

Mr. Rauh, who was a genuine legend and a hero of mine, readily agreed to meet me for lunch and share some his vast wisdom on Washington lobbying in general and civil rights advocacy specifically. We met in the basement of his office building, and I cherished our meeting. In addition to offering lobbying advice, he told me about the Leadership Conference on Civil Rights (LCCR), where he served as legal counsel. The Leadership Conference included more than 120 member organizations and was precisely the sort of prestigious coalition group I was interested in having the gay and lesbian community join. However, Joe explained that it wouldn't be simple to secure membership.

A couple of years earlier, the National Gay Task Force, directed by Bruce Voeller, had applied for membership and been rejected. NGTF, which was based in New York City, was the larger and older national gay rights group but, according to Mr. Rauh, the Task Force failed to understand there was a chance of being rejected. They applied much like an individual would if he or she was joining the Rotary. Their request came up at the Leadership Conference Executive Committee without any prior notice, even among women's organizations which could be expected to support our position. They had not bothered to alert those on the executive committee who could expect to be supportive, nor work to ease any objections by others. The U.S. Catholic Conference and the AFL-CIO, two of the largest and most powerful of the member organizations and critical to the funding of the Leadership Conference, both objected, essentially vetoing membership by a gay organization.

Although NGTF had the advantage of being the larger group, their broad agenda for gay freedom posed a challenge for those that might accept civil rights but not endorsement of the lifestyle. I thought that the Gay Rights National Lobby, which was specifically working for nondiscrimination legislation, was perhaps a little easier "sell" for the members of the executive committee to accept. Rauh indicated he'd help as we sought admission but strongly suggested that we mobilize our friends on the executive committee and try to get the objecting organizations to reverse course before even thinking of moving forward. I stored the information away, and over the next few months I began securing the support and leadership of the various women's organizations who were part of the Leadership Conference. They agreed to help as soon as we were ready, but it would take a couple of years rather than months to get all our ducks in a row.

The Gay Rights National Lobby built good relations with the civil rights coalition by vigorously working against President Reagan's nomination of right-wing, antigay Rev. B. Sam Hart to the U.S. Civil Rights Commission. Hart was not only quite bigoted on gay issues but was at loggerheads with the entire civil rights community on affirmative action. We also used our grassroots network—through field associates and through phone banks to supporters—to urge constituent pressure for the Voting Rights Extension. We got the National Coalition of Black Gays, which had neither the staff nor a large mailing list, to join us in the project. But we also issued a joint press release to the gay press urging readers to actively support the Voting Rights Extension. Susan Green, who helped direct both coalition building and constituent mobilization, coordinated these projects.

I also tried, initially in vain, to reach the chairman of the conference's executive committee, Bayard Rustin. I'd long known of him as a pivotal be-hind-the-scenes coordinator of the 1963 Civil Rights March as well as countless other civil rights activities, but not until I moved to Washington, DC, did I learn he was a gay man. In fact, in the early 1960s Rustin's sexual orientation had been used against him by Senator Strom Thurmond and per-haps by others as well. Perhaps because of these difficult experiences, Mr. Rustin was hardly pleased to hear from me when I reached him in New York. I sensed that he would not go so far as to work against our admission, yet it was clear that he was unwilling to help advocate our membership like Mr. Rauh would.

Next, I began to explore how to defuse the opposition of the U.S. Catho-lic Conference. Frank Scheuren, the national president of Dignity (the Catholic gay group) and a board member of the Lobby, thought we could make some headway within the church, depending on how we approached the issue. Frank arranged for a meeting and flew in to join me in meeting with Monsignor Francis Lally, who directed the Catholic Conference's leg-islative advocacy. The meeting, in the Catholic Conference's impressive Washington offices—which struck me as almost a fortress—was very posi-tive and cordial. Once we assured Lally we weren't asking for endorsement of the "gay lifestyle," nor even immediate support for our legislation, Lally agreed that the Catholic Conference would withdraw its objections. Only some years later did I learn that Lally's investment in the issue was deeper than I'd suspected, with rumors labeling him as gay himself.

Finally, we were ready to face what might well be our most difficult test: eliminating the opposition of the AFL-CIO. The AFL-CIO not only con-tributed a great deal of money to the Leadership Conference but also had ex-cellent on-the-Hill lobbyists and a massive network of constituents. George Meany, the longtime president of the AFL-CIO, had been an outspoken op-ponent of gay rights and was given to making antigay slurs. Yet Meany had recently died and was succeeded by Lane Kirkland, a far younger and more progressive leader.

I reported our success with the Catholic Conference to Bill Olwell, who had indicated that if we could somehow overcome Catholic opposition he'd try to turn AFL-CIO around. Olwell, a vice president of the United Food and Commercial Workers (UFCW), was the highest ranking openly gay union official in the country. A cigar-smoking pol, Bill hardly fit anyone's stereotypes of who gay people were. He agreed to discuss the matter with John Perkins, the effective and progressive director of AFL-CIO's Committee on Political Education (COPE). The report came back that AFL-CIO would end their objections as well. However, there was a condition: we must agree not to raise the issue of official Leadership Conference endorsement of the national gay civil rights bill within two to three years. Since we were a long way from real action on the bill, that was no problem at all.

The very able executive director of the conference, Ralph Neas, was uncomfortable with the issue, but I would not describe his discomfort as real homophobia. His discomfort may have revolved around the need to hold together a broad-based coalition of over 120 groups with diverse agendas. They had played a very active role in the ERA and its extension, but they'd avoided contentious battles over abortion at this time.

We still faced one last barrier when Mel Boozer, the Washington representative of the National Gay Task Force, stumbled into this delicately arranged situation and demanded that NGTF had to be admitted for membership as well. Informal discussions suggested that it might upset the whole apple cart. Were we going to demand that every national gay and lesbian group in the country be allowed to become a member? Finally, we convinced them that we would not and both groups were admitted. Short-term, our membership has meant we've often tried to help deliver for various civil rights bills on the Hill. The Human Rights Campaign Fund, which took over GRNL, regularly bought a table at each year's Leadership Conference banquet for about $1,500.

It has also helped establish the gay civil rights movement as a "player" within the broader civil rights community, providing tremendous opportunities for invaluable networking with other progressive groups and lobbyists. At this writing, the Leadership Conference on Civil Rights has not yet taken a position on the National Gay and Lesbian Civil Rights Bill but is expected to endorse it shortly. In fairness, that probably has had as much to do with the necessary preoccupation of gay lobbyists with AIDS issues as any LCCR reluctance to support gay civil rights.

Securing Support from AFSCME and the Labor Movement

A key aspect of Joe Rauh's advice was not only to eliminate labor union objections to our participation in the Leadership Conference, but also to secure their active support. Rauh stressed that the struggle for black civil rights would never have been successful without the leadership of the labor union movement. Most progressive lobbies either focus on very specific issues—such as the environment—or just don't have that much political clout to impact the outcome. But labor has historically taken a broader view of the public interest than many other organizations. Now, with Meany's death, we no longer had to deal with attacks on "fairies" from the top AFL-CIO leadership.

Lane Kirkland, and the new generation of leaders that came in with him, was very forward-looking. Kirkland was an individual who might well recognize that nondiscrimination in jobs for lesbians and gay men was completely consistent with workers' rights advocated by the labor movement. So, in the early 1980s we began exploring how to secure labor movement endorsement. Discussions with UFCW's Olwell convinced us that our best starting point was with one of the more progressive unions with large and openly gay memberships, probably either of the two public employee unions—the Service Employees International Union (SEIU) and the American Federation of State, County and Municipal Employees (AFSCME). The two groups often competed with each other over organizing and the bargaining rights of public sector employees. SEIU is particularly strong on the West Coast, where we could expect strong support.

Eventually we decided that while we'd seek support from both, we'd focus our initial attention on securing AFSCME's endorsement, in part because we felt we had more immediate avenues of access. Susan Green, our hardworking, intense legislative assistant, and Vic Basile, a new gay activist with a background in union organizing, agreed to spearhead the effort.

Both AFSCME's national leadership and grassroots are quite progressive. The then-new national president of AFSCME, Gerry McEntee, had a strong record of support for gay civil rights in the 1970s, even when it wasn't as popular to be supportive of gay rights. Bill Lucy, the black secretary-treasurer and second most powerful person in the union, met with us and agreed to lend his support to our drive to get AFSCME's endorsement. McEntee and Lucy had been competitors for the presidency so we had to make sure that, by working with Lucy, we weren't walking into any internal conflicts between them.

Looking back, although our preparation and organization for the AFSCME endorsement drive seems almost extreme and overdone today, we just did not know what to expect as we moved forward in 1982. Susan's board report in January 1983 summed up the effort:

> One of my proudest moments to date was the victory in Atlantic City on June 23, 1982, when the American Federation of State, County and Municipal Employees (AFSCME) passed a resolution endorsing lo-

cal, state and federal gay civil rights legislation. This came as a result
of a six month behind-the-scenes operation. . . . Together, we wrote
the resolution and developed the strategy for passage. We also lined
up support from many AFSCME locals, district councils, and key union leaders prior to the convention.

Susan went on to point out the broader significance: "This single victory
has mushroomed, in great part due to support from Bill Lucy, AFSCME's
International Secretary-Treasurer and the highest ranking black labor union
official in the U.S." Because of AFSCME's resolution, the entire Industrial
Union Department of AFL-CIO, which represented the so-called hard hats,
adopted a similar resolution supporting gay rights.

Later we learned that the entire AFL-CIO, at an executive committee
meeting, passed a national resolution putting organized labor on record in
support of lesbian and gay rights. Although Bill Olwell again played a key
role in its adoption, the actual executive committee resolution was put forward by John Sweeney, the international president of the Service Employees International Union (SEIU), and passed October 3-6, 1983.

This resolution has continued to be strengthened over the years; it was
not treated as just another progressive social issue but instead as consistent
with the labor movement's trade union responsibility to their workers.
There's still much to be done to translate these resolutions into real legislative help, and again much of that is due to the gay community having to set
aside our civil rights agenda temporarily in order to address the AIDS crisis.

Creating a "Think Tank" for Education and Research

In 1991, as I was meeting with fellow panelists at a forum on the national
lesbian and gay civil rights bill, I heard the familiar refrain and was deeply
saddened to hear that most gay men and lesbians across the country didn't
even know that there was a need for a national bill, let alone know about the
actual bill itself. Little had changed, at least nationally, on this problem—in
terms of educating either nongays or gay and lesbian people—in more than
ten years!

We tried to address this issue before I left the Gay Rights National Lobby
by establishing a 501(c)3 research and educational foundation, the Right to
Privacy Foundation. We designed RPF as our tax-exempt, tax-deductible
unit to carry out critical research and educational initiatives associated with
GRNL's mission. It would work closely with both the Gay Rights National
Lobby and, after 1980, the Human Rights Campaign Fund. At the time, we
wrote,

The Foundation will serve as a "think tank" for the lesbian and gay civil rights movement, providing research and analysis services. It will be, in some ways, analogous to the Heritage Foundation's or the Free Congress Foundation's service to the New Right movement.

As in other movement organizations I've helped to run, RPF was to operate by "Goals and Objectives" which clearly stated our intentions:

Documentation of anti-gay discrimination in employment and possibly other areas addressed by the federal Gay and Lesbian Civil Rights Bills. The approach is through case histories rather than statistics. The results will be printed in a short brochure and made available to the public.

This project implements the Foundation's objective of assembling information and presenting it in a clear and effective way so as to educate both the gay and the non-gay public.

In addition to producing the informative pamphlet, we planned to create ads for the gay and nongay print media illustrating the basic unfairness of such discrimination. Also, we would prepare brief memos analyzing both the strengths and weaknesses of our arguments for lesbian and gay civil rights legislation as well as those put forward opposing said legislation. Finally, RPF would provide vital education to the gay community in terms of skill development training, including organizing skills and persuasive techniques; RPF, in fact, helped plan significant skill enhancement seminars for the first national field associate meeting.

To implement these and other research, education, and analysis functions, RPF hired Rick Davis as our education and research director of the think tank. Rick had lobbied with me at the Minnesota state legislature in 1973, 1975, and 1977, and assisted in the unsuccessful defense of the St. Paul ordinance in 1978. I stated then, "Rick has an unusual combination of strong academic background and good practical political sense and experience." Davis summed up the tasks before him by saying,

The people working on national lesbian/gay civil rights legislation necessarily get caught up in the frantic scramble to fight daily battles. They often don't have time for careful analysis. They have to be too close to daily developments to see long-term trends clearly, and they're too battered and exhausted to do painstaking, detailed research. The Right to Privacy Foundation will provide these essential services.

Unfortunately, I finally convinced Rick to move to Washington, DC, just a short time before the conflict began in earnest between David Goodstein and Larry Bush and the group of organizations that I ran, and the funding for the Right to Privacy Foundation became one of the earliest victims. The Lobby was suffering badly from the steady drumbeat of attack, and although the board and many connected activists felt the attacks were unfair, funds dried up because many others felt that where there was that much smoke there surely was fire. I became preoccupied with responding to the attacks and fell into a siege mentality, unable to effectively handle fund-raising for either the Lobby or the Right to Privacy Foundation.

Among the many sad developments from my pitched battle with Goodstein and Bush was our inability to fulfill our commitments to Rick, who had moved east at my request and at considerable sacrifice. Just as important, the foundation never had an opportunity to reach its enormous potential. Many of the projects planned for the foundation still haven't been addressed effectively since the foundation collapsed.

I have often reflected on those times and tried to figure out how I could have better handled the problem of RPF's funding, but I've never arrived at another approach. Although we knew that I couldn't be the primary source of fund-raising on a long-term basis and anticipated hiring resource development staff, we hadn't even reached that stage of development. But I have never stopped feeling guilty.

A Fund-Raising Primitive Goes National

Although the GRNL board had many good points, I realized that I had made the same mistake the Task Force had made earlier. Many, if not most, of our board members were preoccupied by their efforts for their local or national groups and failed to do fund-raising for GRNL. We were only slowly beginning to move to a more fund-raising board in 1982 with the inclusion of noted gay California fund-raiser Sheldon Andelson when we began facing internal community attacks; while many national nonprofits raised the overwhelming majority of their funds by the retention of resource development staff, GRNL didn't yet have the funds for such a position.

When I arrived in Washington, DC, it became clear that my lobbying efforts on behalf of the Gay Rights National Lobby would depend on my ability to scrape through and raise enough funds at least to make ends meet. What I found at "my office" was a disconnected phone on a desk in a space we rented from the Universal Fellowship of Metropolitan Community Churches' Washington office. When I went to the bank, I found only nine dollars left in the account. There was a membership of almost 1,000 people, but the group—whose sole function was to lobby Congress—had never had a full time lobbyist. Also, members hadn't even received a newsletter for more than nine months; they'd been badly treated as members and I told them so, promising a "New Beginning for GRNL."

Although finances were desperate and it's hard, in hindsight, to see how we made it, we gave all GRNL members a six-month extension on their memberships. We told them that if at the end of that time they couldn't see progress, they shouldn't renew, but if they did see the progress we planned, I hoped they'd give generously, as we certainly needed it to keep going. Somehow, it all worked out. Happily, it was many months before we also discovered over $9,000 in preexisting tax liabilities.

After my major donor sent the first $2,000 to $3,000 of his $25,000 pledge, the pledge of the big donor that brought me to Washington fell through. I was devastated and scared to death the whole effort might collapse. During this early period, money to keep going and pay my salary was hard to come by, but somehow we made it, often by bizarre means. My roommate Eric charged me very low rent. One man picked up one of the GRNL brochures we'd put out on a cigarette machine at an adult bookstore in DC and sent in a $2,000 check; when we met years later, I discovered he was anything but rich or pretentious and instead was a very down-to-earth guy who simply cared about making a difference and believed in what we were doing. He actually continued to give generously for many years, and his gifts were truly sacrificial.

We occasionally got letters from a woman in Kansas City, with jagged handwriting at a slant. She would say things like, "I've just sold my furs, here's $1,000." A few months later, I'd get another, "I've just sold the last of my jewels and enclosed is a check for $2,000." "Crazy Alice," as someone in our office dubbed her, never even gave me a return address to write to thank her, but years later, while traveling through Kansas City, I found out that she had probably heard about GRNL from her participation in the local Metropolitan Community Church. Although most of my friends would pooh-pooh the notion, I think such contributions were direct gifts from God, much like I found a $100 bill in a neighborhood restaurant years after I'd left GRNL and was unemployed.

GRNL Becomes One of the Earliest
in Gay Direct Mail

Largely because my roommate's boyfriend, Dan Schellhorn, owned a mail house handling hundreds of thousands of pieces of direct mail, the Gay Rights National Lobby began to explore a direct-mail strategy to raise funds nationally. From my time on the board of directors of the Task Force, I knew they had tried direct-mail fund-raising, although I didn't know then how they had done.

You had to have the names and addresses of potential donors, however, and those sorts of lists did not really exist in the gay community when we started direct mail. We began to change that situation by asking current donors to give us the names of their friends and others who should be asked to contribute, which brought in a remarkable number of names. In addition, we took advantage of the various legislative developments—the passage of the McDonald amendment to Legal Services, the so-called "Family Protection Act," urging support for the national gay and lesbian civil rights bill, etc.—to circulate petitions across the country.

By the end of my time at the Lobby, we'd collected more than 100,000 names and addresses of people who signed such petitions. Although they ended up having a negligible direct legislative impact, they became sources of our later success in direct mail. When circumstances forced me to leave GRNL, my successors failed to use the lists or regularly clean them of bad addresses and they grew outdated; despite later efforts to repair them, they never really produced effectively again.

Successful direct mail required not only lists but also the up-front capital to pay for it. Because we had no start-up funds, Dan front-ended resources to us and helped to teach me how to write direct mail. Our first prospect piece, "We Can Have Reports Lost and Opportunities Missed or . . ." went to about 20,000 people and did very, very well—I think our response rate was almost 3 percent. In addition to Dan's ongoing advice, I took several seminars on direct-mail writing and our administrative assistant, Alan Fox, took seminars on the administrative and financial ends of a successful direct-mail operation.

As things progressed, I would write a first draft based on recent political developments with the secondary goal of educating our constituency. Then Dan reviewed it and suggested changes. As time passed, I began to get the hang of the process and became better at my drafting, and Dan made fewer changes. Unfortunately, I never got into a position to follow Dan's most important advice of establishing a revolving fund to be used exclusively for future direct mail because we were broke and had to have some of the resulting proceeds of every mailing to pay pressing bills. Nonetheless, we finally had the beginnings of a real donor base around the country.

Maybe we got a little cocky because the next major roll out, which we referred to as the "Gloom and Doom" mailing about the impact on gay rights of Ronald Reagan's election, truly lived up to its name. To say it bombed is to seriously understate the case. There is a very thin line between creating a picture showing a compelling need and totally immobilizing the reader with a sense of hopelessness. We'd painted such a bleak picture people couldn't figure out why they should give. Also, timing can sometimes be the difference between success and disaster: our "Gloom and Doom" package actually got to people shortly before Christmas in the flood of holiday cards, when most people were saving every penny for holiday presents. We were doomed.

As Dan had warned us, with no funds in a revolving account for "prospecting," we were in debt and in trouble. Generally, prospecting is doing well to break even with the real revenue coming in as a result of quarterly "house appeals" and the annual renewal of donations. Unfortunately, much of our debt was to Dan's mail house and it put a significant strain on our relationship (by then I had moved in with him and his lover David). In his search for a solution to get us out of debt and his firm paid off, he opted for more prospecting.

But again, the mailings did badly and our debt became even more severe. Dan and I are both control freaks and each of us was concerned about the whole situation. I insisted on a halt to all prospecting until we retired the debt and until I felt more in control of our destiny. Dan is a terrific guy; I and the community owed a great deal to him and, after a brief period of strain, we reestablished our friendship, seeing each other not only at church but also at Georgetown basketball games.

We had to find a way to pay off more than $45,000 to our creditors, so we wrote a very important special appeal to the GRNL donor base, which was then only about 5,000 people. Since we could not count on the normal help we had on drafting the package, I borrowed the opening from a NOW mailing and borrowed more extensively from a Moral Majority appeal. I'd long since gotten myself on the list of every antigay and New Right group in the country to see what they were saying on gay rights issues and figure out how to use it to mobilize lesbians and gay men.

The survival of the Gay Rights National Lobby was on the line, but it was tricky to make the situation sound sufficiently scary but still give people a sense of hope. I had learned my lesson from the "Gloom and Doom" mailing that direct mail that sounds too overwhelmingly hopeless will freeze contributions. People have to have a sense their contribution can make a real difference. Also, people don't give to organizations or individuals. They give to respond to their own needs, so aside from GRNL's life-and-death situation I had to include plenty of programmatic motivation.

The so-called Family Protection Act, which had become the New Right and Moral Majoritarians' "wish list," provided this substance. I began the letter:

I only have a few days before I must make a very serious decision about the operation of Gay Rights National Lobby. What I am referring to is a drastic cutback of lobbying efforts in Washington, D.C. Unless I can find a way to pay the bills, I can't see any other way.

But I thought I had to show people that we really had made progress:

It won't mean the death of GRNL—we've come too far, grown too rapidly, and accomplished too much for that. But it would mean a severe and dangerous reduction in operation right now, and just when we are needed most.

The recent efforts against the antigay McDonald amendment to the Legal Services Corporation bill had cost GRNL massively, and I quoted Rep. Barney Frank (who hadn't come out yet) about the job we'd done. Then I explained what was at stake if the right wing passed the Family Protection Act and said, "This just isn't the time for Gay Rights National Lobby to be cutting back our operations." I was completely candid when I concluded,

Frankly, I hesitated in sharing the full dimensions of our plight. Your past support has been essential to our enormous growth and what I think is a strong record of accomplishment, and it's been appreciated. I don't like having to come to you again, but the need has just never been so severe.

By then GRNL had moved a couple of times and although we were housed in a townhouse on Capitol Hill, it was a rough neighborhood across from a housing project. Because GRNL's finances were so difficult and its ability to pay my modest salary was so shaky, my lover and I actually rented a room in the GRNL offices for a few tough months. I worried about the image it could convey of unprofessionalism, and neither Will nor I felt safe walking to and from the apartment to the grocery store at night. But we didn't really have a lot of choices, and GRNL needed the modest rent from us as well. The fact that the entire complex was unbelievably infested with cockroaches made it hazardous to go into the kitchen at night.

When the first business reply envelopes (BREs) from our emergency appeal began coming back I was out sick, meaning I was up in bed in Will's and my room. Susan, our wonderful legislative assistant who doubled as everything else, too, insisted I come down from "our apartment"; since only the small GRNL family was around, I struggled down in my bathrobe—hacking, coughing, and sniffling.

Instead of the normal small stack of business reply envelopes, there was a huge mailbag absolutely filled with BREs and checks from our donors. I felt like we were living a scene from *It's a Wonderful Life*. We had a morale-boosting strategy of ringing a little bell every time a check for $100 or more came in. Well, Susan sat down and the bell was ringing all afternoon. Knowing it really represented salvation for our organization, we all cried. It's been hard to get even close friends who know direct mail to believe me, but the final figures showed we received responses from over 23 percent of our donors! The average contribution was well over $40, far greater than the $25 low gift option. We'd exceeded the goal we'd stated in the letter, which was a little more than we'd needed. The response was so unbelievable we wrote each a thank you letter, stating:

> I discover that, for once in my life, I am almost at a loss for words. Thanks to your contribution, and those of hundreds of other individuals, we have met the challenge and will be able to continue to aggressively work for justice and civil rights for lesbians and gay men. . . I only wish you could have been in our offices when the return mail arrived and we knew we could continue our work—it was pure joy.
>
> We will always work to get maximum impact for every dollar given to Gay Rights National Lobby. And second—I will never come to you proclaiming crisis if one does not exist.

One of my favorite prospecting pieces, which I thought was fairly creative, was known in-house as "We Won't Go Like Frogs!" One of the major goals of the outer envelope is to get the package opened, and we had a cute drawing of a frog outside; but on the enclosed letter that cute frog was in a pot of boiling water and the letter began,

> If you drop a frog in warm water, he'll swim lazily around. Increase the temperature slightly and he'll relax even more. When the water is hot, he'll fall asleep. Raise the temperature even further and, eventually he'll die in lazy comfort. DO YOU FEEL A LITTLE DROWSY?

Although most acknowledged it as an innovative letter, I think, in hindsight, the letter both reached and offended those reading it. It's hard to remember my emotional state at the time, but perhaps it was a time when my frustration and irritation at the lack of financial support got the best of me. If so, I wish my friend Jim had been around then to remind me that bitterness and anger aren't motivating. Needless to say, this mailing did even worse than the "Gloom and Doom" letter and brought a number of complaints as well.

If you heat the kettle slowly enough, it's been said, frogs die in
lazy comfort. They just fall asleep.

DO YOU FEEL A LITTLE DROWSY?

The Moral Majority and their cohorts are stoking up the fires. Especially in Washington, D.C. They know that the Nation's Capital fosters the trends and national publicity that sweep through the land. No place — not even San Francisco — is immune. A change in national law can cook us altogether.

Gay Rights National Lobby is at the heart of the current battle in Washington, rallying our friends in Congress to put out the fires. We're the only full-time lobby at Congress devoting full attention to civil rights and equal justice for lesbians and gay men.

We've had success — expanding support and co-sponsorship of gay/lesbian civil rights bills, generating thousands of letters to Congress, fighting anti-gay bills, and bringing together coalitions who feel a common danger.

With your help, we've produced these results with a growing budget — getting a huge impact for each dollar contributed.

The heat is on now more than ever. With millions of dollars in the "New Right" warchests, the opposition is determined to turn back the clock on human rights. We are all at a critical point in our history — a time when we must step forward to meet the challenge.

But we must step out together.

Let's not go like frogs!

"We Won't Go Like Frogs" letter. Courtesy of HRC.

The issue of direct mail is one that is badly misunderstood by many, if not most, public interest advocates. I was very fortunate to be guided in my direct mail initiatives by two excellent individuals, Dan Schellhorn and Alan Baron, and I sometimes benefited from the informal advice of Roger Craver of Craver, Mathews and Smith, who is a close friend of Baron's. It's difficult, if not impossible, to summarize a set of "rules" about direct mail but I did have some general guidelines:

1. Keep the paragraphs short and to the point.
2. Use "helper" words and phrases to make sure the reader continues to follow along, and sometimes use underlining selectively for emphasis.
3. Make sure the entire direct-mail package—outer envelope, letter, response form, and so on—are coordinated in an integrated package.
4. The central theme must be easy to grasp.
5. People don't give funds via direct mail to individuals or to groups per se.
6. It's essential for the writer to speak with the readers' needs in mind and not those of the group soliciting the gifts.
7. While it is, of course, important to create a compelling need, it's also absolutely essential that the letter is not based on appeals to guilt.

We initially received a 2 to 3 percent rate of response for "prospecting mail" to untested lists (the average contribution usually was close to the lowest dollar figure option listed). This was far better than normal as well as better than most at the time, and it has since slipped dramatically for almost all groups. We also secured an 8 to 12 percent response to appeals to proven donors to our organization. The dedication of our core base of donors is largely what was responsible for building a viable organization. However, because of the severely limited universe of gay direct-mail names and the fact that those donors grow weary of solicitations, the prospecting rate dropped to between one-quarter and one-half of a percent, and repeat appeals no longer got more than a 4 to 6 percent response.

At the same time, the Lobby's referral program produced quite well, but it was the source of the single most embarrassing moment I've ever had in the lesbian and gay rights movement. Shortly after coming to Washington, DC, we asked the current members of GRNL to refer others to us. We told them that we could include their names as the people referring them (i.e., "Sally Smith has suggested we write you . . .") or we could simply send out the appeal without the referring person's name.

Two lesbians from New Orleans, among the most esteemed people in that wonderful city, sent in the names of everyone on their Christmas card list. In our small cluttered offices, a volunteer somehow had misplaced the note asking that we not use the referring people's names in the appeal, so we did. And so, in short, we brought these two women out as lesbians to many of their nongay friends and family members.

When I spoke to one of them shortly after the blunder, she cried and I felt horrible. Although I've talked with these two women since and they seem to be forgiving, I know that what we inadvertently did caused them serious pain. Even now, more than a dozen years later and after all the time I've been involved in the gay and lesbian movement, I've never made such a mistake. There is no way I could ever appropriately apologize or make up for this mistake. It taught me to be far more sensitive to any such situation in the years since.

We escaped disaster, and GRNL's annual budget was growing from our start-up of just $9 in the bank (and $9,000 tax debt) to a little more than $20,000 in the first year and about $40,000 in our third year. By the fourth year, we'd exceeded $120,000 and our projected budget in the fifth year was just short of a half-million dollars.

Shortly after the direct-mail failures (and some successes, too), we decided to diversify our fund-raising and brought in a consulting firm for major donor fund-raising who had previously worked with the Universal Fellowship of Metropolitan Community Churches. However we quickly concluded that the consulting group wouldn't work out, and even would be a bit unethical, so the program was put on hold until one of our board members took it on.

Terry Bean, from Eugene, Oregon, agreed to see what he could do to get the program off the ground. Terry, who is about forty years old now, must have been in his early thirties at the time. At 5'10" and about 160 pounds, he was quite attractive. His sandy brown hair had just a touch of gray to lend a distinguished look, and his deep tan and Cary Grant smile made it easy to see how potential donors had a hard time saying no to him. The word "class" comes quickly to mind when you think of Terry, and he could sell anything to anyone. He had owned an Alaskan fishing boat, sold real estate, and owned several gay bars.

We had first gotten to know each other when he was running the gay community's side of the Eugene gay rights referendum and I was helping run the St. Paul referendum. For years I teased him that he'd swindled me out of about $30,000, as he conned a staffer on the St. Paul retention fight to share the proceeds of a national mailing for the three gay rights ordinances on the ballot although St. Paul had actually done the mailing. Terry seemed like the fictional character "Cash McCall," but he was an excellent board member.

The idea was to set up a prestigious, exclusive "club" of major donors who would give at least $1,200 a year to the organization for its ongoing work. MECLA, the Municipal Elections Committee of Los Angeles, had become the first gay and lesbian group to establish a major donor club about a year earlier and had done quite well. Los Angeles was hardly typical of the nation, though, and none of us knew if a national group could recruit major donors who cared about what happened in Washington, DC. Since this was long before the AIDS crisis—and even longer before we'd have a realistic chance of winning any congressional battles—the jury was out.

Terry traveled to San Francisco and Los Angeles to enlist people on a few weekends in "The 48," the name the earlier consultants came up with for the major donor club. He pledged to try for six months and, if it went well, he'd continue. If not, we would give it up. We couldn't even have considered such an effort if Terry had not graciously agreed that he would assume all risks, and we'd pay his expenses and payments based on his success. By the time Terry began, we had an annual budget of about $265,000, but we struggled to meet such a meager budget. Much needed to be done but staff were in various states of exhaustion from excessive hours; so if we didn't get reinforcements we were in danger of people burning out, collapsing, or leaving their jobs.

The first time Terry went to San Francisco, he called toward the end of the weekend to report he'd enrolled twelve people: most were at $1,200 a year and a few were at either $1,800 or $3,000 a year. The second weekend, just a couple of weeks later, went almost as well, and we were shocked. Once Terry got people to join, he got their advice and suggestions of other people who they thought might join as well. With such good initial success, he soon returned to San Francisco for another round of solicitations. My visit to our West Coast regional office coincided with Terry's and we got together with GRNL board member Larry Bye in between Terry's fund-raising pitches, which usually happened around meals. He'd signed up another thirteen people in "The 48" and had several more appointments before he flew back to Oregon. Whether he was just making me feel good or not, he reported that these were some of the easiest sales he'd ever made. Later, when it came my turn to actually do such face-to-face fund-raising, it became clear it wasn't so easy—unless you had Terry's charm, salesmanship, and masterful ability.

My own role in the development of the major donor group was pretty limited. I joined Terry in a couple of meetings, but excused myself before he closed the sales. Even then, Terry knew this would be a temporary undertaking on his part and he tried to teach me how to do such encounters. He stressed that he spent most of his time listening to the people he met about what they thought and about their needs in the context of the movement.

Listening wasn't my strength, so this was tough when I later had to take on the one-to-one efforts. Terry also reminded me of the old sales technique: Once you've asked for the contribution, be quiet. The saying goes, "the next one who talks loses."

I vividly remember one night when Terry and I were both in San Francisco but I had already gone back to the hotel (I seldom stayed in hotels during my years in the movement, usually opting for friends' spare beds, but Terry had arranged the stay as a comp). There was a knock at my door and I woke up to see Terry at the door. He had a potential major donor downstairs who wanted to meet me. I got dressed and wiped the sleepy ticks out of my eyes and the cobwebs from my brain. When I met this gentleman, I realized that potential major donors come in a range of styles. The donor, who went on to pledge $1,800 a year, was a blue-collar worker from the East Bay. His intense desire to make a difference offset any shortfall in terms of his resources—and he honored his commitment.

Later, as various occasions arose, I got to know many of those who'd joined "The 48" and made such major donations to our work. They were mostly terrific people who cared intensely about what we were doing. Often, no one had ever asked them to contribute at that level before. Joining an exclusive club might have been a factor for a few, but the primary motivation for most was the desire to help us win on a range of national battles.

The only limitation on the size of our donor club seemed to be how much time we could get Terry to devote to the task and which cities he would visit. He went to Los Angeles, where the fund-raising was a little tougher, but he still did pretty well. A little later, he flew to Minneapolis, where I still had a pretty good base of supporters. Terry carefully cultivated the "local boy makes good" angle and he came back with about ten more major donors despite the relative lack of gay wealth compared to the West Coast.

Even though we agreed he would do very well and raise a lot of money in New York City, Terry would not go there because he disliked the city so much. Dan Bradley, a GRNL board member, once promised to match Terry, major donor for major donor, but while Dan was certainly charming enough, he never really had that special killer instinct it took to close the sale. Aside from his own generous participation, he never got GRNL major donors, including one of his best friends who had millions on top of millions.

The "privileges" of being in "The 48" were modest: a monthly report from me on current Capitol Hill developments, occasional cocktail parties in San Francisco to meet other major donors and help us solicit additional ones, acknowledgement in our publications of their participation, and an annual meeting in Washington, DC. In addition to reviewing the group's goals and objective, those that attended "The 48" meeting met with various

Steve in his element with fellow activists. Photography by Jim Marks.

members of Congress, both informally and at presentations at our lun-
cheons. For instance, when "The 48" met in Washington just before our
board meeting, Senator Tsongas invited all of them to his office for a private
meeting; Rep. Waxman, who was an emerging power in the House and the
leading congressional expert on the then-mysterious disease AIDS, addressed their luncheon.

Many of those contributing these significant funds to the Gay Rights National Lobby and/or the Human Rights Campaign Fund (after 1980) were
also donors to a range of state and local gay and lesbian and AIDS organizations. This speaks to one of the most central themes of effective fund-raising: "givers give." The idea that there's a single dollar out there and if you
get it, I can't, is misguided at best and silly at worst. The simple truth is that
we haven't even scratched the surface of the potential financial resources
that can be mobilized for the human dignity and equal justice of lesbian and
gay Americans.

Chapter 3

Money Talks:
Gay and Lesbian Political Clout
and the Founding
of the Human Rights Campaign Fund

We launched the Human Rights Campaign Fund in 1980, which has now, by 1993, become the largest gay and lesbian organization in America, with over 80,000 members. The Campaign Fund slowly evolved from being a political action committee alone to the nation's largest direct Capitol Hill advocacy group. In addition, as modest as its grassroots organizing component is, it's more extensive than any other in the community.

Looking back, I think there's general agreement that the creation of the fund marked a substantial breakthrough for the community. For far too long, we'd gotten along with blowing blue smoke at mirrors. Finally, with the advent of the Human Rights Campaign Fund, we had an organization whose performance could be measured, and that could not only talk the talk but could actually walk the walk!

In earlier years, elections were a time when the gay community had to lay low, since politicians and police targeted gay people for special harassment and abuse during these periods. But reflection on the emergence of countless movements and political action committees convinced me that elections could become the time when our clout forced elected officials to respond to our demands for justice. It would take a lot of hard work and a wholly new mind-set, though. We would have to produce both campaign contributions and volunteers, no small task in a community that was in short supply on self-esteem at the time.

It was hard then to see just how we could get from there to here. A genuine movement pioneer, Jim Foster, was leading similar efforts in electoral politics in San Francisco. A charming man (if you agreed with him), he was the political director of the Society for Individual Rights, one of the more establishment-oriented groups during this period of counterculture and protest. Jim decided one avenue to such clout was a specifically gay Democratic club, an unheard-of idea at the time. Foster's goal was not just to build local clout but also to help repeal California's sodomy laws.

A short time later, in the early 1970s, I made a pilgrimage to San Francisco to meet key activists I had read about in *The Advocate*. Although some were a bit of a disappointment, Jim was politically savvy, full of Irish blarney, and completely delightful. He was dedicated to using the mainstream political process to make a change for the gay community, something I never heard Minnesota activists discuss at the time. Our meeting was everything I could have hoped for, and I flew home with a new hero and an important role model. At the same time, I was acutely aware that what worked in San Francisco might well have far more serious limitations in the Twin Cities.

A short time later, in 1972, I watched Jim on TV, speaking at the Democratic National Convention (even if it was 2 or 3 a.m.). Despite that liberal convention's rejection of the simple gay rights plank Foster advocated, Jim's speech was one of the early breakthroughs for a young, struggling movement. It was also at this 1972 Miami Democratic convention that some other gay activists were protesting what they saw as George McGovern's backtracking on the gay rights issue.

Much of our later national effort was based on our experience in mobilizing electoral support at the state level in Minnesota; as our Minnesota movement grew stronger and the state lobbying campaign went well, the simple knowledge that Jim and others were also using the political process to advance our agenda gave me strength. We sought pledges of support for a nondiscrimination ordinance in Minneapolis from alderman candidates and, once we got them, we turned out volunteers for their campaigns. Although so many nongay groups talk a good game in this area, few really deliver, so our small handfuls of volunteers, whom we dragged all over town, were noticed. Although gay rights buttons were popular with that generation's activists, I insisted our people remove any buttons before we went door-to-door for our candidates, because we wanted politicians to see not only that we could produce bodies but also that we understood political realities and were genuinely there to help. Usually the campaign served chili or some other snack to volunteers afterward and it gave us a good chance to get to know other people involved in the political process and vice versa. Since the gay rights issue was so new and the stereotypes still so prevalent, this interaction, which might now seem trite, was critical to changing ideas about who gay people were.

The most important race that year was for mayor, where a low-key, effective guy from north Minneapolis, Al Hofstede, was the Democratic-Farmer-Labor (DFL) party's nominee to challenge the right-wing incumbent, Charles Stenvig. Stenvig was a police officer who proudly said he took his orders

from God and if he were reelected, any gay rights ordinance would be vetoed. Hofstede might sign a gay rights ordinance but certainly didn't want to
commit to it before the election. That was not good enough for me. I'd take
a private pledge but nothing less. Because liberals were so desperate to get
rid of Stenvig, my position was very unpopular—but I did not care!

Our chance to get a pledge from Hofstede came when we learned he was
seeking the endorsement of the liberal Americans for Democratic Action;
ADA's "sample ballots," showing preferred candidates, had been distributed over the most liberal parts of the university community. Every vote was
likely to count, and ADA's open endorsement process gave us our opportunity. We had several gay activists at the poorly attended ADA screening of
Hofstede, we had three of the six votes and, when Hofstede refused to commit to signing a gay civil rights ordinance, we blocked his endorsement by
ADA. And once the committee had been constituted it couldn't be changed,
so Hofstede had either to satisfy our concerns or go on without the ADA endorsement and sample ballots. Hofstede was livid and our action wasn't
popular with our liberal friends, but I frankly didn't care. Since the decision
could be reversed Hofstede agreed to meet with me, and this time he agreed
privately to sign the ordinance if we wouldn't publicize that fact. With this
pledge, we withdrew our objections, Hofstede was included on the ADA
sample ballot, and we quietly worked to ensure a large gay and lesbian turnout for him. When the city elections came, our candidates swept into the
city council seats and Hofestede defeated the right-wing mayor. He fulfilled
his pledge to sign the ordinance and then appointed me one of the first three
openly gay people to a human rights commission in the country.

In subsequent years we largely duplicated and tried to expand on our effort to mobilize volunteers for supportive candidates at the state legislative
level. This was tougher because we had to drag them all over the Twin Cities
and that still didn't get to the key, undecided legislators in outstate Minnesota (now called "Greater Minnesota"), where it was hard to find out gays
and lesbians, let alone ones who'd volunteer for that nitty-gritty work.

When I moved to Washington, DC, we explored a range of strategies to
influence the national elections. The Gay Rights National Lobby was the
first national gay and lesbian group to put out congressional ratings on gay
and lesbian issues, with much of the focus on three areas: the almost constant antigay amendments by Rep. Larry McDonald (D-GA); the D.C. Sexual Assault bill repealing the sodomy and fornication statutes; and the
cosponsorship of the National Gay and Lesbian Civil Rights Bill. Rather
than either a percentage or a letter rating, instead our ratings just listed the
votes and how the incumbents had voted, because we sensed legislators
were still afraid that a positive 98 percent rating on the gay group's chart
might hurt them. Although the myth of political suicide was just that, we

were at an early stage of development and had to be sensitive to their concerns until we really were prepared to help them with money and bodies.

We also explored national gay and lesbian voter registration drives but eventually backed away from joining another major national group because it appeared to me that what they wanted was more smoke and mirrors, a public relations effort. I did not want to just pull a number out of the hat and say we'd registered 2 million voters (which I thought was essentially fraudulent), but instead help coordinate a real national effort with gay and lesbian political groups and clubs, for massive registrations and also massive lists with the names and addresses of supporters for future political efforts. Eventually we would have gotten around to this sort of voter registration drive on our own, but both the AIDS crisis and then the internal battles with David Goodstein and Larry Bush meant it would have to wait.

To move the issue, we had to prove to members of Congress, and their political consultants, who are largely liberal but a real and serious barrier, that supporting fairness isn't political suicide. Joe Cantor helped prepare an amazing study, "Does Support for Gay Civil Rights Spell Political Suicide?" showing exactly what happened to city council members, state legislators, and members of Congress all over the country who supported gay rights. With lots of local ordinances and state legislative efforts, there was now plenty of evidence on the subject, and finally we could prove that candidates weren't hurt by their support for gay rights. When Joe did discover a couple of instances that suggested candidates had, in fact, been hurt, I initially argued for their deletion. Joe refused and properly pointed out that, of hundreds and hundreds of potential situations, the exceptions would actually help and prove the study was no whitewash.

To our dismay, the study was virtually ignored. The GRNL just did not have the communications staff to get the study the visibility it deserved, and lesbian and gay civil rights simply wasn't yet a "relevant" enough issue. AIDS began to help change that fact but it also preoccupied everyone, and this kept updates of the study from ever getting completed. More recently, President Clinton's commitment to end the ban on gay people in the military and the press it has generated has pushed gay rights into being a front-burner issue.

When our study of the political impact of supporting lesbian and gay rights failed to get legislators' attention, I concluded that our only logical course of action was to take the bull by the horns and begin an initiative that neither legislators nor political consultants could ignore: the creation of a political action committee that would contribute to defending our friends, beating our enemies, and moving those on the fence into our camp. Research at the Federal Elections Commission pointed to two options, an "associated" or "unassociated" PAC. An associated PAC would allow GRNL to pay related expenses, but an associate could raise money only from GRNL's members, which was only about 5,000 people at that point. An unassociated PAC, which is what HRCF became, had to absorb all the administrative expenses itself but it could raise money from anyone. With sophisticated fund-raising plans in mind involving black-tie dinners and new, major donors, the choice seemed clear for an unassociated PAC. We knew that we wanted to maintain a close working relationship with GRNL, however.

What should we call the group? Years later, I was both amused and irritated to hear a wide range of stories about why the Human Rights Campaign Fund didn't have "gay and lesbian" in the name. Some said it was founded by closeted gay men who wanted to hide its real purpose. The simple truth was, since I was running both the parent group of the Gay Rights National Lobby and the new PAC, I just did not want to face marketing problems between the two and, for that reason, did not want "gay" or "lesbian" in the new PAC's name. Also, as a gay activist my entire adult life and the community's lobbyist, I hardly qualified as a "closeted gay man."

Those who said HRCF's name made it easier for candidates to take our contributions were closer to the mark. I understood that a number of candidates might have initial reluctance to taking money from a gay and lesbian PAC, but I had no intention of hiding what kind of PAC we were. However, I did feel the name would make it a little easier to make the initial breakthrough and get candidates to take our money—and harder for their opponents to use the issue—and, since we were reaching out to upscale gay donors, the name might also help with them. Again, though, the key reason for HRCF's name was to avoid marketing confusion between the two companion groups and avoid a sense of competition.

The name actually resulted from a phone conversation with a friend. We each scribbled down a variety of names, trying to find one that appealed to us. I had recently heard of the Women's Campaign Fund and liked the simplicity and clarity of the name so I began the top of my page with "_____ Campaign Fund," so the name would clearly indicate that the new group's purpose was to contribute to candidates. Rick Davis, my friend, also suggested we try "_____ Political Action Committee." Agreeing we would not include gay or lesbian in the name, we focused on words such as "Justice," "Civil Rights," "Human Dignity," "Equality," "Fairness," and "Human Rights." We agreed that a key task was to show both legislators and their constituents that "gay and lesbian rights" wasn't some bizarre idea but a simple extension of the existing principles of civil and human rights and basic fairness. We went through countless combinations and none really thrilled either of us, but the "Human Rights Campaign Fund" sounded best to me. Another option was "Human Rights Political Action Committee" but another new PAC, focusing on international affairs, had just started with that name. We didn't have a board yet, so I made the decision and the PAC was named the Human Rights Campaign Fund.

Even before we could get the group off the ground, one congressional race in the 1980 elections cried out for our attention. Just as I had come on at GRNL, our movement had faced tremendous setbacks with the repeal of local lesbian and gay rights ordinances in Miami, St. Paul, and Eugene, Oregon, and I had had this brainstorm to convince the House members from each city to become cosponsors of the National Gay and Lesbian Civil Rights Bill. Congressman Bruce Vento from St. Paul would not cosponsor then (he did later), but we got both Rep. Bill Lehman from Miami and Rep. Jim Weaver from Eugene on the bill. Now Weaver was facing his toughest reelection battle, gay rights was a major issue, and I felt like a class A jerk. We had to find a way to help him win reelection.

We didn't yet have much money, although the glamour of a PAC made fund-raising much easier than it was for the Lobby. But no sooner had we registered with the Federal Elections Commission than we gave Weaver the legal maximum and I flew to Eugene to speak at a gay fund-raiser hosted by GRNL board member Terry Bean. The event raised a couple thousand more and Terry, the best fund-raiser I've ever known in the gay community, raised several thousand more for Weaver before the election. We worried right up until Election Day, though. The 1980 elections were anything but a good Democratic year, and although Eugene is liberal, they had repealed the gay rights ordinance by a margin of two to one just a year earlier. Further, the rest of the district was rural and conservative. Weaver's opponent had run full-page ads talking about Weaver's arrogance in cosponsoring the gay rights bill, flying in the face of the will of his constituents. A fundamentalist group did a 100,000-piece mailing on gay teachers, which hit the day before the vote.

We hoped our rhetoric about gay rights not hurting candidates was correct. We contended that most people voted based on the issues they think directly affect their lives; therefore, only gay people, their families, and friends on the one hand, and fundamentalists on the other, vote based on a candidates' stance on gay issues. For others, jobs, the economy, farm issues, even constituent service mattered more. In the abstract, we were right, but candidates do use certain issues to create a "we/they" in the electorate and, if the candidate on our side was afraid or inept, the outcome could be disastrous. Would we prevail this time? If Weaver was beaten because of his support for gay rights, we thought it would set us back years. When President Carter conceded early and many presumed West Coast Democratic voters left the voting lines in droves, our hearts sank. Weaver won, however, and by as big a margin as he had ever had. We had dodged a bullet. The Human Rights Campaign Fund had its first important victory.

Setting up boards of directors has always been a hassle for me. The GRNL board was wonderful, but I didn't relish having yet another board to be responsible to. We included some GRNL board members—cochair Jerry Weller, treasurer Paul Kuntzler, Jack Campbell, and Ginny Apuzzo—and I was particularly excited about Jerry because we'd become very close in recent years, he had excellent mainstream political judgement, and I trusted him completely. Two lovers of GRNL board members, longtime NOW leader Lois Reckett from Maine and Bettie Naylor, the lesbian and gay rights lobbyist in Texas, also joined the board (see Appendix A).

Since I wasn't paid by HRCF, I became a board member and treasurer. GRNL staffer Kerry Woodward also joined HRCF's board and became, with Jerry Berg, a cochair. I didn't believe in setting up "miniature United Nations" boards with each member having different pictures and goals, but instead tried to bring together like-minded people to accomplish shared purposes. In hindsight, some of my conversations held while recruiting founding HRCF board members were amazingly casual, if not bizarre. For instance, during my conversation with Ginny Apuzzo, which took place at a 1980 Democratic Party Platform meeting, I told her we were starting a new, officially distinct group and I'd like her to serve on the board. Distracted, she seemed bored with the subject at best and just kind of waved me off in the regal manner Ginny sometimes has, saying sure, if I've got to, or something to that effect.

The recruitment of those who did not already have a close association with GRNL was very different and challenging. I met with Jerry Berg, a prominent gay lawyer in San Francisco, for two or three hours, first in his law offices and then in his magnificent Twin Peaks home. Jerry was a tall, good-looking man of about forty-five with a full head of prematurely gray hair, and he simply radiated class. Already having a strong reputation as a mainstream, establishment-oriented community fund-raiser, Berg agreed about the need for the project but seemed dubious about his own participation unless he could be sure we would be successful. Eventually he not only agreed to serve but ended up as our first cochair of the board as well. We couldn't have been more different and our relationship sometimes seemed like a tug of war, but we ended up complementing each other well.

Jerry Berg's best friend was a very nice man who happened to be quite affluent: Jim Hormel. A slender, distinguished man of about 5'10" with short gray hair and abundant warmth, Jim was already involved in many community efforts, including The Advocate Experience. Although Jerry and Jim were close, Jim's decision rested solely on being convinced of a compelling need for a new group. He had a "donor's attitude" about new groups, meaning the fewer, the better. Once Jim was convinced that PAC contributions couldn't be handled by an existing group, and he understood my commitment to reaching out to the broad community (including people of means who had never felt included), he enthusiastically agreed to serve.

Finally, I wanted to reach out to the minority communities more effectively than the movement had generally done. We didn't do as well as I wanted, but we still ended up with three of the original thirteen board members being people of color, including Gilberto Gerald of the National Coalition of Black Lesbians and Gays (NCBLG). Betty Powell, who'd originally agreed to serve, resigned because of overcommitments before the first meeting, and Rev. Jeri Ann Harvey, an elder of the Universal Fellowship of Metropolitan Community Churches, is a Native American.

Despite the original composition of the Human Rights Campaign Fund board, it quickly became clear that we were entering the period when board members of groups, and particularly those like the Campaign Fund, increasingly would have to raise funds for their groups. This "give, get, or get off" approach has been key to HRCF board membership since the early years. In candor, I can now see that Vic Basile, as the eventual director of the Human Rights Campaign Fund (1983-1989), was far more effective at bringing in either affluent donors or those who could raise funds—people like Vivian Shapiro, John Thomas, Duke Comegys, Randy Klose, and others. However, although the aforementioned people were terrific and insightful, boards who think their primary responsibility is fund-raising can have a different set of weaknesses: if they help raise $10 million but don't have the political or legislative judgement to oversee the strategy and tactics, much of those funds could be wasted.

Once we'd assembled a strong board, we had to find time to get the group off the ground, which now sounds easier than it was at the time. The linkage between HRCF and the Lobby, which had to be unofficial, was always a somewhat awkward matter. In fact, before the board finally met, not only had Betty Powell resigned but Ethan Geto also had decided to step down from the board to be our dinner consultant for the New York Waldorf dinner. Dallas Coors, cousin of Joe of the Coors Brewing Company, agreed to join the board, bringing important diversity as a conservative Republican. So because the Campaign Fund unofficially was to work hand-in-glove with GRNL, and also because of the incredible onslaught we faced on Capitol Hill, we kept putting off the initial board of directors meeting and the real launching of the organization. A few board members, particularly Jerry Berg, pushed me hard to get the board to meet and probably wondered if I could handle both jobs.

Those delays ended immediately when we learned that a Southern California political consultant was suddenly talking with the director of National Gay Task Force about starting a competing PAC, which made me furious. The Gay Rights National Lobby was the only national lobbying group and, as of that moment, NGTF had honored its commitment to stay out of Congress. Further, they knew we were launching a PAC, so it was just a power play. I felt—and still feel—very, very strongly that the community is best served by effective division of labor and not duplication of services and mission. We didn't need two national lobbies—as we eventually had—and I was determined to avoid similar confusion that would be caused by letting someone else create another political action committee. (Remember, this comes from a member of the first national board of the Task Force and a former cochair.)

So what Jerry Berg couldn't do by patiently pushing me was done virtually overnight when I learned another PAC could emerge. I worked nonstop to address what I saw as not only a challenge but also an insult. First, we created and announced an extremely impressive national advisory committee that included several big-city mayors and bishops of major religious denominations, making the Campaign Fund as real as we could before we'd actually gone through an election cycle. Second, I flew to San Francisco to meet with longtime friend and top-notch political consultant Larry Bye about the organizational and fund-raising efforts. Larry's not only a brilliant organizer; I knew firsthand that he always found a way to get the job done. Initial conversations suggested he'd be part of a fund-raising group built around a small group of close friends, who were also close to board members Jerry Berg and Jim Hormel. As those conversations proceeded, Larry begged off the bulk of the venture, citing an overwhelming workload, but agreed to consult with us from October 1981 until the second board meeting in April 1982. Without his leadership, I doubt the Campaign Fund would exist today.

These conversations suggested we'd retain a new consulting team called "Friends and Associates" which included longtime activist Jim Foster. The Campaign Fund's anticipated fund-raising strategy—modeled after the large banquets of the local gay PAC in Los Angeles, the Municipal Elections Committee of Los Angeles—would rely on black-tie dinners and/or concerts. By the time we actually met, however, the other participants in Friends and Associates had reconsidered and Jim proposed that he serve as a consulting "field coordinator" for fund-raising.

Jim had been a personal hero and role model, but I had serious reservations about retaining him. First, although Jim had helped coordinate such black-tie dinners in San Francisco and he had charm and the gift of gab, I wasn't sure if he'd work the long hours or be able to get along with the diverse dinner committees he'd have to create and rely on in five to seven cities. If Jim, and our dinners, didn't work out, we'd have a huge fund-raising hole and no time to repair the damage in time for the 1982 elections. More-over, I might be described as the problem rather than Jim, who was clearly strong-willed and difficult to supervise—he might have been the only per-son more difficult to supervise than me. Among his best friends were some of the most powerful people in the movement: *Advocate* publisher David Goodstein, Larry Bush, a stringer for more than a dozen gay papers around the country, and Ginny Apuzzo, the new executive director of the National Gay Task Force.

I felt that retaining Jim might be dangerous not only for me personally but also because I wasn't certain if he could deliver, organizationally. Yet we didn't have a lot of options, there were very few people in the gay and lesbian community then who had such fund-raising experience, and Jim re-ally wanted the project. Later, when problems led me not to recommend his retention in 1983, it was one factor in my fall from amazing grace, but that's a story for a different time and chapter (see Chapter 4). HRCF board mem-bers Hormel and Berg were close to Jim, but they approached the issue very professionally and we discussed his strengths and weaknesses and moved forward.

While I was in San Francisco, I also met with the owner of *The Advocate,* David Goodstein, to enlist his support. Goodstein was attracted to the glam-our of a PAC and liked our plans, and his long association with Foster, Berg, and Hormel convinced him we were reaching out to the sort of people he wanted to see involved. He didn't want to serve on the board but would con-tribute generously, and coordinate (along with his able assistant and later lover David Russell) our Los Angeles fund-raising. I found him pompous and I had no doubt that I wasn't his cup of tea, either. Yet, I have—when I've been able to catch myself—tried to set aside my own feelings and do what I thought was in the best interests of the movement, including getting David's help. As the multimillionaire owner of the nation's only national gay news-paper and a guru to a small but emerging network of upwardly mobile, newly out gay people, he could contribute the $10,000 legal maximum, raise funds from affluent friends in Los Angeles, and be a powerful asset for the Campaign Fund's success. So when he agreed not only to spearhead our Los Angeles fund-raising but also to take a tour to rally his contacts in cities where we anticipated key fund-raising efforts, I quickly agreed.

Overestimating how much of a draw he'd be, Goodstein decided to speak at kickoff events to launch the Campaign Fund in key cities across the coun-try. He didn't draw big crowds and had many movement enemies, but he also had a very loyal following among "graduates" of The Advocate Expe-rience, which was described by many as a gay EST-type "self-actualiza-tion" program. Many of these Advocate Experience grads were brand new to the movement, had terrific energy, had the resources to attend such fund-raising banquets, and were connected to networks of similar people. Although Goodstein was extremely opinionated, overbearing, and far less politically astute than he thought he was, he was also brilliant and unique, to say the least. At the time, I defined his decision to participate with us as a success.

So with little time, no strong base of large donors across the country yet established, and AIDS not yet a primary motivating factor for giving, we had to hope our idea for major "big-ticket" banquets would catch on in cities with no track record of raising funds from the sort of affluent donors on which we'd have to depend. Many, including some of us on the board who were counting on its success, seriously questioned whether a strategy that seemed so perfect for rich, glitzy Los Angeles could work elsewhere. We had to hope our doubts were unfounded, since in addition to raising large amounts of money quickly, HRCF's black-tie dinner strategy had another key advantage, from my point of view: it wouldn't compete with the ongoing fund-raising of our semi-parent organization, the Gay Rights National Lobby. GRNL had grown enormously over the previous five years but, if we were going to be able to undertake essential grassroots organizing and coalition building effectively, we had to keep growing and adding staff. HRCF's fund-raising obviously needed to be very successful, but it also had to complement the Gay Rights National Lobby's own efforts.

We were ready for our first board of directors meeting in October 1981: fund-raising consultants were ready to begin, Goodstein was enrolled, plans for kickoff events were in place, and Larry Bye lent a steadying hand. Also, our assertive efforts around the creation of the advisory committee seemed to have scared off those contemplating starting a competing effort. Even with so much important groundwork done, though, we were still a very, very long way from being ready to play the role we all envisioned in the 1982 elections. With the recession dampening enthusiasm for Reagan, it was already clear 1982 was going to be a good Democratic year and we had to be ready to take advantage of it.

The first meeting went well, but it was clear GRNL's small staff couldn't handle all the administrative tasks that were quickly presenting themselves, even if it had been legal within FEC guidelines for them to do so. So we hired Farley Peterson, a former IRS official, to serve as HRCF's first administrative assistant. I was unsalaried, so Farley was our first staffer and he did a tremendous job. I knew him from involvement in the Metropolitan Community Church and we shared an attraction to black men.

The Human Rights Campaign Fund rented a room in the Lobby's offices—in fact, the room that had been my and Will's bedroom a couple of years earlier. For the next nine months I seemed to spend much of my time shuttling up and down those stairs between meetings with my HRCF AA, my GRNL AA, or other staff and the new director of Right to Privacy, our 501(c)3 educational and research foundation. We rented an additional floor in the townhouse then serving as our offices. My hours increased from sixty to seventy hours a week to well over a hundred hours a week for the remainder of the election cycle. It's a good thing I have a well-developed martyr complex, because I've never worked harder or probably packed as much into so little time. Partly, it was important to me personally that I won the absolute confidence of every HRCF board member, including those who'd been unsure whether I could run both organizations. Although some criticized me severely for insisting on leading both groups, my decision to do so wasn't about being a control freak (although I am indeed one); rather, I saw myself as the available human link. Serving in that role was one of the hardest things I ever tried to do and it did leave me vulnerable to attack, however.

(After our first election cycle, external forces—largely *The Advocate* and the dishonest reporting for them by an unscrupulous reporter—eventually led me to give up the leadership of the Campaign Fund and later GRNL. Although both boards remained firmly supportive, I came to fear, ironically, that my continued presence could lead to the destruction of all that I'd sought to build at that point. As a result, the two groups went separate ways, an outcome that seriously hurt the movement for a brief period. Some years later, Vic Basile undid this damage by reuniting the two groups, with the "mother group" of Gay Rights National Lobby merging back into the Human Rights Campaign Fund. His efforts, which were more politically astute than my own, vindicated my perspective and ensured that the Campaign Fund's political clout would be used to maximum advantage for the community's legislative objectives.)

One of the things I remember about the Campaign Fund's first board meeting was the insistence of cochair Jerry Berg that we clearly define, write out, and later review our mission statement. I thought our purpose was already clear and was impatient with taking up valuable time even discussing it, but Jerry wanted to make sure we were all "in alignment" about our mission. It was one of the smartest things we ever did. We repeatedly used the mission statement to avoid taking on other worthwhile tasks which were, nonetheless, off purpose for the Campaign Fund.

Another special feature of Campaign Fund board meetings was "sharing," a process in which board members took turns talking about what was going on in their lives, how they felt about the tasks at hand, etc. I'd never been involved on a board that functioned this way before and it initially seemed a little "California touchy-feely" for me, but it helped build strong bonds and allowed us to function better as a team. Other movement boards I'd seen often represented a wide range of views and approaches and there had been constant battles for control. The GRNL board was not one of these "mini-UNs" but, with thirty members and only two or three meetings a year, we weren't as able to build quite the sense of family as the much smaller Campaign Fund board was doing.

From the beginning, before the AIDS crisis unfolded, it wasn't hard for the Campaign Fund board to agree on our legislative priorities, including the top priority—advancement of the national lesbian and gay civil rights bill. In addition to supervising our fund-raising consultants, my own responsibilities included the direct-mail aspect of our fund-raising, public relations, and candidate relations and disbursements recommendations.

The board approved broad targeting priorities for candidate support and disbursements, and we generally didn't make many contributions to candidates unless we thought they had a real chance of winning. With more than fifty House sponsors of the lesbian and gay rights legislation, and most of them scared to death they wouldn't win by three-to-one margins, we made a tough but gutsy decision to make only token contributions to safe incumbents (including our chief sponsors). Only if cosponsors had serious races did they get major gifts, but they then became our top priorities. We anticipated we'd have far fewer resources than we'd need, and we wanted the bulk of these monies for tight races to retain friends, beat enemies, or capture open seats.

If the candidates were relatively even, we usually opted to stay out of the race or perhaps support the incumbent. Although we used roll call votes on various antigay amendments as a criterion, our top priority, advancement of the lesbian and gay rights legislation, meant helping elect or reelect cosponsors. Although political viability was a key criterion for getting our support, there were times when we felt a candidate's track record was so strong we simply had to back them in order to maintain credibility with either local activists or the local political community.

I thought, and think, that business PACs' "inside-the-beltway, almost-always-support-the-incumbent" approach had no relevance to cause-oriented PACs such as the Campaign Fund, since we're fighting to transform the status quo. Also, I hate term limitations and the current unthinking anti-incumbent rage, but I agree this is, at least significantly, a generational issue and we have to change radically either the composition or the positions of Congress. However, it's easy to slip into the approach of supporting incumbents I personally think fall far short of reasonable standards (and I'm usually seen as a political hack, so it's not because I'm much of a purist). We'd have to take risks. Talk about "100 percent voting records" of incumbents often just shows the weakness of voting records that don't even penalize the gutless wonders who refuse to cosponsor our bill or otherwise speak out against antigay discrimination. The message they get is that they can get away with their silence.

Our direct-mail program hit it rich when a friend, who wrote some of the best direct-mail copy in town for progressive groups, quickly agreed to write an appeal and to help me arrange a line of credit for a direct-mail rollout. The outcome was a direct-mail letter signed by famous playwright Tennessee Williams. The letter, in our first major electoral campaign season in 1982, effectively summarized the case for the Campaign Fund, stating,

> The Weaver victory (in 1980) sent a message to other politicians: that support for individual rights is *not* self-defeating, even in conservative areas. And more importantly, *that those concerned with individual rights are now organized and active . . . and unwilling to sit quietly by while their friends are defamed and defeated.*

In the years that have passed since, the story has been told that we secured Williams's signature by hiring a hustler. Although it was absolutely not true, it is correct that we got Williams—who had never been publicly identified with the gay movement before—to sign the appeal by having an attractive young man he was fond of, Sean Strub, make the request in person (and, if I remember correctly, I was told that Williams was about two-thirds "in the bag" when he agreed to sign on).

Although there may have been assumptions on Williams's part, there was no return of the favor nor any indication there would be. Sean would eventually become a very, very important figure in the evolution of lesbian and gay fund-raising and direct mail, raising literally millions for a range of national lesbian and gay and AIDS groups. In the meantime, Williams's Campaign Fund direct-mail solicitation did very well.

However, in hindsight, it became clear that Williams—who didn't know a lot about direct mail and was probably drinking extensively during these discussions—didn't understand that the letter would be mailed to a couple hundred thousand people. Years later I heard that Williams repeatedly called Sean but Sean didn't return the calls because he was afraid Williams would demand that all future letters be stopped; until we received official word demanding we stop, we could keep mailing the very lucrative piece.

In the meantime, David Goodstein made an exception to his longstanding rule about not sending subscribers movement appeals. I suspected he was far less popular with subscribers than he thought and we'd probably have done far better if we could have just sent the standard Tennessee Williams appeal to *The Advocate* lists instead of the one by Goodstein. But we still did well and it was the very first time *Advocate* subscribers had ever received other gay direct mail.

Fund-Raising: With the Campaign Fund, We Shifted to "Serving Food"

Electing friends and beating enemies was the "meat and potatoes" of the Campaign Fund's program, but none of it could work unless we went out and raised the needed funds. The AIDS crisis wasn't yet visible to give our fund-raising urgency, only Los Angeles and San Francisco had done the sort of upscale, expensive-ticket dinners we envisioned, and none of the existing gay groups had established the base of major donors that would be so vital for the future. We had our work cut out for us if we were going to raise the two to three hundred thousand dollars I figured we'd need.

Jim Foster plunged into his task as our lead fund-raiser and traveled the country nonstop trying to get dinner operations going in Atlanta, Houston, Chicago, Philadelphia, Boston, and New York. MECLA had already put on such a dinner in Los Angeles, so we settled instead on a boat cruise in Los Angeles, with Goodstein's birthday party being the theme; it was held in the spring when we needed the resources. Under Goodstein's guidance, Los Angeles didn't produce the resources that should come from affluent Southern California but David's efforts were still terrific and played a key role in assisting our cash flow. We quickly determined that Foster could also forget San Francisco, where Berg and Hormel would make things happen. With the glut of banquets in San Francisco, our Bay Area board members argued we should opt for other ways to raise significant funds there. Unfortunately, with the exception of a few major donations, we never came up with a viable fund-raising plan for San Francisco during that first election cycle. They also ran into an undercurrent of resentment toward Washington, DC, particularly because everyone knew San Francisco was the center of the universe.

Washington, DC, itself was a different situation. Knowing the city was very closeted (and boy, were we wrong!), the local committee decided they couldn't pull off such a black-tie dinner. Instead, they opted for a series of private fund-raisers in people's homes. Joe Cantor (who'd already coordinated the historic study "Does Support for Gay Civil Rights Spell Political Suicide?") served as a key player on the local committee. Each fund-raiser was supposed to raise at least $1,000. The committee got more than thirty people to agree to host them, and more than twenty-five actually came through. Overall, the DC committee exceeded their $25,000 goal. Of course, subsequent years taught us that Washington, DC, could do such a dinner, and it became the home of the Campaign Fund's largest black-tie dinner.

As HRCF treasurer, I attended many of the DC events and played a key role in two. The first was held in the home of a major political commentator and was quite successful, raising about $5,000. The only blemish on the evening was when one of those present told my then–best friend, who happened to be black, to clean up the dishes as if he were hired help instead of a very successful and proud lawyer. The individual hadn't meant offense, but I rightly heard about his comment for a long time to come. Another fundraiser, held at the home of the owner of a Washington, DC, black gay bar, marked another breakthrough. The purpose was not only to raise funds but also to reach out to the black gay and lesbian community. We had strong support from the local Black and White Men Together (BWMT) and the cooperation of the National Coalition of Black Gays. Representative Julian Dixon (D-Los Angeles), who was then both the chair of the Congressional Black Caucus and the chief sponsor of legislation ending the antigay immigration prohibition, was our honored guest and speaker.

In fact, most of the members of the Congressional Black Caucus were cosponsors of the national lesbian and gay civil rights bill and many were asked to speak at gay fund-raising events. Far too often, the crowd was virtually all white, but this event, which cost only $25, was very well attended and almost half of those attending were black. Rep. Dixon confided in me privately how happy he was to see such large black participation. *The Washington Post* had a picture of the event in their "Style" section the next day, reflecting the racial diversity that was present.

Atlanta did some good preliminary fund-raising but wasn't yet ready to hold a major dinner and was set aside (they've come a long way, with the 1992 dinner drawing 1,200 people and having former President Jimmy Carter and Bishop Desmond Tutu as honorary cochairs). Houston just didn't come together (nor has it since, either), and a couple of visits to Chicago convinced us we just didn't yet have a base of potential big-time donors to make such a dinner work there in 1982 (again, Chicago's just blossomed!).

The Goodstein tour and my contacts helped establish the dinner committees bases in both Philadelphia and Boston. The events marked the first time the local communities had done black-tie, upscale dinners at $150 per seat. Their success was a result of both Foster's good efforts and those of the local committees he'd helped establish. Longtime gay activist Tony Silvestre spearheaded the effort in Philadelphia, where Foster got his old friend Senator Alan Cranston (D-CA) to be the keynote speaker to more than 200 people. Noted gay lecturer Brian McNaught and lawyer Vin McCarthy played important roles in Boston, and we secured chief sponsor Senator Paul Tsongas (D-MA), who helped in every way he could, to be the keynoter there before almost 300 people.

Dinner at the Waldorf

New York City, as usual, was a bigger challenge. Banker Chuck Nesbitt, who was brilliant if somewhat politically inexperienced, and at least as high-strung and difficult as I am, spearheaded our efforts as dinner committee chair. Nesbitt was not getting along well with Jim Foster and, as it turned out, Foster had to devote large portions of his attention to the New York dinner, which was to be held September 29 at the prestigious Waldorf Astoria. Because of the magnitude of the event, we retained the consulting firm of Ethan Geto, who was Attorney General Bob Abrams's campaign manager and a real public relations wizard, to handle many of the details of the evening. Initially, we didn't have a big-name keynoter and organizers were struggling to sell tickets. More than a few local "blue-denim elitist" activists were publicly saying (and hoping) it would be a disaster, pointing out that there had never been a gay black-tie dinner in New York.

In order to help with the creation of dinner committees, enroll major donors, and otherwise help publicize the importance of the Campaign Fund, Foster convinced Mike Farrell, who played "B. J. Hunnicut" on M*A*S*H, to do a fourteen-minute "talking head" video for the Campaign Fund, explaining the importance of HRCF's effort. It was terrific, sending a solid message of professionalism to those who saw it, and was particularly useful in cities where there weren't special fund-raisers.

Foster had been slated to handle major donor fund-raising in addition to the dinners, but a couple of facts quickly became clear. Despite his charm and gift of gab, Foster just couldn't seem to do one-to-one major donor solicitations. Ironically, he didn't have the killer instinct to close the sale, which turned out to be okay since the dinners were so critical and required all of Foster's time and attention. To my surprise, then, the major donor fund-raising fell not only to Goodstein (who was never short on the assertiveness needed to solicit big gifts) and cochair Berg, who had both the polish and a good deal of experience at such solicitations, but on me as well. I'd always left GRNL's major donor fund-raising to Terry Bean and didn't think I could do it, but I used my aggressiveness to good effect and dug in to help. When the dust cleared, we'd probably gotten about twenty contributions of $5,000 each, one such gift coming from Abigail Van Buren of "Dear Abby" fame as a result of Goodstein's friendship with her.

Our problem of getting a big-name speaker for our New York dinner at the Waldorf was solved when former vice president Walter Mondale agreed to speak. Mondale was a leading candidate for the 1984 Democratic nomination for president and a hot property. With the recent inclusion of the lesbian and gay civil rights plank in the national Democratic Party platform, we obviously wanted to consolidate support for the issue. A wonderful opportunity to affect Mondale's views developed when Alan Baron, a highly regarded political commentator and former executive director of the Democratic National Committee, spoke with one of Mondale's top assistants, Jim Johnson. When the subject of gay rights came up in their conversation and Johnson complained about gay activists' protests of Mondale during his vice presidency, Baron countered that he knew that I, as the executive director of Gay Rights National Lobby, was well-disposed to Mondale. Johnson, who was from Minnesota, remembered me as a pragmatist from our days in the same Democratic-Farmer-Labor party ward organization.

When Alan told me about their conversation, I contacted Johnson to see if there was any room for growth and movement on the issue. We got together for lunch and I cited some of the recent expansion of support for gay rights—by members of Congress, by the AFL-CIO, our inclusion in the Leadership Conference on Civil Rights, and new national opinion polls. I also gave him a copy of the study we'd recently completed, "Does Support for Gay Civil Rights Spell Political Suicide?" documenting the fact that support for gay civil rights didn't hurt candidates across the country.

I stressed that we weren't seeking Vice President Mondale's endorsement of "the gay lifestyle" but simply support for nondiscrimination in jobs and housing, which was consistent with his longstanding support for civil rights. Jim's a nice guy and the meeting went well. As a result, he arranged a lunch for me with one of Mondale's law partners and a top political advisor at an expensive French restaurant. That lunch also went well (although McDonald's was actually more my style) and we arranged for the vice president to meet with four of us to discuss the issue.

The group we put together was Kerry Woodward, Dan Bradley, Jim Hormel, and myself, and was very much tailored to the vice president. Although I didn't know it at the time, when Hormel learned he'd be part of our efforts to move Mondale he secured an invitation to a small, intimate cocktail party on the Peninsula where Mondale was the honored guest. Dick Blum, the husband of San Francisco Mayor Dianne Feinstein, provided a superb introduction to lay a solid base. Although they didn't really get much of a chance to talk at that point, Jim had laid the foundation he wanted.

At the time of these conversations and negotiations, the vice president was still anticipating a major nomination battle with Senator Ted Kennedy. Kennedy had a built-in base among liberals and I'm convinced that Mondale, who was seen as liberal but very cautious, felt a need to demonstrate that he was gutsy and willing to take risks on controversial social issues in order to make inroads. In hindsight, I think we were lucky that Kennedy had not yet withdrawn from the race. If he had, I doubt whether we could have secured as much movement as we did.

The four of us first met for about an hour and a half to make sure we knew who was going to say what, what issues we might want to avoid, and so on. As I recall, our premeeting get-together was in a cheap restaurant near the vice president's prestigious law offices. We then went together to meet with him in their conference room. We wanted Vice President Mondale not only to publicly clarify his support for gay civil rights but also to actually speak at the Human Rights Campaign Fund's first major black-tie dinner in New York City. Because Mondale and his political handlers wanted him to look courageous on a tough issue, we knew this was a viable request—no matter how uncomfortable he appeared to be with the issue.

Our meeting with him was about an hour long and each participant did an excellent job. We demonstrated that support for gay rights was not a radical step but instead was consistent with his own proud civil rights record. Our recent political gains and a willingness to approach the issue in a moderate, constructive fashion contributed mightily to the meeting. However, Kerry reminded me years later that Mondale had seemed to focus unusual attention on her, which she initially thought meant lesbians were being taken seriously. But she concluded that it was really because Mondale was really so uncomfortable with gay men that he tried to focus on her. Yet, despite this discomfort, the meeting generally went well. We agreed to get him additional materials and to continue the dialogue through staff persons. In a brief letter of June 21, 1982, Mondale wrote, "I appreciated our candid discussion and I did find it very beneficial in helping me to understand the problems and needs of the gay community."

As a result of the meeting, Vice President Mondale agreed to be the keynoter at the New York dinner. From the day the former vice president agreed to speak, two months before the actual affair, we felt his presence would ensure both a great crowd and fabulous national public relations. Almost nothing could screw it up, we thought, but about two and a half weeks before the New York dinner, it seemed we'd found a way. Shortly before the dinner, the lingering conflicts between Foster and the dinner committee finally blew up. The dinner committee, in the middle of key ticket sales, called to demand that we get Jim Foster out of New York within twenty-four hours or the entire dinner committee would quit. Foster, a very proud man and real movement pioneer, was beside himself with rage and, of course, refused.

The last couple weeks before a dinner are prime time for ticket sales and New York was our flagship dinner. So I convinced the Campaign Fund cochair Jerry Berg, who had been a close friend of Foster's for years, to join in a conference call with the New York committee to discuss the problem. We listened to their complaints and then asked for some time to discuss the situation privately. We got back to them and reluctantly agreed to ask Jim to step back from involvement in the final days; in return, they had to allow him to be present at the dinner, and they agreed, even more reluctantly. It was tense but we finally struck a deal both sides could live with. The committee continued the vital ticket sales and more than 600 people ended up attending (although Ethan Geto—who could sell screen doors to submarine captains—successfully convinced all the media that more than 1,000 were present, at $150 per ticket).

Despite settling this feud, we were still worried. Fritz Mondale had a long record in support of civil rights and I've come to be a real fan of his. However he is, or was, an uptight, personally straitlaced guy for whom "gay rights" was hardly second nature. As a U.S. Senator from Minnesota, he'd never been particularly supportive of gay rights; like many other politicians of his generation, he probably grew up with the stereotypes about gay people and probably thought of them as "perverts." Further, although Mondale had a very strong track record on civil rights, he didn't really see the gay rights issue in this context. Although there weren't any Senate floor votes during his tenure, his views were reflected by his meetings with Minnesota's gay and lesbian activists, which were difficult. He once commented on the election of state senator Allan Spear, who later came out publicly, "If we can elect him, we can elect anyone."

The fact that the gay rights issue had emerged in the context of the "radical" McGovern period, and that the longtime leader of Minnesota's movement, Jack Baker, was more prone to drama and confrontation than moderation and conciliation, did nothing to settle the misgivings of this liberal, cautious Minnesota politician. Now, as the likely 1984 Democratic presidential nominee, he would be in a key position to have an impact on the issue. If his nervousness came through as much as we feared, the news stories the next day might focus on that fact or, heaven forbid, even a hostile reaction from the audience—hardly the story of emerging gay and lesbian political clout we wanted.

We had extensive meetings with Mondale's aides leading up to the dinner to ensure the evening was positive for both sides. Knowing Mondale's discomfort with the personal aspect of the issue, we stressed that it was critical for him to actually say the word "gay" during his speech. Even though those attending the dinner would be affluent and well-disposed to him, it wouldn't help either him or us if he gave a speech like that of former Rep. Mario Biaggi (D-NY), who when running for mayor of New York had told a large gathering of cutting-edge gay activists, "I got no problem with your problem." Such a statement or obvious discomfort might prompt a negative reaction from the crowd. If that happened, his discomfort rather than his appearance would become the next day's story. Mondale's staff people understood our fear and concurred.

They finally settled on a foolproof way to ensure he'd at least say the word "gay." Mondale would open his remarks by acknowledging me with the words, "My good friend, Steve Endean, the executive director of the Gay Rights National Lobby." When the vice president arrived for the VIP reception before the dinner he was clearly very nervous—either because of the issue or because his appearance seemed to be getting much more publicity than he'd expected. When it was time for him to begin his address, he screwed up all the advance planning to get him to say the word "gay" by just saying, "My good friend Steve Endean." The crowd could see that Mondale was uncomfortable but also saw the event as a historic occasion they desperately wanted to be successful. His speech was not brilliant or gutsy, but the crowd knew the real issue was that a former vice president of the United States was speaking for fairness at a gay banquet. They were happy he'd come, wanted to be supportive of him, and responded affirmatively to his presence.

With New York City being the national media capital, Mondale's appearance ensured critical publicity. *The New York Times, The Washington Post,* and countless other papers covered it the next day. In part because of the excellent spin put on the event by New York media expert Ethan Geto, the stories focused on Mondale's courageous leadership for gay rights and on the emerging political clout of the lesbian and gay community across the country.

For instance, *The New York Times* ignored the fact that Mondale couldn't seem to get the word "gay" out of his mouth and instead reported, "He drew applause from the audience in the hotel's Grand Ballroom as he recalled the 1980 Democratic National Convention's platform plank opposing discrimination based on 'sexual orientation.'" The *USA Today* article pointed out that Mondale had been booed off a stage at a 1977 Democratic gathering in California because of his hostility to gay rights, and aide Ralph Whitehead denied that the appearance marked a change in Mondale's support, stating, "Had such an event (as the gay fundraiser) occurred in 1970, would Mondale have attended then? The answer is no. But the more fundamental question is could such an event have been held in 1970. And the answer is no."

In addition, ABC's *Nightline* used the occasion to focus on emerging gay and lesbian political clout. Reporter Betsy Aaron taped a long segment with me on lobbying Capitol Hill and the anticipated impact of HRCF contributions that was used in the show, and Dan Bradley and Virginia Apuzzo were interviewed live from the dinner.

Financially, the combination of the former vice president's presence and a strong and determined, if difficult, dinner committee, resulted in a whop-

Steve on television. © 1982 Leigh H. Mosley.

ping $400,000 for supportive congressional candidates. It was great, but thank God it was over.

Establishing Priorities and Procedures:
The 1982 Elections

So fund-raising was going great. Somewhat earlier, the board had begun to address a range of key program questions: Would we undertake independent expenditure campaigns, where a group goes in to advance its agenda without making contributions to specific candidates? Should we launch a major voter registration drive which could not only help the candidates we backed but also help us identify potential donors who could be solicited again and again? Should we undertake a "bundling operation," which a number of other groups had used to collect far greater resources for the candidates we backed than the $5,000 limit otherwise imposed by the FEC?

By "bundling" some groups were able to raise more than $100,000 for key candidates with the group asking its members to write checks directly to selected campaigns and then send them into the PAC, which forwards them on. It'd be perfect for groups like ours, which then didn't have too many candidates who either deserved or wanted our support but had a few heroes who might well desperately need our help. EMILY'S List (Early Money Is Like Yeast) may be the best known of the breed right now, although they didn't even exist at that time.

Many of these ideas were very appealing to me and, left to my own devices, I might have been tempted. But board cochair Jerry Berg quickly saw that one of my weaknesses was to take on too much and he vigorously argued for us to confine ourselves, for the first election cycle, to simply contributing to the candidacies of our friends and trying to defeat our enemies. I was beginning to get a sense of just how much work I'd have to do to handle even this limited responsibility as well as GRNL's work and I didn't argue. The board wisely demanded that we should learn to crawl or walk before we tried to run. Just reviewing the range of political newsletters, talking with activists around the country who advised us about potential contributions to congressional campaigns, working with other progressive PACs, and meeting with candidates when they breezed into town was a massive task. I'd always thought I was a hard worker, but I have never before or since worked so hard just trying somehow to keep all the balls in the air.

Defending friends and beating enemies was only one part of our task. The Campaign Fund would make us real players with other lobbies and progressive political action committees. Liberal PACs had "targeting" meetings to review congressional races and to meet with candidates, and we were quickly included in these meetings. The National Committee for an Effective Congress, the granddaddy of all progressive PACs, started these meetings to discuss candidacies and their viability, but the best such meetings (and probably most frequent) during the 1982 elections were put together by Peter Fenn, director of Democrats for the '80s, for a group of fifteen to twenty PAC leaders. Democrats for the '80s, which was sometimes privately called "Democrats in Their 80s" because it had been founded by Averill and Pamela Harriman, made a real difference because of Fenn's leadership. It was one of many new Democratic PACs founded to offset the previous Republican advantage. Fenn, an astute young political consultant, was secure about the gay rights issue and felt we should always be included. The networking that took place during this period, and which HRCF's Political Department has expanded tremendously in recent years, played a key, if hard-to-define role in advancing our efforts.

The targeting meetings were particularly vital in our first election cycle because they really helped us sort out the candidates. Every candidate cited self-serving information to show PAC directors they had a good chance; of course, it wasn't just scam since they'd all invested much of their lives in these efforts and they really had come to believe what they were telling us about their great chances. Such sales jobs by candidates made it challenging for all PACs trying to ascertain viability, though, and particularly those of us that anticipated having very limited resources. Because of my leadership of Gay Rights National Lobby, with our well-developed network of grassroots organizers, as well as other local gay and lesbian groups, I often brought solid, independent information to these meetings of PAC directors and therefore contributed to the collective intelligence about candidates' viability and developing trends in their districts.

There were also the so-called meet and greets, where sometimes very small groups of PAC directors met with candidates who were in Washington, DC, to solicit our support. Our attendance at these meetings and the ensuing dialogues really played a central role in educating candidates in not only the legislative issues they'd face on gay-related public policy but also on the political viability of the issue. Our study "Does Support for Gay Civil Rights Spell Political Suicide?" was very useful in this context. Many candidates were open and accessible during the elections in ways that they simply wouldn't be once they'd won election. If we were able to establish solid relationships—and assist their campaigns when that was the most important thing in their lives—it could well carry over to future congressional relationships.

There were also several occasions when I thought the candidates were practically going to run out of the room rather than deal with a real, live homosexual. One such candidate was the New Mexico Democratic senatorial candidate Jeff Bingaman, who was so uncomfortable I almost felt sorry for him. He came into town on very little notice and there were only about six of us at the meet and greet. He had a hell of a time avoiding dealing with me, but tried his best. Once elected, his voting record was mixed—with fairly good votes on AIDS issues and almost always bad votes on strictly gay issues—and his gay and lesbian constituents have been generally hostile to him. Despite these sometimes awkward meetings, our inclusion within the progressive PAC community sent a positive signal to the candidates and their campaigns that has continued and been strengthened.

From the first days of the Human Rights Campaign Fund, we were very concerned about the image of the Campaign Fund as a bipartisan political action committee. We decided to make our very first 1982 contribution a symbolic one, to a Republican, Senator Lowell Weicker (CT), for the primary. He'd played a key role in killing the McDonald amendments when they came from the House to the Senate. Partly because he was so liberal, Weicker was now facing a Republican challenge from George [H. W.] Bush's brother, Prescott. Because his general election opponent, Rep. Toby Moffett, was also a deeply committed House sponsor of the lesbian and gay civil rights bill, we didn't plan any general election contribution. Unfortunately, Weicker's handlers were nervous about taking our contribution during the Republican primary season, so our plan of making our first contribution to a Republican was foiled.

A short time later, we spotted a key race that just demanded Campaign Fund involvement. Redistricting had thrown two incumbent House members into the same Philadelphia congressional district. One, Rep. Tom Foglietta, was a cosponsor of the National Lesbian and Gay Civil Rights Bill, while the other, Rep. Joe Smith, was a cosponsor of the so-called Family Protection Act, a virtual wish list of right-wing demands, including several antigay provisions pushed by Falwell's Moral Majority. Unfortunately, it would be an uphill race since redistricting seemed to favor Smith, who maintained much more of his old district than Foglietta did. The May primary would determine the Democratic nominee, with the nominee almost sure to win the fall election. When I talked with other liberal PAC directors, they described the Foglietta-Smith race as a loser for liberals. They didn't say we should stay out but certainly argued we wouldn't be getting into a winner.

However, my conversations with Tony Silvestre, who ran our Philadelphia dinner and was a very politically astute observer, suggested not only that this was precisely the sort of race for which we created the Human Rights Campaign Fund, but also that it might be more doable than the conventional wisdom suggested. Although the new district was generally pretty conservative, there were pockets of the gay community. Moreover, many of the conservatives the Smith campaign was counting on were Italian, and we thought there was a fair chance Foglietta, because of his surname, would do better with Italian-American voters than his political stances might otherwise justify. Finances were tight and we had a lot of upcoming expenses associated with our dinners, but I polled the board and we decided to contribute the legal maximum of $5,000, making us his single biggest contributor. When we learned this, we asked Rep. Foglietta to pose for a picture with us delivering the check to him, as long as we didn't release the photos until after the primary. Somewhat to my surprise, he agreed and came over to our offices and Tony came down from Philadelphia.

On primary night, I finally got through to Tony about 11 p.m. and learned that our gamble had paid off. Foglietta had upset the odds, winning by about 1,500 votes. The next morning, we put out our press release, with photos, to every gay and lesbian paper in the country. Those articles and photos went a long way to helping define the mission and purpose of the new national group in their midst. Foglietta's race became one classic part of our pitch as we solicited major donors as well as dinner committee members, table captains, etc. Only later did I realize just how much of a gamble we took and the fact that most of my fellow PAC directors thought I'd been crazy. They were right, but I got the last laugh.

Since we weren't well-known yet, congressional candidates weren't beating down our doors for donations during the spring and summer (but it was great then, since our few resources were needed for fund-raising). Not only were we new, but candidates also were unsure whether they should take contributions from us (in fact, a couple of candidates turned down contributions from the Human Rights PAC, which focused on foreign affairs, because they got confused). If they wanted our money at all they tended to want to take it late in their campaigns when the opposing candidates, who could and often did monitor Federal Election Commission records to learn who'd contributed to their opponents, wouldn't have a chance to use the issue against them in the elections. The board had decided we wouldn't funnel contributions to candidates who weren't willing to take contributions openly from a gay PAC, but we did make several contributions one day after the last actual FEC filing deadline so our contributions wouldn't show up on candidates' FEC reports until after the elections. I knew they were going to have to grow up on the issue, but I tried to be flexible with candidates during this first go-round. More than a few of our donations were handled this way and, happily, I can now report that the overwhelming majority of those candidates, who went on to serve in Congress, became firm, public supporters.

Practically, the vast bulk of the money we raised during those first eight months wasn't available for candidate contributions until the last two to three months anyway, so the situation worked for everyone. Some candidates wanted our contributions only late in the game, but others declined them altogether. In general, we didn't make major contributions without advance conversations with the candidates, but we did send some small contributions of $200 to $300 each to candidates simply based on their records. That was particularly true when we could find Republicans who had voted with us on the McDonald amendment and/or the D.C. sodomy repeal vote. We hoped it would serve as encouragement and we could somehow make this a bipartisan issue.

Although we attempted to develop dialogues before just sending a check, sometimes it just didn't work out. Rep. Bill Frenzel (R-MN) returned our $250 check with a note saying we'd obviously misunderstood his intentions on the D.C. sodomy repeal vote and that he was in no way supportive. About a dozen contributions were returned, with at least one coming back as a result of the congressperson not taking any PAC contributions. A couple of times, challengers asked for our support but then held the checks. When they'd seen they'd won, they returned the checks. In both cases these new members of Congress were severe disappointments once elected. One had pledged to gay and lesbian constituents, who volunteered in large numbers for her, that she would cosponsor the National Gay and Lesbian Civil Rights Bill, but once she won, she returned our generous check, reneged on her pledge, and ended up as an erratic vote on various antigay amendments. Some excuse her because they say she suffers from rumors about her own sexuality, but I can't find it in my heart to forgive her. To this day, there are now-former activists who have never recovered from her betrayal and can't get themselves to step back into a political process that so undercut them.

The other candidate, an intellectual challenger in an uphill race in a southern state, told me he didn't think he'd be willing to cosponsor the National Lesbian and Gay Civil Rights Bill given his blue-collar district, but he assured me he'd never vote for antigay amendments like the one Rep. Larry McDonald (D-GA) was regularly offering then. On the day after the election, he returned our check and claimed there had been a misunderstanding, which was virtually impossible, since he'd personally solicited the contribution from me.

The political newsletters helped us determine which incumbents were locked in tough reelections. When the incumbent was strong on our issues and his or her opponent was not, we didn't just jump in but first tried to use their tight reelection battle to increase the level of their support. Would they not only vote with us but actually cosponsor, too? In a couple of cases, however, the races pitted liberal Republican incumbents who'd voted with us on antigay amendments—but who were unwilling to cosponsor the National Lesbian and Gay Civil Rights Bill—against aggressive Democratic challengers who pledged to not only vote against antigay amendments but also to cosponsor. Those were much more difficult choices because we tended to favor incumbents, and we also had to search hard to find Republicans worthy of our support.

In the case of both Rep. Larry DeNardis (R-CT) and Rep. Harold Hollenbeck (R-NJ), I initiated meetings with them to discuss their records and their willingness to cosponsor the national bill. I explained our priority on the civil rights bill and my hope they would cosponsor. Instead each one, in separate meetings, not only declined to do so but warned us that if we decided to back their Democratic opponents, we'd better hope those opponents won because neither Republican would ever vote with us again. Although I thought both incumbents were unnecessarily harsh, I guess I understood. I hesitated to take a chance and almost opted to go the safe route of either supporting the incumbents or just staying out of the races. But our top priority, the nondiscrimination bill, was very clear and two new cosponsors would help.

I met with the challengers, Bruce Morrison, a Legal Service lawyer, and Robert Torrecelli, a former Mondale aide, and they, like every other candidate I met, had convincing polling data suggesting a good chance of victory. I saw HRCF as a change-oriented PAC and we ended up vigorously supporting both challengers, in fact becoming one of Morrison's largest contributors. Happily, when the votes came in on election night, both Morrison and Torrecelli had won. We again had rolled the dice successfully and they both cosponsored.

One personal priority during the 1982 elections was to support as many viable black congressional candidates as possible. As it turned out, there weren't many key races for the black community in 1982, but we were able to help both Rep. Ron Dellums and Rep. Bill Clay, cosponsors who faced difficult primaries. The other notable race in which we supported a black candidate was in Kansas City, Missouri, where we gave Alan Wheat $3,000 in his difficult initial race. He won, has been a cosponsor of the lesbian and gay civil rights bill ever since, and, I'm told, has played a helpful role in facilitating communication between gay activists and the black community regarding efforts to enact a local ordinance. All in all, despite the limited number of races, we contributed more than $12,000 to about ten black candidates—more than the Congressional Black Caucus PAC gave.

Thus, 1982 was a major watershed year: the recession, dragging the Republicans down badly, gave us many opportunities to make a difference. At the same time, it seemed an awkward time for me to be going through a first election as a PAC director let alone run the Lobby as well. Also, none of us really knew how much money we'd have to give, making disbursement decisions tricky at best, but we hoped to contribute at least $100,000 to candidates. In order to be able to really have an impact on the modest number of races we selected, the board of directors made a decision, at my urging, which I felt helped us enormously: we decided we would make only small contributions, rather than major ones, to safe incumbents, even our leading congressional supporters. It sounded reasonable as an abstract concept, but it was tough as a practical reality. For instance, it meant we had to limit our contributions to Rep. Ted Weiss (D-NY) and Rep. Henry Waxman (D-CA) to just $250 each, but only such discipline would leave us with the resources for the really big races. Because we did want to come out of the 1982 cycle with a good winning percentage, however, we made lots of token contributions to safe incumbents, in addition to our small contributions to encourage Republicans who had voted with us on McDonald. I still have a hard time swallowing $5,000 contributions to safe incumbents.

We worked with our leading advocates, and particularly with Rep. Henry Waxman, to try to broker our contributions to their close allies in return for their strong support for lesbian and gay rights. By doing so, we strengthened their hands on our behalf. One race that Rep. Waxman got us into was that of Rep. Marty Martinez, a leading Hispanic member of the so-called Berman-Waxman machine, who hadn't previously been a cosponsor. He reviewed the bill at Henry's request and decided to cosponsor, so we contributed the legal maximum of $5,000.

Had the legendary Phil Burton not faced a difficult reelection in his San Francisco district, he might have played a similar role in distributing our contributions and building our clout, despite the fact that his time of being the premier wheeler-dealer in the House had come and gone. In fact, the Campaign Fund had already made the uncomfortable decision to stay out of Burton's race because he was facing a challenge by State Senator Milton Marks, a Republican who also had a very good record on gay rights; to do anything else would have damaged our reputation as a bipartisan PAC. When it became clear that Burton would face a tough reelection, we saw an opportunity to increase his level of support. Although he'd been the leading liberal in the House, was one of few genuine power brokers on the Hill, and represented one of the largest gay constituencies in the country, his support had been minimal. Sure, he'd voted against antigay amendments and was a cosponsor of the national bill, but he had never used his massive clout on our behalf. We met to have a candid conversation about the matter.

I explained that although the Campaign Fund would have to stay out of the race, I could help him personally as the director of Gay Rights National Lobby if there was a reason to do so. He knew our help could be very important since the district included huge numbers of gay voters—voters who actually knew Marks much better than Burton. The primary argument for helping Burton, though, was what he could accomplish on our behalf on Capitol Hill and we had to be able to point to something. Marks was a nice man and a genuine supporter, but couldn't "deliver" his mother. If Burton helped us get, say, ten new cosponsors, then I could argue more effectively to gay and lesbian voters that they'd be better served to reelect him because of his clout.

My meeting with Phil went very well, he liked our blunt, hardball logrolling, and he readily agreed to deliver. He got us the ten new cosponsors in no time, including Rep. Harold Washington, who had previously avoided cosponsoring but who later became a champion of gay rights as mayor of Chicago. In addition, he took me under his wing and occasionally would call me—on about ten minutes' notice—to come over to his office to talk political and legislative strategy. Even though Phil was no longer in his heyday and some in Congress saw him as a shell of his former self, I still felt like I was sitting at the feet of the master. For all of his weaknesses, he was a hero to me and I was honored by the time he gave me—and I'd like to think he finally began to really care about lesbian and gay civil rights.

When the time came, I gave Phil a strong quote for literature that was distributed throughout his district, spoke at a gay fund-raiser in the district, and was interviewed by each of the gay papers. Phil won reelection, and I still believe that if he hadn't died a short time later, the AIDS crisis and the national fight for lesbian and gay civil rights might have been far, far different.

Our very top priority election of 1982 for the Human Rights Campaign Fund was the reelection of Rep. Barney Frank (D-MA). Barney hadn't come out yet publicly, but I'd known him for years, even when I was Minnesota's gay rights lobbyist and he was the presumably straight cigar-smoking chief sponsor of the similar bill in Massachusetts. His incredible legislative ability made him one of the most effective advocates we could ever have.

Redistricting had thrown him in with Rep. Margaret Heckler (R-MA), however, in a district that overwhelmingly favored her. The Democratically controlled state legislature didn't have to screw Barney, but his extraordinary wit, used against some of these legislators, had alienated too many of them and it was time for payback. Heckler wasn't a firm opponent of gay rights—in fact, Barney joked about her gutlessness (some said you could tell where she had last stood before a vote because of the little puddle she left)—but she did vote against us on more than a few occasions and faced our best friend in the Congress. We contributed almost the entire $10,000 allowed ($5,000 in the primary and $5,000 in the general) to his campaign. Contrary to the prevailing political wisdom, which had Barney locked in a very tough, uphill battle, he ended up winning by a substantial margin and I felt like Joe Kennedy Sr. when he joked that he never intended to pay for a landslide.

The Campaign Fund went all out for the candidates we really cared about. Of the top twenty races we entered, our average contribution was over $4,500—not bad for a new PAC. We supported several incumbent cosponsors facing tough reelections, and against some the gay issue was used, including Rep. Bob Edgar (D-PA), Rep. Peter Kostmayer (D-PA), and Rep. Les AuCoin (D-OR). In the case of Edgar, who represented a conservative, suburban GOP Philly district, we mobilized volunteers who drove out to work for his campaign. It was a good Democratic year and each won.

We also got into a number of pivotal races for open seats as well as taking on a handful of vulnerable homophobic incumbents. We backed a young candidate, Doug Bosco, in the Russian River area of California who was trying to take an open seat. We gave my old fraternity brother Gerry Sikorski $5,000 for his candidacy for the reconfigured 6th District in Minnesota. After Gerry and I left school, I became the gay rights lobbyist and he became a very able state senator who thought seriously about the issue of gay rights for a bit but then never backed away from it, even when he received hundreds of phone calls from constituents. In fact, in addition to the

Campaign Fund's own direct contributions, we were able to secure several individual contributions of $500 or $1,000 from donors such as Jack Campbell, Jim Hormel, and even David Goodstein to key races such as Sikorski's.

George Sheldon, who'd been selected the most effective state legislator in Florida by statewide magazines, convinced us he could win the new open seat in the Orlando area against George Biklarias. The district seemed to tilt GOP, but we thought this smooth bachelor had a chance. If he couldn't do it now, the district would stay in conservative, and probably homophobic, hands for years. We also decided to get in big into the race between an old-time New Jersey Democratic pol, Joe Merlino (who had supported the state bill), and one of the young darlings of the anti-choice movement, Chris Smith. I can't actually remember any conversations with Merlino, but he had to have committed to cosponsor or we wouldn't have gone into the race as strongly as we did.

In other races, GRNL board member Terry Bean, who'd gotten us into our first race for Weaver in 1980, joined HRCF board member Jerry Weller in pressing me hard to go all out for a wonderful candidate, Ruth McFarland, against homophobic incumbent Denny Smith. In the contest for the open seat left by Rep. Toby Moffett's Senate bid, we vigorously backed an anti-nuclear power leader, Bill Curry. Normally, we tried to support women candidates, but Curry's opponent, Republican state legislator Nancy Johnson, had voted against the state bill.

On election night we held our breath. We hoped we'd made the right decisions and gotten into the important races. Even before that night, I saw that we had supported one likely losing race in Mary Gojack of Nevada, a good woman in an unwinnable district. Despite the polls she cited, Gojack got creamed and we blew more than $3,500! In general, though, we could look back and realize we had made good decisions and got into the right races. In our top twenty-two races, only Gojack's loss and Barney Frank's victory were won or lost by more than a 52 to 48 percent margin. Sikorski, Morrison, and Torrecelli slipped through to victory, while Sheldon, McFarland, and Curry all lost by the narrowest of margins. Moreover, by the combination of winning some of these tight races and using the persuasive powers of the dollar, we were able to parlay the 1982 elections into sixteen new cosponsors!

A few gay activists gave me grief because we didn't get enough publicity, and I wasn't experienced enough to know whether the criticism was valid or not. But a review of all the news articles shows we got a huge amount of publicity, mostly because of Mondale's appearance. Some people just never stop bitching. Since then, under several different directors, some have continued to complain that HRCF doesn't get the publicity that its impressive program deserves. They're right, but we can do only so much with the staff available (I usually just want to tell them to grow up and get a life). In some ways, the Campaign Fund, then and now, could have gotten more publicity, but I think much of the problem revolves around the fact that steady, within-the-system initiatives seldom get the attention of major media, who are looking for the more dramatic, confrontational events. Further, while the name "Human Rights Campaign Fund" has had many major benefits, the fact that we don't have "gay" or "lesbian" in the name has hurt us in terms of the media turning to us.

Because many political action committees face criticism for not giving a large enough percentage of the funds raised directly to candidates, we kept pouring out contributions to candidates. In part because we got unanticipated bills late, we ended up giving an excellent percentage of the funds we raised directly to candidates, but we also left ourselves short of operating funds for the next election cycle. Although I thought there was some room for legitimate concern here, I still believe this mistake was just used as a justification for an upcoming power play.

What was next? From a personal point of view, it was difficult even to think about—having just finished the most exhausting period of my life I was definitely burnt out. The Lobby had continued to flourish, largely because of the excellent staff who kept everything going. My lover and I had just bought a house on Capitol Hill and were preparing to move in. But more than anything else, I was just completely beat. It was hard even to focus.

Jack Campbell's fiftieth birthday party in Miami in December became a command performance for movement leaders. Jack's support had been central to our getting off the ground so, despite feeling like a complete vegetable, I went down for it. The fund's 1982 success was the culmination of years of trying to win elections that began way back before the Minneapolis ordinance. Moreover, I thought the Campaign Fund's success had helped us start to turn the corner—bringing the gay and lesbian rights movement into the mainstream. It was certainly a key topic of discussion, and the accolades poured in. Of course, I was satisfied.

I remember, while lying around Jack's pool, all the positive feedback we received for the Campaign Fund's efforts. We'd had an incredibly successful run, raising about $600,000 in about eight months' time and contributing about $145,000 to 119 candidates. In the areas for which I had direct responsibility the direct mail had gone extremely well. More to the point, we won 81 percent of our races, and about 65 percent of the smaller number of pivotal races where we threw in our biggest contributions. Later, I found out that some people, particularly Jim Foster, thought I was grabbing all the credit. I've searched my soul over this point, but I still don't think that's true or that I was doing so intentionally. I never doubted that our efforts had been those of a really terrific team, including not only Foster, Goodstein, and the board itself, but countless dinner committee members across the country. (But while Foster deserved credit for his hard work, my knowledge of the things that didn't happen and the near disastrous dinner blowups we'd barely sidestepped made it hard for me to bubble over.) The truth was that I was still so exhausted that I just lay there and absorbed and enjoyed the positive feedback (which is always great and particularly sweet to someone who's a bit unsure).

How should we build from this point? When David Goodstein insisted we meet immediately, I foolishly flew to the West Coast. Goodstein's primary efforts for the Campaign Fund had ended in the spring and he obviously didn't share my exhaustion—or fully understood just how exhausted and vulnerable I was then. So in this meeting with him and Bruce Voeller late in 1982, I made the mistake of suggesting that the black-tie dinners might be used for funding GRNL in the nonelection, off years. Of course, they'd be devoted to funding the Campaign Fund during election years, but I made it clear I was just thinking out loud and knew I was still so exhausted that even I couldn't trust my own judgement then. I later heard that my statement was being held up as proof that I was undercutting the Campaign Fund for the Lobby, and that I wanted to put the Campaign Fund efforts on hold. They didn't say much at the time, but in hindsight I'm convinced that quite some time earlier they had decided that now that these groups were truly becoming successful, I wasn't the person they wanted to run them. I've never been good at internal fights, though, and didn't see what loomed just ahead.

Even before the 1982 elections were over, I realized that the renewal of Jim Foster's fund-raising contract posed a serious challenge for the organization. Although he'd thrown his heart and soul into it and, as I've said before, he was not only a pioneer but also a hero of mine, he wasn't nearly as strong in this area as we'd need for ongoing operations. Moreover, although I knew we could find stronger fund-raisers for the coming year, I also realized making such a change could pose serious challenges, perhaps from both within the board and among his circle of influential close friends in the gay media. My conflict with Foster, along with my idle conversations with Goodstein and Voeller, became the basis for what was essentially a power struggle over our emerging groups.

Ironically, it was the Campaign Fund's very success in 1982 that set up this situation. As the year came to a close it was increasingly clear that no good deed goes unpunished and the overwhelmingly positive gay media coverage we'd gotten for more than three years would be changing. At that exact moment, however, I just didn't want to think about any problems, our future, or anything beyond sleeping for a week or two nonstop. Maybe a couple months' vacation would revive my spirits and help me rejoin the land of the living. We'd have to see.

Chapter 4

We've Met the Enemy . . . and the Enemy Is Us: Internal Conflicts Can Be Far More Painful Than Fighting Homophobes

In the early 1970s you simply had to have a very strong ego to play a leadership role in the gay movement or you wouldn't have gotten involved. For people with well-developed egos, the real challenge became sorting out the issues, disagreements, and conflicts and trying, as much as possible, to let go of those issues based only on ego and retain those where the outcomes could truly impact the best interests of the community. In other words, the serious challenge is to keep our eyes on the prize. I've always felt it's essential to place the civil rights, human dignity, and justice for lesbian and gay Americans before our own agendas and best interests. However, that's often easier said than done. Since I tend to feel deeply about issues, it was very difficult to evaluate what was really going on before I went to war on the wide array of issues.

A short time after I joined the first national board of directors of the National Gay Task Force in the mid-1970s, an activist I knew (who probably was tired of fighting me) taught me an excellent rule: before getting into internal battles, consider whether the issue or point of contention would matter five years down the road. If so, the chances are that the issue is a real and important one and discussing/negotiating it is worthwhile. However, if I concluded that the issue wouldn't matter or even be remembered five years hence, it was likely that the driving force in the debate was ego, and I'd let my ego go and move on to real issues. Despite this rule, my ineptness at fighting such internal fights, and the fact that I hate fighting other gay people, I do fight for my positions because I have strongly held views and I am stubborn. So, if I wanted to just get even or vent my spleen, I could easily devote several chapters to such internal conflicts.

In the earliest years there were conflicts, such as the battles my roommate, Steve Badeau, and I had with the Socialist Worker Party (SWP), which I viewed as a fringe and ultimately parasitic group (much like today's New Alliance Party) in the way they try to exploit the legitimate aspirations of oppressed people. Also there were the clashes with activist Jack Baker, who was then much more prominent in the movement than I was, over the language of both the Minneapolis and the state lesbian and gay civil rights bills. I felt that his proposed language was unnecessarily cumbersome and might jeopardize the ordinance's passage, but talking with the city council members showed that Jack's language wouldn't cost us votes, so I backed off and let my ego go.

In recent years, I've often found myself at odds with younger activists over terminology. I hate the term "queer" and am unconvinced by the arguments of the activists who use the term. But, although I find it offensive, it's clear the disagreement is fundamental and there's little chance of convincing these young activists of the wisdom of my position, so I've let it go.

Yet among all the clashes both big and small, two stand out as far more significant in my movement life than all the others. In the first, our state legislative effort, we faced a range of innovative but destructive efforts from activists who had never even worked for the lesbian and gay rights bill. In the other, I failed to understand a fundamental political rule: never fight with people who buy ink by the barrel. Because of my conflict with David Goodstein, then publisher of *The Advocate,* and a few others, I was eventually forced to resign and leave the movement I love and to which I have always felt called. Both of these battles were incredibly painful personally as well as seriously destructive to the gay and lesbian movement.

The first of these two conflicts took place during my years lobbying the Minnesota legislature, in the 1975 session. Our first effort, in 1973, had gone well, since we passed local ordinances in both Minneapolis and St. Paul and thought we had a good chance at winning at the legislature. The first indication of potential problems came when a guy named Tim Campbell—who previously hadn't been involved in the lobbying effort or gay activism in general—came to the board of the Minnesota Committee for Gay Rights and demanded that we include transvestites and transsexuals in the bill. We declined, pointing out that the bill would be lucky to pass and just couldn't stand the additional political weight of such an inclusion. Tim was furious and denounced us.

The next we heard of Tim and his cohorts was when the nondiscrimination bill came up before the House Judiciary subcommittee. Tim and Thom Higgins, another activist whose wit was matched by his nastiness, testified that they were happy the bill included "public accommodations" and "public services" because that would legalize gay marriage and gay adoption. This seemed farfetched at best, but the members of the subcommittee were clearly spooked and I sensed that putting off the vote was our best, in fact our only, hope. State Representative and Subcommittee Chairman Neil Dietrich (D-St. Paul) shared our concern and adjourned the subcommittee. Conversations with the subcommittee members quickly made it clear that only drastic action had any chance to save the bill. We got a state representative, who was being pressured by a conservative monsignor in his district, to move to delete the public accommodations and public services sections and to go forward with employment and housing only. In return, he'd vote for the modified bill. Although I wouldn't compromise on many areas, such as the exclusion of the gay teachers from the employment section, most of the protected classes didn't get across-the-board coverage. But Campbell, Higgins, and Jack Baker were beside themselves with rage.

Campbell's retaliation included several tactics: a press conference in the men's room the legislators use (two swing votes were actually using the facilities when the press had the bad taste to come into the restroom to cover the "press conference" so, needless to say, we didn't get either vote); a so-called hunger fast and sit-in (during daytime hours only), with offensive signs about those supporting us; transvestite parades through the halls of the legislature; and use of the women's room, scaring the secretaries. We'd heard rumors they were going to throw fruit from the galleries, so we had to alert security each time they went into the galleries. We'd worked hard to maintain a low-key, dignified lobbying effort for more than three years, but in a matter of two weeks Campbell reduced the issue back the level of a joke. On more than one occasion, I left hearings and faced several of these individuals chanting "Uncle Tom, Uncle Tom." I was devastated and thought I was going to have a nervous breakdown.

Given these circumstances, we used one of the few options available to us. We got the *Minneapolis Star* to editorialize that the gay civil rights bill was so moderate that the gay radicals didn't support the bill. Our lobbying team stressed that theme with legislators. In the final analysis, the antics of Campbell and crew made our lives more difficult and gave some legislators an excuse to vote against us, but I seriously doubt that their bizarre behavior cost us the legislative victory we craved so badly. The problem was, as it had been, a combination of bigotry and political cowardice. For some reason, Campbell and his friends did not return during the following legislative session in 1977.

If I thought our conflict with Tim Campbell was the worst possible internal battle we could ever face, I learned some years later—after I'd moved to Washington, DC, to assume leadership of Gay Rights National Lobby and launch the Human Rights Campaign Fund—that I hadn't seen anything yet. Ironically, this painful battle took place in 1983, shortly after one of our community's greatest victories to date, the successful launching of the community's political action committee, the Human Rights Campaign Fund. Not only had the direct mail I'd supervised, with a letter signed by playwright Tennessee Williams, done extremely well, but we'd won 81 percent of our races, were deeply involved in every key race in the country, and had secured commitments for sixteen new cosponsors of the national lesbian and gay civil rights bill. In the process, we'd worked with a range of new major donors within the gay and lesbian community and with the directors of the other key progressive political action committees.

As the Campaign Fund efforts unfolded, I felt it was essential to secure the participation of *The Advocate*'s owner, David Goodstein, even though many said that it would lead to future difficulties. I knew that David's image of a lobbyist was of a big business lobbyist—and not of a very informal Midwestern boy such as myself; in sports terms, Goodstein was looking for a soccer or rugby player while I was a bowler. But I was naive enough to think our performance would convince him to alter his picture.

The problem was compounded when, as the treasurer of HRCF, I wouldn't recommend a renewal of Jim Foster's contract as our fund-raiser. Although Jim was a personal hero, a genuine pioneer, and had worked hard on the various black-tie dinners he supervised, he'd ruffled many feathers unnecessarily and failed completely in his other major responsibility of major donor fund-raising. And Foster, who was extremely close to David Goodstein, had warned me that I'd pay a price in the press if I didn't recommend an extension of his contract. The Goodstein/Voeller letter stated,

> Farley's call for money several days ago was a real shock to us. It is difficult for us to comprehend how HRCF could be short of money for its own meager overhead two months after the most successful fund-raising drive in our community's history. . . . Momentum is being lost daily . . . Thus the impression we have is that the entire Washington gay apparatus is on the brink of financial disaster. . . . This is 1983, not 1973. The success of HRCF in 1982 makes it more urgent that the Washington gay operation not resemble amateur night on the Gong Show. . . . And it is clear that if GRNL and HRCF fail to do what is needed and wanted, other organizations will step in. We will support what works. All the best.

Copies of the letter were sent to all members of the boards of the lobby and the Human Rights Campaign Fund.

We'd probably made a strategic error by giving out so many campaign contributions so our record would be good. Miscalculations by administrative staff led us initially to think we had more money left than was actually the case. So I can see how Goodstein and Voeller would be surprised, but we were able to give out a large percentage of the funds raised. Goodstein, who hadn't done much of anything for the Campaign Fund since the previous spring, was also very critical of the fact that the board wasn't going to meet until March, but I'd been working 100 to 110 hours a week and badly needed a break. (In hindsight, a conversation David Goodstein and I had in the spring of 1982 convinces me he was already planning for my removal. We were alone and he kept asking what sort of personal support systems I had in case I faced criticism.)

Even though my down-to-earth style wasn't consistent with Goodstein's warped image of what a lobbyist was like, and I'd opposed Foster's future retention, the Goodstein/Voeller attack took me a bit by surprise. I'd received so much praise, from both the gay and nongay press alike (including *The Advocate* and Goodstein himself)—and we'd just come off such an extraordinary success—that I couldn't really believe I was facing this situation. I was probably most deeply offended by the reference to *The Gong Show,* given our strong performance for both the Campaign Fund and the Lobby. In hindsight, I was getting so much positive publicity and I think I was guilty of the sin of hubris.

The *Washingtonian* magazine in 1982 listed me in an article on "Future Leaders of Washington," describing those cited as, "100 men and women in their twenties, thirties and early forties who are likely to be among Washington's most powerful people of the future." Other praise included statements such as, "On an absurdly low budget, Gay Rights National Lobby is producing miracles. Imagine what they could do if we really supported them" (*Advocate* owner David Goodstein); "Increasingly one hears from Congressional sources and others that GRNL is doing a job nothing short of miraculous" *(The Advocate);* "His style is professional. When he talks tactics, it's as a seasoned lobbyist" (*The Washington Post,* referring to Steve Endean).

Still hoping to avoid a wholesale war, my letter of response to David Goodstein and Bruce Voeller was extremely temperate, particularly given my propensity for pugnaciousness:

> Your letter seems to indicate that you don't have all the necessary information on the finances of the two organizations, or that misinformation or misinterpretation is involved. I can certainly understand your concern. I regret that the press of events here on Capitol Hill has kept me from communicating with you and other important people as often or thoroughly as I should have. Looking back, the Board of GRNL should have been informed of our difficult financial condition.
>
> As you know, I've been working for many years to lay the critical foundation that we all agree is essential for our future success. The success of HRCF in 1982 coupled with the strong record of accomplishment by GRNL in the past year should remove all doubt about our efforts resembling "amateur night at the Gong show." I'm confi-

dent the aforementioned organizations *will continue to function professionally and effectively.*

I'm certain the points raised in your letter come from a position of basic support and concern for myself, the Campaign Fund and the lobby. Thank you for raising them. I look forward to seeing you soon.

I too sent copies of my letter to the boards of both the Campaign Fund and the Gay Rights National Lobby. Some board members in each organization were personally offended by Goodstein and Voeller's implied criticism of the board for inadequate fund-raising (Voeller certainly had no room to talk given his lack of fund-raising for GRNL as a board member), but it seems fair to say the predominant sentiments among board members were shock and anger.

Some months into the protracted attacks by *The Advocate* and journalist Larry Bush, several progressive PAC directors jointly signed a letter, which went to all the gay press, strongly defending me, particularly in terms of my political judgement, strategy, and ability to work with both candidates and other PAC directors. But when it was printed in *The Advocate,* it was followed by a vicious attack by either Goodstein or Bush. It was probably at that precise moment when it became clear to me just how futile my defense was when there was only one national gay paper and with Bush writing for so many of the other major local gay papers. Although the attacks didn't seem to fit with the either the recent widespread praise and the success of the Campaign Fund, all Goodstein and crowd had to do was to create enough doubt and people would sit back and wait until the dust settled.

Given the fact that Goodstein had abandoned GRNL in the first place when he didn't get exactly what he wanted, had publicly and repeatedly praised my leadership of the lobby over the past several years, and had remained completely silent when the leaders of other national gay groups ran their groups into the ground, I initially had a difficult time understanding why he'd lead an attack on me. But friends who are much more savvy on the ins and outs of internal battles pointed out that it was precisely our success that made it worth his time and energy to attack.

So Goodstein and Bush's stated grounds for criticism and the real motives were starkly different. The earliest behind-the-scenes criticism focused on board members not raising enough money, which I found particularly irritating. HRCF board members such as Gil Gerald and Jerry Weller had worked hard at it, plus Goodstein's own efforts represented a small percentage of what he was capable of. Also, I've never believed that a board's sole responsibility was to raise funds. There are more than a few examples of boards, including present ones, who do a great job at raising funds but don't seem to have the first clue about effective program implementation.

As I've said to more than a couple of people recently, if the board plays a key role in raising $10 million but then allows $9.7 to be spent unwisely, I question how good a job they've done.

The attacks quickly shifted to my own overextension, running both the Lobby and the Campaign Fund. It seemed unfair, given the continuing strong performance of the Lobby and our outstanding success (winning 81 percent of our races). However, this criticism didn't have much shelf life because I was absolutely exhausted and completely agreed with and had long planned for the hiring of additional staff, including a director for the Campaign Fund. The issue of overextension was interwoven with the supposed loss of momentum by the local HRCF committees. As has been proven in the years since, committees function at various levels of energy and activism at different points during the course of the year.

If "loss of momentum" sent Goodstein and Foster ballistic, my off-the-top-of-my-head suggestion to them that the dinners go to funding the lobbying effort instead of the HRCF political action committee contributions went over like a lead balloon. Ironically, as things worked out with the merger of the Lobby into the Campaign Fund, that's exactly what has happened. Finally, criticism for our supposed failure to get publicity in the nongay press seemed overstated at best, since we had coverage in *The Washington Post, USA Today, The New York Times, Los Angeles Times,* and ABC's *Nightline.* But there I go again, trying to approach it rationally when it was primarily a power struggle.

Eventually, when it became clear that these issues weren't providing the justification for the venomous attacks, Larry Bush turned to AIDS. By November 1982, I'd worked over a hundred hours a week for months—to help ensure the successful birth of the Campaign Fund, the continuing growth of GRNL, and the yet-unveiled emergence of our new tax-exempt, tax-deductible foundation, the Right to Privacy Foundation—and didn't immediately understand the demands AIDS would put on our galaxy of groups. Fundamentally, the Gay Rights National Lobby was a civil rights lobby operating to carefully build a solid foundation for our long-term goal of enacting national lesbian and gay civil rights legislation. Suddenly, with the onslaught of AIDS, we were expected to be a knowledgeable health lobby familiar with the complex appropriations process.

AIDS was a weird new disease that seemed to be attacking the gay male community far more than any other population. In most respects, we just were not prepared for such a challenge. However, because of several years' work we did have some advantages we could employ quickly in the battle against the disease. For instance, a GRNL press release asked grassroots constituent lobbyists to press for immediate AIDS funding:

Since the end of September, nearly 100 more people have contracted AIDS and about 35 more people have died, bringing the total number of cases to 691 and total deaths to 278. Two new cases are reported every day.

We ended up securing $2.5 million in AIDS funding in a supplemental appropriations funding bill for fiscal 1982, but only because the CDC shifted resources from other programs, which simply could not provide the long-term funds necessary and could only increase tensions and competition with advocacy groups working on other diseases. Also, no new funds specifically for AIDS research were allocated in the House's proposed health appropriations bill, so securing any funding was an accomplishment, due in large part to Rep. Waxman's excellent leadership. Yet it was clear that the Reagan administration just wasn't prepared to do what was necessary (hell, he couldn't even get the word "AIDS" out of his glib mouth!) and our advocates were not shy about saying so. "In 1982 the overall funding for the Centers for Disease Control was effectively cut by 20 percent," said Rep. Henry Waxman (D-CA), chairman of the House Subcommittee on Health and the Environment. He went on to say, "The Reagan Administration's 1982 budget does not even keep pace with inflation and will mean a further effective cut of 7%. The study of these relatively rare and poorly understood diseases will surely suffer."

In a December 1982 press release to the gay and lesbian press we were able to point to the valiant efforts of grassroots organizers and groups across the country, who had been alerted by GRNL. Our efforts met with real success when Congress passed a Continuing Resolution funding the government for the rest of the fiscal year (through September 30, 1983). Virtually no other new health-related programs were funded during the entire 97th Congress. We stated clearly who the real heroes were in this instance:

> Without the persistent efforts of GRNL's Field Associates and other key contacts, particularly in those states with Senators and Representatives on the Appropriations Committees, the GRNL lobbying effort would not have met with the same degree of success. This victory demonstrates that the gay community must continue to utilize the same constituent lobbying techniques which are effectively used by other grassroots organizations.

While these grassroots lobbyists played a key role, gay congressional staffers almost always were overlooked. Bill Krause, a leading San Francisco activist who'd been hired by Rep. Phil Burton but then went on to serve Phil's successor, Sala Burton, was short of patience but deeply dedicated. Sadly, Bill eventually passed away from AIDS. Tim Westmoreland, Rep. Waxman's key point person for AIDS, may have done more in combating this dread disease than any human being alive, with hardly any credit for his tremendous work.

GRNL also assembled a coalition of groups that pledged their support to the lobbying effort. This included the American Public Health Association, the American Psychiatric Association, the National Association of Social Workers, the American Psychological Association, and the National Hemophilia Foundation. In subsequent years this core of groups expanded into NORA, the National Organizations Responding to AIDS.

But to be honest, most of us still didn't have a clue as to the magnitude of the health crisis that was to come (though perhaps those from New York City, San Francisco, and Los Angeles understood earliest because they were losing friends in large numbers even then). A worst case, we thought at the time, was that it might be similar to Legionnaires' disease, which certainly cost lives but in no way matched the tragedy AIDS has become. So initially we resisted dropping the rest of our agenda to focus full attention on AIDS, but as soon as its extent became clear we tried to respond. We immediately assigned a staffer, Bart Church, exclusively to the AIDS issue, while legislative assistant Mike Walsh and I also focused increasing attention to the issue.

In March 1983, AIDS developments continued to spin forward at a dizzying pace. Representative Waxman, who was quickly emerging as the leading expert on AIDS in the House of Representatives, introduced a new bill that could put $40 million into national public health emergencies such as AIDS—not much by today's standards but massive at the time. Citing the dramatic worsening of the AIDS crisis, GRNL agreed that it had to dramatically increase its AIDS initiatives even though Congress seemed extremely reluctant to properly fund the AIDS crisis—at least until the death of Rock Hudson shocked the nation several years later.

When both the National Gay and Lesbian Task Force (NGLTF) and the Gay Rights National Lobby appeared before the U.S. Conference of Mayors meeting in Denver, Colorado, the Task Force chose to chastise the mayors, while the focus of GRNL's presentation was on a set of positive recommendations. Jerry Weller, who had recently stepped down as cochair of GRNL's board of directors to move to Washington, DC, and become our deputy director, presented the Lobby's recommendations before a packed meeting. Jerry had been the preeminent gay activist in Oregon, and his move represented a major favor to me and a significant risk for him, particularly because I was already under serious attack by Bush and crowd. He immediately stepped in, though, telling the mayors, "In fact, the $12 million [recently approved by Congress] is really only an opening salvo in the war against AIDS. Next year, in the fiscal year 1984, the federal government must begin the real research battle." Happily, with the advantage of advance coordination with San Francisco Mayor Dianne Feinstein's office, the conference overwhelmingly approved a resolution incorporating virtually all of GRNL's recommendations.

In August 1983, I testified before the House Subcommittee on Intergovernmental Relations and Human Resources, stating that "the federal government's commitment for AIDS research [is] a joke." I went on to remind members of the subcommittee that for a public health crisis that the HHS secretary described as the number one health priority, "only one tenth of one percent of the entire NIH research budget has been spent on AIDS." And in a statement as true in 1992 as it was when I made it in 1983, I went on to criticize federal education efforts: "The pitiful attempts that [the Department of Health and Human Services] have thus far made at educating the American public about AIDS appear to be nothing more than media hype."

During that time one of the criticisms put forward by Larry Bush was that I didn't even attend AIDS hearings, even though I was, in fact, present the entire time. Larry was one of the brightest people I knew; nonetheless, he seldom let the truth get in his way when he had an ax to grind, and the nature of GRNL's AIDS lobbying efforts were grossly distorted. Later I was told that his primary employer, David Goodstein, had no idea how much of what Bush said in that period were flat fabrications. I only regret that I was convinced to not sue for libel, as I'm told the two key criteria for proving such libel are inaccuracy and accompanying malice. The facts were clear, and no one doubted that what motivated Bush was malice.

The internal community attacks we faced more than took their toll by seriously eroding the resources we had available to bring to this vital task and by generally weakening an already fledgling effort. Ironically, those who even remember the attacks I and GRNL faced on AIDS have generally failed to recall that they were just the final criticism to justify what was more fundamentally a power struggle and a vendetta.

Ginny Apuzzo, then director of the National Gay Task Force, was based in New York City and was already losing friends, including her best friend, Peter Vogel, to the crisis. So what was still a bit of an abstract issue to me was far more personal to her. I remember Ginny accused me of major denial because I'd always led an active sex life and, in hindsight, she may have been partially on the mark on that particular criticism. But more to the point, I think, people react very differently to the AIDS crisis once they've lost friends to it.

Further, everything I'd learned in my lobbying was that I had to have some rational basis for my advocacy. At that early stage of the crisis, even the scientific experts weren't sure what we were facing, let alone what it would take financially to even begin to unravel the puzzle before us. To make matters even worse, GRNL was a very young lobby without either the number or quality of staff that would be necessary to meet the challenge.

One step we took to beef up our direct lobbying effort was to secure the assistance of two former members of Congress. Jim Corman, who represented San Fernando Valley, California, for twenty years, had been a leading advocate of both civil rights and national health insurance during his time in Congress and had recently picked up many political chits as the chair of the Democratic Congressional Campaign Committee (DCCC). The fact that Jim's daughter Tanyan worked for us played a key role in his pro bono assistance. Unfortunately, the fact that Corman's assistance was a favor to his daughter and to me personally meant that when I left, and Tanyan was so thoroughly demoralized, Corman stepped back from his earlier commitment and instead lent his pro bono assistance to others who faced their challenges more maturely.

The other former member of Congress, Robert Bauman (R-MD), didn't work out as well. He had been defeated for reelection after it was revealed that he frequented a go-go boy bar and hired male prostitutes. Initially he hid behind claims of chemical dependency (and that no doubt was one part of the problem) and denied that he was gay, and only later, after he claimed to have come to terms with his sexuality, did we decide to try to utilize his services. Despite his longstanding right-wing orientation, including antigay stances, he was a very bright and talented individual who appeared sincere when he said he wanted to make amends. So, despite the fact that we knew it would cost us support with certain elements of the activist community, we felt it was important to use his services and truly reach out to Republicans as well as Democrats. It was only later that Bauman demonstrated that his sole concern was with Bob Bauman.

Despite the full scope of GRNL's AIDS lobbying, though, activists called for a new, separate AIDS lobby. Although my first instinct wasn't positive, I supported the move and the AIDS Action Council came into existence. Initially I hoped the new group would not only dramatically enhance the community's response to the AIDS crisis but also relieve some of the pressure on the Gay Rights National Lobby. Such hopes would be realized, though, only if the real concern of the critics was an effective response to the health crisis instead of just another excuse to be used in the power struggle.

I confess that the attacks against me on this subject have continued to irritate me profoundly over the years. Several books, apparently depending on the inaccurate gay media portrayals and the groupthink of the time, criticized me severely. These attacks were particularly galling to me when I knew they came from activists and authors, particularly in California and New York, who had consistently refused to help build the Lobby in our early years, which would have better prepared us to address AIDS or any other national issue. Now it seemed almost more than I could stand to get the sanctimonious criticism in the best-known AIDS books.

So it wasn't until I launched the Fairness Fund in 1986 to generate dependable and ongoing constituent mail to Congress that I got marginally involved in AIDS-related issues. By then, GRNL had merged into the Campaign Fund (sort of like the mother merging back into the child), and Jeff Levi (who'd been my volunteer coordinator at GRNL) was running the National Gay and Lesbian Task Force; later, Jeff became the lobbyist for the AIDS Action Council. I decided that the Fairness Fund's contribution to addressing the AIDS crisis was to generate the relevant and timely constituent mail we needed to finally begin to win on what were life-and-death issues.

Although I never felt that GRNL was doing enough or was nearly well versed enough in the intricacies of appropriations lobbying, I did feel we often got a bum rap—in part because of the internal struggles and the fact that the AIDS crisis gave our critics their only really legitimate grounds for criticism. But if these were only justifications, what was really going on? I now think there were several key factors. They included Goodstein's inclination to try to maintain control and ensure that reality looks like his advance picture (in this case, the subject was my down-to-earth approach); the not-insignificant factor of revenge for Foster's removal as HRCF's fund-raising consultant; and the fact that Ginny Apuzzo, who had all the class that Goodstein thought I lacked, had recently assumed leadership of the National Gay Task Force. The Task Force had long wanted to break their agreement with GRNL to stay out of congressional lobbying, but I'd always raised hell about it. With me out of the way, either the Task Force could merge with the Lobby or they could simply move into Congress without facing my pugnaciousness. I could never be sure if Ginny was behind or supported the attacks on me, but she certainly benefited from them.

The boards of directors of both the Campaign Fund and the Lobby remained strongly supportive, and the GRNL board felt compelled to issue a joint letter defending me from the continuing distortions. In a letter released to the gay and lesbian press and printed in full in GRNL's newsletter, *Capitol Hill,* they wrote:

> These criticisms, primarily aimed at Executive Director Steve Endean, have continued unabated, to the point where we—members of the board of GRNL—feel compelled to respond to what we discern to be the major issues at stake in this matter. Admittedly, responding to

these charges is no easy task, in view of the differing perspectives as to their nature or in what might lie behind them.

Indeed, some criticism has been based on legitimate philosophical differences over future directions for the gay rights movement; other criticism has originated in understandable frustration with the difficulty facing any issue group seeking to influence the legislative process; and still other criticism appears to have emanated from petty personality disputes which do not serve the interests of the gay and lesbian community.

After citing an extensive list of the Lobby's accomplishments, the board addressed one of the areas of criticism that Goodstein and Bush had eventually settled on when other lines of attack failed: the Lobby's response to the AIDS crisis. The board wrote: "In the past year, GRNL has had to move from being a lobbying group working steadily but quietly on a gradually emerging civil rights issue to the role of supplicant for millions and millions in federal dollars relating to a rapidly emerging health crisis."

They cited the positive feedback of members of Congress, including Rep. Bill Green (R-NY) and Rep. Henry Waxman, chair of the House Subcommittee on Health and the Environment and the chief sponsor of a bill GRNL actively worked on to appropriate $30 million in public health emergency funding. Waxman wrote,

> Over the past year, GRNL has moved directly to meet the AIDS crisis. It mobilized congressional action for more federal research funding. GRNL began contacting constituent lobbyists across the country. These key contacts coordinated lobbying and led other efforts designed to affect Congress. They achieved tremendous success.

Their letter concluded,

> Our loyalty must be to the cause above any individual, and it is precisely because of this higher loyalty that we want Endean to remain at his post. Indeed, it would be unfair to him and a gross disservice to 20 million gay men and women to relieve him of his responsibilities when his greatest victories—for all of us—lie ahead.

Coordinated by board cochair Kate McQueen, the letter was signed by almost all board members, including Metropolitan Community Church founder Rev. Troy D. Perry, gay rights pioneers Barbara Gittings and Frank Kameny, Dan Bradley, and the National Gay Rights Advocates' Jean

O'Leary, who had been close to Bruce Voeller and probably risked the most by standing firmly with her embattled executive director.

Despite the solid loyalty of both boards, it was increasingly clear to me that the Campaign Fund, the Gay Rights National Lobby, and the movement in general were suffering badly from the attacks on me, not only in terms of fund-raising but also the grassroots constituent network GRNL's national field director had worked so hard to build. With over 200 local congressional district organizers, known as field associates, our constituent network had resulted in well over 300 grassroots lobby meetings between concerned gay and lesbian constituents and their members of Congress. But these individuals were volunteers whose primary reward was to be part of an increasingly successful national organization. Obviously, the Goodstein-Bush attacks seriously undercut this advantage.

Although I didn't feel that my work was done, or that we'd even laid all the key aspects of our foundation for future enactment of the national lesbian and gay civil rights bill, I finally decided there was little choice but to resign. Only by such a resignation could I help end a battle that was threatening to immobilize the entire movement. Therefore, I resigned in the early fall of 1983, with my resignation to take effect by early 1984. In a letter to the board and the gay and lesbian press I defended myself one last time, summarizing the sense of accomplishment and the unbelievable pain caused by the internal conflicts:

> I believe that I still have the support of the majority of the Gay Rights National Lobby's Board of Directors [actually, it was almost 100 percent, as well as similar support within the HRCF Board]. While this continued support has been gratifying, I've concluded nonetheless that my continuation is not in the best interests of the Gay Rights National Lobby, the lesbian and gay movement in general or for me as an individual.
>
> While internal politics are inevitable in any movement, it is apparent that the atmosphere has been so poisoned that I can only anticipate continued power plays, maneuvering, backbiting and bickering which absorb precious time and energy better spent fighting our real enemies.
>
> I entered this movement years ago to fight for gay/lesbian rights and to make a difference in the lives of gay people. I did not get involved to either fight other gay people or spend my time and energy defending myself and my staff. If self-defense becomes the highest purpose, it is time to go.
>
> While I obviously leave with strong emotions stirring within me, I also leave with a sense of peace. Frankly, neither the criticisms of de-

tractors nor even the kind words of praise from colleagues are necessary for me to judge both my accomplishments and shortcomings.

When I came to Washington, D.C. a little more than five years ago I had a mission. Today I can look back with the conviction that I've been able to make a difference. Hopefully, not only our past successes but the groundwork and infrastructures we've sought to build will help our movement win future victories. Few endeavors could have been so rewarding and satisfying. I thank the gay and lesbian communities for the opportunity of having served them.

Leaving the Lobby, the Campaign Fund, and the movement for which I'd worked full-time virtually my entire adult life resulted in extraordinary pain and unbelievable insecurity. Looking back, I can see I probably had a nervous breakdown but was just too stupid or stubborn to lie down. That period is still painful to write about, even years later and after we have many more achievements under our belts.

A number of factors helped me somehow survive. By far the most important lay in my deep and abiding sense that the good Lord had called me to do lesbian and gay rights work. And, although it seemed a bit sadistic of him given the fact that our movement in those days didn't seem to want me, I did trust him and tried to stay on the path he set for me. I've never regretted it.

As I write this chapter, I'm reliving the incredible pain my friends and I lived through, yet I also can see considerable irony in the fact that some of the greatest accomplishments in which I played a role came after I'd gone through the wringer and returned to the movement, first via the Fairness Fund and then as director of the Campaign Fund's Field Division.

Chapter 5

Beginning Again:
Building an Effective Capacity
to Generate Grassroots Mail to Congress

After leaving GRNL in 1984, I had plenty of time to reflect on our movement's progress. Our on-the-Hill advocacy was strong, the Human Rights Campaign Fund was flourishing under Vic Basile's direction, and the community was raising plenty of money to contribute to congressional candidates. However, despite the success of our constituent lobbying and other grassroots initiatives, GRNL had failed miserably at the critical task of generating constituent mail to members of Congress. Few members of Congress were likely to vote with us—no matter the merits or how much money we could give to their campaigns—if they thought their votes would incur the wrath of their constituents. The utter silence of our supporters, even on AIDS bills, compared to the massive quantities of antigay mail, convinced legislators again and again of the danger of standing with us.

Also, when our lobbyists pointed to national public opinion polls, which have shown majority support for amending human rights laws to protect gay people from job and housing discrimination, they heard, "Not in my district!" or, on a few occasions, "Yes, but those who support your rights don't even care enough to write. And your opponents pour in antigay mail." Legislators assumed that if our opponents could generate that much mail, they could well become a factor in their next election. Further—and this is hard to hear—if our supposed majority did not care enough to write a letter, could they be expected to mobilize to defend courageous elected officials who stuck their necks out and encountered trouble because of it?

Although I'd often attributed our difficulty to the fact that most lesbians and gay men remain closeted, our failure here isn't unique. I have since learned most progressive groups fail to get the grassroots mail needed to back up their direct lobbying efforts, especially when compared to the avalanches of mail produced by right-wing groups. As a result, many progressive groups have had to hope members of Congress would have the courage to fly in the face of overwhelming constituent mail from their districts. Unfortunately, such members of Congress are few and far between, and rare is the cause that prevails on conviction alone.

Our ability to generate mail to Capitol Hill faced serious obstacles. Many local gay and lesbian activists were overwhelmed with state and local challenges, and even the few who worked on national projects gravitated to short-term, more glamorous projects such as protests, vigils, and marches. Nonactivists, by definition, were unlikely to write to Congress. In addition, many of the early congressional votes were essentially legislative potshots against us via right-wing amendments. Such votes came up on short notice, making it difficult to even reach people in time, let alone have their mail get to Congress in time to influence members' votes.

Even on those few occasions when time, resources, and volunteer power had permitted GRNL to generate mail to Congress, new issues often came up within a few days or weeks and the whole effort had to be repeated. To the overburdened local activists on whom we depended, these repeated demands for help seemed unreasonable and unmanageable, while even for us it felt like emptying the ocean with a teacup. The problem became overwhelming as the AIDS epidemic grew, since not only did vital AIDS research, protection, and education legislation come up but also hostile amendments that could cripple these efforts. But the biggest barrier, by far, was "the massive gap of good intentions." Time and again, no more than a third of those who were contacted, who were committed to the issues, and who pledged to write actually got around to writing those letters to Congress.

In this context I stumbled onto a strategy I thought might address our inability to generate mail. About a year and a half after I left GRNL, I was retained as a consultant for direct lobbying of members of Congress. My duties there required me to attend a tedious four-hour coalition meeting, which unfortunately is a necessary part of a Capitol Hill lobbying effort. During the meeting, there was a brief discussion of how the National Organization for Women (NOW) had previously generated mail on the equal rights amendment extension. By getting people to preauthorize "Public Opinion Mailgrams," which were charged to their phones, NOW could produce the massive quantities of mail they needed. This proxy-type system, using Western Union's overnight mailgrams, also had the advantage of the modest charge, $4.25. The system was both very appealing and painless, but when I looked around the room to see if others were as excited about it as I was, there wasn't a ripple.

I was stunned to learn that a single approach addressed so many of the problems we had encountered. With a preauthorized approach we'd be able to respond to quick-breaking legislative emergencies. Also, if people authorized more than one mailgram, it would allow us to respond to the multitude

We Don't Care.

Members of Congress don't hear from us, and wonder if we don't really care.

Our community's organizations and lobbyists are hard at work, advocating a vigorous, effective and non-hysterical response to the AIDS crisis. But, despite opinion polls showing support, legislators seldom receive mail from constituents supporting our positions.

What's worse, our Far Right opponents are exploiting the health crisis for political gain—

mobilizing hostile constituent pressure. While our advocates work the halls of Congress, our opponents work the streets and avenues of Congressional districts across the country. And, as a result, legislators too often are afraid to stand with us on controversial and emotional issues.

With critical AIDS funding decisions, the defeat of countless AIDS hysteria measures and basic fairness questions hanging in the balance, we just have to turn this situation around!

Finally, Here's an Easy Way to Give 'em a Piece of Our Minds

The Fairness Fund's Public Opinion Mailgram campaign now gives us an easy way to make our voices heard on Capitol Hill on the issues we care about. A POM is a 50-word mailgram that costs just $4.50 each (the same 50-word message would cost almost 3 times as much outside this system). They are charged to your telephone bill. You don't even have to know who your legislator is—that'll be taken care of for you.

Too often, there just doesn't seem like there's time to write a letter. And sometimes you're just not sure what to say or when to write. Now, by signing one of our Public Opinion Mailgram authorization forms, or by calling the 800 number we have established, you can ensure that your voice will be heard in a timely, articulate fashion.

And, because the Fairness Fund works in close cooperation and with the support of the Human Rights Campaign Fund and other national gay/lesbian groups, your mailgram will reflect

our community's current lobbying strategy and priorities.

Won't you take just a minute, right now, to make a difference. Let's prove that we really *do* care.

The National Mailgram Campaign

Public Opinion Mailgram Authorization for Fairness and Privacy

Please print

| Last Name First Name | Telephone Number |

| Address | City | State | Zip |

I support fairness and privacy for lesbians and gay men and adequate AIDS funding and therefore authorize the Fairness Fund to use my name to send _____ (2-12 or unlimited) Public Opinion Mailgrams (50 words) during the next year at a cost of just $4.50 each. (The mailgrams will be charged to the phone number authorized. CANCEL AT ANY TIME.) The mailgrams will be sent to elected officials (at all levels) at critical times on the general categories of increased AIDS funding, defeat of AIDS hysteria measures, and support for justice for gay men and lesbians.

Signature

The Fairness Fund, P.O. Box 1723, Washington, DC 20013

Call
1-800-257-4900,
Oper. 9184 to send AIDS Mailgrams or Oper. 9188 to send Fairness Mailgrams.

THE
FAIRNESS FUND
(202) 347-0826
(Save for future reference)

Example of the Fairness Fund's Public Opinion Mailgram. Courtesy of HRC.

of votes coming up on the Hill. Because it was simple and easy, I thought we might be able to get a significant number of people to participate. However, I wondered why, if the program could work so well, were other groups not using it? I knew the conventional wisdom that members of Congress are less affected by orchestrated mail than personal and heartfelt letters, but was such mail totally ignored?

As I began to research the issue, I started with a hunch that since people had to pay for the mailgrams, they might have a greater impact on Capitol Hill than the conventional wisdom would indicate. Mailgrams, after all, suggest a higher degree of commitment than preprinted postcards. My research led me to talk with a range of groups, read studies, and consult with experts in the field, but the answers were not uniform. Some, including a number of gay congressional staff people, were pretty negative about the value of such efforts. The members of Congress I talked with were generally negative as well (but in my experience they rarely admit voting based on anything other than principle and it seems to be particularly "shameful" in their minds to admit to responding to such orchestrated mail).

Despite this negative input, my research revealed studies and analysis by experts showing such orchestrated mail was surprisingly effective:

> Some members of Congress, especially those from marginal districts or junior members, are afraid to risk alienating large constituencies. They dare not ignore any major pressure group, even if its pressure looks contrived, for mass mail usually shows organizational force, and that threatens to touch the politician's lifeline of survival and re-election. Any group that can mobilize masses of people to sign letters—or get their proxies—can mobilize those people to vote, or so the logic goes.[1]

> *The Power Game,* Hedrick Smith

> . . . the public relations firm of Burson-Marsteller interviewed 123 Congressional staffers and found that constituent letters, telegrams and calls counted more than anything else in influencing their bosses. . . . Richard A. Viguerie [a conservative leader and direct-mail expert] used the technique of bombarding Congress with thousands of preprinted post cards or clip-out coupons. He admitted that Members of Congress would recognize his campaigns as orchestrated and that they did not value the opinions expressed in a standardized post card as much as a thoughtful individual letter. But neither could they ignore them, he argued.

His [Viguerie's] view was supported by the Burson-Marsteller study which found that "orchestrated mail," while not so effective as spontaneous constituent letters, ranked "surprisingly high" as an influence on lawmakers.[2]

The Washington Lobby, Congressional Quarterly, Inc.

I also learned that NOW wasn't the only organization to use the proxy system. At least a couple of other groups, including the National Realtors' Association, had tried it as well. Almost as important, I found that a variety of groups, both liberal and conservative, used a Western Union product called "Action Hotlines" to generate overnight mailgrams to members of Congress. The hotline approach was different in that people had to call an 800 number to authorize mailgrams to Congress, but it clearly showed that other lobbies shared my growing belief in the value of the mailgrams generated this way. Further, when members of Congress received mailgrams they would not know whether it was as a result of a proxy system such as the one I envisioned or because concerned voters responding to a hotline option cared enough to pick up the phones and call in mailgrams on a given issue.

Members of Congress use their mail not only to judge public opinion in the district but also to ascertain how well organized people are on both sides and how much they care. A mailgram campaign—in which people have to pay a significant amount for the overnight message—differed from a postcard campaign in that the mailgram signals a greater intensity of interest by the sender. Besides, most postcard campaigns face a similar difficulty in terms of that "gap of good intentions"; even when hundreds of thousands of the postcards are distributed, huge proportions never get mailed into Congress.

Finally, for the gay and lesbian community, in judging the effectiveness of this program, I would ask the question, "Compared to what?" Our past failures to generate grassroots mail—500 letters on a specific bill from 435 districts seemed to be the high-water mark I could document—which meant almost anything would seem good by comparison.

After I had reviewed the studies on the subject and the other options available to us, I became convinced that a preauthorized system could make a tremendous difference in our ability to generate mail. I decided that the misgivings of those who objected to such orchestrated mail approaches were more the results of buying into conventional wisdom rather than looking at the studies or the options. In some cases, the objections looked like excuses and a way of avoiding the hard work and extensive organizing required to create such a system and secure the broad participation that would give it clout. My analysis also convinced me that such a system would work only as a part of a comprehensive grassroots effort, with constituent meetings in the district, phone calls, and personal letters all complementing the orchestrated mail side of the initiative.

The Challenge Was to Get Someone to Take on the Project

After reaching the conclusion that a preauthorized mailing program could make a big difference, the challenge became finding a group to tackle the project. A major selling point was that this effort would help build valuable mailing lists. My first thought was to take the idea to the Gay Rights National Lobby. In my report to executive director Nancy Roth and the board on September 8, 1985, I stated:

> Although oversight of GRNL's grassroots constituent mobilization is not my responsibility as a consultant retained to do the lobbying, the connection between the two is quite obvious. . . .
>
> I believe that, without dramatic steps to fundamentally improve GRNL's ability/performance in this area, we will continue to find ourselves in the uncomfortable position of having to ask Members of Congress to take the lead on a controversial social issue without any apparent constituent backing, let alone actual pressure. Members of Congress are not generally noted for such courage and those that are either already cosponsors or are ideologically opposed. . . .
>
> GRNL's field system was never all we would want but it was improving. But the erosion of GRNL's network in the last couple of years and the fact that at the very same time the New Right and the moral majoritarians in particular are doing such strong field work makes this development even more serious.

Nancy Roth just did not get it, however. She was in the position I'd once occupied, but her strengths centered around public relations and "feel good" stuff. She loved to travel around the country as GRNL's executive director and clearly had a flair for public relations, but her lack of political savvy and failure to take grassroots mobilization seriously damaged the organization. For instance, she forced the staff person ostensibly assigned to grassroots work to spend all his time scheduling her travel, calling local activists to set up meetings with her, etc. GRNL's field associate system collapsed and the network of 140,000 supporters—which had been so useful in direct-mail solicitations—fell into total disarray. The real grunt work that had previously been GRNL's hallmark (although it was anything but fully developed even at its best), which was necessary to build ongoing, effective grassroots mobilization, was completely ignored. In addition, GRNL was headed for dire financial problems and clearly lacked the funds and ability to help build such a proxy-mail program.

It broke my heart when I couldn't convince either Nancy or the board members to make it a priority. Eventually I decided my only option was to leave the Lobby and try to build the grassroots pressure and network we needed somewhere else. There were three other groups to approach as possible sponsors: the AIDS Action Council, the National Gay and Lesbian Task Force, and the Human Rights Campaign Fund. I met with the directors of each to try to convince them to take on the program, but they all declined. I realized that their concerns were based in part on the negative image that resulted from my highly publicized fight with David Goodstein and *The Advocate* as well as some conflicts I'd had over the years with them.

Gary McDonald, executive director of the AIDS Action Council, expressed mild interest at best. Then over lunch I met with Jeff Levi, executive director of the National Gay and Lesbian Task Force. Although he thought the idea had potential, the Task Force did not have the resources to undertake such a massive new program. Also, given the fact that I had spent the first three or four years with GRNL trying to make the Task Force honor its earlier promise not to engage in congressional lobbying, it would be tough for Jeff to retain me to run the project. This difficulty was increased by the fact that I'd tangled with Ginny Apuzzo, the former executive director, who was now on the NGLTF Board.

Finally I approached the Human Rights Campaign Fund, the best-funded group in the country. HRCF's director, Vic Basile, doubted whether a preauthorized mail program would make any difference legislatively but was interested in its potential for bringing in new names that could be used in direct mail. Yet, here too, my history made things tough. I'd founded the Campaign Fund and, when I stepped down as CEO, I had supported Jerry Weller rather than Vic. Although we'd made peace, he was uncertain if we could work together on an ongoing basis, and he doubted that I'd be easy to supervise. In addition, the Campaign Fund was preparing to absorb GRNL and its lobbying functions. Vic clearly thought that the Campaign Fund would have its hands full assimilating GRNL's direct advocacy efforts without also tackling a new constituent mail program.

I had two choices: either I could give up the idea and leave unaddressed a serious void in our movement, or I could start my own group to focus exclusive attention on grassroots organizing with the mailgram campaign as its first priority. After some serious soul-searching, I launched the Fairness Fund, taking care not to compete with the Campaign Fund or NGLTF. Happily, once I decided to create a new group, both the NGLTF and the Campaign Fund lent support, if not money, and both groups urged their members to participate in Fairness Fund initiatives. As tangible evidence of their support, both Vic Basile and Jeff Levi supplied positive quotes for use in the press to show that this wasn't a competitive effort.

These quotes were quickly supplemented by others. Chicago's *Outlines* newspaper stated, "The Fairness Fund does not duplicate the efforts of other groups, but instead focuses its attention on 'filling the gap' of generating grassroots constituent pressure/mail." Likewise, Dan Bradley, chair of the Fairness Fund's advisory committee and a former board member of both HRCF and the Gay Rights National Lobby stated,

> While our community's advocates are doing an excellent job in the media and in the halls of Congress, our opponents work the streets and avenues of the districts across the country. As a result, legislators too often are afraid to stand with us on controversial and emotional issues. We must translate the opinion poll majorities into tangible grassroots mail.

Despite the support from movement leaders, establishing such a new program from scratch, in a market where people thought there already were too many groups, was difficult at best. The program was new and unproven, and there wasn't much evidence to suggest that major donors cared a lot about grassroots organizing. In addition, my own reputation was still suffering from the contentious and highly visible battle I'd had with David Goodstein.

The Fairness Fund

Generating constituent mail to Congress was our sole purpose when we launched the Fairness Fund in 1986. The first task was to assemble a board of directors and find the funds to get the project off the ground, including paying my salary. And, if it really was to be successful, I had to set aside past conflicts and bitterness with the handful of key activists I'd been battling, so I got together with Ginny Apuzzo and Larry Bush to explain the program and to ask for their support. They graciously agreed to lend their names to the Fairness Fund's advisory committee, which was widely reported in gay media.

Next, the Rev. Troy Perry—an old friend and former GRNL board member who'd joined the Fairness Fund board—arranged a dinner meeting with David Russell and his lover Niles Merton, the current publisher of *The Advocate*. Russell had been the lover of David Goodstein, who'd since passed away, during my feud with him. Russell is extremely bright, and our conversations often gave me new insights and perspectives I might never have thought of otherwise. Despite our disagreements, we liked and respected each other, and when I asked him to serve on the Fairness Fund board, and to raise and give funds, he agreed.

I had a pretty good handle on the range of techniques of fund-raising by this time, but I soon was reminded that knowing them and implementing them are not one and the same. Grassroots mobilization often isn't the sort of work for which most donors really like to contribute. In addition, my group's key project of preauthorized mail to Capitol Hill was untested. All of this was in the context of a time when most people still cared primarily about local initiatives, thought there were already too many national groups, and, to the extent they were contributors, were more likely to be giving to AIDS groups.

I simply put to work every technique I'd learned which seemed applicable, setting up a monthly pledge club and establishing a major donor club called the Founders' Club. I have always believed that assertive, one-to-one fund-raising can result in unimagined resources, but I had never done this sort of major donor fund-raising before, since at GRNL I had relied on the class and charm of Terry Bean—who could sell anything to anyone—to build our major donor program. Terry gave me advice, but he would not do it for me. Although I met lots of rejection, there were enough successes to keep me going, and what I lacked in grace and class I made up in sheer brass.

The Fairness Fund's 1986 April-May progress report to board members and major donors reflected my mixed emotions:

> It's frustrating to be back at essentially square one, where I'm doing everything myself and no matter how many hours I put in I can't get everything done. But if you also read in these lines of "update" an incredible joy at again being involved full-time and preparing to enter an undertaking that could make such a difference, you're sure right. Thank you for helping make this possible!

I turned to anyone I knew who I thought still believed in me. My bowling coach, my best friend, and an old political crony each made vital contributions that helped me get off the ground. I also ran up massive expenses for the Fairness Fund on my personal credit cards. Eventually, I realized I had put myself into an incredible hole and I was forced to declare bankruptcy, not a strategy I'd recommend to anyone. But with the help of patient friends in Minnesota, the support of just enough former major donors to GRNL and HRCF, a handful of donors in Washington, DC, and an eruption of goodwill and massive financial support from previously untapped Chicago, we were able to get the Fairness Fund going and show that we could make a difference.

A key reason for our Chicago success was the help of a close friend, John Chester. I'd first met John when I was the gay rights lobbyist in Minnesota and came to Chicago every couple of months for a mental health and "outreach" break. John was then masterminding gay rights legislative efforts in Illinois. He'd been a gay activist for more than twenty years and knew virtually everyone, activist and nonactivist alike. With his stocky frame and receding hairline, a couple of friends of mine said John reminded them of what they pictured Chicago machine politicians looking like. A Notre Dame graduate, John had lived in Chicago for many, many years, and his knowledge of Chicago politics probably matched that of anyone in the city, machine or otherwise. And in a city that can be very polarized, John not only had good relations with the leading reformers but was also seen as Mayor Richard M. Daley's favorite gay activist. John gladly let me stay with him but told me he doubted he could assist me, since his strength was not fund-raising strategy. During my visits, however, he would think of one after another potential donor. I'm certain that he didn't realize he had so many leads, but as we sat I picked his brains, and his incredible knowledge of who had contributed significantly to which local groups just spilled out.

Years later, the Human Rights Campaign Fund honored John at their annual Chicago gala, but I suspect very few people still understood the key role he'd played in helping find major donors for the Fairness Fund (which became part of HRCF). Several local gay groups also honored John for his incredible, if sometimes low, visibility and pioneering role in so many vital initiatives.

Another player in the emergence of Chicago's gay movement was a terrific bar owner, Art Johnston, one of the people I met early on. Art assisted financially and also took the time to assure me he'd followed the battles I'd been through at GRNL and felt I'd gotten a rotten deal. As someone who was still suffering from a very painful and very public denouncement by the movement I loved, Art's gracious words meant more than he possibly could know. Later, Art threw his substantial energy and charm into passing Chicago's lesbian and gay rights ordinance.

Also, two of the board members of Chicago House, an excellent AIDS residence organization, opened their home and their hearts to me and often put me up. Jack Delaney and Pat Griffin practically became a second family to me. Chuck Renslow, the owner of the local baths and several bars, a former GRNL board member, and an old friend, helped tremendously. One Chicago major donor grilled me hard and asked every tough question he could, but he then gave me terrific support and I've come to view him not just as a donor but as a friend.

There were two other reasons for our Chicago success: the fact that Chicago's movement had just reached a new level of sophistication, and the national groups' focus on donors on the East and West Coasts, ignoring much of the great Midwest. So although the terrific help from friends was a major factor in our success, it also helped that national gay and lesbian groups had never really "worked" Chicago. These groups had solicited major gifts in Los Angeles, San Francisco, and New York for years, but this was one occasion when the movement's coastalism spared Chicago's potential donors.

Eventually, Chicago was the site of the first Fairness Fund chapter, which was kicked off at a major event in early 1987. The event received great publicity and was attended by virtually every major gay and lesbian leader in town. Yet overall, fund-raising for the effort proved difficult. During much of this period, I felt fairly desperate, which made me more difficult than usual. Many friends begged me to give up, and friends and foes alike probably wished I could accept the fact that my time in our movement had come and gone. I sometimes thought they were right. Because I am religious, I prayed for guidance and strength. Was I really supposed to continue working in the lesbian and gay movement? The answer seemed to provide the assurance I needed that this is what I was supposed to be doing.

During this early stage of the Fairness Fund's development, we were handed the opportunity of a lifetime to prove the worth of mailgram campaigns. In June 1987 President Reagan nominated Judge Robert Bork of the U.S. Court of Appeals to serve on the U.S. Supreme Court. Bork had a reactionary record, including extreme insensitivity to civil rights and civil liberties. In addition, he was very clear about his opposition to the idea of a constitutionally based right to privacy. One of his best known lower court opinions stated unequivocally that "private, consensual homosexual conduct is not constitutionally protected."

Almost immediately, lesbian and gay rights advocates joined a broad-based coalition of civil rights, civil liberties, and women's groups who pledged all-out opposition to the Bork nomination. Yet our preauthorized, proxy-type system did not yet have enough people participating to really make a difference, so we settled on establishing a Western Union 800 Action Hotline so people could call a toll-free number to send overnight mailgrams to members of Congress. We also utilized both free and paid ads to urge lesbians and gay men to call the toll-free number to send overnight mailgrams against Bork's nomination.

The hotline connected the caller to a Western Union operator, who read the caller three fifty-word mailgrams, and gave the caller the option to choose one. The price for the first mailgram was $4.50 and additional mailgrams cost $4.00, which was applied to the caller's next month's phone bill. (During later 800 campaigns Western Union kept screwing us up by continually changing the number, but during the Bork controversy the number remained the same for the duration of the nomination fight.)

With the help of gay papers, over 3,500 mailgrams were generated—far more constituent mail than came as a result of all other national gay and lesbian groups combined. In fact, Western Union was running 800 numbers for several different groups, including the umbrella coalition against Bork, and Western Union indicated that our hotline produced much more mail than any of them.

Many people, even on our board, thought the action hotlines were much easier than the proxy system I'd been advocating, but the hotlines still left us too dependent on people's initiative to call the 800 number. I viewed our hotline success as just buying us time so we could finish creating the National Mailgram Campaign. However, in addition to the organizational problems of finding the resources and staff to build such a program, we also had to overcome that thousand-pound gorilla of barriers—the closet. My exploration at the front end of the mailgram program focused not only on its impact on the Hill but also on whether we could get gay men and lesbians to sign up. I spent a lot of time talking to nonpolitical friends to get their views.

Since I have always felt that gay activists spend too much time talking with one another and not enough dealing with the broader community, I often tried out my ideas on my bowling buddies or friends from the gym. This reality check brought bad news. One after another, people told me that most people they knew would not be willing to be "out" enough to have their names put on constituent mail to their congressional representatives. In hindsight, I am convinced they would have been right, and that gay men particularly wouldn't have signed up in large enough numbers had the AIDS crisis not dragged them by the thousands from their closets. The onslaught of AIDS showed how much was at stake, in life-and-death terms, in influencing public policy.

In contrast to gay men, lesbians were initially much more supportive, but I do not pretend to understand all the dynamics that contributed to the difference in response. Whether it was experience in the women's movement or a less competitive, suspicious nature, the fact that lesbians so willingly signed up and participated even when many of the mailgrams sent were on AIDS issues (which did not impact them directly) is testimony to how generous and supportive they were.

Our next big opportunity to get people to sign up in large numbers was the 1987 March on Washington for Lesbian and Gay Rights. The march promised to bring tens or even hundreds of thousands of the most committed people in the country to Washington for a massive display of strength and unity. For us, it offered the possibility of securing a large, quick enrollment in order to jump-start a program that had already taken too long to get

CONGRESS MUST GET THIS MESSAGE!

Just call
1-800-325-6000
and ask for
operator 9188.
It's quick.
It's easy.
It's inexpensive.
And it makes
a difference!

RICH JONES
652 72ND STREET
DES MOINES, IA 50312

THE HONORABLE
UNITED STATES SENATE
WASHINGTON, DC 20510

SENATOR

STRONGLY URGE DEFEAT OF ROBERT BORK
NOMINATION TO SUPREME COURT. RECORD SHOWS
INSENSITIVITY TO CIVIL RIGHTS, CIVIL LIBERTIES OF
RACIAL MINORITIES, WOMEN, GAYS, ETC. FEAR CIVIL
RIGHTS ACHIEVEMENTS COULD BE OVERTURNED IF
HE'S CONFIRMED. AWAIT WORD OF YOUR DECISION.

RICH JONES

Congress must hear from each of us!

Call 1-800-325-6000 and ask for operator 9188. Tell the operator tha you want to send the Public Opin ion Mailgram (POM) listed above Other POMs are available. The cos is just $4.50 per mailgram, whic! will be charged to your telephon bill. You don't even have to kno who your Senator is, they'll tak care of it for you.

Won't you take just a minute, rigl now, to make a difference.

THE NATIONAL MAILGRAM CAMPAIG
Sponsored by The Fairness Fund, in coope
tion with the Human Rights Campaign Fu
and many other national gay and lesi n rga
izations. For further information on g
mobilization, write The Fairness Fun,
1723, Washington, D.C. 20013, (202) 347-08;

Defeat Bork Supreme Court Nomination

Citing Judge Bork's extreme right-wing record and past insensitivity to civil rights/civil liberties issues, a broad cross-section of civil rights and women's groups have pledged to oppose him. They argue his confirmation could tip the Court balance and lead to erosion of past civil rights gains.

Advocates of lesbian/gay rights point to his record of opposition to gay protection. One of his best known opinions states, "Private, consensual homosexual conduct is

not constitutionally protected." He described arguments of pro-fairness advocates as "completely frivolous."

Activists point to high stakes. The Court will not only address privacy and gay employment cases, but critical cases relating to the AIDS crisis. Gay lobbying groups have joined the coalition opposing Bork's confirmation. But they need our help! One civil rights leader said, "There's no question the mobilization of the grassroots is one of our most critical tasks."

Congress Public Opinion Mailgram. Courtesy of HRC.

SEN. SPECTOR MUST GET THIS MESSAGE!

Just call
1-800-325-6000
and ask for
operator 9188.
It's quick.
It's easy.
It's inexpensive.
And it makes
a difference!

RICH JONES
652 72ND STREET
PHILADELPHIA, PA 19123

THE HONORABLE ....
UNITED STATES SENATE
WASHINGTON, DC 20510

SENATOR ....
STRONGLY URGE DEFEAT OF ROBERT BORK
NOMINATION TO SUPREME COURT. RECORD SHOWS
INSENSITIVITY TO CIVIL RIGHTS, CIVIL LIBERTIES OF
RACIAL MINORITIES, WOMEN, GAYS, ETC. FEAR CIVIL
RIGHTS ACHIEVEMENTS COULD BE OVERTURNED IF
HE'S CONFIRMED. AWAIT WORD OF YOUR DECISION.

RICH JONES

Defeat Bork Supreme Court Nomination

Citing Judge Bork's extreme right-wing record and past insensitivity to civil rights/civil liberties issues, a broad cross-section of civil rights and women's groups have pledged to oppose him. They argue his confirmation could tip the Court balance and lead to erosion of past civil rights gains.

Advocates of lesbian/gay rights point to his record of opposition to gay protection. One of his best known opinions states, "Private, consensual homosexual conduct is

not constitutionally protected." He described arguments of pro-fairness advocates as "completely frivolous."

Activists point to high stakes. The Court will not only address privacy and gay employment cases, but critical cases relating to the AIDS crisis. Gay lobbying groups have joined the coalition opposing Bork's confirmation. **But they need our help!** One civil rights leader said, "There's no question the mobilization of the grassroots is one of our most critical tasks."

Congress must hear from each of us!

Call 1-800-325-6000 and ask for operator 9188. Tell the operator that you want to send the Public Opinion Mailgram (POM) listed above. Other POMs are available. The cost is just $4.50 per mailgram, which will be charged to your telephone bill. You don't even have to know who your Senator is, they'll take care of it for you.

Won't you take just a minute, right now, to make a difference.

THE NATIONAL MAILGRAM CAMPAIGN Sponsored by The Fairness Fund, in cooperation with the Human Rights Campaign Fund and many other national gay and lesbian organizations. For further information on grassroots mobilization, write The Fairness Fund, P.O. 1723, Washington, D.C. 20013, (202) 347-0826.

Senator Spector Public Opinion Mailgram. Courtesy of HRC.

off the ground. With the resources from a matching grant from Jim Hormel, we hired consultants to help run a major March on Washington enrollment project. We next convinced Western Union to contribute signs and thousands of buttons to promote the program. Assuming the march really drew the crowd that organizers had been predicting, we would be able to sign up between 5,000 and 10,000 participants.

Less than two months before the march, the consultants—who had proven to be as useless as tits on a boar anyway—walked out to accept a more lucrative offer from Jean O'Leary's National Gay Rights Advocates (NGRA). Sensing that my dream might be going down the drain, I was going crazy. One of my best friends, Eric Martin, and a hardworking young man from Connecticut, Ethan Felson, stepped in to help. We quickly found that potential volunteers to assist with the canvassing were more attracted to the march committee itself, although I later heard that volunteer turnout at the march was extraordinarily low as well. Others promised to help but did not follow through. Most people, I later learned, can't stand to do the canvasser-type work that we needed, and most wanted to enjoy and be a part of the historic event that was unfolding. In the end, we also tried to "hire" people to help us approach and sign up participants, but we could pay only 25 cents a name—wholly inadequate for this sort of assertive work. Looking back, I can see just how green and unprepared we really were, but we had few choices.

Despite these problems, we mustered about twenty volunteers, clad in some of the ugliest bright orange T-shirts I'd ever seen, to sign up people. The efforts by this small, solid core of friends and associates allowed us to enroll about 2,300 people. I counted the petitions at Metropolitan Community Church that Sunday evening with my friend Eric Simpson and thought that surely some of the petitions got lost. I now realize it was our rationalization to face the reality that we'd signed up so few out of a crowd of over 600,000 people. I just about cried. So while we publicly heralded the results as a good beginning, I was devastated, even as thousands of other activists reveled in the success of the march.

Several years later, as I brainstormed how to cover the 1993 March on Washington for Lesbian and Gay Rights with our assistant canvass coordinator, Tom Swift, I realized my 1987 expectations had been far off the mark. Not only had we been unable to pay an acceptable amount for each person they signed up, but no matter how much people were paid, few lesbians and gay men wanted to miss the "event of a decade" in order to work it as a canvasser, which is sort of like being a vendor. Tom and I figured that even with all the changes we later made in the system, all of our experience, and the thousands of people who have canvassed for us since, we'd still have a hard time finding the thousand canvassers we'd need in order to take advantage of an event that large. But I'm getting ahead of myself. After the 1987 march, I briefly but seriously questioned whether it was time to give in to the prevailing wisdom and abandon the project and my involvement in the movement.

However, shortly after the 1987 march, another key legislative battle took place that demonstrated the importance of grassroots mail to Congress. Senator Jesse Helms (R) of North Carolina had offered an amendment to the 1988 AIDS appropriations bill to bar the use of federal funds to purchase educational materials as "promoting a sexual lifestyle other than monogamous marriage." Despite the fact that the Helms amendment would have a devastating impact on candid AIDS educational materials being prepared for use in the gay community—and would therefore result in many unneeded deaths—it passed by the overwhelming vote of 96-2.

At the time I explained to the gay press:

> What happened with the Helms amendment is that it came up with almost no notice. There was no way to call people across the country—or even use our 800 numbers to generate mailgrams. If we had five or ten thousand people we need around the country, we could have generated a mailgram in one day's time on behalf of each of those individuals and it would have made a difference.

After the fact, the Human Rights Campaign Fund ran beautiful ads in nongay papers all across the country focusing on the Helms amendment as a classic example of AIDS hysteria. The ads included a reference to our 800 number and resulted in more than 2,000 mailgrams.

With the Helms amendment as incentive, I decided we needed to expand the Fairness Fund staff, even if our finances didn't logically allow it, to build our constituent operations. Therefore, I hired two terrific people, Steve Dwyer and Lee Bush, who had worked for the march. Steve and Lee brought invaluable administrative and organizing experience to the venture and remained with the undertaking for several years. Kate McQueen, the chair of the Fairness Fund board who had also served as cochair of GRNL, stated in a widely covered press release, "Lee brings to the Fairness Fund expertise, commitment, and a wealth of fresh contacts with some of the best organizers in our movement from his experience with the tremendously successful March. . . . we're confident his efforts will be every bit as successful as his tireless work with the March on Washington."

Lee Bush was about thirty-five years old at the time and stood about six foot two, with a medium build, reddish brown hair, a twinkle in his eyes, and an impish and charming personality. Having served successfully as the national coordinator of the march, Lee was now poised to help spearhead the program's development. In a Fairness Fund press release, Lee stated,

> October 11 was the beginning of the march on Washington, not the end. The event spawned a "new generation" of activists and a new, energized spirit of activism. I view the Fairness Fund as the best and most logical step to build on the momentum of the march.

Steve Dwyer took on the thankless task of administering the Fairness Fund and implementing our mailgram program. Steve, who was low-key, had been the office manager of the march, and he'd been largely responsible for the terrific bucket brigade that raised so much money the day of the march. I was certain he could handle the administrative details that go with establishing a complex system such as the mailgram program, although I was less certain he could work with someone as high-strung as I can be. I knew I was not the easiest person to get along with right then. I could be a difficult, demanding control freak, and I was particularly tense at that point since I was growing increasingly desperate at the possibility that our undertaking could fail.

About that time, Randy Klose, one of the newest board members of the Human Rights Campaign Fund, asked me to go out for drinks with him and talk about my movement experience and what I thought our movement was missing. Randy had gotten involved in helping defeat Lyndon LaRouche's AIDS initiative, Proposition 64, and was from a wealthy family. I had tried, unsuccessfully, to solicit his financial support for the Fairness Fund. Although I had initial concerns about him—probably because I have always resented people with wealth—I had learned to respect both his extraordinary commitment and his savvy. He was green as grass but eager to learn, and he learned quickly.

The conversation was free-flowing and inconclusive, but quite pleasant. I have loved my time in the movement and have developed pretty strong opinions on a range of issues. Randy asked lots of questions, sometimes tough ones, and after two or three hours of chatting, we went our separate ways. At the time, I did not know why he'd wanted to meet, but I had always enjoyed talking about my work. Later I realized Randy had pursued the subject because he was exploring the idea of adding a grassroots mobilization component to the Campaign Fund. Apparently, even though people at the Campaign Fund were uncertain how to do this, after our conversation Randy decided that merging the Fairness Fund into HRCF was the best way to go.

The Fairness Fund had rented space from the Campaign Fund some time earlier, but Vic Basile might have had reasonable doubts about supervising a strong-willed individual such as me. Despite misgivings, though, just before the Thanksgiving break in 1987 Vic asked me to consider merging the Fairness Fund into the Campaign Fund as its field division; given the Campaign Fund's strong fund-raising base—and the Fairness Fund's financial difficulties, which included some significant tax liabilities—it seemed like an easy decision. The Human Rights Campaign Fund had established a very strong and positive reputation that could attract people with the resources necessary to make a significant difference. Nonetheless, I knew it would be strange to work for a group I had originally founded.

As I considered the possibility of a merger, I knew I would have to avoid becoming involved in other aspects of the Campaign Fund operation. I knew not to observe closely our lobbying efforts, and this proved not to be so difficult since the Campaign Fund was preoccupied with AIDS at the time, while I remained more interested in the enactment of lesbian and gay rights laws. I also could not allow myself to focus on how or to whom the Campaign Fund gave its political contributions. Further, even though I had doubts about some aspects of the fund-raising program at the time, I knew I could not get involved in that either. In short, I had to be very clear that I was not returning to head the organization. Instead I had to continue to focus on how to address our movement's longstanding, and probably biggest, failure: its inability to move beyond platitudes about "grass roots" to real mobilization. That effort alone was more than enough to keep any two or three people completely preoccupied for years to come.

Lee Bush, on the other hand, preferred that we merge with the National Gay and Lesbian Task Force, an idea I was not inclined to accept. I remained angry that the Task Force had broken the agreement that the Gay Rights National Lobby would handle the national lobbying effort, while the Task Force would handle general education, media, and coordination and clearinghouse functions for local groups. Further, I knew that the Task Force had failed to establish the funding base necessary to undertake the task effectively. Merger with the Campaign Fund was the only way to build the proxy mailgram system I envisioned.

In the meantime, Steve Dwyer was working frantically with Tom Bastow, a member of the Fairness Fund board, to assess our debts and work out the details of the merger. The Fairness Fund board of directors, which was made up largely of longtime friends, former GRNL board members, and a sprinkling of others in key cities, had not shown a great collective capacity to raise funds. And, in fairness, most of them had reluctantly agreed to join the board as a means of supporting me. As part of the merger agreement, Vic Basile insisted that we help pay off any debts that we brought with us. Since Vic had not secured the financial advantages he had envisioned from the takeover of the Gay Rights National Lobby a couple of years earlier, he seemed determined not to make the same mistake twice. He was a tough negotiator.

To help with this effort, Tom Bastow—along with several terrific friends—agreed to hold a fund-raiser, which he pitched as a tribute to me. The event was very successful, though Tom explained later that it was far easier to pull off because the proceeds had gone to the Campaign Fund. Once the merger was accomplished, Vic insisted that I work to convert Fairness Fund major donors into Campaign Fund donors, and become involved in other one-to-one solicitations. Although I found it frustrating at the time, because it kept me from focusing full attention on grassroots organizing, eventually we were able to get out of debt and clear the way to build the constituent mail program.

Vic gave me some latitude to run the grassroots program, but initially we didn't get the financial support I had expected or needed to build participation in the mailgram program. When Steve Dwyer shifted to become the Campaign Fund's comptroller, we were not allowed to hire a successor due to limited resources. Somehow, having two, not three, people working on grassroots organizing was not the well-funded support I had in mind.

Back Home at HRCF

Our maiden legislative effort after the merger was on behalf of the first comprehensive AIDS legislation since the epidemic began. The bill, S. 1220, was authored by Senator Edward Kennedy of Massachusetts. With strong support from the board and Randy Klose in particular, Vic decided to put every possible effort into the campaign to pass the legislation. However, when the division director met to discuss various grassroots strategies to support the bill, I learned how little of my commitment to the National Mailgram Campaign was shared by the Campaign Fund.

To my surprise, HRCF decided to spend more than $25,000 on a mailing to senior citizens, who were proven letter writers. The mailing, pressed by the Campaign Fund's development director, Dick Dadey, generated over 1,000 personal letters. However, even though this mailing accomplished its purpose, these people had very little understanding of the issues they were writing about and had no ongoing commitment to AIDS or gay and lesbian rights. To say that Lee and I were frustrated and upset is a serious understatement. Had the Campaign Fund invested a similar amount of money in building the mailgram program, we would have had a network of about 4,000 to 5,000 people committed to sending repeated multiple mailgrams to Congress. But it was the first lesson in learning to be humble, which might have been part of Vic's point: I was not the boss.

Nonetheless, the Fairness Fund division, which eventually became the field division, accomplished important work in generating grassroots pressure in support of S. 1220. Lee worked the phones frantically to help initiate constituent lobby visits with key senators in more than fifteen states, and the Campaign Fund spent large amounts of money for advertising. Although I felt that too much emphasis was placed on creating the right organizational image and not enough on generating mail to Congress, the ads included the 800 number for our action hotline, and more than 1,500 mailgrams were generated from across the country.

When it was clear we couldn't get the Campaign Fund to fund our ambitious plans for building an ongoing proxy system, Lee and I settled for signing up as many people as possible for mailgrams on S. 1220 alone. As with most legislative battles on Capitol Hill, the exact timing of floor debate and vote continued to be a mystery. We heard—and spread—word of one deadline after another; no doubt some people began to wonder if it would ever really come up, and we looked uninformed and stupid more than once.

Finally, on a Wednesday, we were told that the vote would come up on the following Tuesday, posing the question, "How many people could we sign up in just five days?" Also, one had to allow a one-day buffer for Western Union to deliver the mailgrams. Our theory was that we would get people to preauthorize mailgrams on S. 1220 to their senators, in addition to whatever mailgrams were called in on our 800 Action Hotline. We telephoned everyone we could find in the key states: local gay and lesbian political groups or activists, AIDS organizations, local Metropolitan Community Churches, gay bars, etc.

The idea was that we would get people in each key state to sign up as many people as possible in the following three to four days and then call in the names, addresses, and phone numbers of each person. Because the mailgrams were charged to the senders' phone bills, our key volunteers didn't have to collect the money and participants did not need to send any payment. Lee and I made the calls to recruit these key volunteers from Wednesday through Saturday morning, and these organizers were supposed to call me collect at my home any time on Sunday.

After we finished our calls, all we could do was wait, but as the return calls started coming in that Sunday, chills raced down my spine. In some of the least-traveled highways and byways of gay and lesbian America, these dedicated organizers called in long lists of people agreeing to authorize mailgrams in support of S. 1220 and against any amendment offered by our most vicious opponent, Senator Jesse Helms. More than 2,500 mailgrams were called into me from all across the country in one day. I'm not particularly into abstract discussions about "empowerment," but this was the real thing. It may sound corny, but I felt like I was living the movie *Mr. Smith Goes to Washington.*

So many people helped in that effort I could never remember them all, but I recall some extraordinary people from some surprising places. They included Mark Bryant, an attractive, outgoing gay man who went out to the gay bars in Birmingham, Alabama, and signed up more than 100 people from that conservative Southern state. A lesbian MCC minister from Eureka Springs, Arkansas, doing the Lord's work, signed up almost 100 people for grassroots mail. A terrific community leader in Kansas City, Kay Madden, rounded up people there, while a former Washingtonian I had known, Gary Hoggard, got more than twenty-five people signed up from Springfield, Missouri. A bar owner in Tallahassee, Florida, even gave away free beers to anyone who would sign up and managed to bring on more than forty people in that conservative and closeted town.

Miracle workers just kept calling that day. A terrific woman in Augusta, Georgia, signed up forty folks, even though that city didn't even have an active gay and lesbian group at the time. Pat Coleman, then the publisher of *Etc.,* an Atlanta-based magazine, signed up more than 100 people. Don Randolph signed up more than sixty people in Omaha, Nebraska. Rev. Charlie Arehart, the pastor of the MCC in Denver, helped us enroll over ninety people, while Dr. Audrey Kick secured an additional seventy-five people to authorize from the rest of the state. The whole Illinois Fairness Fund crew, led by state chair Curt Hicks, enrolled more than 200 people. Brian DeWitt, who has worked tirelessly and usually without thanks in Cleveland gay activism for years, got more than 100 to participate and send mailgrams.

There were no doubt many others I now forget, but shortly after the conclusion of the effort, we gave "Make A Difference" Awards to a "dynamite dozen" of the most effective recruiters. The "Make a Difference" Awards were meant to say that everyone can change things if she or he chooses to do so, no matter where they live or what they do for a living.

The simple, easy, and inexpensive system we had advocated played a central role in the successful response to S. 1220, but it was the dedication of people all across the country that reinvigorated this old tired activist. When the vote finally came, Helms was defeated and S. 1220 became law. Probably for the first time, constituent mail and pressure had played an important role in the passage of a bill favorable to the gay and lesbian community. Senator Kennedy, the chief sponsor of the bill, spoke about the impact of the proxy mailgram program. He said, "the Fund's mailgrams were an extremely effective signal that the American people were urging prompt congressional action in the face of this public health epidemic."

While I regretted the misplaced expenditure for onetime letters from senior citizens, the positives of our new association with the Campaign Fund
outweighed the negative. Not only was I proud to be a part of such a committed and effective lobbying organization, I continued to fight for more resources for grassroots organizing in general and the National Mailgram
Campaign in particular. Because HRCF still was not providing the support I
felt we needed, I turned to the idea of getting gay businesses to sponsor our
outreach materials by offering them the opportunity to include their businesses' names on those materials. Although gay bars are constantly solicited for contributions to the large number of gay and AIDS groups, this approach offered participating businesses high visibility and, perhaps even
more important, a tax write-off for advertising.

I started with the Washington, DC, Eagle, a local bar I patronized that I
thought might agree to sponsor various promotional materials. I met with
the owner, Dick McHugh, and he agreed to sponsor the printing and distribution of great posters and hundreds of thousands of brochures on the
Mailgram Campaign, to be put in gay bars across the country. As part of the
package, we would include acknowledgement of the Eagle's sponsorship
on every single poster and brochure. In part because Dick felt he'd reached
his local market and would benefit from the national visibility, they agreed
to a several-thousand-dollar sponsorship package, and because of the Eagle's leadership, we were able to turn to countless bars and other businesses
across the country and secure their sponsorship as well. In return, we acknowledged the Eagle with one of our Community Service Awards for
helping build the program. Dick is an extremely nice guy with a good social
consciousness and we related very well, but the fact that he often saw me in
his bar probably didn't hurt us, either.

Unfortunately, mailings to local groups seeking help in building the
Mailgram Campaign met with almost stony silence, though there were a
few exceptions. I chalked up our original lack of success to badly drafted
letters, but the simple fact is that local groups were clearly too busy or too
disinterested to respond. On the other hand, religious groups such as Dignity and the Universal Fellowship of Metropolitan Community Churches
did a great deal to promote the program, including "piggybacking" the
proxy-mail program in their mailings. In fairness, when we directly called
—and reached—local gay and lesbian groups we sometimes got them to do
these piggybacks of brochures also. The gay and lesbian press across the
country also helped by printing free ads, and running articles and editorials
about the program. *The Advocate,* which had been my nemesis in the past,
was particularly supportive.

In the fall of 1988 we got a real break. The San Francisco–based NAMES
Project announced that it was bringing the massive Quilt display back to

Washington, DC, to appear on the grounds of the Ellipse (the large lawn area on the Washington Mall between the White House and the Washington Monument). The Quilt had last been displayed in Washington during the 1987 march, and its return promised to bring tens, and maybe hundreds of thousands of gay men, lesbians, and friendly supporters streaming into Washington for its display. This was a large pool of people who might be willing not only to participate in our mailgram program but who, in fact, were anxious to do whatever they could to help end the AIDS crisis.

Vic Basile wanted the Campaign Fund to use the presence of the Quilt to raise their own visibility. Although Vic had never been particularly close to NAMES Project executive director Cleve Jones (I'd even heard someone around our offices describe Cleve as "MLQ," standing for "Martin Luther Queen"—although Vic has since denied ever saying it), he retained consultants to help promote the Campaign Fund. While I thought they overcharged for their services, they did design a dynamite button with the pink triangle replacing one of the stars on the American flag. We have since distributed hundreds of thousands of these buttons to people enrolling in our program, and the design later became the ongoing symbol of our Speak Out program.

Largely because of Cleve's good relationship with Lee Bush, Cleve agreed that the Campaign Fund would be the only other national group allowed to participate in the momentous occasion. Our booth was on the way to the actual display of Quilt panels. Determined to seize the opportunity, Lee and I decided we'd get out there and try to sign up as many people as possible during the three days of the display. While we didn't think of it as "canvassing," and have always considered our later trip to Ohio as the trip that pioneered the canvass approach, we poured our hearts and souls into getting as many people as possible signed up.

I challenged Lee to try to beat me. While he was more lovable than I was, that hardly left him short on competitive spirit. In addition, several other people helped us sign up people for the National Mailgram Campaign, although most of the other Campaign Fund staff focused on other efforts, including a ploy called the "world's largest mailgram," which was designed to build an enhanced mailing list. In order to avoid getting teary eyed, I had to avoid looking at the Quilt panels until the very end of the weekend. Otherwise, I never would have been able to muster the assertiveness it took to sign people up for constituent mail. Over the three days, we signed up more than 1,200 people. Years later, I found out that at least two of those that I signed up that weekend in October went on to become cochairs of the Campaign Fund dinners in San Francisco and Philadelphia. In both cases, their enrollment was their first contact with the Human Rights Campaign Fund.

Chapter 6

Speak Out

Despite the boost from the AIDS Memorial Quilt display in Washington, the mailgram campaign still was not making the quantum leap in numbers we needed. Although the misconceptions about organized mail campaigns not working were overstated, we clearly needed to enroll some threshold number of participants in each district and state across the country in order to be taken seriously. Our current approach was not getting these numbers, and we had to find a way to transform the program.

Ironically, the impetus for that transformation came from a phone call I got from a former Western Union representative, Emily DeWitt, who had moved to a new firm and wanted our business. During that conversation she outlined a prepaid approach in which overnight messages would be purchased in advance and the decision of when to send them and on what issues was delegated to us. Although there were distinct advantages to such a system from our point of view, it didn't have the advantage of the easy, painless "charge on the phone bill" approach. The question was whether people would pay in advance; but if participants were most attracted to the convenience of someone else doing the work of writing to Congress rather than to the billing system, then the change would probably fly. Most important from an organizational point of view, the new prepaid approach offered the possibility of building significant resources that could be plowed back into this organizing venture, resources for direct mail to expand the base of participation and to pay people a decent fee to sign up others.

We explained to Vic Basile that if people responded positively, we could totally transform the program, turn it into a revenue producer to pay for all of the associated expenses, and even hire the full-time regional organizers we needed; he agreed to allow us to do the test mailing. Besides Lee Bush, Steve Dwyer, and myself, however, nobody really believed that the new approach would work or paid much attention to the idea. The test results came out better than we could have hoped, with the mailing more than breaking even and a good number of people signing up. So HRCF agreed that we could go forward. The challenge was to come up with effective marketing strategies to expand participation. When we told the board about the change and the potential it would give the field division—in terms of both grass-roots organizing and as a revenue producer—the only request was that we develop a catchy name for the program. Thus, the National Mailgram Campaign became Speak Out.

We tried inserting Speak Out brochures in local gay newspapers, but our efforts were unsuccessful. Then, as we considered the glut of gay direct mail in a far too limited market and explored what other marketing strategies might work, an intern, Eric Peters, suggested that we should consider an assertive canvass-type effort at various gay community events such as gay and lesbian Pride days. Given our previous experience, I thought that it was a pretty farfetched idea.

Before I knew it, however, we had a chance to try Eric's suggestion. Lee learned that the NAMES Project Quilt was scheduled to visit Cincinnati and Columbus, Ohio, on successive weekends. The Quilt was drawing huge crowds across the country, so it seemed likely that a lot of people would be present. Despite the fact that neither of us had actually done this kind of enrollment before, Lee and I decided to drive to Ohio for the two weekends of Quilt appearances. In between the weekends, we could visit both Toledo and Detroit, for grassroots organizing as well as "personal outreach."

When Lee talked with activists in Cincinnati and Columbus, they all warned us that Cincinnati was very conservative and politically apathetic. Although most thought Columbus would be better, they were not sure that the NAMES Project people would let us canvass there. Since many of the people attending the Quilt would not be lesbian or gay, NAMES Project people assumed that no one would sign up and that our goal of 200 to 300 people might be overly ambitious.

The organizers of the Cincinnati display were apprehensive about the presence of political groups, but after a heavy dose of Lee's Irish charm, they agreed to let us stand outside the large downtown civic center where the event was held. Lee had arranged to get some help from the gay youth group, but it turned out that only one of them was really able to assist significantly. The young man, Martin, was very young but quite dedicated (he also had a furious crush on Lee). Because the showing of the Quilt stretched over three days, people trickled in and out during the course of at least twelve hours each day.

Lee and I took a place near the entrances with clipboards and the enrollment petitions in hand. As people headed in, one of us would approach them and ask for a moment of their time. Although people were often surprised to be solicited—and were probably worried at first that we were fundamentalists—they had not yet been hardened by constantly being canvassed, as are people in cities such as New York or Boston. We gave everyone who signed up one of the leftover buttons from HRCF's efforts at

Speak Out Brochure. Courtesy of HRC.

the Quilt the previous fall, so we could tell who had signed up and who hadn't. I concluded that the label of "apathetic" was quite unfair and, in fact, the people we met in Cincinnati were among the most polite people I'd ever met. But that isn't to say that a small minority—both gay and nongay alike—wouldn't have preferred to enter as quickly and unobtrusively as possible, and some went to great lengths to avoid us.

After the first day's work we rushed back to the Holiday Inn and counted how many names we'd gotten. Our first day's total of almost 200 people was amazing to both of us and indicated a solid success. We were just as exhausted as we were happy, so although we had planned on going to the bars, raising hell, and, hopefully, getting laid, we could barely stay awake for our room service burgers to arrive. We were asleep by 8:30 p.m.

Over the course of the weekend, we had some amazing moments. Once, as a large family came to the entrance, Lee gleefully pointed out that it was my turn to make the approach. Even though other nongay people had already signed up during the weekend, getting over our own ingrained homophobia and fear of rejection was not easy, even for a brazen, longtime activist such as myself. I put a friendly smile on my face and stepped forward to talk with the family, which consisted of about ten people—not an ideal size to canvass. I concluded that it was a grandmother, several aunts and uncles, and a couple of their kids. I don't know if they had a relative who had died of AIDS or what it was that brought them to the Quilt that day, but every single adult in the group of ten signed up. After they were safely out of sight, Lee and I just looked at each other in amazement. I think at that precise moment we knew that canvassing for Speak Out would work. When we went back to the hotel room after the third and final day, we counted again. Even though it was early March, the weather was great and we got results far better than we could have hoped. In the competition between us, I'd narrowly beaten Lee's total, and overall more than 600 people signed up that weekend!

I have done a lot of direct canvassing since that weekend, but I will never forget our experience in Cincinnati. It was tough work, even for two brassy folks like us. We tried to be sensitive to people's "Quilt experience"—for example, we would not approach people who were leaving in tears—but we quickly found that countless people left wanting desperately to get involved, and they thanked us profusely for being there. (It didn't occur to me until later, but my only preparation for this sort of assertive task was selling salted-in-the-shell peanuts and ice cream in the stands of Minnesota Twins and Minnesota Vikings games as I grew up. Since we were paid on commission, it was imperative to really hustle.)

Before our return the following weekend for the Quilt display in Columbus, we headed off to Toledo, where we had a lunchtime meeting with local activists, and then went to Detroit, where we planned a little recreational and personal "constituent outreach." The highlight of our Detroit trip came as Lee and I were driving to the Michigan Organization for Human Rights (MOHR) offices to meet several activists for lunch. En route, I pulled into a drugstore lot to check under the hood because the rental car was suddenly running very poorly. When Lee lifted the hood, we discovered a very large, confused raccoon. Freaked out, Lee dropped the hood, which probably further irritated the raccoon. I ran into the drugstore to borrow a stick or something to get him out of there. When I came back, Lee again opened the hood, while I poked the raccoon with a stick until he took off. Suddenly, this Detroit neighborhood had two gay men, who liked to think of themselves as "butch," screaming as we tried to figure out where he'd gone. When we finally concluded that he was gone, we discovered that he'd chewed half the engine wires to shreds. We had to return the rental car and get a new one.

With the excitement of our Detroit trip behind us, we headed back to Columbus. Unfortunately, the early spring weather went from T-shirt mild in Cincinnati to snow and parkas in Columbus. This meant we could not stand outside and stop people casually walking in and out. Instead, people rushed to and from their cars to get inside and they did not want to be stopped.

The weather was not our greatest logistical problem, however. The local Quilt committee in Columbus included several control freaks, determined to exercise their decision-making authority, regardless of the consequences, on the issue of whether mail could be generated to Congress to combat AIDS. We had already proven we could be sensitive to people's "Quilt experience," but it was precisely the people who came to such displays—gay, lesbian, and nongay alike—that we needed to reach. Our experience in Cincinnati showed that these people would be most likely to sign up to help impact public policy on AIDS. Happily, Lee was a smooth talker, the Columbus committee included a number of people also associated with the Campaign Fund, and the committee even had one well-connected, well-liked HRCF board member, Steve Shellabarger. We were allowed to continue to canvass, and even though a couple of difficult people on the committee kept forcing us to move our location, we still signed up more than 600 additional people in Columbus.

Overall, people have been quite nice when our canvassers have approached them, and lesbians have responded far better than gay men have. Tens of thousands of gay men have been supportive, but women have been far more likely to sign up. One explanation might be that many lesbians have already had experience in the women's movement and are therefore more politically responsive. Another might be that men may be more competitive and somehow think the person trying to sign them up is trying to put something over on them. But, no matter how you slice it, the lesbian community has responded wonderfully, even though many of the messages we activated have been regarding AIDS rather than lesbian and gay rights.

The Columbus event was the first of many occasions where we encountered a problem that arose at Quilt displays and even at some gay events, including a few Pride Days. Event organizers were often more concerned with calling the shots and setting up rules than with the impact of those rules. Few seemed to consider the possibility that they might adversely affect the community's ability to generate constituent mail which can help translate pride into political power.

A few months after our trip to Cincinnati and Columbus we hit the high-water mark of selfish control for its own sake at the display of the Quilt in Pittsburgh. Lee was busy somewhere else on enrollment, so Damien, a high-strung but nice guy that had come on staff as canvass assistant for the Pride period, another guy, and I drove to Pittsburgh. They had planned to go alone, but because the organizers of the Pittsburgh display had told us they didn't want anything "political" there, I was apprehensive and thought my presence might help straighten it out.

After they first tried to turn us down over the phone, we explained that we would be happy to stay outside the civic center. Damien further pointed out that we could do "free speech" activities outside without their permission. With the help of the director of the local AIDS group, we reached an agreement with the local Quilt organizers that we would stay outside. Or so we thought. But when the Quilt opened Friday evening, Committee Chair Robert Masacone, whom I later discovered was very, very unpopular in Pittsburgh, raised holy hell about our presence outside. The director of the local AIDS group, who was both powerful and very supportive, wasn't there and was unreachable. After some negotiations, Masacone finally agreed that night that we could stay—but only at one of the two doors.

Despite Masacone's concerns about the event not being political— which is absurd since the entire issue of AIDS is political—I later learned that the person he had permitted to read names at the opening ceremonies was the city councilperson who had betrayed the community by casting the deciding vote in killing the local gay and lesbian rights ordinance. And I found out that Planned Parenthood had a pro-choice petition inside, so his hassles weren't about anything except his desire to control things. However, people responded very well, and we concluded Friday night with good numbers of new Speak Out participants.

The next day, Saturday, we discovered that Masacone was now insisting we move further toward the street. Although initially we were concerned that this would hurt our chances of getting people enrolled, we acceded to his demands because we did not want any controversy that might hinder our ability to participate at other Quilt appearances. Despite these restrictions, we continued to get a great response from those attending. In part because he saw this great response, Masacone then insisted that the local police stop us from continuing to canvass on the grounds of the civic center at all, and because we had no solicitation permit they could do it. The police were very nice and told us they did not want to enforce the permit requirement, and suggested that if we just move out a little further, which put us almost in the street, Masacone might not force the issue.

In spite of our efforts to appease him, Masacone forced the police to return, and at his insistence we were told to stop canvassing or face arrest. Reluctantly, we stopped, went back to the motel, packed, and drove back to Washington, DC. Because of his outrageous behavior, we missed the opportunity to enroll 500 to 600 people for repeated mailgrams to Pennsylvania Senators H. John Heinz (R) and Arlen Spector (R), who were key and often undecided votes. Later, Masacone was virtually ridden out of town on a rail by the gay community, and his treatment of us was only one example of his outrageous behavior.

For all the difficulty with Quilt committees in some cities, we were warmly received in others Also, we got plenty of support and help from the national NAMES Project staff in those critical early years. Cleve Jones, the founder and initial director of the NAMES Project, was a longtime gay activist I'd known and respected for many years. Cleve understood the value of what we were doing and, to the extent that national organization affected local committees, we usually benefited. We also received help from Joe Van Ness Balleros and Mike Bento, who played key roles with the national group as the Quilt traveled. Unfortunately, when Cleve, Joe, and others left the NAMES Project staff, that measure of cooperation was replaced with almost across-the-board resistance, despite promises to the contrary. While the Quilt continued to travel the country and visited many smaller communities where constituent mail was even more important, we usually were not permitted to canvass the crowds. At one point, the NAMES Project established a post card campaign. Aside from the fact that post cards don't have the impact of mailgrams, they were one-shot deals. Over time our canvass people tired of the constant resistance and we stopped even spending much energy on trying to get in.

By April 1989, Lee and I decided to put together enrollment efforts at various Pride Days in June. By then, we had shifted from the charge-on-the-phone system to the prepay system, which meant that resources previously handed over to Western Union now stayed with us to handle associated overhead. So, while suddenly we could afford to pay Speak Out volunteers or canvassers $1 per name, we had no time to find these people in time for the 1989 Pride days. Much of the pressure for direct canvassing still fell directly on Lee and me.

One opportunity that came up that spring was the first March on Austin for lesbian and gay rights. There had long been discussions about having state-level marches across the country, but this one in Texas was one of the first. Neither of us had been to Austin before and no one could know whether the march would be well attended. We decided it was worth the gamble and that we would have a good time, regardless.

There were countless events leading up to the Sunday march. Lee and I arrived in Austin on Wednesday—in part to get a feel for things, in part to raise some hell. It was a very exciting weekend. To get ready for the march, Lee approached Austin's professional canvass groups to find experienced canvassers who wanted to make spare money. With the promise of help from the pro canvassers of groups such as the Peace and Justice Coalition, Greenpeace, and Sane Freeze, Lee held careful training sessions so they'd be adequately prepared. Robert Bray, the Campaign Fund's new public relations director, also came down and spent a fair amount of time helping Lee and I sign people up at the various pre-march events. Although he did not understand the program at first, he quickly caught on and proved to be as assertive as Lee or I.

It was during this initial march in Austin, in April 1989, that I first noticed a connection between my own canvassing and those unpleasant HIV-related canker sores in my mouth. With more than twenty-five sores, I was in no shape for personal "constituent outreach," and the night before the actual march, I went to bed at 7:30 p.m. unable even to eat because of the discomfort in my mouth.

The day of the march, Lee and I got up very early. While he went to round up the other canvassers, I convinced myself to get my mouth working enough so that potential enrollees could understand me. Even so, I was so early that I was one of the first five people there. As people arrived and before there was any real action, I had tremendous success in signing up new participants. The incredible responsiveness of the crowd led me to shout out my explanation of the program and to hand out my four clipboards with sign-up sheets like playing cards. When the march itself started, I gave up on trying to canvass the moving crowd and ran ahead to sign people up at the rally site.

Once people assembled for the rally up on the grounds of the state capitol, we ran into an unexpected if reasonable barrier—people actually wanted to hear the speakers and didn't want to be bothered by us. I finally figured out that we could position ourselves at the head of the long lines to the porta-potties a little ways off, and there I yelled out "nobody goes to the john till they sign up for grassroots mail to Congress." Luckily, everyone laughed and grabbed the clipboards.

Our canvassers took advantage of every line at the festival. Lee, Robert, and I were joined by Randy Klose and his sister, Carole Lee, who were from Texas, and Hilary Rosen, Campaign Fund cochair, who was one of the key speakers. Each of them pitched in to help sign people up after the rally. With the heat, people were backed up forty to fifty deep in the beer and soda lines, so Hilary and I just started a few people from the front and worked our way back, signing up people all along the way. By the time the day ended almost twelve hours later, I had signed up more people than I ever had before, or have since—about 310 new people. It's funny, but as Lee and I went out to dinner with Randy Klose, Carole Lee, and her lover, I noticed my sores seemed much better.

Usually when I got past my psychological and physical barriers, I was vividly reminded of why the work was so worthwhile. Even though we sometimes ran into difficult, unpleasant, or rude people, far more often people overcame their initial reluctance at being approached by strangers and heard us out. Many signed up, giving this far-away, national group authorization to send mailgrams to Congress on their behalf. Actually, when you think about all the barriers, it's amazing people have been so responsive. I was moved by the countless people who were so thrilled to make a difference.

With the march on Austin behind us, we had almost no time for the war-like planning that we have come to learn is needed to take full advantage of lesbian and gay Pride Day festivals. Nonetheless, Speak Out enrollment continued to swell. Lee covered Los Angeles as well as several other Pride days. David Simmons, who had come on some time earlier as the administrative assistant to the division, coordinated our outreach at the Boston, New York, and Washington, DC, Pride Days with the energetic assistance of Damien Alexander. I coordinated our Long Beach; Portland, Oregon (on Saturday); and Seattle (by driving up that night to cover it on Sunday) Pride Days, and then flew into Chicago for the next weekend's Pride events. All in all, despite the short notice we had to prepare for the Gay Pride festivals, and despite the retention of a difficult and incompetent assistant, we signed up about 13,000 people in a handful of cities across the country. Finally, we were on our way!

Finding Canvassers

A major challenge was to find enough canvassers to sign up new Speak Out participants. Even though we could now afford to pay canvassers a decent part-time wage, we had a hard time finding enough dedicated people to help us, particularly on an ongoing basis. But with most gay and lesbian crowds fairly responsive, we had learned that the key variable to how many people we signed up was how many canvassers we could find. Under Lee's leadership and then that of Cathy Nelson, our approach to finding canvassers became more structured and more successful.

To enlist canvassers we tried placing flyers in gay bars and other gathering places, and in mailings to gay, lesbian, and AIDS groups, so their people could make spare money or raise funds for their groups. We advertised in local gay and lesbian papers, as well as in the alternative press, and tried both classified and space ads; *The Advocate* even ran our ads for free, which helped us reach out nationally. We also wrote current Speak Out members to remind them of the chance to make extra money while making a difference. Our canvass staff phoned thousands of potential canvassers across the country, and, as our local Speak Out coordinators got into place, they did the same thing within their communities. We wrote letters to the editor and op-ed pieces for numerous newspapers promoting canvass opportunities, and we even established a toll-free 800 number so potential Speak Out canvassers could call in to explore the opportunities.

Yet often we were not able to find people to cover a community event or we came up with far fewer volunteers than we needed for large events such as Pride Days—and then most of them didn't show up. We heard some of the innovative, bizarre explanations and excuses for why they didn't come: I remember one woman who explained she'd been hit by a car.

While we fought like hell to find the canvassers we needed, we were also fighting a rearguard action in the form of criticism from a few activists who argued that our proxy system "took people's power away." I saw it as completely the opposite. I've always felt that most people don't especially want to be "activists" but they do want to make a difference, particularly in the context of the AIDS crisis. Most lesbians and gay men live very busy lives and far fewer are "political" than I might wish, but that's probably the same as within most other constituencies, with the apparent notable recent exception of fundamentalists. To anticipate that large numbers of gay men and lesbians, scattered across the country, would carefully monitor congressional developments and sit down and write thoughtful letters to their members of Congress each time a key vote came up seemed to me totally unrealistic at best.

"Empowerment" is an idea far too many people like to talk about but far too few truly work to implement. It takes a lot of hard work to turn "grassroots" into a reality. One of the most empowering things I could think of was success, and for too long gay activists had expected people in the community to keep fighting after getting their teeth kicked in again and again. We had to break the cycle.

Some activists' demands that people spend countless hours on activism and/or take to the streets in order to prove they aren't apathetic are not only unrealistic, they aren't "empowering." Self-righteous demands that everyone must come out or be denounced as "closet queens" are also hardly words of empowerment. So, although the criticism of a handful of activists that Speak Out and the Campaign Fund were not empowering people irritated me, I didn't seriously worry that their criticism was valid. Instead, we employed the old sales axiom of "taking people from where they are" by making it simple and easy for people to participate. Once we got people in the door and made them feel good about their participation, showing them the tremendous difference they were making, I felt we could plug them into other grassroots organizing efforts. In fact, many who originally signed up for Speak Out have gone on to meet with members of Congress when they're back in the district, volunteer for supportive congressional candidates, host house meetings, help sign up other people for Speak Out, and so on. Later, in recognition of their contribution to our overall mission, HRCF made each Speak Out participant an automatic member of the Campaign Fund.

Once we'd transformed the finances of Speak Out, we finally convinced Vic to let us fill the administrative assistant vacancy that had existed since Steve Dwyer had become comptroller. We got extraordinarily lucky, finding a young, pleasant man named David Simmons, who had recently come on Campaign Fund staff as the receptionist. The two of us could not possibly have been more different, with David being a vegetarian and a donor to animal rights groups and me then living on fast food and feeling a bit negative about such politically correct positions as "animal rights." David sometimes came into work with his hair sort of "spiked." On the other hand, he clearly possessed an unusual degree of maturity and stability, and cheerfully handled the countless details and loose threads that a so-called big-idea person could not; and, despite his rather unusual approach, he was actually somewhat conservative for a movement person. We agreed far more often than not, and he came on just in time to help save a good idea from collapsing from the weight of its own administrative details—or lack thereof.

If Speak Out were to reach full potential and secure a strong renewal, we had to straighten out all the administrative complexities of such a program. Reports on the Speak Out messages had to go out often and regularly, and we began publication of an attractive newsletter for Speak Out participants called "Capitol Hill Update." Our new system may have freed resources to support the program, but it also meant that we'd have to create and handle a billing system. Soon we'd also have the opportunity, or challenge, of renewing people—most of whom had signed up for only three messages initially. David arranged the insertion of Speak Out brochures and space ads in the gay press, which is no minor task. Finally, there were the actual "activations" themselves, in which we sent three different versions of these overnight messages to members of Congress from their own constituents.

It sounds easy, but it sometimes included sending messages only from "people with five messages or more left" in selected districts and states, with different messages going to committee or subcommittee members. All the nuances may be confusing to outsiders, but it ensured we'd "spend" people's messages carefully, saving messages for key issues coming a bit down the road. David's mastery of the computer system allowed us to carefully juggle competing concerns, and his pleasant, patient personality helped Speak Out to survive and thrive. There's no way to explain David Simmons's pivotal role in the successful creation and growth of the Speak Out program.

A classic example of the program's impact came up when a new congressional session began. Each session, our lobbyists had to undertake the tedious task of re-signing all of the previous session's cosponsors of the national lesbian and gay civil rights bill, as well as get many more. One senator who had previously cosponsored was facing a tough reelection and didn't seem to be coming back on the bill. After weeks of lobbying brought no action, our legislative director asked us to send Speak Out messages to the senator from everyone signed up in his state.

The next day we sent three versions of an overnight message to him from the 600 constituents in Speak Out from his state. A call the very next day from his Washington staff person demonstrated the effect our "orchestrated" mail could have: "Enough already! Call off Western Union. The senator is back on the bill." That case was but one example of what Western Union and the other vendors of these overnight mailgrams mean when they say "high impact." The senator subsequently won solid reelection, with a Campaign Fund contribution and the help of HRCF-volunteer mobilization, and he's signed back on again, without prodding. This was duplicated when three House members agreed to cosponsor the National Gay and Lesbian Civil Rights bill during 1991 as a direct result of receiving Speak Out messages. In two of the three cases, we were able to identify additional factors, but the Speak Out messages clearly played a key role in their taking the final hurdle.

If we'd proven that the program worked, and dodged the bullet by finding David Simmons and cleaning up our administrative messes, we had a new trauma thrown at us when, amazingly, Western Union—which was the vendor for our overnight messages to Congress—challenged the constitutionality of California's lesbian and gay civil rights ordinances. We learned of this impending doom when a Campaign Fund staff person happened to notice a small article in one of the gay papers about how Western Union was, in the process of defending themselves from a charge of antigay discrimination in San Francisco, contending that California's local lesbian and gay rights ordinances were unconstitutional. Since we had built the Speak Out system on the sending of Western Union mailgrams, it was clear that their action could have a clear and quick negative impact on our constituent mail program.

California activists can be a bit pure and strident, to the rest of us anyway, but they'd surely have a right to go nuts if the Campaign Fund continued doing business—or sending messages on their behalf—through a company actually trying to take away their rights. We immediately contacted our account representative, Ed Locke, to demand that they end their challenge to the ordinances in order to keep our business, as well as avoid a potentially nationwide boycott. We'd worked with Ed for two or three years; he started out pretty uncomfortable with the issue but was a good guy and had slowly grown more relaxed. He promised to pursue the matter vigorously and we had no doubt he would, since he had a lot of commission riding on it. However, when he'd taken the matter up the corporate ladder and exhausted all avenues of recourse, the answer was that they would not end their challenge.

Our new executive director, Tim McFeeley (1989-1995), who'd been a corporate lawyer himself and is a hell of a negotiator, entered into dialogue with Western Union's legal counsel in New Jersey, but to no avail. We had no choice but to announce publicly that we were leaving Western Union over the issue, thereby turning lemons into lemonade within the community. After some searching, we settled on a new vendor, Telepost, and discovered, to our surprise, that the change resulted in a net savings.

The publicity that resulted from our departure—which was covered not only in the gay press nationwide but in nongay media in California and in the *Wall Street Journal*—resulted in serious pressure on Western Union. To our shock, we received a call out of the blue three or four months later from Western Union. They flew in, met with us, and gave HRCF $100,000 in free services, a clumsy attempt to clean up the public relations mess they'd created. Of course, we accepted their gift, but didn't shift back to them. Despite our good feelings for Ed, our account representative, we were now getting a better deal and couldn't afford to return to them if we wanted to. It's no wonder that Western Union was on the verge of bankruptcy.

With the administrative details coming together under David's leadership, Western Union's gift of services helped us undertake important Speak Out direct mail. In addition, with the change in the program creating resources to devote to grassroots organizing, HRCF's new director, Tim

McFeeley, was letting us hire the field staff we needed to build Speak Out and generate other forms of grassroots pressure.

We ran into a serious bump, though, when Lee Bush, now our national canvass manager, had to leave staff and go on disability at the beginning of 1990 after lingering illnesses associated with AIDS the previous fall. Lee had done a very good job and had been a constant partner as we pioneered the program. We'd counted on his charm and good humor to offset my aggressive, goal-oriented, "type A" approach. His easy-going style complemented my own relentless approach. I've been blessed with lots of close friends but none has been quite like Lee, who was like a brother to me, both in terms of how close we were and how furiously we could fight. And we were both primarily attracted to black men, so going out cruising in our spare time was great fun—even if it was a little competitive. Much of that early period had as much to do with our great times together as it did with the extraordinary energy and love we poured into the creation of Speak Out. Despite our furious and loud fights in the office, I counted on his friendship tremendously. We did the work but also ran the streets, raised hell, and generally had a great time. I doubt if he realized how hard it was for me to go on without him. When he passed away in September 1991, it was a very difficult personal loss.

Instead of hiring a national canvass manager to replace Lee and his assistant, Damian (who had also left a couple of months earlier), we hired two new people to serve as the eastern and western state canvass managers. Their task was to build on the previous year's experience and sign up many more people than the 25,000 we had enrolled in 1989. To do that, they'd have to be less dependent on HRCF staff canvassing and get people around the country to lead these efforts, and this hadn't been particularly successful in 1989. Generally previous experience had shown that if Lee, Damien, or I directly undertook the effort, we could count on a dramatically higher number of people signed up than if we left it to others. So any change would be a serious challenge, but we really had little choice if the program was going to grow.

To assist our new canvass coordinators and reduce direct staff canvassing, we added a new level of "staffing" across the country. Basically, the idea was to find ongoing Speak Out coordinators, which we called area canvass supervisors (ACSs), everywhere. Their job would be to recruit the people they needed, train them, and find local events for them to canvass. The change to the Speak Out prepaid approach had created funds for us to pay our Speak Out canvassers $1 a name for people they signed up. Although the idea of getting volunteers to do this task is glamorous, the truth is that this was a task many people didn't particularly enjoy, so the payments were quite important.

Now, with the advent of the ACS system, we'd pay our local coordinators an additional fee per name for all those signed up by the canvassers under them. This change would allow us to create an ongoing presence in countless cities across the country. Even though we were able to provide these modest funds, it's clear that our ongoing local coordinators—as well as the vast majority of those canvassing for us—did this thankless work primarily because they understood how important it was to finally generate sustained and substantial mail to Congress on AIDS and lesbian and gay rights. They deserve the community's undying gratitude.

Since we always needed every possible canvasser, I kept my hands—and aggressiveness—in the direct canvassing. Besides, it turns out that I was a pretty fair canvasser. Although I suspected that my boss, Tim McFeeley, saw it as a sign of retarded management, I knew I could better understand what was happening out there by directly canvassing, at least during Pride time, when we needed everyone we could get. On the front lines, I saw what our coordinators and volunteers ran into, what people were saying about Speak Out and the Campaign Fund. For instance, my experience in direct canvassing convinced me, despite others' doubts, that we could increase the message minimum from three messages to four without it hurting the enrollment. (My physical reaction to canvassing was not pleasant, though. My HIV-positive status and the stress of canvassing often resulted in massive outbreaks of very painful canker sores on and under my tongue just before major canvass events. They made it difficult to talk, let alone canvass. For some reason, these sores always seemed to appear when I went to Texas, which irritated me because I loved the Texas activists and used to get dates there with great regularity.)

Thanks to the new system, and the work of our two canvass managers and their temporary Pride assistants, the number of people signed up during the May-June Pride period soared to almost 30,000 in 1990. Eastern states canvass manager Cathy Nelson did particularly well, and, shortly after Pride, became the national canvass manager. Cathy brought extensive union organizing experience, and tremendous dedication and detail orientation, to her task. She quickly realized how vital the area canvass supervisors were to our success, and hers, and began to create a real team atmosphere—no small feat for a far-flung, long-distance system like ours. She did weekly mailings to her canvass supervisors, including reports on how canvassing was going in other parts of the country and how the constituent mail was being used on Capitol Hill. Sometimes, they included Tootsie Rolls or other candy as a fun idea.

Cathy brought equal parts of nurturing and cajoling to her communications with her coordinators, and weekly she talked with ACSs from coast to coast: Jim McCarthy from Dayton, Ohio; Lena Thompson from Detroit;

John Larkin in San Francisco; John Hedberg, and then Ken Sanes in Boston; and so on. People come and go and burn out is a very real factor in this area, and Cathy understood it was their desire to make a difference, not the modest funds they'd make, which drove them. It was only a good deal later that I realized just how good she was at team building.

Shortly after Pride, one of our temporary Pride assistants, Tom Swift, stepped up to become her assistant, bringing extraordinary enthusiasm and innovation. The first thing one noticed about Tom was his bright red hair and pinkish complexion but also as quickly one could sense an incredible fire in his belly to make a difference. He had been an actor, performing in prisons among other places and, in fact, had had very little experience in organizing. But what he lacked in experience or formal training, he more than made up in butt-busting dedication. Tom would simply do whatever it took to get it done. If it couldn't be done, well, he wouldn't let that stop him, either; he'd just find a way. Beneath the incredible commitment, I discovered that he was also pretty good at "constituent outreach," and, like Lee and me, was attracted primarily to black men.

Before 1990 ended, Cathy's and Tom's efforts had brought almost 50,000 people into Speak Out. Our canvassing initiatives continued to diversify, focusing on much, much more than just lesbian and gay Pride Days, Quilt appearances, and AIDS walks. Our task was to directly, and assertively, get to our supporters wherever they gathered, and although Speak Out included nongay people, our top priority was to reach lesbians and gay men. Since most often the gay community got together to party, our people had some very unique canvassing "opportunities."

There was the time our southeast regional field coordinator, Cathy Woolard, tried to sign up the thousands of scantily clad, very nonpolitical boys at the Hot Atlanta Raft Races and at Splash Day in Austin, Texas, where they skinny-dip. There were the nights in the early days when our Illinois state coordinator, Curt Hicks, set up an ironing board in front of the gay bars on Chicago's Halsted Street, yelling, "We're pressing for change!" There were the sign-up efforts at any number of bike-a-thons for AIDS, including one in the Rockies. I still don't really understand how our canvassers could get bikers signed up, but then our people did the same at roller-skating parties as well. And, of course, there have been dozens of times when our dedicated volunteers have charged into the often dark and noisy recesses of gay bars to reach the community where it often gathers. It's among the more difficult challenges to scream over the blare of the music to sometimes loaded customers about constituent mail when they came in to dance, cruise, or just get laid. Finally, there's our persistent Provincetown canvassers who not only get people at the night spots and throughout town, but who actually trudge through the sand dunes to approach buck-naked gay men and bare-breasted lesbians sunbathing. More than once, from what I've heard, they've tried to sign up the director of our sister and somewhat competitive national group, the National Gay and Lesbian Task Force.

The 1991 task was to build on previous experience—and sign up far more people than before. Although the system of local Speak Out coordinators or ACSs had worked well, we could see that more staff for direct supervision of such coordinators and canvassers was critical. We especially needed a West Coast–based staffer, as there were so many gay and lesbian community events in the region. Also, the weather was warm and there were concentrated gay areas where we could have street canvassing. Finally, with recent population shifts, there were many marginal districts in California, Oregon, and Washington State.

We built the position of a full-time West Coast canvass coordinator into the 1991 budget; but, because of cash flow, Cathy wasn't able to hire for the position until the spring—too late to fully utilize for the quickly approaching Pride season. Cathy flew west and eventually hired our dynamic San Diego ACS, Rene Narvaez, as our West Coast coordinator. She came on quickly and did a great job. In addition, we ran full-page ads in the gay press to make sure people knew about Speak Out, and sent out press releases and op-eds. Classifieds were placed to find paid Speak Out volunteers, providing a toll-free 800 number so would-be canvassers could call in. In many places, Tom Swift managed to secure unbelievable help from professional canvass groups—the CLEC network, Greenpeace, Clean Water Action, Sane Freeze, local PIRGs, and so on.[1] He directly coordinated armies of canvassers in Boston and New York, as well as supervising outreach at Philadelphia.

By hook and by crook, we'd talked with probably more than 3,000 people interested in canvassing, and more than 1,000 people actually canvassed. We signed people up at more than ninety Pride events in a little more than a month. Our canvassers probably directly asked several hundred thousand lesbians and gay men to sign up for vital mail to Congress, and our canvassing took place in more than forty states, meaning that our constituent pressure would be applied to members of Congress across the nation. As a result of all of this, we added almost 50,000 new Speak Out enrollees during 1991's Pride events alone, and to date have signed up 150,000 to 200,000 people across the country.

As I look ahead, there is much yet to be done. We have to find a way to reach and sign up the hundreds of thousands of lesbians and gay men we don't seem to be able to reach at Pride events and other gay community events; maybe we'll get them by increased efforts at the bars. If we don't sign up at least 100 to 200 people in a congressional district of 550,000, I wonder if the system will reach its full potential.

Looking back, we can take satisfaction at the help of national groups such as Dignity, MCC, and PFLAG, who have played important roles in building the initiative. Old friends Dignity president Jim Bussen and UFMCC founder and moderator Troy Perry received our first community service awards and richly deserved them. Both institutions understand the concept of "Christian social action," and PFLAG logically could be the next organization to be recognized for its support and contributions. However, when we started all this, we thought local gay, lesbian, and AIDS groups would be a key to the program's success. Unfortunately, with the exception of a small handful of local groups who have taken the minimal step of doing piggybacks of brochures, the sad truth is that Speak Out wasn't built with their help but, more often, despite their resistance.

AIDS groups, who should understand better than anyone how much is at stake in national public policy, have been particularly difficult. Groups such as the AIDS Project in Minnesota have consistently refused to be helpful by even allowing us to be present at their events. As I write this book, I still plan to set up a picket and create havoc at their AIDS Walk next spring if I'm still alive. A full ten years into the crisis, far too often we still face officious proclamations that "this event isn't political so your Speak Out volunteers can't be here" and usually from people who quickly and proudly state, "I'm an AIDS activist, not a lesbian/gay activist."

On the other hand, we couldn't have dreamed that we'd receive the continuing help we have from the gay and lesbian press. In fact, *The Advocate*—with which I had fought furiously during the days when David Goodstein ran it—received one of the first HRCF Community Service Awards, which are given annually for helping advance Speak Out. Nor at the beginning could we have ever imagined that gay businesses—the DC Eagle, Gene's TV and Video in Los Angeles, the Encore and Elite in Seattle, the Saloon and Brass Rail in Minneapolis, Badlands in DC, to name just a few—would have shown such community consciousness and pitched in to sponsor Speak Out outreach materials.

When we began, members of Congress told our lobbyists that they had never heard from gay and lesbian constituents. If nothing else, we've taken that excuse away from them, but Speak Out has done much more than that. Just the mail it has helped generate has allowed us to reach tens of thousands of people who have never before been political. For some, their participation in Speak Out is all they would ever do, while many others go on to sign up with us to do constituent lobbying, volunteer for HRCF-backed campaigns, write to Congress on their own, and even become ongoing volunteer coordinators for our other grassroots efforts.

As we began to reach large numbers, the system proved itself and our coalition openly envied our capacity to not just talk grass roots but actually deliver. We heard less pooh-poohing and snickering about the program, both internally and from the outside. Instead, the question increasingly was how often we could "activate" the system and on what issues. Since the conventional wisdom when we began was that such a system wouldn't make any difference, this transformation has been very satisfying. We have come so, so far! Our Speak Out outreach has been absolutely historic. Many now realize that our Speak Out canvassers have been present at hundreds of community events, both big and small, in virtually every state in the country in the past four years, and some even realize that more than 150,000 people have sent in well over a half-million pieces of constituent mail as a result of the program.

Yet another, more intangible, benefit of the program is that for every person who signs up, many others have been approached and told about the program. Our canvassers have probably directly explained the program and solicited participation from over a million people. I don't think any of us could have predicted quite what we were starting or how far the program would come.

We're still exploring many innovations for the program, including having the messages hand delivered to Capitol Hill to ensure they reach members of Congress, even when things come up on very short notice. Countless additional changes and improvements will be made as the Speak Out program marches forward. I'll miss "my baby," but these changes will be led by a new director of the HRCF field division.

The incredible disappointment of signing up only 2,300 people at the 1987 March of Washington, with its 600,000 attendance, was not repeated at the 1993 march. This time, because canvass manager Tom Swift knew what to expect and where he'd run into pitfalls, the Human Rights Campaign Fund enrolled over 15,500 in Speak Out, and this was especially critical in the context of the hotly contested ending of the military ban. I must confess that I've taken great satisfaction at the number of those who were negative, snide, and patronizing about such orchestrated mail programs who have since come back to us urging us to activate the program to try to prevail on one of their pet bills or amendments. I remain extremely proud of the program and the people who inherited and built on it.

Infrastructure and Leadership

Before merging into the Campaign Fund, a top priority of the Fairness Fund had been the reestablishment of the infrastructure for other aspects of grassroots organizing. I felt that such a structure should include hiring a national field manager and eight regional field coordinators across the country, and implementing a renewed field associate program. In other words, I still had deep faith in the battle plan formed by me, Susan Green, and the rest of the GRNL field staff, and I was committed to helping get it reestablished.

These grand designs had to wait until our finances were significantly improved, but before that could happen, the Fairness Fund became part of HRCF and we turned the National Mailgram Campaign on its head to help pay for our grassroots organizing. With this last change and the resulting increased revenues, HRCF's new executive director, Tim McFeeley, agreed that we could move forward, so we hired both the midwest regional field coordinator and the national field manager in the fall of 1989. I'd gone along with having GRNL's Midwest person based in Madison, Wisconsin, but as I reflected on it I decided it had been a mistake to have the person in any Midwestern city other than Chicago.

Eventually we settled on Laurie Dittman, who had just played a key role in the passage of Chicago's human rights ordinance. Laurie is solid, able, and an excellent strategist. My later trips through her region allowed us to travel together a couple of times and we became good friends. More than a year and a half after Laurie joined the HRCF staff, the local gay and lesbian PAC in Chicago, Impact, had a vacancy for the executive director's position. Because of her prominence and reputation as an excellent strategist, Laurie was recruited for and accepted their position (and the increased salary associated with it). In her new position, Laurie remains a good friend and continues to work closely with the Campaign Fund.

When we filled Laurie's vacancy, we decided to follow the lead of many other progressive lobbies and base our regional field organizer in the national offices, with outreach by constant phone and extensive travel into the region. Although we were concerned that some people in the Midwest might feel slighted, we concluded that we could best serve both our mission and the region by opting for the substance rather than the symbol of real organizing.

We settled on excellent organizer Marcie Wasserman, who quickly established relationships with activists throughout the region by phone and traveled to Iowa, Michigan, Illinois, and Missouri within just four months. Precisely because she is not based in any one of the region's big cities and doesn't get caught up in local initiatives, Marcie can work the entire region more thoroughly. And because she's based right in the national offices, there's no lag time before she finds out about what's happening on the Hill.

Our search for the national field manager led us to the door of Tacie Dejanikus, who'd worked on the 1987 March on Washington and who also served as national coordinator of the Sharon Kowalski Day protests. Tacie is able, extremely dedicated, and has poured her heart into the difficult task of building this national system up from scratch and supervising far-flung staff. Tacie not only has had to endure my constant remembrances of how things worked for our grassroots "infrastructure" during the GRNL days, but we probably couldn't be more different. She is as politically correct as I am a pragmatist, she's as sensitive and process oriented as I am insensitive and "just get it done," yet we built a remarkable bond that helped reestablish the grassroots infrastructure we agreed was so desperately needed.

Just a short time later we hired Cathy Woolard as southeastern regional field coordinator, in part because she had so impressed our executive director. Cathy is probably the most prominent activist in Atlanta and is extraordinarily witty and committed. Eventually she transferred to the legislative department as a lobbyist, and Mandy Carter from North Carolina was hired to replace her. A young black woman, Mandy had an extremely impressive resume of organizing on a wide range of causes. Shortly after the 1992 elections, where the Campaign Fund's field network and Speak Out program provided the backbone of a very strong gay and lesbian volunteer effort to elect Bill Clinton (as well as countless pro-fairness Senate and House candidates), it was decided that Mandy would maintain some oversight of the Southeast. Because the region simply didn't have a sufficient number of marginal districts, however, Mandy also took responsibility for a number of other marginal districts or states across the country.

We still hope to have eight regional field coordinators eventually, but getting them will have to be a gradual process. As I write this book, the next two regions likely to have full-time regional organizers are the West Coast and the Northeast; the Northeast person probably will be based in the national offices, while the West Coast person would almost have to be based in Los Angeles or San Francisco. So our program could fairly be described as a hybrid, with some regional organizers to be based in the region and others based in the national offices.

I'm very impressed with the job Tim McFeeley has done for the Campaign Fund, taking the budget to almost $5 million annually, and he's certainly been good to me personally. Yet I'd quickly confess that even now, more than a year after I retired on disability with AIDS, I continue to find myself frustrated by Tim's unwillingness to hire the additional regional field organizers necessary to take a serious run at enactment of a national lesbian and gay civil rights bill. I haven't always felt that our infrastructure has functioned quite as well as I'd like, but I'd think a program that has so effectively proven itself shouldn't have to fight so hard to attain the most basic level of growth.

On the other hand, Tim clearly understood the value and importance of a solid grassroots organizing program, while my sense is that the board hasn't been helpful here. This is natural enough, since many of them came on board when the Campaign Fund was a political action committee alone. Also, I think in some ways we're victims of our own success, and that both the staff and board have come to depend on the Speak Out proxy-mail program.

Close examination of other progressive lobbies or our moral majoritarian opponents shows that others understand the value of constituent pressure. The mail that moral majoritarians generated in the early 1980s will be a mere drop in the bucket compared to what they'll produce based on lies if it looks like our nondiscrimination bill really can pass. I realize that I tend to have strong opinions, but I think that failing to prepare for the coming assault is a serious error. It almost smacks of the politically ignorant view that if you have thirty staff people, they should all be lobbyists, an inside-the-beltway view that, unfortunately, is far too common in DC. I can say without hesitation, though, that while other groups talk grass roots the Human Rights Campaign Fund—for all its shortcomings—still does ten times more in grassroots organizing than any other national group!

One of the first tools we decided to utilize to build the Campaign Fund's grassroots mobilization efforts was a "house meeting program." The house meeting approach had been used effectively by many causes and groups, such as the Stop AIDS Project, Neighbor to Neighbor (which works for peace in Central America), and the National Abortion Rights Action League (NARAL). A typical house meeting begins with the host inviting friends to their home. Those attending review the issues and discuss how they can affect government action on AIDS policy and on lesbian and gay civil rights. The program was designed to complement other Campaign Fund field initiatives, generating immediate letters to Congress, mobilizing campaign volunteers for supportive congressional candidates, and stimulating in-district constituent lobbying. Such a "Tupperware party" approach seemed to be perfect for such a social community. At the time, I described one of the major advantages of the effort in this way: "House meetings have the potential to reach countless individuals who have never considered themselves activists."

Longtime friend Suellen Lowry, who previously had served as the lobbyist and political director of NARAL, was particularly helpful in this aspect of grassroots organizing. She described the program somewhat differently than I had, in a Campaign Fund press release aimed at the gay and lesbian press: "House meetings are terrific opportunities for personal contact, conversation, awareness building and action. Federal legislation may seem remote to many of us but house meetings bring national AIDS policy home and demonstrate how each of us can make a difference."

However, NARAL's house meeting program had been implemented by an organization with state-level staff able to help with many of the details leading up to the parties and also to speak at each meeting. Not only did we have no state staffers, we had regional staffers in only two of the anticipated eight regions, and to try to compensate for this shortcoming we tried to enter into partnerships with state groups. To our disappointment, we found that most groups looked at such endeavors through a prism of overwhelming work and little or no staff or volunteers.

To most of them, when they looked at the house meeting program, all they saw were burdens and barriers rather than opportunities or the new people and resources that could be reached. Even the few groups that tentatively agreed to participate with us quickly abandoned the initiative and it died on the vine. Our Southeast regional field coordinator, Cathy Woolard—who is very outgoing and loves public speaking—has continued to use the house meeting program in a pared-back manner, particularly as she's traveled through her region. If Tacie hadn't been so busy launching the entire infrastructure, or grassroots network as she preferred to call it, she too could have used the system well. Laurie Dittman was far more reserved, however, and the program just didn't seem to work for her.

Further, our field associate system simply wasn't well enough developed at that point to provide the seasoned volunteers that would have to have pitched in to make it work. Looking back, I can see that the system is extremely useful but also that we simply weren't ready to take it on at that point. I hope our early disappointment doesn't poison the well for future attempts at house meetings, because a well-established field associate program and more seasoned regional staff should be able to make it work very well in the gay and lesbian community.

On a day-to-day basis, HRCF's regional field staffers helped generate constituent phone calls and letters on a range of issues, much like the GRNL grassroots staff had done years earlier. Among those issues were the hate crimes legislation addressing antigay violence; the Americans with Disabilities Act (which included protections from discrimination for people with HIV); countless appropriations bills; the constant antigay Helms amendments; the Ryan White CARE AIDS legislation; and Jesse Helms's amendments to censor homoerotic art funded by the National Endowment for the Arts (NEA).

In fact, as this partial list suggests, one of my greatest tasks was to try to find the balance between such short-term mobilization around pressing congressional issues and the need to find the field associates and other grassroots organizers that would provide the long-term backbone for our program. Our legislative department constantly wanted us to drop everything to respond to these emergencies, while I often tried to limit the number of occasions on which we'd respond so we could go about the time-con-

Anti-Helms Action Hotline Advertisement. Courtesy of HRC.

suming work of truly building an infrastructure. It was a natural tension but didn't always make things easy.

Some board members had doubts about the value of the non–Speak Out aspects of our field operations and their persistent focus on resource development, and refusal to appreciate a comprehensive constituent mobilization program certainly put more pressure on us. Despite regular reports to the board of directors, I felt that many, if not most of them, really didn't share my commitment to this aspect of our program. I doubted whether we'd ever have the resources necessary to fully develop the grassroots infrastructure, unless I—or my successor—could convey more effectively the urgency of developing this program. These concerns often dampened morale within the field division, but we hoped that things would evolve.

In the meantime, we realized that it's much easier to get local activists to help on various projects and a range of bills once they establish a personal relationship with our organizers. Although we had to rely on the phone to some extent, face-to-face meetings were by far the best, so our field staff traveled across the country—meeting with activists, speaking at local groups' meetings, and building that vital infrastructure that so obsessed us. During the first two years of our grassroots network development, HRCF's noncanvass field staff traveled to over thirty states, often to several places in the state, and in many cases the visits were repeated. This program slowly began to transform the Campaign Fund's image; now, activists could see firsthand that we were putting our resources into vital nuts-and-bolts grassroots organizing.

Another initiative the field division threw itself into was mobilizing volunteers for supportive congressional campaigns. Although the Campaign Fund was one of the largest progressive PACs in the country, making massive direct contributions to campaigns, another currency at election time is campaign volunteers. In the past two election cycles, the Campaign Fund's political department had sent HRCF staffers out to work in campaigns for a couple of weeks as an in-kind contribution; these staffers sometimes tried to get HRCF members involved in the campaigns, but it was not a major priority.

We simply took the concept another major step forward, with field staff charged with mobilizing our membership to find volunteers. Actually, we had begun the effort to identify potential volunteers long before with the distribution of what we called a Next Step mailer, as well as a similar mailer—called the HRCF Action Card—to other Campaign Fund members. The purpose was to inform those getting involved in one aspect of our grassroots program about other aspects and additional steps they could take to make a difference. It included options for hosting house parties, helping us canvass, referring friends to become members, and agreeing to volunteer for targeted congressional campaigns. Without putting a massive amount of energy into it, we signed up more than 600 volunteers.

Because 1990 marked our first major attempt to mobilize volunteers, we limited our efforts to a few congressional races, in part so we could do the sort of thorough job that was needed. Of course, we poured massive energies into defeating Jesse Helms—and electing dynamic Harvey Gantt—in North Carolina. Tacie and another staff person traveled to Salem, Oregon, to work on the campaign of pro-gay rights challenger Mike Kopetski and called HRCF members to volunteer to help defeat moral majoritarian Rep. Denny Smith (R-OR). Field staffers Tom Swift and David Simmons flew to Colorado to try to help long shot Josie Heath's campaign against antigay Hank Brown for the vacant Senate seat; Heath did not prevail, but I continue to hear positive feedback about their organizing for her and the Campaign Fund's commitment to grassroots organizing in the area.

In Chicago's gay and lesbian community Laurie played a key role in fund-raising as well as in mobilizing volunteers to help reelect Senator Paul Simon (D-IL), who was a cosponsor of the national gay civil rights bill. Although his race was expected to be one of the closest in the country, Simon ended up winning rather handily. In addition, Laurie played a valued role in community efforts for Rep. Cardiss Collins (D-IL) and Rep. Sid Yates (D-IL) in their primaries.

Countless other staffers from other divisions also went out and worked in campaigns across the country, and this time they called HRCF members and helped recruit critical volunteers from the gay and lesbian community. Increasingly, politicians would learn that we put not only our money but also our bodies on the line for those that support us.

My own small piece of the puzzle was to mobilize volunteers for Jim Moran, who was running an uphill campaign against entrenched antigay incumbent Stan Parris. Moran, as a councilperson and then mayor of Alexandria, Virginia, introduced and then signed a local gay civil rights ordinance. I hadn't coordinated such a volunteer mobilization for over ten years, and the fact that I'd recently ruptured a disk in my lower back definitely slowed me down a bit. But, with the help of a couple of other staff people, my strong friendship circle, and a large Washington, DC, and northern Virginia membership, we were able to mobilize large volunteer crews.

Actually, we put together a team of six key coordinators who were charged with helping do the phone call recruitment and follow-up. We assumed the "one-for-two rule": if we wanted ten volunteers to actually show up, we needed to have commitments from twenty people. I'm not quite sure how the other organizers did it, but I wanted to make sure that the Moran campaign—and the northern Virginia political community—had no doubt about our ability to turn out volunteers, so I didn't let our volunteers just trickle in and meet at the campaign headquarters. Instead, we carpooled out from the District and from all over northern Virginia and met at a fast-food restaurant right next to the headquarters. From there, we went over in mass, not only to help but to do so rather ostentatiously. We turned out volunteers on eleven separate occasions, with more than twenty-five people on four of those occasions. Our high was almost fifty people the Saturday before the vote, and in all, we turned out more than 100 different volunteers for ten different occasions in Moran's campaign. (Lots of groups talk about turning out such numbers but very few actually are able to do so these days.). The point, I kept stressing to our team, was not only to beat an enemy and elect a proven friend but also to show the entire political establishment of northern Virginia (and the national political establishment as well) that we could both raise big money and turn out the troops. The campaign culminated with several of us agreeing to hold signs urging support for Moran as voters drove into their jobs in the District at 6 a.m. and then as they headed home at 4 to 6 p.m.

Although the election was seen as increasingly close, most observers still thought the antigay incumbent would prevail. The day before I'd stuck my neck out and predicted that Jim Moran would upset Parris. When the votes came in, Moran had won 54 percent. Our hard work paid off and now we have not only one more vote against Bill Dannemeyer–type amendments, but also the first cosponsor of the national gay rights legislation from Virginia. Just as important, he knows that we were there for him. The Campaign Fund gave him the legal maximum of $10,000, the local gay and lesbian community raised several thousand more, and we were able to mobilize a small army of volunteers. Clearly our election efforts were a new but important form of grassroots mobilization.

Shortly after we all returned and recovered from our massive election efforts, Tacie began to tinker with the grassroots network. She settled on the establishment of telephone trees by each field associate to generate quick phone calls from the district or state. Each field associate was urged to go out and recruit at least twenty people for their phone tree, and in some cases they were able to get many more. In addition, Tacie argued vigorously for establishing a congressional action alert program again and, after significant discussion, I gave in.

Although the action alert system had not worked for GRNL, at that time people had not consciously signed up for the system nor had they ever really indicated that they'd write to Congress. This time, with people actually signing up for the program, I felt there was a far greater chance that they'd follow through and write when we urged them to. I remained the voice of doubt—which successfully led Tacie to try a range of strategies to confirm people were writing—but the truth is that I think the telephone tree and action alert systems might become important complements to other aspects of our program.

When 1991 began we started an assertive constituent lobbying program on the federal lesbian and gay civil rights bill. Other groups claimed to be undertaking such initiatives, but our contacts across the country suggested that most of their grassroots efforts ended up taking the form of a postcard campaign. Our constituent lobby kit stressed that people didn't have to be professional lobbyists in order to make a major difference, and we strongly urged constituents to meet directly with their senator or representative rather than their staff persons. So during this first year of our constituent lobbying project, we initiated and oversaw countless in-district meetings between gay and lesbian constituents and their members of Congress. It's remained amazing to me how often, even in districts with extremely sophisticated, capable local gay and lesbian groups, it hasn't occurred to the group to initiate such a constituent lobby visit.

The strategy, which should be used in each new congressional session, is to use the period immediately after the congressional elections to plan and set up countless constituent lobby visits on the national lesbian and gay civil rights bill shortly after the first of the year. The meetings should all take place in the first three months of the year because after that the legislative department will demand that the field operation drop all long-term efforts and focus exclusively on pending and imminent bills and amendments, including stopping Helms.

So far there have been constituent lobbying meetings in more than ten states, and as a result of important efforts of the gay and lesbian constituents who undertook those meetings, several members of Congress agreed to cosponsor the nondiscrimination bill. Rep. Louise Slaughter (D-NY) from Rochester, Rep. George Hochbrueckner (D-NY) from Long Island, and Reps. Henry B. Gonzalez (D-TX) and Albert Bustamente (D) from San Antonio each cosponsored the federal lesbian and gay civil rights bill because of the Campaign Fund–initiated constituent lobbying. Many additional visits are planned which hopefully will result in additional cosponsors, but I think that future efforts will be able to carry out many more meetings as staff gets used to the process.

Rep. Ben Jones, a moderate Democrat from the Atlanta area, is a classic example of a member who endorsed the bill because of constituent input and lobbying, and it's worth taking a much closer look at what sort of grassroots campaign it took to secure his sponsorship. This is not to suggest that he doesn't care about fairness for lesbians and gay men, though, since no matter what we had done he would not have decided to lend his name to the bill if he didn't support nondiscrimination.

During Jones's 1990 campaign, Cathy Woolard, our southeastern regional coordinator, made sure that members of the Campaign Fund and of LEGAL, Atlanta's lesbian and gay Democratic club, each hosted campaign fund-raisers for his reelection. HRCF's Political Action Committee donated $5,000 to Jones's campaign prior to the 1990 general election. In addition, Cathy found a core group of dedicated people who subsequently hosted a biweekly HRCF volunteer night at the Jones campaign headquarters for six months prior to the election. As Cathy has said, "Our members proved to be highly skilled phone bank volunteers, ace mass mail envelope stuffers and yard-sign distributors extraordinaire!" A short time after the elections, local Campaign Fund volunteers met with Congressman Jones to ask him to cosponsor the national nondiscrimination bill. Then Cathy mobilized other forms of grassroots input to show Rep. Jones that significant constituent support existed in his district. We activated overnight mailgrams from more than 200 Speak Out participants in Jones's district. Cathy then proceeded to help generate more than 100 heartfelt letters and countless phone calls from gay and lesbian constituents.

In no time, the Campaign Fund's annual Atlanta banquet gave us another chance to move the congressman. It's a very impressive event to savvy politicians: more than 750 people in black ties and gowns who care enough about lesbian and gay rights to pay $150 each. When we heard Rep. Ben Jones would be attending, we thought we could take the occasion to enhance Rep. Jones's understanding of the impact of discrimination. Southern restaurant chain Cracker Barrel had recently issued a national policy of antigay discrimination and had dismissed several lesbians and gay men. Probably the best known and most widely publicized victim of such discrimination was lesbian cook Cheryl Summerville, and we decided to invite Cheryl to the dinner and let our executive director, Tim McFeeley, talk about her case, describe the nature of antigay discrimination, and introduce her. Tim is extremely articulate and can be quite compelling, so I was confident that the whole situation could be very moving for the crowd in general and Rep. Jones in particular.

It worked just as we'd hoped. Moreover, Rep. Jones was extremely moved by the thunderous applause he received from the assembled crowd. Afterward he spent time listening to a number of individuals who impressed him with their knowledge of the issues, and he told several people that night that he would become a cosponsor. However, faced with more immediate attention on redistricting, Jones didn't get around to cosponsoring. But Cathy Woolard, who is as persistent as she is creative, again met with Rep. Jones when she came to Washington, and he agreed to come on the bill. He became the ninety-fifth cosponsor in the House of Representatives before the day was out.

It always bothered me that the gay press, including the national columnists that could—and I think should—find out how things really happened, never bothered to report how members of Congress came to cosponsor the national lesbian and gay civil rights bill. Often their articles about increases in cosponsorship simply mentioned or quoted both national organizations ostensibly working on the legislation. Also, because the Human Rights Campaign Fund is best known as a PAC that contributes to candidates, the articles usually cited our political clout while referencing the National Gay and Lesbian Task Force in the context of constituent lobbying. That's particularly galling because the Task Force has maintained the mythology of helping coordinate constituent lobbying while actually doing very, very little of it, but has a long track record of taking credit. If the Task Force is simply giving lip service to this central mandate of their mission, either that should be pointed out or they shouldn't be getting credit.

Some argue that fair journalism requires that both groups get mentioned in the articles, but that is just crap. Give people and groups credit for what they do. For instance, the Task Force—which did virtually nothing meaningful around the 1992 elections—called a press conference to discuss lesbian and gay involvement in the elections after Clinton's victory. Although most of the focus was on the venomous disruption of Michael Petrelis, I question more fundamentally why the Task Force called the press conference in the first place, and the Campaign Fund had to ask to be included.

Such coverage is demoralizing for our national field staff, as well as the thousands of HRCF-generated volunteers, given the extensive hard work it takes the Campaign Fund to get the constituent lobbying going and help along the way. More important, the failure to credit the constituent lobbyists also fails to empower them and removes one motivation for taking on other important national projects. Likewise, it doesn't encourage other potential constituent lobbyists to take on this vital work. I personally believe that the national gay and lesbian civil rights bill will not pass until this effort is dramatically increased. Such scenarios should be duplicated in districts across the country.

So with just two of the eventual eight regional field coordinators currently in place, there was much to be done. As the Pride period approached in the spring of 1991, I decided to undertake a 6,000-mile, twenty-seven-city tour. In addition to directly supervising our canvass efforts and attempting to set up constituent lobby visits, we decided that I would speak at a number of "Campaign Fund Community Forums" across the country. Our executive director had recently become enamored of such forums and, I think because he was a bit stung by criticisms that the Campaign Fund was out of touch with its constituency, he had begun to hold several such forums. I quickly decided that my trip would provide an opportunity for me to speak to gay and lesbian constituents and to get input from them. My preference was that the forums would be cosponsored by a key local gay and lesbian group, and one of our very able administrative assistants, Joe Cabush, agreed to contact the groups that I suggested in order to explore their willingness to do this. Joe did a spectacular job with the various logistics of setting up nine community forums. When I returned to Washington, DC, more than five weeks later, I had been vividly reminded of the fact that we are working with and for an incredible collection of people around the nation. My trip, although longer than most that our other organizers take, is very similar to what our regional organizers go through on an ongoing basis.

In part, because the entire Campaign Fund is growing so rapidly and resources are tight, the field division still hasn't been able to grow as rapidly as some of us would want. We're by far the biggest division and we've been teased by others on staff about "building empires," but our job is to mobilize the 200 million people around the country, so it's going to take more staff people than mobilizing the legislators. However, I recently had the opportunity to do a videotape on the evolution of our grassroots program, and I could see that we had really come a very long way. Our full-time regional field coordinators are not only actively building this entire infrastructure but also using it as it grows for countless legislative emergencies. We now have a network of proven letter writers participating in our action alert network, and each day brings more ongoing field associates who, in turn, recruit telephone tree people and so on. In more and more races, both HRCF staff and our best field associates will continue down the trail we've blazed of campaign volunteer mobilization.

It has and will take unbelievable hard work, including a commitment to staying at it for the long haul rather than instant gratification. Anger, rage, and protest activities certainly have an appropriate role in our movement, but no one can deny that there's a very, very important place for the nitty-gritty grunt work of simply putting the pieces in place for our long-term victories. It's now clearer than ever that we must not only continue but dramatically increase our movement's grassroots organizing if we're ever going to pass national lesbian and gay civil rights legislation. While the Campaign Fund must continue to apply its dedication and resources to this task, the rest of our movement must overcome institutional jealousy and join in the various aspects of all the groups' effective organizing strategies to increasingly mobilize the majorities that the polls say are on our side of the issues.

Finally, although we have had some success—if too many starts and stops—in many forms of grassroots organizing and mobilization, until recently we continued to fail miserably at the challenge of generating ongoing and short-notice constituent mail to members of Congress. Unfortunately, our failure was further magnified by two factors. First is the recent trend to describe organized initiatives as "special interests," so that too often legislators try to make light of some forms of grassroots pressure as contrived. Second, our own failure to generate mail stands in stark contrast to the extraordinary capacity of our fundamentalist opponents to generate literal tidal waves of citizen mail from members of their congregations who seem to have little else to do but spew their hate on the issue to their legislators.

Upon returning to the staff of the Human Rights Campaign Fund it was difficult to let go on a number of issues associated with grassroots organizing. With the pain of our loss at the Minnesota legislature forever etched into my consciousness, and only reinforced by the floods of grassroots mail generated by the so-called Moral Majority on the DC sodomy repeal bill, I've fought vigorously with both HRCF executive directors I served, as well as with the board of directors. My vigorous and almost strident advocacy of additional staff and funding for grassroots organizing has to have been quite irritating, and my reputation for being difficult was probably well deserved (although these issues clearly fit my criteria of whether the issue at hand would still seem important five years down the road). I've often felt badly about the strained relations that might have resulted, but I'm quite clear that national groups often talk a good game on grassroots organizing but usually gravitate to glitz and glamour, seldom putting their resources where their rhetoric is.

Simply stated, I believe that we won't be able to enact federal nondiscrimination laws in jobs, housing, and public accommodations without finally funding the organizing to mobilize the majority that polls show supporting lesbian and gay rights. There have been at least a couple of occasions when I've seriously considered resigning, making my distress public, or both.

Part II:
Reflections of an Old, Tired Activist

In this section I share my thoughts on aspects of the movement. First I review a number of key aspects to effective lobbying efforts, including having to demonstrate a compelling need for the nondiscrimination laws we're working so hard for. After a brief chapter on some of my experiences in one-to-one lobbying, I discuss the role of hearings in the process, and share my thoughts concerning fund-raising.

In the concluding chapters I look at some of the pitched battles we've usually lost as we're in the process of winning the war, and at the ways our opponents have inadvertently advanced our efforts. I also look at the issues of coming out and "outing," and consider the role of protest activities in an otherwise insiders' game. Finally, I reflect on recent events and bring a satisfying career to a close, a bit early.

Steve Endean in Speak Out Office. Photography by Jim Marks.

Chapter 7

If It Ain't Broken . . . :
Demonstrating a Need
for the Gay and Lesbian Rights Legislation

Early on, our goals didn't focus on specific legal reforms but on visibility. Millions of young gay men and women had grown up like I had, thinking they were "the only ones." In 1970, you couldn't find much on the subject of homosexuality, and most of it argued that gay people were sick, sinners, or criminals—or some combination of all three. Our small group of activists believed, I think correctly, that we'd eventually win if we could just force people to deal with an issue they desperately wanted to avoid.

The gay movement, which was just emerging from the tumultuous 1960s and 1970s and the antiwar movement, had the potential to show young lesbians and gay men struggling with their identity that there were proud, assertive gay people willing to stand up publicly to fight for our rights. Moreover, we hoped to break down society's incredibly destructive stereotypes. We wanted to show nongay people that gay people were from all walks of life and, in most respects aside from our sexual orientation, just like them. It was also important, at least from my point of view, to demonstrate to gay men and lesbians themselves, who'd been brainwashed about what it means to be gay, that we came in all sizes, shapes, and varieties.

I was certain our progress would come in relationship to society recognizing that lesbians and gay men are their sisters and brothers, sons and daughters, co-workers and clients. In short, that—with the exception of our sexual orientation—gay people are just like them! That's certainly a controversial idea within the lesbian and gay movement, with many arguing vehemently that the last thing we want is to become just another piece of the "rotten American pie." Despite growing up in a time when I saw America's injustice to racial minorities, perhaps it was my suburban upbringing that led me to reject this negative view. I an still convinced Americans fundamentally believe in fairness.

I also quickly came to believe the best public education takes place in the context of some specific initiative. After reading of Gay Activists Alliance/NY's fight for a local gay rights ordinance, it became clear that passing statewide legislation in Minnesota as well as citywide ordinances in Minneapolis and St. Paul prohibiting discrimination against lesbians and gay men should be a top movement priority, and in the process we could answer our pressing need to reeducate the public about who gay and lesbian people were.

That led us right into the old legislative axiom, "If it ain't broke, don't fix it!" It's one of the more commonsense ideas legislators have ever created, since it's only reasonable for there to be a "need" before legislators go to the trouble of passing a bill. God knows there is no abundance of political courage on Capitol Hill, even for those issues where the most compelling need has been proven. Protecting gays from discrimination is right up there with abortion, gun control, and the legalization of marijuana as explosive social issues which legislators would give their right arms to evade. So we had our hands full proving the need.

Legislators only have to contend there's no need for the bill, or suggest the existing law—in the form of the constitution or existing statutes—protects lesbians and gay men, in order to avoid taking a courageous, principled stance. In my experience, however, most legislators initially settled on the argument that there was no discrimination, that we were just trying to give gay people special privileges. Their demands that we demonstrate the need seemed unreasonable because the problem was so self-evident to most of us, so initially this challenge took many of us by surprise. But "If it ain't broke . . ." has remained a central challenge for the entire time I have been in the movement.

For instance, then-Governor George Deukmejian (R) of California contended there was no evidence of discrimination when he vetoed lesbian and gay civil rights legislation in the late 1980s. More recently, even Governor Pete Wilson, a moderate Republican who had supported the bill, ended up vetoing it in 1991, again contending there wasn't enough evidence of need. It became clear that any nondiscrimination laws for gays would have to come in the context of the public's understanding of discrimination in general, which tended to be in the form of discrimination against blacks and, secondarily, against women.

Certainly there were similarities, particularly in the devastating impact, but there were a number of key differences I always felt gay activists ignored or failed to understand. We faced a significant challenge in explaining to legislators, and society in general, how discrimination against lesbians and gay men happens: since gay people could, and often did, hide, and therefore often initially got into the workforce, many people assumed discrimination took place only if gay people "flaunted" their sexuality. Any linkage of the civil rights bill with "coming out" would almost certainly be politically suicidal because it was clear that most people didn't even want to think about the existence of gays.

Since most lesbians and gay men don't fit society's stereotypes, employers generally weren't initially aware of the sexual orientation of their employees at the point of hiring. As a result, most gays didn't face the same difficulties that women and minorities have in getting into the workforce. Because those of us who were young, gay activists wanted to demonstrate the unfairness of the discrimination we faced, too often we made a serious strategic mistake in failing to acknowledge the differences between racial and sexual discrimination on the one hand and that based on antigay sentiment on the other. It made us vulnerable to homophobes and undercut critical potential support from racial minorities who might believe gay people are trying to "get a slice of the affirmative action pie," even though affirmative action makes no sense for gay people. In those early years, some activists also tended to refer to gays as minorities, which I always thought was misguided and hazardous.

Affirmative action, particularly in terms of goals, numbers, etc., ignores the nature of antigay discrimination. Not only do we not generally have a problem at the point of entry where women and minorities often face discrimination, but it also sets up illogical remedies. What are you going to do, give a bisexual a part-time job? Antigay discrimination usually takes place once employees are on staff and have a chance to prove their abilities and establish job performance.

Acknowledging the differences—which even then were obvious in terms of economic conditions (just take a look at the Hollywood Hills or most gay "ghettos")—could only help ease tensions with racial minorities, both non-gay and gay and lesbian minority people who feel the differences in very real terms. Honest analysis of the differences as well as the comparisons would help people understand the fundamental unfairness of antilesbian and antigay discrimination.

Happily, the leaders of the black movement and women's movement were very patient with an immature gay movement because they had already gone through so much, or perhaps because they understand the gay community has the growing resources to contribute to vital coalition building (the Human Rights Campaign Fund has probably contributed more money to minority candidates for Congress than any other political action committee in the country). Despite minorities' patience, lesbian and gay leaders must modify our rhetoric and acknowledge the differences as well as the similarities.

Further, it will not only help us avoid conflict with racial minorities but will stop us from either attacking or defending affirmative action programs in a time when there seems to be a growing backlash against them. I am told that our side on the recent Colorado initiative failed to separate itself effectively from affirmative action, so our fundamentalist opponents were able to portray the vote as for or against quotas for gay people.[1] If I understood correctly, we lost an unnecessary fight by a modest margin of 53 percent to 47 percent when we should have won. I support affirmative action for racial minorities and women very, very strongly, but that's not what the issue was. In some ways, discrimination against gay people is more like discrimination based on religion. Once enacted, gay and lesbian rights laws probably will not result in many large "pattern and practice" cases but will provide legal recourse for those gays who face specific cases of discrimination.

Sometimes opponents of gay rights try to point to the modest number of cases resulting from the state and local lesbian and gay rights laws to argue there is no need. But in fact, civil rights laws cannot be judged by the number of times they are violated but by their deterrent effect. I'd like to believe businesses have begun to learn that discrimination is not only wrong and immoral but also doesn't make sense from a business perspective.

During our first campaign at the Minnesota legislature in 1973, we explained the distinctions and similarities between discrimination against racial minorities and women, and gay people. Moreover, we also had to begin to document antigay discrimination, because state legislators claimed there was no antigay discrimination and no need for a bill (but if there was discrimination it was, of course, justified). We got through the 1973 legislative session without much solid documentation or any good case histories; our failure to demonstrate a compelling need did contribute to our loss, and I resolved then that we would have to do better in demonstrating discrimination if we were ever going to win.

Between the end of the 1973 legislative session and our full-scale assault on the Minneapolis City Council for the local ordinance in 1974, a great discrimination case fell into our laps. The *Minneapolis Star*'s "Column 1" reported on a situation in which a gay man, Byron Schmitz, had been refused employment because of his sexual orientation alone. Several friends brought it to my attention (I guess that was one of the few advantages of being one of the best-known activists in town). None of us actually knew Byron, but we were able to track him down and get a far more complete picture than the few lines in the paper had revealed. In addition, if we were going to make this case the major cause celebre, we also had to have his permission to pursue the matter publicly.

In the spring of 1973, Schmitz had applied for and tentatively been accepted to the position of an interoffice errand person for Northwestern Bell Telephone. After he was hired and before he was to start, he was sent to the company nurse to take a physical. His 4-F draft status came up during the course of the physical, and when the nurse asked about it Byron replied it was because he was homosexual. Nothing more was said at the time, but when Byron reported to find out his starting date, he was told he couldn't be hired because "Northwestern Bell has no medical policy for homosexuals." "Column 1" quoted Northwestern Bell spokesperson Wy Thorson as stating that Northwestern Bell

> has a policy to not employ admitted homosexuals. Until society rec-
> ognizes homosexuality as socially acceptable behavior, we believe
> that employing known homosexuals would tend to have an adverse ef-
> fect on how our company is regarded by other employees and the gen-
> eral public.[2]

We felt that everyone knew Northwestern Bell had large numbers of gay people already on staff, which made Thorson's statement remarkably stupid and gave us a strong basis for protest and enormous public relations possi-bilities.

After meeting with Byron, a group of gay activists decided to mount a major effort around the case. But first we met with William Stock, the vice president of personnel for Northwestern Bell, to seek a reversal of their pol-icy. The policy was so obviously absurd that, even in the early 1970s, we ac-tually hoped a reasoned discussion could reverse it. Stock just pointed out repeatedly that there was no legal prohibition to such discrimination, ex-plaining that Northwestern Bell policy was consistent with both city and state law; in fact, he specifically cited our own failure to secure reform of the state civil rights law during the previous session. They would con-tinue to abide by the law, and if we wanted to end their discrimination, we'd have to secure amendment to either the city or state laws.

With polls showing 70 percent of Minnesotans opposing antigay dis-crimination and many locally based firms such as Pillsbury and General Mills already having nondiscrimination policies, we felt we had a particu-larly strong case. Also, because Byron had not "come out" but been discov-ered via his draft records, we didn't have to deal with the widely held but silly view that openness and honesty somehow represented "flaunting." Al-though there were, indeed, many differences between discrimination based on race and antigay discrimination, in this instance, Northwestern Bell's own statement highlighted the similarities. Just substituting the word "black" for the words "known homosexuals" reminds one of the sinister nature of the discrimination of other companies, particularly in the South, and how outrageous it is.

With our conversation with Mr. Stock in mind, our small band of activ-ists met to lay plans for what ended up as an extraordinary campaign of pro-test and public relations. We picketed on every weekday for a month (downtown Minneapolis was largely deserted on weekends). On some days we'd have up to sixty picketers, while on others it would be just a small handful of us. It was a lot of hard work, but it was also exhilarating. After each day's picket, we'd all adjourn to a popular German restaurant, the Black Forest, to talk about our experience and socialize. The Black Forest was a quaint old place and its heavy wooden booths and chairs were anything but comfortable, but it was also a liberal hotbed and had a somewhat womblike feeling—very safe and good.

Because the Northwestern Bell offices were just a block from Minneapolis City Hall, virtually every alderman, their aides, and the mayor could hardly avoid the pickets as they went to and from lunch. Moreover, our leafleting of the gay bars to find picketers and the general publicity our campaign brought helped clarify for the gay community why we were fighting for nondiscrimination legislation in the first place. Activists understood the need to educate nongay people about antigay discrimination, but I think too many of us thought such education wasn't necessary in the lesbian and gay male communities. However, many, if not most of us, assumed the Constitution protected them from discrimination and that there was no need for any special legislation.

So our campaign against discrimination was very, very visible. Beyond the general picketing, we held press events and had people dress up as telephone booths. Within a matter of a few days, bright yellow stickers were plastered across the coin slots of hundreds of pay phones throughout Minneapolis:

> THE PERSON NEXT TO YOU MAY BE GAY
> Doesn't That Person Have a Right to a Job?
> Gay people never know when they'll lose their job or be passed over for promotion.
> Support the "Equal Job Rights Bill." Write your legislator today.

Both our volunteering in the city elections and the Byron Schmitz/NW Bell case were critical to eventual victory in Minneapolis. A solid majority of the incoming aldermen as well as the election of a more progressive incoming mayor resulted in the enactment of the third such nondiscrimination ordinance in a major city in the nation. One of our flyers explained how antigay discrimination compared to that against racial minorities, stating,

> Gay people do not face the same type of employment difficulties as do Blacks—we can hide. We can pretend we are heterosexuals, we can smile or laugh when a co-worker makes an anti-gay joke or slur such as "damned faggots." But to do that is to internalize the guilt and hate

that society has put on the gay person. That is to say, if only to your-self, that there is something wrong with being who you are. . . . It fur-ther points out that many . . . face the cruel choice between honesty and dignity on the one hand and their vocation and livelihood on the other. Policies that precribe fear and anxiety and proscribe openness and honesty must be reversed.

It was honest, but I now see it probably wasn't the most effective legisla-tive advocacy. Any argument by lesbian and gay activists that suggests non-discrimination laws are an "out-of-the-closet" measure fails to understand how much society still hopes we won't keep throwing it in their faces. When I met with candidates for alderman, I didn't focus on the need to be able to come out but instead explained what had happened to Byron. I asked them if they really felt what happened to Byron was fair. Sometimes there was an uncomfortable silence, but I didn't let them off the hook and they usually had to admit it wasn't fair. Although I have never underestimated the impact of working in eleven of the thirteen city council races, I also believe our month-long picket and resulting publicity was the primary reason we were able to enact the Minneapolis Gay and Lesbian Civil Rights Ordinance.

One day after enactment of the ordinance, Bell's Mr. Stock called me at my home to let me know that, as a result of the ordinance, they were revers-ing their policy not only within Minneapolis but within the five-state region they represented. It was enormously satisfying and today the Bell system is among the most enlightened in the nation.

Despite the Byron Schmitz case, we struggled with state legislators' de-mands to document discrimination statistics in our largely invisible com-munity. Responding to legislators is essential and I didn't then think much about it, but it's clearly part our opponents' malevolent strategy to slow us down. Without civil rights laws to provide recourse or document both the number and nature of discrimination cases, it's very difficult to demonstrate a pattern and practice of discrimination. But in more recent situations, in which governors have appointed "blue-ribbon commissions" to hold hear-ings and collect such information, it is my impression that it didn't seem to build momentum for the bill. Instead, it took tremendous time and attention away from far more fundamental initiatives to win the bill.

Early on, we had one set of statistics, from a study done in the early 1970s by Dr. Evelyn Hooker, who had been associated with the National In-stitute of Mental Health Study on Homosexuality. Her studies showed that 16 percent of all gay people face employment difficulties and 9 percent lose their jobs simply because of their sexual orientation. I cited those studies for years without serious challenge, but when I again cited them in the early 1990s, I faced criticism from other Campaign Fund staff who felt, correctly, that they were seriously outdated. Although I felt some of the resistance was to this old-timer, I agreed that more timely, well-documented statistics—and, more important, solid cases—would be useful. Ironically, *USA Today* cited those precise statistics within just one month of our internal debate.

Some time after the Byron Schmitz/Northwestern Bell case, we discovered an even better job case—that of Rob Balfe. It turned out to be the one I would use for years to come, one which had almost every element I could hope for. Rob had been fired when he was discovered to be gay so there could be no contention of "flaunting." He had an excellent work record of more than seven years, and his job was not related to children, which has been a silly but touchy point for years, so we didn't have to fight that fight. Finally, his termination left him blackballed in his field and unemployed for months. The case simply screamed unfair, and as a Metropolitan Community Church member, he was active in the community and not afraid to stand up.

Minneapolis had passed its ordinance, but Rob was employed in the suburbs—so his case was a perfect one to argue for the enactment of state legislation. We used Rob's case on a lobbying brochure, stating:

> Rob Balfe was fired several months ago. Not because he wasn't doing his job. And not because he didn't get along with his associates and clients. He was fired because he's gay. And, at present, most gay people are not legally protected against this kind of discrimination.
>
> Rob Balfe worked for an insurance company for seven years, first as a claims adjuster in the Grand Forks, North Dakota office, and then as a claims examiner at the company's suburban Minneapolis, Minnesota office. Like most gay people, Rob kept his personal life to himself and nobody suspected that he was gay. He was well liked at the office. He worked hard. And he was the kind of guy who finished a job no matter what it took to do it. In 1975, Rob closed more cases that anyone else in the company.
>
> Then, through a rumor, his supervisor found out Rob was gay. He tried to "freeze" Rob out of his job by refusing to talk to him. Then one Monday morning an associate told Rob that his supervisor wanted to see him. "I don't want any homosexuals working here. You're fired," his supervisor told him. "We'll arrange for a time after working hours for you to come in and pack your desk."
>
> Since that time Rob has applied for jobs with a number of other insurance companies, hoping that his experience and good work record would help him continue in his vocation. Their initial interest soon

vanished after they check with his former employer. Rob now realizes that he may never be able to find another job in his professional capacity . . .

As we pointed out in the brochure, people do not often hear of cases such as Rob's because most discriminating companies aren't as candid and blunt. More important, most lesbians and gay men who face such discrimination have to go on to find another job, and since most states do not protect lesbians and gay men from discrimination, very few of those who have faced such discrimination are willing to come forward and fight back.

My own experience with city council members, state legislators, and members of Congress and their staff suggested that their eyes just glaze over when gay rights advocates cite statistics, but they respond very well to a few good cases. With effective presentation, elected officials and their staffs, or at least those that were not complete bigots, had to agree that being refused employment or being fired because an individual is gay is unfair. It often wasn't hard, then, to get them to agree that such discrimination should be illegal. In that context, I was surprised when Ross Perot candidly expressed reservations about gay people and indicated he would never employ adulterers.[3] I assume that he would also include fornicators in the group that should be disqualified, leaving "full employment" at maybe 10 percent at best. I wasn't happy with his initial views but was pleased he expressed them honestly.

One of the big advantages of Rob's case was that he'd been discovered to be gay only after years of excellent work performance. As I first heard it— and told it for many years—Rob had been seen going into a gay bar by a co-worker who happened to be driving by and who subsequently reported it to Rob's supervisor. Some time later, I heard the story somewhat differently, with Rob and his lover of many years inviting a couple of Rob's co-workers to a holy union ceremony at MCC. According to this version, one of the co-workers was less supportive than Rob had thought and reported the nature of Rob's relationship to his supervisor. Although the later version was fine, I would be the first to admit the initial story felt much "cleaner" because of society's screwed-up notions about what constitutes "flaunting." I never found out what the correct story was and, over time, I stopped referencing any gay bar but instead simply stuck to the basic fact: Rob's boss had learned of his sexual orientation and summarily fired him despite years of strong work performance and good relations with co-workers and clients alike. When I moved to Washington, DC, to direct the Gay Rights National Lobby, the Rob Balfe case went with me. The case was getting old, but it still accurately reflected the general nature of the problem of antigay discrimination—discovery once employed.

The whole issue of documentation led into another trap set by our opponents. National opinion polls showed that the American people believed there was serious discrimination against homosexuals, but if we couldn't document the discrimination for legislators, they'd use it to duck the issue. However, if there were too many cases of discrimination based on sexual orientation, opponents would try to pit one protected class against another, arguing the inclusion of "sexual orientation" would put an unreasonable burden on the enforcing civil rights agencies. Happily, the facts showed enactment of local ordinances didn't result in a huge avalanche of cases. Instead, the value of lesbian and gay civil rights legislation rests largely with its deterrent effect on employers. Legislators sometimes seemed dubious about the point until I pointed out that we didn't judge the effectiveness of murder laws by the number of times they were violated, but by the deterrent effect.

A short time after I took over GRNL in 1978, we acknowledged the need to educate the lesbian and gay community about the importance of the non-discrimination legislation. We designed an ad—which was to be part of a series we never completed—to run in the gay press. Called "She Paid the Price," it focused on the eviction of Barbara Love and her lover from their apartment in New York City because the landlord "didn't want their kind." Since neither New York City human rights laws (at the time), nor national laws protected taxpaying gay and lesbian citizens from arbitrary discrimination, they had no recourse. We also established the Right to Privacy Foundation, and one of its top priorities was to document job and housing discrimination, not only in terms of numbers but also in terms of specific cases.

Unfortunately, the combination of a shortage of resources, internal community battles, and the AIDS crisis forced us to set aside both these initiatives and the overall drive for national lesbian and gay civil rights legislation. Of course, there were—and are—countless efforts going on across the country to document discrimination against gay and lesbian citizens. Studies were undertaken in Omaha, Boston, Baltimore, and New Jersey, to name just a few. These commissions sought to clarify the nature of discrimination against lesbian and gay citizens and whether there was a genuine need for statewide legislation.

The mayor of Kansas City, Missouri, who had slowly become a supporter of fairness, appointed a similar blue-ribbon commission to investigate the matter and report back on the need for local legislation. Although I admit events have kept me from following it as closely as I might have wanted, I believe the Human Rights Project (HRP) still exists, suggesting that they haven't yet enacted the ordinance. But I was deeply impressed with the dedication and political savvy of the political activists in Kansas

City and hope they continue to press for the legislation, no matter what barriers they encounter.

The National Gay and Lesbian Task Force did a great job of demonstrating a serious problem in terms of antigay, antilesbian violence, which resulted in countless legislative efforts, at all levels, for the enactment of hate crimes bills addressing bias-motivated violence. Many bills have passed, including the federal statistics bill, and have helped get legislators used to the idea of including sexual orientation as a category. The outstanding job done by the Task Force's Kevin Berrill on the effort is precisely the model we need to follow in documenting discrimination against gay men and lesbians in jobs and housing.

With the collapse of the Gay Rights National Lobby—along with its 501(c)3, the Right to Privacy Foundation—and the Human Rights Campaign Fund's shift to the AIDS crisis, national efforts to document discrimination in jobs and housing had to be set aside. Only years later, when the Campaign Fund had refocused attention on passage of the lesbian and gay civil rights bill, was there serious national attention to the vital task of documenting job and housing discrimination to members of Congress and their staffs. HRCF is now undertaking an assertive national campaign to pick up the pieces from years before, collect the wide range of documentation that already exists across the country, and mobilize local groups to help identify strong, relatively current case histories.

The need for documentation and solid efforts to explain the nature of such discrimination was reinforced by Senate Majority Leader George Mitchell (D-ME). A solid, progressive legislator from Maine, whom I'd always considered thoughtful, Mitchell has shown just how easy it is, even for people of good will, to seriously misunderstand the nature of antigay discrimination. In a letter to a voter, Mitchell wrote,

> Our civil rights laws rest on publicly ascertainable behavior and appearance. They rest on public events, public behavior and relations between people which are in some way in the public sphere. . . . I do not know what the experience is of states where human rights statutes at the state level bar discrimination on the grounds of sexual orientation, but it would seem to me that only those individuals who are willing to make plain their orientation can benefit from such statutes.

However, without the inclusion of sexual orientation in existing civil rights laws, those who have been fired from their jobs simply because of their sexual orientation or *presumed sexual orientation* would have no standing or legal recourse. Rob Balfe was not out to his employers until he was discovered. Had there been a state law, he would have had recourse to arbitrary and unfair discrimination. Rob's strong work record and ability to get along with co-workers and clients alike would have made for compelling evidence that some other factor was at play in his dismissal. During the first referendum on the St. Paul lesbian and gay civil rights ordinance, we learned of a case of a woman who was fired from her job because her employer concluded she was a lesbian. Because the ordinance was in effect, she had recourse and won her job back. Most interesting, she claimed that in fact she was not a lesbian, yet the ordinance protected her.

Fortunately, Iowa's excellent gay rights lobbyist Michael Current has drafted an amendment that, although totally unnecessary, should satisfy the need to explain and respond to the strange concerns of Mitchell. An opinion by the Lawyers Committee for Civil Rights would also be helpful.

Another widely publicized case of discrimination, at the Cracker Barrel restaurants, gained major national attention and generated massive protests when the management announced a national policy not to employ lesbians or gay men and proceeded to fire about ten employees. The ongoing series of protests, which have taken place across the country at Cracker Barrel's far-flung chain, helped spark considerable national attention, with *USA Today, The New York Times, The Washington Post,* the *Oprah Winfrey Show,* and ABC's *20/20* all doing major features on the outrageous discrimination.

Cheryl Summerville, a cook with a terrific work record, has become a national spokesperson against such unfair discrimination. Campaign Fund executive director Tim McFeeley arranged for Summerville to attend the Fund's Atlanta fund-raising dinner and introduced her, stating,

> And speaking of heroes—what about the Cracker Barrel employee of three and half years who went to her boss after management had fired her gay coworkers and told them that she was a lesbian and they'd have to fire her, which they did. And when Cracker Barrel tried to hire her back, she refused unless they hired the gay men back as well. She put her job on the line—not once but twice—she's a real hero and she's with us tonight with her lover of ten years and her mother as well.

Partially because of learning of Cracker Barrel's discrimination that night, a member of Congress from Georgia finally decided to cosponsor the national lesbian and gay civil rights bill, and Cracker Barrel was the final straw in helping convince several others to become cosponsors, demonstrating the real need. The Cracker Barrel case proved that "it was indeed broke," and will give important new impetus to the national drive for nondiscrimination laws. We need to find more cases like this and to devote the time, attention, and resources to ensure adequate public relations around them.[4]

Another example of "compelling need" centered around our efforts to pass consenting adults legislation, repealing sodomy and fornication laws. Since they were virtually never enforced except when they took place in public, there simply was no "compelling need." Again and again, we heard from legislators, "These laws are never enforced, so why should we stick our necks out when it's only symbolic anyway?" We tried to show them that the existence of sodomy laws caused real and serious problems, both in terms labeling gay people as "criminals" and contributing to bigotry and discrimination.

Further, maintaining such unenforceable laws in the mid-1970s, regulating what people do in the privacy of their bedrooms, bred serious contempt and disrespect for the law itself. Despite my own belief in this principle, I had to admit that the then–Minnesota attorney general, who was a liberal but pretty straitlaced, certainly didn't seem impressed. He seemed obsessed with why "we took a good word, gay, and destroyed it." I again pointed out that these laws, as they pertain to consenting adults in private, were virtually never enforced. Nothing seemed to move him.

Years later the U.S. Supreme Court, in the now-famous case of *Bowers v. Hardwick,* rejected, by a narrow margin, right to privacy arguments and upheld the constitutionality of the sodomy laws.[5] I was shocked, not by the decision but by the huge public outcry. I had been living in Washington, DC, for a long time by then and I wondered where this public outcry had been when advocates of consenting adults legislation had fought for reform for years. Of course, the *Hardwick* case—with its police intrusion into the privacy of a real citizen who could face imprisonment—again showed the public "it was indeed broke" and had to be fixed. Unfortunately, our movement was not then prepared to capitalize on that fleeting outrage.

Chapter 8

One-to-One Lobbying

As with virtually all other aspects of my later lobbying of Congress, I relied on my Minnesota experience to guide me. With the help of my friends from the Minnesota Americans for Democratic Action and the DFL Feminist Caucus, I began to learn the process and realize that these legislators represented not only the "best and brightest" but also some of the most stupid human beings I'd ever met. I also quickly discovered, however, that while there was significant carryover from the state to the national level, there were plenty of significant differences as well. One of the most formidable was the fact that it remained extremely difficult to get lesbians and gay men to care about what happened in Congress. This was also somewhat true at the state and local levels, but national efforts seemed so remote, and the chances of meaningful change so slim, that I had to be as pushy as I ever remember being simply to get attention to our efforts.

Equally difficult, from a tactics point of view, was the reality that as a lobbyist in Congress, I no longer would get to meet directly with real decision makers, the congresspersons; on Capitol Hill, lobbyists spend most of their time talking with staff. Because gay rights is such a "gut issue," I felt that no matter how much I was able to convince the staffer I was relegated to see, it was unlikely at best that they could convey this information as effectively to their boss, or answer his or her more serious misgivings, as I had to them. Of course, I was right but, with the exception of creating a PAC operation (resulting in direct meetings) and carefully coordinating effective constituent lobbyists (whom members of Congress almost always would see), there was darn little I could do about it. But I'm getting ahead of myself. Before I could even contemplate, let alone face, these challenges, I had to learn how to lobby a legislative body on the issue of fairness for lesbian and gay Americans.

In Minnesota, the first challenge for a beginner like myself was to figure out how to secure meetings with legislators. Now such a small challenge seems silly, but I just didn't know then and had never lobbied before. My only claim on the lobbyist position was that I was a real "political hack" who kind of took to this stuff, cared very deeply about the issues I was lob-bying, and simply wouldn't let any voice of sanity deter me.

Most state legislators had small offices and no staff to "protect" them from assertive lobbyists. Protocol called for advance appointments with state senators, but you could get direct access to House members. With the goodwill of the receptionist, Roxanne Chenoweth—and by citing the bill number rather than subject matter—I usually got in to meet legislators who might otherwise have tried to avoid me. The alternative, which I used after I got a bit more self-confident, was to simply wander through the halls out-side the legislators' offices and just drop in when it appeared that they had time to meet with me. A couple of times I even lobbied legislators on eleva-tors, but the nature of the issue—and usually the amount of education nec-essary on it—made such lobbying less advisable.

While I'm on the subject of staff, many of those serving as staff at the legislature, including secretaries, were DFLers (Democrats) who'd been swept in when the DFL finally took the legislature in 1972. With a fair num-ber of them progressive, I worked hard to build friendships with them and more than a few proved to be very valuable allies, letting me know when their bosses were getting antigay pressure or were just vacillating. I tried similar tactics at Congress but generally didn't meet with nearly as positive results. The fact that congressional staff circles looked like a local gay bar, with many "knowing Dorothy" (as the old expression goes), even seemed to work against me; gay staffers in the earliest days seemed to bend over back-ward not to be accused of operating based on anything but their bosses' best interests. Gary Aldridge, who worked for Senator Alan Cranston (D-CA), was shunned by other gay Capitol Hill staff when he came out publicly in the early 1980s.

In those first days at the Minnesota legislature one of the first legislators I met with after I began lobbying in 1973, Rep. Harry Johnson, turned out to be a tough challenge and a real learning experience. I got in to meet with Johnson, a DFL legislator and farmer from rural Minnesota, by having the receptionist refer only to the bill number so Johnson had no idea what the subject matter was. I later learned Johnson had barely survived attacks from his Republican opponent for the DFL's "radical platform" and specifically the support for gay rights. Johnson had prevailed only by denouncing the platform, and with special venom on the gay rights issue.

Once I explained my agenda—extension of the nondiscrimination laws for gay people and repeal of the sodomy laws—Johnson quickly let me know in no uncertain terms of his opposition to "the queers." Beating a quick retreat didn't save me from being hit in the back of the head with my lobbying booklet (Johnson may have been old and cranky but he still had a hell of an aim). This lobbying business was a little more hazardous than I'd thought. Looking back, the encounter was funny, but I also learned the important lesson of getting as much information as possible about legislators' records and views. Had I done such research on Johnson I would've learned that he was one of the most conservative DFLers in office and that his recent election had only hardened his hostility to gay rights.

A couple of state representatives were so appalled and disgusted by gay rights (we hadn't grown up enough yet to remember to reference lesbian regularly then) that when they figured out I wanted to talk to them about gay rights they actually left their own offices to avoid me and refused to return until I left. Maybe I should've made myself at home, using their phones, etc., but I wanted to create goodwill if at all possible. So I'd just leave. In fact, despite some legislators' ignorance and bigotry I went out of my way to be courteous, even inviting them to lunch. I didn't think I'd turn them around (and I didn't), but I thought I might at least minimize their hostility and active work against our bills. I was wrong, but it allowed me to better understand their arguments and have the answers prepared. Without this preparation I thought we'd be at a serious disadvantage, and I still believe this is one of the pieces that progressive advocacy lobbyists most often overlook.

One legislator who was never openly hostile but did remain a challenge for some time was State Senator Hubert Humphrey III, known by everyone as Skip. Lesbian and gay rights was a new issue for Humphrey and he was unsure of its merits. However, he was willing to discuss it and his concerns, most of which centered around gays and youth. After an extensive lobbying visit, I'd leave thinking I'd turned him around, only to learn later from other lobbyists that Skip had changed his mind again and needed more work. I suspected someone in Humphrey's family, maybe his wife, might have had a problem with the gay teacher issue. Some were critical of Humphrey and thought he lacked guts, but he was always open to listening and learning; you almost couldn't help liking the man. Despite those early reservations and tremendous constituent pressure to oppose us, Humphrey eventually voted for the state civil rights bill. Nonetheless, the next session I assigned our best lobbyist, a therapist named Doug Elwood, to work with Senator Humphrey. In later years Humphrey, who was by now the state attorney general, became a regular attendee at the Human Rights Campaign Fund banquets in the Twin Cities. In 1992 he brought his wife, who seemed lovely and quite at ease. My mother, who's as talkative as I am, talked their ears right off.

Sponsorship

One of the issues we had to deal with from the very beginning was how to choose sponsors. Sponsorship of the nondiscrimination bill in the state senate was essentially handled by Nick Coleman, the senate majority leader who served as chief sponsor. As the most powerful senator and a wonderful, articulate man, we couldn't have gotten luckier. In hindsight, we weren't as lucky when we settled on Rep. Gary Flakne (R-Mpls.) as the chief sponsor of our consenting adults bill in the House. We were happy to have his lead sponsorship because he was a Republican and the consenting adults bill (repeal of the sodomy, fornication, and adultery statutes) is a logical Republican, less-government-intervention bill.

At first I didn't understand that, despite his official leadership role in the GOP Caucus, Flakne was seen as too liberal by most other Republican legislators even while DFLers viewed him as rabidly partisan. Although Flakne taught the important KISS rule—Keep It Short Stupid—DFL legislators concluded that Flakne was sandbagging the bill and using it to put DFL legislators on record in favor of a controversial social issue. No one but Gary himself could ever know the real facts of the matter, but his inept floor management clearly cost us a few votes, and repeal of the sodomy and fornication statutes was defeated.

Flakne's performance stood in stark contrast with that of State Representative Linda Berglin a few years later. She was sponsoring a rape reform bill that also included repeal of the sodomy and fornication statutes as they pertain to consenting adults in private. Berglin's presentation on the House floor was an absolute classic! When right wingers asked tough questions, she just acted spacey and gave short nonanswers. Although they eventually put the fornication law back on the books by a very narrow vote, it was Berglin who really personified the KISS rule Flakne preached.

By the 1975 legislative session, Senator Allan Spear had come out publicly and was the obvious choice to carry the nondiscrimination bill in jobs and housing in the state senate. Allan, who is an excellent speaker and well respected by his colleagues, did a terrific job and almost carried the day.

We weren't as lucky in the House, where we had a tough time finding a good sponsor. I didn't want a legislator from one of the well-identified gay areas or one who was seen as too liberal, so we settled on state Representative John Tomlinson. John was an exceptionally nice man but didn't want to serve as the sponsor and it showed. John's strong suit was his extensive preparation, but it was more than offset by his utter lack of intensity about the issue. I learned an important lesson from the Tomlinson sponsorship. If we could find a lead sponsor from an unpredictable area who really is committed on the issue, great, but having a lead sponsor who cares deeply is far more critical. John did a respectable job and worked hard at his preparation, but his heart wasn't in it.

When I arrived at Congress I faced a somewhat different problem. We asked Rep. Henry Waxman (D-Los Angeles), who showed all the signs of becoming a new "Phil Burton–type power broker" of the House, to serve as our lead sponsor, but before he could get the bill introduced, Rep. Ted Weiss (D-NYC) introduced it. Weiss represented the same district that Bella Abzug had, and then Ed Koch (when he was still a liberal), and though he cared deeply about the issue Ted was completely predictable. We settled on the rather unwieldy setup of both acting as lead sponsors, referring to it as the Weiss-Waxman bill.

Unlike the state legislature, there was no limit on the number of cosponsors you could have in the U.S. House of Representatives. So because it was already obvious that it would take a very long time before the bill would actually pass, increasing sponsorship became one of our tactics and measuring sticks. Part of my reasoning was based on other groups' and bills' experience and my philosophy that members of Congress who were already on record as cosponsors were more likely to stick with us when we'd finally have the strength to get it to the floor.

Tenacity As a Strategy

Even in the early years lobbying the Minneapolis and St. Paul city ordinances, long before I'd thought about lobbying Congress, I used tenacity as one of my major techniques. I call it the "bulldog" approach to lobbying: get ahold of them by the ankle and hang on till they're sick of you. There was one Minneapolis city councilman who essentially asked me, "If I vote for this stuff, will you go away?" because I haunted the council so much of the time until enactment. Another told me, "I spend more time with you than I do my wife! Can we just pass this bill and you'll move on?" which was particularly amusing in the context of the issue. I don't know if anybody will ever be able to say, "We picked up seven votes because of it," but I remain convinced that tenacity is pretty central to my own brand of lobbying.

It wasn't ACT UP or Queer Nation stuff because, with the exception of the Northwestern Bell month-long picket, I always saw my role as that of an insider. In fact, I never went to the legislature without being in a suit and tie and I remember my real horror when the MCGR cochair of our board, Kerry Woodward, who is very attractive, nonetheless came over to the Capitol on her motorcycle and in her black leather jacket. Although it wouldn't bother me today, at the time I was far more obsessed with breaking down stereotypes.

I quickly learned there isn't a great demand to be taken out to lunch by the gay rights lobbyist. If I couldn't find the ADA lobbyists, DFL Feminist Caucus lobbyists, or my friend Allan Spear to eat with, I just took a newspaper or a good book to read in the inexpensive cafeteria in the basement of the Capitol. I also quickly learned that I'd have to listen politely to a lot of bigoted and ignorant stuff, but there were days I just couldn't take their stupidity and I'd avoid the legislature. On a few occasions, the ADA or DFL Feminist lobbyists allowed me to vent my rage to them in private.

The weekly "sanity breaks" were the only fun social occasions associated with my lobbying at the Minnesota state legislature. Begun and led by the DFL Feminist Caucus lobbyists, who were always a lot of fun anyway, they consisted of meeting at a local drinking pub on Wednesday nights with five to fifteen of the most progressive legislators and a very small handful of other progressive lobbyists. We purposely didn't do much business, although you'd occasionally get a chance to mention some emerging problem, etc., so that the legislators would feel they could really let their hair down, too.

In 1973 we had a small lobbying team of four or five, and by 1975 we expanded it to twelve. Sixteen years later, I still stay in touch with almost all of those who served on our lobbying team then, even though they now live all over the country, from Seattle to Chicago. A weekend-long, intense training session was central to our operation, with lobbyists coming to provide insights. This training also focused on our arguments for the legislation and what responses they were likely to get back, as well as any other objections they were likely to encounter. With my rotten experience of Harry Johnson behind me, we took care to teach them the value of extensive knowledge of who they were going to lobby—what their philosophies, views, and voting records were—as well as any knowledge about their previous stances on gay issues. Finally, I felt it was important they have some sense of the districts they represented.

Another major focus of the training was what I referred to as the great myth: that support for lesbian and gay civil rights spelled political suicide. It was already quite clear that we couldn't prevail if legislators thought their votes could cost them reelection. We cited the president of the state Farmers' Union, who explained that when people vote for elected officials they do so based on the issues that impact their lives—farming, taxes, and even constituent services. Little did I realize then how much the issue would follow me for the duration of my gay rights lobbying career.

In fact, most of the lessons we learned at the Minnesota state legislature served us well as lobbyists for years, including at Congress. One of the weaknesses of most lesbian and gay rights lobbyists, particularly when they're just beginning, was to tend to think that their presentation to the legislators was the bulk of their responsibility. In fact, one of the most critical factors in good lobbying is to probe the legislator to discover his or her views, questions, and misgivings. Only when we know where the barriers are can we address them successfully, so it's essential to get the legislator talking, even if we have to ask a series of questions in order to get them talking (and even if we're going to hear stupid and bigoted remarks). I've seen a number of beginning lobbyists misunderstand silence and report back that "we had a good chance to get X's vote" when we didn't even really have a clue what they were thinking. Fundamentally, lobbying is a sales job—just one where we're selling a tough issue to a group of skeptical legislators.

Another thing we learned early on was how critical it is to address the issue of gay youth in general and gay teachers specifically. Because legislators don't want to betray either their ignorance or bigotry, they're seldom willing to actually raise the issue, but make no mistake: it's probably the number one topic of concern (with political impact second) as they deliberate about nondiscrimination laws for lesbian and gay Americans. If it doesn't come up in our one-to-one meetings, it certainly will when the floor votes come!

Just because someone was gay or lesbian, or even because they were effective activists, doesn't mean they necessarily would be good lobbyists, so role-playing was part of the training. Although we'd initially tried role-plays in front of the full group, they were just too intimidating, so we set up private appointments and the lobbyist-trainees would come in and do two role-plays—one with a legislator who was neutral and one with somebody who was hostile and often uncommunicative. A former high Republican official, who wasn't out, had the perfect demeanor to play the state senator in role-plays and helped by doing so in private sessions. I'd critique the role-play at the end, but wouldn't interrupt until each session was complete. If they weren't doing too well, I'd suggest that we reschedule another role-play in a week or so. Each of the team members, if they'd passed muster, took responsibility for five to thirteen legislators and I took the rest. Their lobby assignments were based on an assessment of their skills, with those less able getting about half those who were likely votes and half those who would be tougher to get.

Doug Elwood, the therapist who could get legislators talking and then effectively answer their concerns, got ten to twelve of the most pivotal legislators. Mike Garrett, who'd given the money to help get the lobby off the ground in the first place, reluctantly lobbied, though he hated it. Kathy Cota discovered she was so good she went on to lobby for the nurses' association. Rick Davis, a deeply dedicated activist who took his task seriously, faced some of the toughest assignments and held his temper remarkably well. One legislator, from Minneapolis, began their meeting by saying, "Oh, you're the faggot lobbyist. Well, you should know I don't like queers!" Although Rick's experience was unique, our lobbyists did put up with a lot of stupid, ignorant, and bigoted statements, so I wanted only those who could face this crap without going off. One lobbyist we had who didn't hear such attacks was a Catholic priest, Father George Casey, who put on a collar (at my request) to go over to the state Capitol (more on George and the pieing of the archbishop in Chapter 12). After we got going, we had potluck dinners at somebody's house every couple of weeks to evaluate our progress, tell our war stories, and generally just build a sense of team participation.

Moving to the National Scene

When I moved to Washington, DC, in September 1978, my top priorities were to put GRNL's financial house in good enough order to keep the doors open and to figure out how to advance the national nondiscrimination bill, thereby giving the lesbian and gay community something to rally around nationally. The other piece of the puzzle was the fact that I was always clear just how many things had to be done to bring the civil rights bill to the floor someday and secure a positive vote: the direct education of legislators; coalition building; development of strong grassroots political pressure and mail; establishing the sort of political clout (in terms of both PAC contributions and mobilization of volunteers); and so on. However, it's always been clear that most of the lesbian and gay public, and people in general, tend to think of lobbying in terms of direct, one-to-one advocacy.

Since we had to show the lesbian and gay community there was reason to focus on national matters, our first attainable goal was simply to increase sponsorship significantly. One aspect which wasn't so different from my previous experience was the way the lesbian and gay civil rights issue broke down along "liberal/conservative" lines to a large extent. So when I assumed leadership of the Gay Rights National Lobby, a couple of my first priorities were to somehow increase sponsorship among Republicans to make the issue truly bipartisan and secure the broadest possible support and cosponsorship from minority legislators. Because we've always known there were a certain number of blue-collar, socially conservative "Reagan Democrats" we'd never get, it seemed particularly important to offset them with the votes and support of more progressive GOPers.

Mobilizing Republican Support

Of the 47 cosponsors in the House of Representatives (there wasn't a bill in the Senate yet), only three were Republicans. We convinced two of the three to sign a "Dear Colleague" letter to fellow Republicans urging their cosponsorship. Rep. Stewart McKinney (R-CT), who died some years later of AIDS, didn't sign the Dear Colleague, but I'm convinced that the matter probably never got to his direct attention. Representatives Pete McCloskey (R-CA) and Bill Green (R-NY) pointed out the proper Republican justifications for supporting the legislation, stating:

> The 1976 Republican Platform states that: "The Government must protect your constitutional rights. The government must assure equal opportunity."
>
> Support of this legislation does not condone homosexuality per se. Ronald Reagan recognized this distinction when he publicly opposed California's Proposition 6 in 1978 (a measure which would have provided for the firing of teachers who "advocated" homosexuality) on the premise that attempts to regulate the private lives of citizens run directly counter to the Republican commitment to lessen the role of government in the lives of the citizens of the U.S.
>
> As columnist William Safire wrote: "Certainly there is a danger in toleration being taken for approval, but the greater danger is in the invasion of everybody's right to privacy . . . when we fail to give them the equal protection of the law, then it is the law that is queer."

Securing more Republican support was a major but largely unsuccessful goal of the Lobby and, subsequently, the successor group, the Human Rights Campaign Fund. In more recent years, antigay fundamentalists—no doubt inspired by Paul Weyrich's Free Congress Foundation—have moved to head off our efforts to secure GOP support for lesbian and gay civil rights. By intensive grassroots organizing, they've significantly taken over the Republican caucuses and organizations in countless states. The result appears to be that moderate to liberal Republicans who might have voted in favor of civil rights for gays are now often too intimidated to seriously consider voting with us. Their fear, rightly or wrongly, is that they would lose GOP endorsement in their next race, or at least face a serious and expensive primary.

The resurfacing of moderate Republicans around the pro-choice issue may give us chances to gain some GOP legislators, but in states where caucuses rather than primaries control the selection of GOP candidates, it will be very tough to break the right-wing vice grip. It's easier to get the zealots of the fundamentalist right to turn out and sit through tedious caucuses than it is the country club Republicans who used to dominate the GOP.

Support from Members of the Congressional Black Caucus

I've always felt it was critical to secure the broadest possible support for lesbian and gay civil rights from racial minorities. Perhaps this was partly because of my own exclusive attraction toward black men, but I think it's really more about my view that our right-wing opponents would at some point almost certainly try to pit gays against blacks and Hispanics. If racial minority leaders opposed the legislation and argued that it wasn't like civil rights for racial minorities, it could seriously undercut our efforts.

With this premise in mind, I targeted the various black congresspeople for cosponsorship, and we were quickly able to secure almost 100 percent of the Congressional Black Caucus as sponsors. As I recall, we ended up with almost twenty black cosponsors, and I think only Rep. Gus Savage, a serious homophobe who represented the South Side of Chicago, and Rep. Harold Ford of Memphis, Tennessee, were not on the bill at the time. Of course, there have been changes since then, including Ford finally signing on to the bill and Savage being defeated in the 1992 primary by gay rights supporter Mel Reynolds. In the early days, Rep. Julian Dixon (D-Los Angeles) and Rep. Mickey Leland (D-Houston) were among our leading advocates. More recently, both Rep. Craig Washington (D-Houston) and Rep. Eleanor Holmes Norton (D-DC) seem to be among our most vigorous friends. (The Campaign Fund, which has probably contributed more money to minority candidates than any other PAC in the country, has continued this as a priority, so many of the new black congresspeople were elected after redistricting in the 1992 elections.)

A short time after we'd secured the aforementioned support, which was the result of a lot of hard work, I had an opportunity to speak to a plenary session of the national convention of Black and White Men Together (BWMT), a group I belonged to. I was introduced to the assembled group by national cochair Charles Stewart, who became a friend of many years despite occasional bumpy times along the way. Those attending were extremely surprised and proud of the leadership of the Congressional Black Caucus, particularly because the black community is seen by many black lesbians and gay men as especially homophobic. I didn't stress my hard work to secure such overwhelming support but privately felt a great deal of pride in helping make this accomplishment possible.

In general, the participation of black gay people lagged substantially behind that of white gay men and women, which isn't surprising. Not only is there homophobia in the black community and some minor traces of racism in the gay community, but there is also the simple fact that black gay people have several oppressions to address and may well devote more of their attention to black issues. Happily, as society's attitudes have improved, it appears to me that the black gay and lesbian community participation has mushroomed dramatically, with people such as Chris Bates, Phill Wilson, Rev. Carl Bean, and countless others playing critical leadership roles. However, that was all a bit later.

One minor downside occurred some time later when people criticized the Lobby and myself for not doing enough outreach to people of color, and they specifically held up the near-unanimous cosponsorship of the Congressional Black Caucus as part of the reason. That seemed a bit unfair in light of how hard I'd worked to secure this support and the fact that we had made concerted efforts to gain broader black community involvement. In hindsight, due to my own involvement with black men socially, I was probably hypersensitive and a bit defensive. Also, all aspects of the gay movement did have to work much, much harder, not only to just be open but then to actually recruit the participation of people of color.

At the same time we worked to increase cosponsorship among minority members of Congress and increase the numbers in general, we also set out to secure the sponsorship of key members on relevant committees and subcommittees. I recall that early in my time in Washington, DC, we overcame the initial resistance of Rep. Don Edwards (D-CA), the chair of the Judiciary Subcommittee on Civil and Constitutional Rights and an extremely well-respected member of the House, to gain his cosponsorship. As a very strong and gutsy liberal, I'm not quite sure why he wasn't already on the bill, but I do remember that UFMCC's Adam DeBaugh had helped turn that around by getting MCC members in Edwards's area to meet with him. In my recent conversations with HRCF director Tim McFeeley I was excited to learn that Rep. Don Edwards would be the chief sponsor of the national lesbian and gay civil rights bill, speaking yet again to the progress we've made over the years.

There were more than a few major disappointments as I sought out increased cosponsorship. I won't soon forget my meeting with Rep. Millicent Fenwick, a liberal Republican from New Jersey who had been immortalized by the Doonesbury cartoon strip. I'd talked extensively with her legislative assistant, who was supportive, but he indicated I'd have to convince her. Actually, her aide was one of the very few gay aides who actually seemed supportive; most seemed to bend over backward to avoid helping.

When I met with Rep. Fenwick I expected the ex–fashion model to be open and sensitive. Instead, I was shocked to learn her real views. She went on at length about the danger gay men posed to children. I tried several different approaches to the issue and cited all the support of educational and psychological groups. Out of the corner of my eye I saw her aide, who I could tell was gay even if she couldn't, practically in tears. It was not only a horrible meeting but I felt just horrible that this young staffer had to go through the experience.

Fenwick wasn't the only liberal legislator unwilling to sponsor. Trying to gain Rep. Barbara Mikulski's (D-MD) sponsorship led me directly into the jaws of a lion, her administrative assistant Ann Lewis. Mikulski was a single Democrat from Baltimore who had won by 70 percent on a regular basis. With the knowledge of her margins of victory and the fact that I understood her special sensitivity to the issue, I tried to press vigorously. I argued that, at worst, her cosponsorship might cut her margin to 60 or 65 percent but Lewis, who I later discovered was Barney Frank's sister, was like a hungry tiger who proceeded to give me a tongue-lashing about Mikulski's Polish district, chewing me up and spitting me out. The facts were on my side, yet I left like a beaten puppy. Years later, after Mikulski had overcome an uproar about one of her aides she was particularly close to, she was elected to the Senate and finally became a cosponsor.

Another woman legislator we tried hard to get was Rep. Mary Rose Oakar, a Democrat from Cleveland. She was vigorously pro-life but was seen as a solid liberal on most other issues. Like Mikulski, Oakar was seen as having a special sensitivity to the issue and she regularly won by wide margins. After several years of our trying, she suddenly came on the bill without prodding or notice. However, we heard from inside sources that some on her staff were trying to get her to withdraw as a sponsor. We determined there was relatively little we could do, but I did come up with one thing. We activated our proxy mail system, Speak Out, to generate more than 300 mailgrams (using several different versions) from her constituents praising her for her decision to cosponsor the bill, essentially trying to pin her in. We couldn't be sure if it had any impact, but she stayed on the bill.

The change in another legislator's views is worth noting. When we first began lobbying the state legislature in Minnesota, State Representative Bruce Vento (DFL-St. Paul) told ADA lobbyist Denis Wadley that gay people were sick and shouldn't be allowed to work with children. Over time Vento, who was a committed liberal, turned around on the issue and became a solid supporter. When we faced the citywide referendum in the spring of 1978, then-Congressman Vento allowed his picture and a quote opposing repeal of the lesbian and gay rights ordinance to be used on our tabloids which were literature-dropped at every door in the district. When I moved to

Washington I tried to get him to cosponsor the national bill. However, he felt it would represent a form of arrogance due to the wide margin by which we'd lost during that referendum. I wasn't happy about the final outcome but liked and respected Vento and understood his decision, and several years later Bruce did indeed sign on the bill. Unfortunately, quite a few members of the House of Representatives were both solid liberals and won their seats by wide margins but failed to cosponsor. Tom Downey of New York, and Texans John Bryant and Martin Frost are three that stick out in my mind at this time.

Utilizing the Support of Nongay Groups and Religious Denominations

We also turned to coordinated letters from supportive groups and religious denominations to help make the case. The American Civil Liberties Union letter spoke eloquently to the need for outspoken support and cosponsorship, stating:

> The American Civil Liberties Union regards discrimination in employment based on sexual orientation as a bona fide civil rights issue, no different morally or legally from similar discrimination against racial, ethnic or religious minorities. Once, biased attitudes against Blacks, Jews and other minorities reigned in this country, and discrimination in employment against those groups was widespread.
>
> Many people, including many legislators, privately voiced their support of efforts to end such discrimination, but found reasons to avoid standing publicly with the victims. Looking back now, their public inaction served to prolong deeply rooted discriminatory practices which are now widely condemned. (May 1981 letter from John Shattuck, the ACLU's Washington director)

When we ran into resistance to cosponsoring a bill that "wasn't going anywhere" per se, we decided to first hold congressional briefings, which aren't an official congressional process but still indicated some limited movement. A short time later, there were actual congressional hearings before Rep. Gus Hawkins's Subcommittee of Education and Labor.

Finally, a Bill in the United States Senate

A nondiscrimination bill had been in the House for several years, but we'd never been able to get a bill introduced into the Senate. So it was with much surprise and more than a little doubt that I received a call from an intern to the newly elected Senator Paul Tsongas (D-MA) saying she thought that the senator might be willing to sponsor the bill. The fact that Tsongas hadn't even signed on the House bill during his two terms there only increased my doubts, but it was worth a try, so I met with the intern and subsequently met with Tsongas's delightful legislative director, Helene Colvin. Our meeting couldn't have gone better and she agreed to recommend to Tsongas that he introduce the bill.

When we heard back, it was good news. However, Senator Tsongas decided it would be more effective for the bill to be a fair employment bill only, rather than one including housing, accommodations, etc., like the House bill. Although I knew we eventually wanted both bills to be the same, I was nonetheless thrilled at Tsongas's willingness to go forward.

Later I found out that movement activist Bob Kunst of Florida had tracked down and angrily confronted Tsongas because the bill wasn't comprehensive. Kunst kept poking the senator in the chest and denouncing him as an uptight heterosexual. The senator tried to explain to Kunst, who was dressed in "Florida casual" of blue jeans and a flowered shirt, that he put the bill in the way he did so it could secure the broadest possible cosponsorship. Kunst neither understood nor cared, however. His hopes for wide sponsorship weren't quite met, although Paul not only put out the traditional "Dear Colleague" letter but also personally buttonholed fellow senators. Only three other senators came on right away: Daniel Patrick Moynihan (D-NY), Lowell Weicker (R-CT), and Bob Packwood (R-OR)—not many, but at least it was truly bipartisan.

Among the many so-called champions of gay rights who refused to cosponsor was Senator Alan Cranston from California. Even after a meeting with a large delegation of gay and lesbian activists the day after the 1979 march, Cranston refused to sign on, and it was several years before he finally did so. The leading liberal in the Senate, Ted Kennedy, steadfastly refused to cosponsor, and this was particularly hard for someone like myself, who idolized him and who was inspired to get involved in politics by John Kennedy, Robert Kennedy, and Martin Luther King.

Years later Senator Tsongas attributed his outspoken support for lesbian and gay rights during the 1992 presidential primaries to our pressing him to serve as our lead sponsor. He claimed that when we "took a chance on a backbencher" he studied the issue carefully and became deeply committed to it. His contention was flattering even if it was a bit exaggerated. I think Paul Tsongas's outspoken gay rights leadership also played a role in Bill Clinton's subsequent unprecedented support, though Clinton's personal friendship with activist David Mixner—and the way the gay community came through with campaign contributions and volunteers—were the primary factors.

After Reagan won his sweeping victory in 1980 and the Republicans took control of the Senate, progressive causes were largely in retreat and many predicted that we'd be lucky to get half as many cosponsors as we'd had in the previous session, so I needed some notable successes. Among those I wanted most were Senator Ted Kennedy, who'd reached out to gays during his primary battles against Carter. In a letter I wrote him in 1981, I cited several factors, including strictly legislative advancement and increased "respectability," which could help expand off-the-Hill support. Finally, I cited the psychological impact on gay men and lesbians themselves. In reference to this last point, I stated,

> With the right wing swing and increased incidents of discrimination and violence against gays, many gay people fear that the last ten years of progress toward civil rights will be completely wiped away.
>
> Gay people, unlike racial minorities, can step away from the fight if it gets too tough merely by going "back into the closet." Many are watching closely (and nervously) to see if things get as bad as it seems they might. In this context, tangible factors such as cosponsorship can have a significant and positive psychological impact on this nation's gay citizens.

Although I heard from Kennedy staffers that he was impressed with my arguments, it was a meeting between Kennedy, San Francisco gay activist Jim Foster (who'd been Kennedy's northern California coordinator in his 1980 challenge to Carter), and myself that finally got Kennedy on board; in the final analysis, it was Foster's friendship with Kennedy that got it. Happily, I'm able to report that Ted Kennedy, who is an excellent legislator, agreed to become the chief sponsor in the Senate during the 1993 session. Unfortunately, for every Kennedy with the guts do what was right, there were many others who either chose to remain silent or, even worse, pledged during their elections to cosponsor the bill only to later break their commitments.

Silence Isn't Always Golden

The final words from the ACLU letter resonated with me:

> Many people, including many legislators, privately voiced their support of efforts to end such discrimination, but found reasons to avoid standing publicly with the victims. Looking back now, their public in-

action served to prolong deeply rooted discriminatory practices which are now widely condemned.

I pride myself on being politically pragmatic and never expected legislators to go to the well for an empty bucket. That is, I haven't tried to convince legislators who barely win reelection to then cosponsor. Not only don't I want them to lose, I also don't want to see the issue of lesbian and gay rights held responsible for costing people reelection, which in the long term would be far more devastating than going without one more sponsor.

Senators such as Chris Dodd of Connecticut, Paul Sarbanes of Maryland, Tim Wirth of Colorado, Bill Bradley of New Jersey, Carl Levin and Don Riegle of Michigan, and Arlen Spector of Pennsylvania are among the many liberal legislators who refused to cosponsor this legislation to ensure basic fairness and civil rights. Although I might have included Senate Majority Leader George Mitchell in this list at one point, I've since learned that he has substantive, if misguided, reservations. Perhaps because of my own liberal orientation, their silence over the years has been particularly galling to me.

So when Senator Tom Harkin (D-IA) decided to run for the Democratic nomination for president in 1992, I saw an opportunity both to secure some richly deserved payback for his silence (and several antigay votes on Helms amendments) and to use him as an example. Before we resorted to more confrontational tactics (which I felt I could employ as an independent agent), we sought one final time to secure his sponsorship. I had supported the Campaign Fund's contributing the $5,000 legal maximum during his tough battle to defeat Tom Tauke a couple of years earlier, and we were lucky to have an extremely politically savvy activist in Iowa, Michael Current, to do a constituent meeting with Harkin.

Harkin remained unmovable, however, and we decided he had to be confronted everywhere he went, at least as long as he was a viable presidential candidate. Activists in Minnesota, gay and nongay alike, confronted him when he spoke in Minneapolis, and Harkin totally lost his cool, throwing down his glasses and breaking them during the confrontation. Gay and lesbian activists staked out the cornfields around the farm from which Harkin made his official kickoff announcement, and they were present most other places where Harkin campaigned. I wrote and distributed a two-page memo summarizing Harkin's failings to speak out. The memo stated, in part, "In the seventeen years Tom Harkin has served in Congress, more than 160 Members of Congress have cosponsored this legislation, which would provide legal recourse against discrimination in housing and employment."

Pointing out that the national Democratic Party adopted a gay civil rights plank way back in 1980, that opinion polls showed well over 60 percent support, and that even the AFL-CIO passed a resolution of strong support, we wondered if something aside from politics was at work:

> Many have assumed that Harkin's lack of support has been based on cautious, political considerations; however, careful examination suggests that something else may be central here. Harkin enjoys pointing out that throughout his career, he has been consistently pro-union, despite the fact that his congressional district and state have not been pro-union. There seems to be plenty of information that suggests Harkin is a politician with the courage of his convictions who speaks his mind. This leaves us with the unmistakable conclusion that his refusal to speak out against anti-gay discrimination is because he doesn't oppose it.

My memo went on,

> . . . there's a difference between "special interests" (Harkin's term) and the public interest—that he can't "show his independence" by refusing to stand up for human rights. Let Harkin know our party is a coalition and we don't pit one group against another, but rather that we work together and we stand together.

Harkin's candidacy—and our confrontations—didn't last very long, because he simply didn't catch on. Nonetheless, one liberal group with a long-standing position in support of lesbian and gay rights, the Americans for Democratic Action, showed what sort of priority they gave to the issue when they still gave Harkin their national endorsement. Since I'd been trained by ADA lobbyists in Minnesota, it made me very sad and I no longer feel comfortable supporting the organization that won't back up its words, even though I remain very fond of a number of their key people.

Confronting such gutless liberals—who address the issue only when the time is right or when forced to—poses a serious challenge for mainstream, within-the-system groups such as the Human Rights Campaign Fund. Because of my now independent status, I've considered starting a group called "Silence Isn't Golden!" to make the point that so many others have made: all that must happen for evil to prevail is for people of good will to remain silent.

One senator who was particularly galling to me was Frank Lautenberg of New Jersey. Lautenberg, who was very rich and poured money into his campaign, won the endorsements of both the gay and lesbian statewide group and the National Organization for Women by responding in writing that he'd cosponsor the nondiscrimination bill. His opponent, Rep. Millicient

Fenwick, was delightful but was deeply homophobic, and Lautenberg's signed pledges (at least two that I know of) won him our support. Once elected, though, he backtracked. It took until 1991 for him to honor his pledge of several years earlier and cosponsor, and I shared the anger and rage of New Jersey activists.

Lautenberg's treachery was duplicated in spades by Rep. Ron Wyden of Portland, Oregon. Wyden had defeated an incumbent Democrat—and cosponsor of the bill—in the primary in the early 1980s and had secured gay groups' endorsements by pledging to be a far more active advocate on Capitol Hill. However, once elected he changed his decision and wouldn't sign on to the bill. Leading gay constituents Jerry Weller and Terry Bean and I met with him without success; only years later did he eventually decide to sign on.

Experience with Georgia's Senators

If I was distressed and upset by legislators who refused to speak out against discrimination by cosponsoring the bill, I hadn't seen anything yet. In 1981 and 1982 I learned of a United States senator who fired not one but two gay staff people. Even if we'd been able to pass the national lesbian and gay civil rights bill for nondiscrimination in jobs, housing, and public accommodations, Congress has consistently exempted itself from coverage of such civil rights laws.

After all these years, the entire issue resurfaced in my consciousness when Senator Sam Nunn (D-GA), the powerful chairman of the Armed Services Committee, spoke out vigorously against President Clinton's intention to end the antigay witch hunts in the military. It all came flooding back to me as I met with two individuals who had been forced to leave Nunn's employment based on their sexual orientation. As it turned out, the two cases came up completely separately and, in both cases, there was no accusation—or even hint—of either inappropriate behavior or that either individual posed any security risk.

Further, both individuals had excellent work records and were out of the closet, eliminating the weak reed on which some of our opponents try to hang: no one could possibly contend that one or both were hiding behind their status as gay men. In two totally unrelated cases, the dismissals had demonstrated the severity of Nunn's homophobia.

The first person I met who had faced this discrimination was Greg Baldwin, who was introduced to me over lunch by a mutual acquaintance. Greg had won a Bronze Star and a Purple Heart during his time in Vietnam. As I sat and listened to Greg's story, it just seemed amazing. I tried to explore whether any other factors could be at play, but concluded that Greg's case was little more than blatant discrimination. I also remember being concerned at Greg's apparent inclination to make excuses for Nunn's clearly unfair approach. We concluded there was little we could do and it got no publicity at the time.

When the issue came up years later in the context of Nunn's opposition, I was surprised at Greg Baldwin's initial willingness to forgive and excuse Sam Nunn. If I hadn't liked Greg and known him as a board member of my Fairness Fund, as well as a major fund-raiser for various AIDS groups in south Florida, I might have concluded that his statement was little more than internalized homophobia. Knowing Greg, though, I just had to conclude that either he was being diplomatic (which I know very little about) or he was just being nice.

In a *Washington Post* article about Nunn's homophobia, it became clear that not everyone was afraid to do what was right.[1] When Baldwin moved back to Florida, he accepted a position in the Assistant U.S. Attorney's office; despite the FBI freaking out, U.S. Attorney Stanley Marcus stood his ground and hired Greg.

Some time after I'd met Baldwin and heard of the hell he'd had to go through, I mentioned the case to a friend and long-time supporter of the Human Rights Campaign Fund. To my shock, he told me that he too had a friend, Ralph White, whom Nunn also had let go. A short time later, I got together with White, who seems to be one of the most genuinely nice guys I've met. Again, we discussed the case and I kept my ears open to see if the removal was in any way based on misconduct or an inability to do the job; and again, it became clear that what was going on here was simple discrimination.

If Greg Baldwin had been, in my view, far too forgiving, Ralph White made no secret of his deep sadness and just how much Nunn's bigotry had hurt. He confronted Nunn and told him that he was deeply offended by the suggestion that he was less patriotic than anyone else. White told me that to be fired because he was gay was like being kicked in the stomach.

When I first met with Wyche Fowler he was the congressperson from Atlanta and was regularly reelected by very wide margins. We'd been working for some time to arrange the proper constituent lobby visit and finally in 1984 had put together the right group, including activist Frank Scheuren, a couple of lesbian leaders, and the leader of the local Black and White Men Together (which was relevant in a 70 percent black district). I flew to Atlanta to join in the meeting.

When the meeting began I learned that Fowler had come up with a strategy to avoid addressing the issue. A short time earlier, the *Congressional Quarterly (CQ)* had done a feature story on the gay lobby, something that normally I would have been very excited about. However, we were right in the midst of the conflict with David Goodstein and with gay reporter Larry Bush. When the *CQ* reporter came to interview me, we had a wide-ranging and generally very positive conversation. (Our new deputy director, Jerry Weller, sat in on the meeting and later told me how deeply impressed he'd been with my performance—no minor statement coming from someone with the political and media savvy Jerry possessed.)

Yet when the article came out, I looked very bad indeed. Clearly, Fowler had read the article and tried to avoid cosponsorship by making me the issue. In the single slimiest legislative performance I've ever personally encountered, he denounced me to the others in the room as inept. I stressed that members shouldn't cosponsor if it might cost them reelection, but I also pointed to Fowler's wide margins of victory. He wouldn't budge and never realized that the other gay constituents at the meeting were personal friends of mine. I was incredibly angry as I left that meeting and swore I'd contribute to Fowler's opponent's campaign, even if the candidate turned out to be right wing and antigay.

In 1992, Fowler faced a supposedly easy reelection. The lesbian and gay community had done a truly impressive job of mobilizing volunteers for the election—but for Clinton and not for Fowler, in part because of Fowler's votes for several of Helms's antigay amendments and on AIDS issues. Massive numbers of gay and lesbian voters, who played a critical role in helping Bill Clinton win the state, sat on their hands and didn't even vote in the Senate race. Fowler was narrowly ahead at the end of the election night, but he hadn't secured the constitutional majority (50 percent plus one) necessary for election in Georgia. In the subsequent runoff, Fowler lost.

In a fitting culmination, Fowler's defeat not only untracked his political career but also virtually stopped any further discussion of Nunn getting the appointment as secretary of defense in the new Clinton administration, perhaps because they were afraid another special Senate election could bring in one more Republican. Instead, Rep. Les Aspin (D-WI), who said the right things about ending the antigay witch hunts in the military, was selected.

Member-to-Member Lobbying

In general, member-to-member lobbying and logrolling takes place around an immediate and pressing issue. Rep. Barney Frank (D-MA) and Rep. Gerry Studds (D-MA), the two openly gay House members, have done a great deal of such lobbying of their colleagues—on the hate crimes issue, on ending the outrageous immigration ban on gays coming into the country, the military witch hunts, and, of course, on AIDS.

Yet another classic case of member-to-member lobbying took place leading up to the 1982 elections. As I mentioned in Chapter 3, Rep. Phil Burton (D-San Francisco), who'd barely lost the position of House majority leader a couple of years earlier, was suddenly facing a serious reelection battle, with gay voters holding the balance of power. His opponent was Republican State Senator Milton Marks, a nice guy who attended virtually every gay or lesbian function imaginable. Burton had his hands full and knew it.

Normally the gay community wouldn't have even considered giving up Burton's clout, but the truth was he'd never used his fabled clout on our behalf; in fact, Burton had never spoken on the House floor when we were fighting antigay initiatives. Burton and I met (I don't remember whether at his initiation or mine) and candidly discussed helping him. My primary argument to San Francisco's gay community would be, "Burton could use his clout on our behalf while Marks couldn't deliver his mother." The snag was that Burton had never done so. He asked me what I wanted, and since this was still pre-AIDS, I told him I wanted him to get us ten new sponsors right away and to start working with me in an ongoing manner to advance the lesbian and gay civil rights bill.

He agreed and produced ten new sponsors very quickly, and from then on he began to invite me to his office for late afternoon chats about strategy. Burton was no longer the power broker he'd once been, but he still had the capacity to make a tremendous difference, and I cherished those meetings with one of my heroes. In return, I spoke at gay fund-raisers in his district, gave him a quote which was distributed everywhere, and generally tried to be as helpful as possible. On election night, Phil told a gay aide to buy me a bottle of champagne for the good work the Campaign Fund had done. He ended up winning reelection only to die a few months later. Although some disagree, I think the entire course of the congressional response to AIDS might have been different if he'd lived and was really engaged.

Some of Our Challenges on the Civil Rights Bill

Three meetings directly with members of Congress come to mind, with each illustrating a specific point. When I met with Rep. Bill Richardson (D-NM) to try to get him back on the bill, Richardson, who's Hispanic, was warm and gracious. He'd been a cosponsor for a couple of sessions but then dropped off the bill. I knew he was contemplating running for governor but asked him why he wasn't a cosponsor and what we could do to get him to turn it around. He acknowledged his aspirations but spoke more forcefully about our failure to do our jobs in terms of generating grassroots mail and pressure. He told me he often ate in a cafe owned and frequented by gay people yet no one had ever thanked him for his cosponsorship. Since he dropped off the bill, no one from his district had urged him to come back on. He candidly told me we needed to produce far greater grassroots pressure if we were going to secure the support of others.

When I started to protest and cite two or three state activists, he cut me off and said yes, he always heard from those same two or three dedicated activists, but if my polls were correct, I should be able to generate at least a hundred letters or set up a meeting of eighty to one hundred people in a district of 550,000 people to urge his sponsorship. I thought he should still cosponsor, but I didn't really disagree with him. It wasn't until some years later, when we had produced the mail he demanded, that he came back on and has been on ever since.

If Richardson was tough, Rep. Bob Borski (D-Phil.) was almost hopeless. We'd originally gotten his cosponsorship when he was running an uphill race against a homophobic incumbent, Charlie Dougherty. The Campaign Fund was one of the few PACs who thought he could win, so we were among the few who weren't surprised by his victory. He agreed that he'd be a cosponsor, and he had indeed done so for a session or two, but his district was blue-collar and growing far more conservative, and there didn't seem to be any significant gay population. Although we pointed to the recent national endorsement of the AFL-CIO, Borski simply challenged our assertion that rank-and-file gay people even cared about such legislation. Our meeting was cordial and fairly long (about forty-five minutes as I remember) but we had no chance with him and he still is not a cosponsor (although he generally votes right).

The other meeting that stands out in my mind was that with Rep. John Seiberling (D-Akron, OH). The most memorable part of our meeting was the sheer length of time he gave us. Members of Congress never give lobbyists more than a few minutes, but this meeting went on and on, to over an hour and a half. Obviously, Seiberling had serious misgivings—he was concerned about gay teachers—and it was also clear that he wanted to keep talking. Unfortunately, we'd arrived early and had two or three cups of coffee. Unsure of the appropriate protocol, I just sat there in growing discomfort and pain, first crossing one leg and then the other, unable to focus effectively on the discussion at hand. Seiberling never signed on the bill, and I was angry with myself for blowing a golden opportunity.

Opposing Antigay Bills and Amendments

Even though our top priority always was the enactment of nondiscrimination laws to protect lesbian and gay Americans in jobs, housing, and public accommodations, the most immediate challenge for the Gay Rights National Lobby was fighting antigay initiatives, such as the McDonald amendment to Legal Services, either on the appropriations or the authorization bill. In a memo to members of the Senate, GRNL stressed that there was no compelling need for the amendment. Equally important, McDonald's amendment violated the basic premise of the Legal Services Corporation: equal access to the law. Moreover, we pointed out the danger of the amendment:

> There can be little doubt that an amendment that would deny gays access to a taxpayer-funded program constitutes a "special persecution." All that we ask is the same access to government programs and services that other citizens take for granted.

We cited a 1980 Department of Justice letter to Senator Fritz Hollings (D-SC), which stated, "If it [the amendment] is construed to deny legal assistance to homosexuals in circumstances where it would be provided to others, then it must be subjected to the Constitutionally-required due process scrutiny." Despite the ultimate passage of the McDonald amendment, GRNL's efforts received wide praise, summed up best by Dan Bradley, the president of the National Legal Services Corporation in a GRNL flyer:

> Their efforts cut the margin of loss, minimized the anti-gay impact of the final bill and—most important of all—insured a historic debate in Congress on discrimination against gay people.

Reform of the Antiquated Immigration Laws

For years and years there had been a prohibition, the McCarren Act, on lesbians and gay men entering this nation either on permanent status or even for short stays. When a number of the antiquated aspects of the INS law were addressed in the early 1950s, the days of the Joe McCarthy witch hunts were still in full swing and legislators simply modified the terminology to reference "sexual deviation" and "psychiatric personality." Now the outrageous ban on gay people coming into the United States emerged as an important issue, in part because it was being selectively enforced. Also, the lesbian and gay movement simply was beginning to have the strength and political savvy to begin to address the problem.

Each of the several gay and lesbian national groups had a pet approach to handling the issue. The National Gay Task Force (which later added the word "Lesbian") had previously agreed to stay out of the congressional lobbying efforts (which they later violated in a wholesale fashion, using the

AIDS crisis as their justification). So they wanted the matter to be handled by the Carter administration and, given coexecutive director Jean O'Leary's close working relationship with some in the White House, there was some small reason to believe such an approach was viable. Groups such as Lambda Legal Defense had had some limited success in selected judicial jurisdictions and wanted to handle the problem through legal cases.

The argument of the Gay Rights National Lobby was that administrations come and go and even the composition of the courts was likely to change significantly over time. Further, as long as the legislative history was so clear as to Congress's intent, the only viable remedy—no matter how difficult it might be to succeed—was through legislative action. Although some of the disagreement was based on legitimate differences of opinion, I'm afraid that, looking back, the more central focus was the desire of each group to get the credit from the community.

In the late 1970s, when a blue-ribbon commission was established to address the wide range of serious immigration issues, we thought we had an excellent opportunity. To our dismay and shock, however, not even the liberals on the commission—such as Ted Kennedy and Elizabeth Holtzman—were willing even to address the issues at hand. We then took the only option that seemed available to us at the moment, the introduction of a separate bill by Rep. Julian Dixon (D-Los Angeles) and Senator Alan Cranston (D-CA). However, although we knew the bills were one way to keep the issue somewhat alive, we also clearly understood the need for another vehicle to eventually change the long-outdated, if ever relevant, prohibition. In his "Dear Colleague" to other members, Rep. Dixon wrote:

> This vague provision, enacted to specifically exclude homosexuals, was based largely on the determination of the American Psychiatric Association, which has long since recanted its opinion that homosexuality is a psychological disorder. Our bill would remove this arbitrary, discriminatory and outdated exclusion. To continue to deny aliens entry into the United States based on the irrelevant factor of private sexual orientation would, in the words of the late William O. Douglas, "Be tantamount to saying that Sappho, Leonardo DaVinci, Michelangelo, Andre Gide, and perhaps even Shakespeare, were they to come to life again, would be deemed unfit to visit our shores."

We suddenly had many advantages that hadn't previously been available to us. Once Franklin Kameny successfully led the effort to repeal the American Psychiatric Association's policy of labeling gay people as sick, the Public Health Service under the Carter administration refused to label lesbians and gay men as sick and thereby took away the justification for excluding gays. (The Task Force took credit for the APA's reversal. Over time, I came to believe the Task Force would take credit for the sun rising if they could get away with it, which was a painful reality for a former cochair of the board!) Franklin, who is a bit idiosyncratic in his rumpled suit and briefcase with a rope handle, is properly seen as the "grandfather" of the gay and lesbian civil rights movement; he defiantly came up with the phrase "Gay is Good!" when most gay people still believed they were sick or criminals, and he's probably done more for lesbian and gay Americans than any other person. Even today, Franklin continues to handle many military and security clearance cases.

Somewhere in this time period, Senator Alan Cranston introduced what is referred to as a "private bill" addressing a single individual, in this case that of the exclusion of a Filipina lesbian, Zenaida Porte Rebultan.[2] Normally, private bills are passed without any difficulties, but a single member of the subcommittee could block action. In an April 1980 letter to senators one of her brothers wrote of the very real and human impact of the law on their family:

> In June 1977, my only sister, Zenaida Porte Rebultan, was denied an immigrant visa by the U.S. Embassy in Manila because she admitted she is a lesbian. . . . She has not committed a crime and has a clean police record. . . . As a result of these frustrations, our mother is suffering from a very emotional illness. She is always crying and hoping that someday, she will be able to spend the remaining years of her life with her only daughter.

To everyone's shock, including Senator Cranston's, the new Senate Judiciary Committee chairperson, Senator Strom Thurmond (R-SC), stopped action on the Rebultan private bill. Some sense of "family values"!

Also at about this time, a significant number of gay Cubans entered the country, fleeing from oppression. What sticks out in my memory now is that Senator Robert Dole (R-KS), who is now seen as a moderate, made a point of referring to the many gays entering at the time as "Castro's scum." Although I do believe we should give people room to grow, it's sheer folly to not keep in mind the legislators' positions, as they may still reflect their current views.

In the meantime, the outgrowth of the blue-ribbon commission resulted in the Simpson-Mazzoli immigration bill. Although initially it appeared likely that the bill would be comprehensive and include grounds for exclusion, it quickly became clear there were far too many controversial aspects to the legislation. The primary focus was on employer sanctions for the hiring of undocumented aliens and the nature of an amnesty for aliens coming into this nation prior to a specific deadline. This bill was fairly complicated and had a range of lobbying groups deeply involved—from Hispanic organizations to business groups to labor unions and civil liberties groups.

As with some of the aforementioned issues, the need for reform was becoming increasingly clear. At best, enforcement was spotty and unfair. Two cases stand out in my memory even years later. One was that of a Mexican dress designer. When he was stopped at the border, the INS officials opened his luggage and, discovering a bag of dresses, detained him in a dumpy motel near the airport for more than two days before finally letting him in, disrupting his work schedule among other things. I don't think we ever even learned whether this dress designer was gay or not, although that wasn't the point anyway.

Another even more outrageous case was that of the Michigan Womyn's Music Festival. The festival, which took place in rural areas of Michigan, drew large numbers of lesbians from Canada. Although the festival had been taking place for some time, the problem really exploded overnight. As hard as it is to believe, the INS officials not only seriously harassed these women but also proceeded to ask a range of incredibly invasive, outrageous questions about the details of their sex lives. These and a range of other cases gave real impetus to changing the law.

In 1982, GRNL's excellent Immigration Task Force chair, Craig Howell, worked closely with both Rep. Julian Dixon and Rep. Phil Burton to hold terrific congressional briefings. Among those testifying were several foreign gay men and lesbians who had come into the nation for a meeting of the International Gay Association (IGA), a lesbian member of Norway's Parliament, and several parents of gay people, including the Caprons, whose son had moved to the Netherlands but now couldn't reenter the country. Like the Rebultan case, the Caprons' was a heartbreaking case and they were very, very compelling.

In addition, Charles Gordon, the former general counsel of the INS, provided a summary history of the antigay provisions of our immigration laws, stating,

> Thirty years' experience . . . have conclusively demonstrated the error of attempting to bar homosexual aliens from our country. The attempt has proved by and large to be unenforceable; and where it has been successful, the result . . . is only individual cases of injustice and family grief.[3]

Our efforts to reform the United States government's immigration policy received support from a range of sources. For instance, two members of the Parliament of the Netherlands, the Honorable Frederik Portheine and the

(Left to right) Harry Van den Bergh, member of the Dutch Parliament; Rep. Henry Waxman (D-CA); Clint Hockenberry, United States Liaison for the International Gay Association; Frederik Portheine, member of the Dutch Parliament; Steve Endean, Gay Rights National Lobby. Photography by John M. Yanson. Courtesy of *Washington Blade*.

Honorable Harry Van den Bergh, came to the United States to meet with the Administration. Their trip to Capitol Hill was coordinated by the International Gay Association and GRNL's Immigration Project director Craig Howell. They met with Speaker Tip O'Neill and presented the U.S. Congress with a petition, signed by 133 of 150 members of the Dutch Parliament, urging support for remedial legislation. Their statement said,

> The Immigration Law also clashes with the free traffic of persons. This is an international principle, which gained fresh momentum from the Helsinki Agreement. We are of the opinion that, as champions of this agreement, the United States ought to follow this principle also in these matters.[4]

If ever there were a clear case for having a seat at the table it was Rep. Barney Frank's participation on the Judiciary Subcommittee with jurisdiction over the pending Simpson-Mazzoli bill. This legislation was very, very important to Rep. Romano Mazzoli (D-Louisville, KY), and Barney was very well respected by his colleagues, particularly those who shared his liberal views. Because of the sheer quantity of issues that come before the Congress, members often depend on the good judgement of those legislators who most closely share their philosophy. This fact of legislative life, and Barney's sharp and witty demeanor, meant his support for the Simpson-Mazzoli bill was quite important to picking up the progressive votes the bill would need in the House of Representatives; Rep. Mazzoli did indeed feel indebted to Barney for his help.

As I understand it, Rep. Mazzoli did not commit to supporting the end of the antigay immigration exclusion but did commit to ensuring that his subcommittee would take up the issue after Simpson-Mazzoli I was completed. Barney opted to approach the proposed change in a different, and eventually more effective, fashion, seeking to reform the entire grounds for immigration exclusion and reduce the then-existing thirty-three grounds down to a rational handful. Barney, who is both a close personal friend and an extraordinary legislative strategist, later came out publicly as a gay man (although he had made no attempt to hide his orientation and many of his colleagues knew he was gay).

As it turned out, ending the antigay exclusion was the least controversial aspect of Barney's bill, with exclusion based on political philosophy proving to be a bit more of a sticky wicket. One final factor that changed the whole context of the issue was the fact that exclusion could also be based on HIV-positive status. We haven't been able to get this issue handled, and Barney was dubious, at least initially, about the chances of changing this situation. One result was that the recent International AIDS Conference, which was to be held in Boston, was shifted to another country. In the meantime, ending the antigay exclusion has become one more accomplishment for a community simply seeking justice and fairness.

Chapter 9

Do Dog and Pony Shows Make a Difference?
How Much Do Hearings Really Matter?

Early in my lobbying career I assumed, like most other beginning lobbyists, that a key to passing our legislation were the hearings. However, over the years, I've come to view them as many other lobbyists do—"dog and pony shows" that require a good deal of preparation and must be undertaken, but which seldom produce additional votes beyond those secured in one-to-one advocacy.

However, hearings can be useful in explaining the nature of antigay discrimination, showing that broad-based support for legislation exists, and so on, and they must be dealt with seriously, in part because failure to do so can only cost votes. Although seldom are legislators actually convinced to vote for a bill just based on hearings, there are exceptions—particularly in terms of complex issues such as business concerns or perhaps AIDS; the same is true of appropriations matters as well. (On AIDS and appropriations matters the Human Rights Campaign Fund has been blessed by the advocacy of their lobbyist, Steve Smith.)

The hearings on the proposed Minneapolis lesbian and gay civil rights ordinance, which became the third such ordinance in the nation, played very little genuine role in the struggle; of course, we had almost all of the thirteen aldermen in the city as cosponsors. As I recall, only one elderly man—who had also opposed civil rights for racial minorities—testified against our ordinance.

During the much tougher St. Paul ordinance battle, the hearings provided a great deal of tension but, in the final analysis, changed nothing at all in terms of votes on the council. Having lobbied all the council members and the mayor, we were certain that we had the votes, so our side agreed to limit our number of witnesses and to address the need for the legislation. But I confess, safe votes or not, we got very nervous when our opponents brought in vast numbers of angry, hateful people who demanded that the council reject these "sodomites."

I remember pacing back and forth, deeply concerned, but it didn't take too long to see that the other side's bigotry was actually working to our advantage. Contrary to our agreed-upon lineup of witnesses, though, a well-intentioned nongay supporter sent me into a momentary tailspin when she testified that if the council enacted the legislation, they'd also better be prepared to add staff to the city's human rights office. This was the last sort of testimony I wanted to hear, but one of the true highlights of the hearing came a moment later when a tall, articulate African-American civil rights leader spoke. He'd been listening to our bigoted opponents using the Bible to justify their hate. He stood and spoke movingly about how the Bible had been used when black Americans had not only been denied their rights but actually were lynched. His testimony not only moved me to the edge of tears but also sealed the matter with the council, who essentially was already solidly with us.

Perfect hindsight suggests that the state legislative hearings didn't generally play too key a role in the outcome on the bills. However, the first consenting adults hearings did raise eyebrows and get lots of media attention when we got both the liberal Americans for Democratic Action and the conservative Young Americans for Freedom (YAF) to testify in support of repealing the state's sodomy and fornication laws as they pertained to noncommercial sex in private. The other notable state legislative hearings were in 1975, when a group of dissident gay activists, who were furious that we would not include a provision in the bill allowing transvestites to go to work in drag, threw us for a loop. As described in Chapter 4, they testified before a subcommittee (happily, one chaired by one of our strongest supporters) about how glad they were that the bill providing protections in "public accommodations" and "public services" included gay marriage and gay adoption. Legislators didn't know if that information was correct or not and absolutely freaked. Eventually we cut a deal with a legislator, who agreed to move to delete "public accommodations" and "public services," thereby saving the overall bill. I was, of course, denounced as an "Uncle Tom," but the history of protected classes showed that most groups did not initially get comprehensive coverage when they were first included for protection.

Perhaps the most dramatic hearings I've ever been involved in were on an issue only indirectly related to lesbian and gay civil rights. When Charles Stenvig, the former right-wing Minneapolis mayor, upset our supportive incumbent, he appointed a far–right-wing black man, Richard Parker, to direct the Minneapolis Civil Rights Department. Fortunately, Parker had a long, clear record that included his opposition to the ERA, serious homophobia (he often called opponents "faggots"), and constant battles with other black activists. As a member of the Human Rights Commission (appointed by the now-former mayor), I got the commission to come out against Parker's confirmation by the city council. Although the black community must have had misgivings about the appointment, Stenvig privately threatened that if Parker were rejected he'd appoint someone worse for them (read: a white woman).

I thought it was critical to keep the battle from becoming blacks versus women and gays. With the black leadership lined up behind him (privately holding their noses), I was the sole lobbyist against his confirmation, acting officially for the ADA. We thought we had a chance to beat him directly in committee but ran into a real buzzsaw. I'd describe it as my first real lesson in how hearings could take on a life of their own. There was a large black turnout, and I'd say that the committee members were both intimidated and guilt-tripped. The vote, to our amazement, was 5-0 for Parker's confirmation.

It looked bleak, but too much was at stake to just give up, so we mounted a massive constituent pressure campaign centered around mobilizing key volunteers for DFL council members. We got a boost when the council majority leader, a friend of mine, goaded Parker into attacking him based on "national origin," one of the other protected classes he'd be charged with enforcing. His statement was that the majority leader was obviously anti-black because he was originally from England, a country Parker saw as particularly racist. For seven days the Parker confirmation battle was a front-page story. Plenty of behind-the-scenes maneuvering finally resulted in our picking up the key vote—we thought. As late as the morning of the vote we still didn't know for certain. The key alderman, who had passed the first time to increase the drama, was a redneck who had recently become a gay rights supporter and was very proud of his principled position. I finally knew we'd won when, just moments before the vote, he gave me a covert thumbs-up signal. We finally prevailed (by a 7-6 vote), but I'll never forget the lesson of those committee hearings.

When I moved to Washington, DC, in 1978 to take over congressional lobbying on the lesbian and gay civil rights bill, "hearings" became a more remote, irrelevant matter, at least at first. But by 1980 we had decided there was real advantage in holding congressional briefings (unlike hearings, which are held before a relevant subcommittee, briefings are unofficial and simply helped to establish a track record and secure visibility). These were our first briefings and we used them to show Congress that there was indeed a problem that needed fixing. "Chaired" by our lead House sponsors, Rep. Ted Weiss (D-NY) and Rep. Henry Waxman (D-CA), the primary purposes were to explain the nature of antigay discrimination and to demonstrate the breadth of support for our bill. Also, we had to create a sense of some movement—to potentially supportive members of Congress and, probably more important, to the broad lesbian and gay community across the country.

Several community leaders were among those testifying: Rev. Elder Troy Perry, the founder and moderator of the Universal Fellowship of Metropolitan Community Churches; Meryl Friedman, the president of Gay Teachers of New York (who addressed an issue too many activists try to pretend isn't on the minds of legislators—lesbians and gay men as teachers and role models); Lucia Valeska, codirector of the National Gay Task Force (her testimony was shallow at best, but it was necessary for internal reasons to include her); Jeanne Manford, representing Parents, Families, and Friends of Lesbians and Gays (PFLAG); and Virginia Apuzzo, a board member of the Gay Rights National Lobby and perhaps the most charismatic spokesperson our movement has ever had (even if Ginny and I weren't close). Ginny spoke about the national public opinion polls, which demonstrated that the American people were again far ahead of their elected officials and strongly supported nondiscrimination in jobs and housing.

Others testifying were Rev. William Sheek of the National Council of Churches (NCC), NOW president Eleanor Smeal (I was somewhat put off by her lack of preparation and felt it was just one more indication she didn't really care much about the lesbian and gay issue, while I felt her successor Judy Goldsmith really committed NOW resources to lesbian and gay rights), and ACLU's legislative director, John Shattuck. By far the most impressive witness, though, was Dr. John Spiegal, former president of the American Psychiatric Association (APA). (We'd paid all the related travel expenses, as we did for subsequent congressional hearings.) We described this congressional briefing as the reason Rep. John Anderson, who was then riding high as a potential third-party candidate for president, cosponsored, though in reality it was probably his need to appeal to liberals that led to his cosponsorship.

I didn't expect additional briefings or hearings for a couple of years, but was surprised when I was told by Rep. Weiss's office that there would be "field hearings" (official hearings held around the country) before Rep. Gus Hawkins's Subcommittee of Education and Labor (one of the two committees with jurisdiction over the bill). My inexperience, and the fact that I was so busy I just didn't think it through initially, kept me from seeing the obvious: the field hearings were a ploy by Rep. Phil Burton to help his brother, Rep. John Burton, who faced a very difficult reelection battle that fall.

Despite my vigorous objections, they took place in San Francisco on October 10, 1980 (transcripts are available). Not only was the timing bad, but the location just reinforced the idea that gay rights was a "San Francisco, Los Angeles, and New York City issue." I'd have much preferred to have them in Des Moines, Denver, Kansas City, or other cities not generally seen as hotbeds of gay rights. More recently, I've argued internally for more field hearings but focused on suggesting "twofers," where our field hearings and the prominent people we could bring in would also help either local or state lesbian and gay rights legislation. But I'm getting ahead of myself.

Although GRNL again was expected to pay for bringing in those testifying, and did, I couldn't make any headway on my view that these particular field hearings should happen neither then nor in San Francisco; it was a done deal, presumably to help Burton, but neither of the Burton brothers did much to gain the positive media attention they could have gotten out of these hearings. Those members of Congress attending all or part of the hearings were Subcommittee Chairman Hawkins, Rep. Phil Burton, Rep. John Burton, and Rep. Weiss. The minority was represented by their senior legal counsel, who was quite hostile to lesbian and gay civil rights.

With our limited funds, I tried to find people we could send to the hearings at a reasonably low cost. Among those testifying were then-Assemblyman Art Agnos; vice president of the United Farm Workers Dolores Huerta; Gwen Craig, a local activist, GRNL board member, and person of color; and Ray Hartman, cochair of GRNL's board, who focused on our recently released study "Does Support for Gay Civil Rights Spell Political Suicide?" Once again, though, the most impressive testimony by far was by a former president of the American Psychiatric Association, the august Dr. Judd Marmor. Marmor's testimony focused on the fact that gays weren't sick but that discrimination and homophobia were, and he spoke specifically about teachers using the "role model argument."

Despite GRNL sending out announcements about the hearings to all three major gay papers in the Bay Area and to the many gay and lesbian groups, virtually none of our supporters showed up. It was packed by antigay fundamentalists, who didn't play a big role except to make me crazy. Probably because gay rights issues were such old news in San Francisco, the nongay media totally ignored the hearings.

Recently there have been serious discussions about holding field hearings, but instead of pursuing my idea of going into the heartland, preferably in cities or states pursuing local or state laws, discussion again focused on the Bay Area. When I rejoined the Campaign Fund as the director of the field division I needed to focus on that job and not second-guess other divisions, so I tried to stay silent. Not only was it outside my own division, but as the founder, I was sensitive to idea that I was a throwback to an earlier generation, difficult to work with, and a control freak; so although I shared my misgivings, I really tried to restrain myself (and my views certainly weren't solicited).

Apparently, the rationale for the location of the field hearings was that the convention of the American Psychological Association was taking place there, but I felt that only increased the problem. I have great respect for APA's lobbyist, Bill Bailey, but I felt we finally were beginning to overcome the whole issue of whether gay people were sick, so to allow or encourage us to refocus on it with field hearings in conjunction with the APA convention—and in the Bay Area, again—just seemed crazy. Since I was never in that loop, I don't know what undid those field hearings, but I was personally delighted.

To this day, I see hearings as most often being "dog and pony shows" that cost massive time and resources, are harmful if not done well, and are seldom able to produce much that is positive. But again, I'm speaking in terms of hearings around lesbian and gay rights, and not more complicated issues such as AIDS or new or emerging issues that really needed to have the light of day shined on them.

Chapter 10

Thoughts on Fund-Raising

The lesbian and gay rights movement faces a number of barriers that are unique to it. Despite the best efforts of people such as Sean Strub, who has done an incredible and largely unheralded job of building the universe of gay direct-mail donors, there is still too limited a universe. The few lists that are available are in danger of being completely tapped out from the constant solicitations; and the universe is not only getting exhausted, it's shrinking. If this situation is going to change, there have to be concerted and well-planned efforts to expand the circle of potential gay and lesbian donors. Also, with many of those who can best afford to make generous contributions still deeply closeted, the challenge of raising funds for lesbian and gay rights remains formidable even after twenty years of tilling the fields. Yet, when one looks at the number of other causes that raise big money—and where so much less is at stake—it's clear we have some advantages, in terms of how this impacts our donors. Certainly the AIDS crisis has dramatically changed the entire context that we face in raising money, at least in the gay male community.

Early on, fund-raising seemed like a pretty distasteful task. Looking back, the primary reason probably was my resentment that others had such resources, coupled with my sense of some people's pretension. Also, in the beginning, a significant douse of rejection, from people who thought they had a lot to lose, no doubt contributed to my negative attitudes. In the final analysis, though, this is a political fight and we simply had to have all available resources, both in terms of human resources and financial support—so I had to get over it. Over the past twenty-plus years, my attitudes in this area have changed completely.

The responsibility to raise funds is a noble one that brings credibility as groups are able to secure broad-based support from the people they are attempting to serve. This fund-raising capacity—and credibility—was what was missing for my early group in Minnesota, the Gay Rights Legislative Committee. Because GRLC was just me and a few friends, it didn't have such credibility and our early fund-raiser was a bomb. The credibility of GRNL, however, allowed us to appeal to donors in a moment of desperate need, and the Campaign Fund has credibility with those attending their dinners across the country or contributing through the mail. As my conflict with David Goodstein showed, credibility can also be taken away. Countless people across the country were unsure whether the criticisms of GRNL and myself were justified, but the attacks were serious enough for people to withhold their support and contributions, at least for a time.

For every person who gives for some selfish motive, many more give, again and again, because of a determination to make things better for themselves and for future generations. The vast majority of the donors I've met over the years have been motivated by the best possible instincts. I came to like most of them, and many of them became dear friends. Also, I cannot stress enough that givers give and we've barely begun to tap the available market of potential donors for fairness for lesbian and gay Americans. The idea that there are limited resources, and if one group gets the contribution another must suffer, is simply inaccurate, yet it's one of the myths that has died more slowly.

This brings me to the next perception I have about fund-raising: I believe fund-raising is, in a very central way, a process of empowerment. People want to make a difference and are looking for ways to do so. Because most people are not that "political" or simply may not have the time to be activists themselves, they are happy to be given the opportunity to make that difference by their contributions.

My world isn't separated into friends on the one hand and potential donors on the other. As most of my friends will attest, I've never hesitated to ask them for support. The reason, I guess, is that I quickly made a critical transition from thinking about "asking for money" to "giving people an opportunity to make a difference." If I could be assured of a good turnout that wouldn't embarrass my family, I'd turn my funeral into a fund-raiser. This explains why and how I've continued to be so persistent and harass my friends and associates so mercilessly to raise funds. I know many polished and able fund-raisers, but I don't have their particular skills. Instead, I've always had to depend on my persistence.

When the Campaign Fund put me through a week-long seminar on the impact of personality type on major donor fund-raising, I came to understand why my own fund-raising sometimes left people—including many who gave—feeling battered and bruised. I had felt that my primary obligation, once someone had given, was to produce the biggest possible "bang for the buck," in other words, to show good stewardship and to communicate that to the donors. However, that obviously was not good enough for some donors. Although I established great relations with a number of donors, my approach didn't work well for a certain subset. I learned from the seminar that my particular personality type is what they call "driven driver"

(I tell people, only half-kiddingly, that what I lack in class I make up in brass). Although it has helped me get a lot done, and allowed me to overcome personal reticence in order to ask people for money, it can leave some irritated or offended—and completely unwilling to give again.

The solution, they told me at the seminar, is not to try to change your overall type but instead to adapt your style on a short-term basis. I felt the seminar was extremely helpful and I have paid attention to the suggestions, but it isn't easy. I've appreciated the contributions of donors more than they could possibly know, and I deeply regret any bruising or bad feelings some might have experienced in response to my aggressive fund-raising style. I confess that I don't regret for a minute the actual fund-raising I've done, though.

Major Donors and Benefactors

No one played quite the same role of benefactor at the national level that Tom Weiser played at the Minnesota level, but Jack Campbell came the closest. I've known Jack since both of us served on the national founding board of the National Gay Task Force in about 1975 (they'd had a New York area board more than a year earlier). As I recall in those earliest years, a few of the Task Force board members tended to look down on Jack because of his vast resources.

Jack, who was then the president and a principal owner of the Club Baths chain, is about 5'10" with sweeping blond hair covering his head like a shell. Despite his height, which is still several inches taller than I am, he appeared short, probably because he's heavyset. Since our first meeting, Jack has led the fight against Anita Bryant during the Dade County referendum and served on the boards of virtually every significant national organization and project advancing the cause of lesbian and gay rights—the Gay Rights National Lobby, the Human Rights Campaign Fund, NGTF, the Lesbian and Gay Democrats of America, the Fairness Fund, National Gay Rights Advocates, and on and on.

Some in the community have disparaged Jack's generosity; because he has made a great deal of money from the community over the years, they argued that he was just returning some of it. Somehow the point escaped them that countless gay businesses profited as much or more but never returned a dime. When the AIDS crisis came along, Jack's connection to the recreational and impersonal sex that often happened at the baths led some activists to trash him (far too often these were puritans who failed to focus on the central point that it isn't where you do it but what you do and how safe you are). I recall one activist, who had never done one damn thing to advance the cause of civil rights and human dignity for gay men and lesbians, nonetheless publicly accuse Jack of being a "murderer."

These Johnny-come-lately activists were still wet behind the ears and had no idea what Jack had done. They didn't know that Jack had fought with some of his partners to accept AIDS education and free condoms in the baths. He argued that the baths could be transformed into health clubs with workout equipment and facilities that might reach and educate parts of the community who do not go to bars or read gay papers. The result was that these fights led to a split. This internal battle, and the attacks by gay activists, must have been very painful to Jack, but I never heard him complain and saw no signs of him pulling back from a movement which too often seemed prone to hateful attacks on its own.

When I came back into the Campaign Fund I realized that some of the largest donors to HRCF also looked down on Jack and the sources of his money. In some cases, these individuals had far greater wealth than Jack Campbell ever dreamed of, but they gave very modestly by comparison. I want it clearly recorded here that the Human Rights Campaign Fund simply would not exist if it were not for Jack's incredible generosity at the earliest, toughest stages of our existence.

Although many, many people lent critical financial assistance, it's really impossible to discuss major donors and benefactors without at least mentioning another HRCF board member, Jim Hormel. Jim, who is one of the bacon and ham family, was not only very generous but also a terrific guy. Also notable is the fact that, contrary to what most people would assume, David Goodstein never was a particularly generous giver (particularly compared to what he could afford to give) and always had strings attached to his contributions. On the other hand, after David Goodstein passed on, his then lover, David Russell, was quite committed to HRCF and gave freely of both his resources and his time.

After I left and later returned to the Campaign Fund I have had the satisfaction of watching the enormous progress the movement has made, and that progress includes fund-raising ability and sophistication. The Campaign Fund now does major fund-raising galas in more than twenty cities across the country, including dinners in both Chicago, where some of the donors I got involved were key players in their early dinners, and in my hometown of Minneapolis. The able development team is expanding the number of dinners and other fund-raising events every year.

However, because the Campaign Fund raises significant funds from major donors and from black-tie dinners, some activists have made disparaging remarks about the "Human Rights Champagne Fund." For some, who object to the high ticket prices of the events, this is part of a broader attack on HRCF as "elitists," and I have grown increasingly impatient with this criticism. Ironically, it is the critics, who often attack both the Campaign Fund in general and Jack Campbell specifically, who are being elitists. Usually the people making those comments are resentful of our fund-raising success because they don't know how to raise funds themselves, because they do not understand its importance, or because they, like my earliest group, GRLC, do not have the broad-based support necessary from the community to raise such funds.

We need a movement that is as inclusive as possible, and that means not only previously excluded groups such as women and people of color but also the broad middle and upper-middle class of gay people who have never before felt they had a role in our movement. For many of these people, their first exposure or real involvement in the gay and lesbian movement is their attendance at one of the Campaign Fund dinners or the major donor group. In a number of cases, they may have previously thought no role existed for them in the gay movement, yet many of them go on to participate in other ways: they write their congresspeople, volunteer for supportive campaigns, even picket and protest.

I took a major cross-country trip to more than twenty-five cities shortly before my retirement, and my conversations with activists around the country convinced me that we may have finally turned the corner on this issue. I think, and hope, that what's happened is that we activists are finally getting over our collective phobias about fund-raising and finally understand that the fight for lesbian and gay rights is essentially a political one in which the maximum utilization of resources—both human and financial—is essential to our victory. Further, I hope we have all grown enough to understand that the best organizing is done when we take people from their present positions and get them to move forward, as opposed to angrily haranguing them because they are not comfortable doing things our way, whether it's protesting in the streets, facing arrest, or whatever.

As good as the Campaign Fund is at development, though, I sometimes wonder why the Campaign Fund—and other gay and lesbian groups— don't search out and hire "Terry Beans" to do one-to-one solicitations to secure increased participation in major donor clubs, as well as actively solicit bequests. Although many people are reached by social contacts and peer pressure, I know that a significant number of people I have solicited (and I'm no Terry Bean) would never be reached by major donor enrollment parties but would respond affirmatively to a personal solicitation. These are people who sometimes aren't very social and are unlikely to be reached by the parties, but whose commitment offsets any shortcoming in finances.

Finally, in order for all of us to be more successful in our fund-raising, we need to look at our efforts more as marketing to our own community. In that context, we need to identify marketing strategies—such as dinners, donor clubs, canvassing, telemarketing, etc.—and better figure out how our efforts address the "needs" and "benefits" of the customer or constituent.

Chapter 11

Of Battles Lost and Opportunities Missed

We had a direct mail appeal at the Gay Rights National Lobby in 1980 that has come to symbolize some of my central concerns: "We Can Have Reports of Battles Lost and Opportunities Lost or . . . We Can have a Strong Effective Lobby Working for Us." I'm sure that it was far too long as a teaser, but it did sum up the issue in a nutshell. Somewhere deep inside, I knew we were winning the war by losing these battles, but I'm very competitive, so it was often tough to feel any victories at the time.

In 1973, 1975, and 1977 we lost on both the amendment to the Minnesota human rights law to protect lesbian and gay citizens from job and housing discrimination and on the consenting adults legislation repealing sodomy and fornication laws; the 1975 loss was largely because we were undercut by a small group in the gay community. In 1977, our head count showed a surplus of eleven votes (although we knew there was a "lie factor"), but unbelievable grassroots pressure from fundamentalists—in a state not thought of as fundamentalist—led to massive erosion and a narrow, two-vote loss in the state senate. Since we felt we had the votes in the House, it was particularly embittering and I didn't really know if I could go on. But, after a week to ten days of screwing my brains out in Chicago (my home away from home), I went back to Minnesota to take a fresh look at our situation.

As it turned out, our loss left us with a bit of a break and, before I knew it, I found myself in Miami volunteering against Anita Bryant's antigay crusade, with my benefactor underwriting my five weeks of volunteer work. I was then cochair of the National Gay Task Force board but just played a supportive role during the Dade County campaign, doing whatever was needed while forging or strengthening friendships.

The campaign arranged for Howard Wallace (who later led the Coors boycott), Chris Perry, and me to stay at the home of a wonderful seventy-year-old gay man. Although Jack Campbell and I served on the NGTF board together, I got to know him much better, of course, during the campaign (in the years since, he's been a, if not the, key funder of virtually every project I've been involved in). Lenny Matlovich, a terrific, selfless man who'd just been on the cover of *Time* magazine in his fight against the bigotry of the military, became a good friend. I was also reminded of the central role of ego in our movement, however, by having to deal with such egomaniacs as Bob Kunst.

Despite the good times and a lot of hard work, by election day it seemed unlikely that we'd prevail. By the time we arrived at our "victory party" we already knew we'd lost overwhelmingly. My most vivid memory of the evening was Lenny repeatedly leading us in singing "We Shall Overcome." Although it was another bitter loss, Bryant's efforts mobilized the national gay and lesbian community as never before and made it a watershed event.

Most of us thought the Dade County loss would turn out to be an isolated event, but some thought it would mark the beginning of a national backlash, and they were right. Shortly after I got home it became clear the right wing would try to duplicate the repeal in countless other cities across the country. Even though the St. Paul ordinance had been on the books for three years without any controversial cases, or what I call "parades of horribles" for our enemies to use, fundamentalist minister Rev. Richard Angwin announced a repeal drive.

Although it ended with a bitter defeat, recent conversation with two of our other key organizers, Larry Bye and Kerry Woodward, helped us all realize just how many of the more positive details we had blocked out of our memories. Larry never held an official title, but his political genius ensured a central, behind-the-scenes role. Kerry, a close friend, was the campaign manager, and I served as one of the two assistant campaign managers. The Twin Cities' gay and lesbian community isn't particularly affluent, but we were able to far exceed our budget goals and raise over $100,000. Although there has been considerable historical revision since then (everyone wants to take credit for victories and point fingers after losses), we benefited from an incredible outpouring of hundreds and hundreds of volunteers and were able to distribute literature to virtually every household in a single day not once but twice (as it turned out, that was one of our mistakes, as we should have left some sleeping dogs lying).

The St. Paul newspapers, which had opposed the ordinance when it first passed, came out firmly on our side. Labor unions, which were a real force in St. Paul, either supported us or stayed out of the race, and Bruce Vento, who in earlier years hadn't been very good on the issue, not only endorsed us but let his name, picture, and quote be used on our literature that went to every household in the district. We convinced the Democratic-Farmer-Labor party, which represented more than 63 percent of the voters, not only to oppose repeal but also to include it on the sample ballot that was sent to every household. Our religious coordinators, Leo Treadway and Craig Anderson, were unbelievable, not only in gaining the support of the bishops of the six major religious denominations, but actually getting four times as many ministers, priests, and rabbis on our side as our opposition had. Leo and Craig even secured more sermons the Sunday before the vote than our opponents (though members of progressive congregations or parishes were far less likely to take marching orders than our fundamentalist opponents).

We also secured the support of the five most recent mayors of the city, a couple of which were pretty far to the right. The incumbent mayor, George Latimer, who was very popular and up for reelection (he won with more than 70 percent), not only let me take him on "walking tours" for the news film clips at 6 p.m. but also helped in every other way we asked. Early on the day of the vote, with the polls incorrectly showing the vote too close to call, I received a hand-delivered note from Mayor Latimer which meant a lot to me, then and now:

> I write this in midday, without benefit of the election results, to compliment you on the fine campaign conducted by the St. Paul Citizens for Human Rights. When the results are in it will be easy for many people to criticize the strategy. However, I feel that the honest, forthright and aggressive campaign you have waged has represented the cause of Human Rights in an intelligent fashion.
>
> To those of us who know this to be a Human Rights issue, it is easy. But to convince others, many with misunderstandings and many more with fears, has been a grueling test of organizing and communication skills as well as endurance and patience. You have my admiration and respect. (George Latimer, April 25, 1978)

Latimer was another of my real heroes and I wish he had become governor. Later he did become national president of the League of Cities.

We believed in the "we/they" of politics—that is, we needed to get people thinking in terms of "we, the good citizens of St. Paul who believe in fairness" versus the "they" of a group of narrow-minded bigots. But obviously I placed too much faith in the "we/they" on this occasion. More important, we failed to give the voters any "self-interest motivation" to vote with us.

Even now, the St. Paul battle is so painful it's tough to review. Recently I met with a key organizer on our side of the 1991 St. Paul repeal vote. While I explained the mistakes I thought we made in the 1978 battle, she kept assuring me that the situation was so different now that it's hard to compare, and that I shouldn't be so harsh on myself. For instance, the AIDS crisis meant that many more people knew they had friends or family members who were gay. In addition, their get-out-the-vote (GOTV), which was critical to their victory, wouldn't have been possible in 1978. I'd like to think she's right, but I still think we made a couple of key mistakes.

The foremost mistake was that we let lesbian and gay rights be the focus when we should have made our self-righteous, fundamentalist opponents the central issue. In a city like St. Paul, which is so overwhelmingly Catholic, the sanctimonious attacks of our fundamentalist opponents made them vulnerable, and in most cases, when a candidate becomes the issue he or she seldom wins. Also, even though I realize voter ID and subsequent get-out-the-vote has come a long way since 1978, we could have done better with voter turnout. Finally, we probably made a serious error by waking sleeping dogs in what turned out to be our worst precincts. The loss broke my heart, and I still feel a lot of responsibility for St. Paul gays and lesbians not having their rights for those thirteen years.

As Larry Bye and Kerry Woodward and I have often discussed since then, the loss—by more than two to one—was very, very personal, at least to the three of us. It was after stumbling through the summer in a real daze (and probably in desperate need of daily therapy) that I accepted the position of executive director of Gay Rights National Lobby and moved to Washington. Larry first left for Florida and then moved to California, and after just a little longer Kerry also moved to the Bay Area. Ironically, eventually we all bounced back, and we have maintained lifelong friendships and worked closely on some important national movement initiatives since then.

Escaping St. Paul was essential to my mental health at the time and also allowed me to get into a better social setting (given my exclusive attraction to black men); politically I was shifting from lobbying a bill on the edge of passage to trying to establish a new national lobby which even the most dedicated activists thought was premature at best. Lesbian and gay rights, at the national level in the late 1970s, was definitely seen as a futile issue. More than a few local activists either thought or told me I was crazy to even focus attention on the matter. But, in light of the later AIDS crisis in particular, I'm awfully glad I did because some important groundwork was laid. At the time, however, it was difficult either to know how to advance the issue legislatively or to try to get local activists to even care. Only stubbornness or stupidity—or both—kept me going during this period.

With Enemies Like These . . .

An old expression goes something like, "With friends like that, who needs enemies?" In our case, I came to believe that the reverse was true and that we were blessed to have the hateful, bigoted opponents we have had, particularly in the early years before we alone had the clout to push our issues to a vote, let alone to center stage. During my years of lobbying lesbian and gay civil rights at the city and state levels in Minnesota, we faced relatively little organized lobbying against us. There were a few "Eagle Forum" women as well as the increasingly strong anti-abortion activists, who also seemed to be easily mobilized against civil rights for lesbians and gay men.

So, shortly after I assumed leadership of the Gay Rights National Lobby, a range of antigay groups emerged, along with their bigoted legislative proposals. I was startled and initially uncertain of the proper course of action; however, because I took great care to carefully monitor right-wing publications, and I knew about Paul Weyrich's plans to mobilize morality zealots as part of the right's ongoing coalition, I discovered a significant silver lining.

GRNL was perfectly positioned to keep the gay and lesbian press informed of a critical development and, in the process, to ensure coverage of the Lobby in the gay press and begin to get rank-and-file lesbians and gay men to really care about national legislative initiatives. Partially because we capitalized on this opportunity, tiny little GRNL got much, much more press coverage in the gay press than the much larger National Gay Task Force, while the various hostile bills and amendments gave us the perfect subject matter for our direct mail.

One of the first clear indications of the emergence of this massive, intense evangelical Christian community as part of the right wing was the upcoming "Washington for Jesus" rally. Although their agenda clearly included a number of secular issues, and more than 200,000 people attended, they'd made the mistake of claiming in advance that they'd get more than a million people. So "Washington for Jesus" ironically did more to mobilize progressive religious leaders (who held a press conference denouncing the right-wing agenda of the rally) and enhance GRNL's coverage in the media.

One interesting sidebar to the march was when my pastor at Metropolitan Community Church, Rev. Larry Uhrig, refused to cede Jesus to the forces of hate and took a placard down to the rally with wording clearly indicating his sexual orientation (the title of Troy Perry's first book, *The Lord Is My Shepherd and He Knows I'm Gay*). Although many in the crowd seemed more motivated by hate than Christian love, and Larry later admitted to more than a little fear and apprehension upon going into the crowd of morality zealots, there was no violence. In part because he approached those in the crowd with genuine Christian love—and didn't hesitate to address a range of misunderstandings about biblical interpretations about homosexuality—Rev. Uhrig effectively made his point that Jesus Christ never said, "Come all ye heterosexuals, for you are the children of God."

Rev. Jerry Falwell's Moral Majority received most of the press attention, but the newly formed Christian Voice posed an equally serious danger, not because of their lobbyist (former Moonie Gary Jarmin) but because of their

"Washington for Jesus" rally. Photography by John M. Yanson.

ability to mobilize grassroots mail to Congress. Christian Voice quickly realized that gay rights was the sort of hot button emotional issue likely to help them raise funds through the mail. Nothing was subtle about Christian Voice's direct efforts to more than five million people:

> I am rushing you this urgent letter because the children in your neighborhood are in danger. . . . I'm mad, outraged, and disgusted—and I know you feel the same way about the sex, godlessness, homosexuality, drugs and violence shown on television.

Some were inclined to dismiss both them and their direct mail as nothing more than a bunch of right-wing kooks, but I tried to get people to take the challenge seriously, stating:

> While Christian Voice is busily reaching out to people who share their views from all over the country, identifying supporters in every Congressional district . . . Gay Rights National Lobby has not yet been able to raise the funds necessary to carry on our direct mail campaign.

Partially because Jarmin was so inept and partially because their "Report Card on Moral Issues" included such things as the creation of a Department of Education, they had little credibility. They did have serious clout, however, because of their ability to mobilize grassroots mail and constituent lobby visits, distorting legislators' views on voters' opinions.

Other groups, such as Public Advocate, attacked the Lobby directly. They stated: "With a massive budget and homosexual pressure groups in almost every city in America, the Gay Rights National Lobby has declared war against your family."

GRNL started warning people about the emerging and dangerous force on the political horizon—the Christian Voice, Moral Majority, and their cohorts (as well as the specific antigay bills and amendments they were proposing). Apparently too many people believed that our warnings were just exaggerations, and they remained silent and failed to assist our efforts to offset these groups.

These weren't just abstract principles and the homophobia of petty bigots such as Rep. Larry McDonald (D-GA) who tried to put them into practice helped us tremendously. His most noticeable efforts were around denying gay and lesbian citizens access to taxpayer-funded programs such as Legal Services. In some ways, it was a largely symbolic vote, but defeat of the McDonald amendment became our rallying cry as we used the issue to establish relationships with members of Congress who were a long way from cosponsoring or even supporting the nondiscrimination bill. Each time the McDonald amendment came up (always without advance notice), we won on a voice vote but then lost overwhelmingly on a roll call.

The Gay Rights National Lobby wrote to Congress, "There is no compelling need for the amendment. Legal Services Corporation repeatedly has stated that they've handled few cases that even relate to the client's homosexuality let alone 'gay rights.'"

When it came over to the Senate, both Senator Hollings (D-SC) and ranking minority Senator Lowell Weicker (R-CT) spoke vigorously against it. Using his Southern drawl to great effect, Senator Hollings was particularly effective, explaining that he didn't know how one would "promote" "homo-sex-uality" (a key part of the McDonald language), but he did know that the amendment would constitute a denial of civil rights and justice. It was deleted from the Senate version.

GRNL anticipated that the House would not preserve the amendment, but we were wrong. The House's ranking minority member, Rep. George O'Brien (R-IL), pressed and House conferees insisted on its retention. Because of the ambiguity of the McDonald amendment, and because the Justice Department's interpretation of it—prohibiting legal services from litigation for "promoting, protecting and defending homosexuality"—could deny gay and lesbian citizens access to the Legal Services program, we came up with a compromise. In more recent years, such compromise language has been referred to as "second-degree amendments."

Senator Weicker offered what we then referred to as "a substantially narrower" amendment prohibiting only those cases seeking the "legalization of homosexuality." Conferees quickly embraced the substitute and Rep. Bill Alexander (D-AR) said that even the Moral Majority would agree with the Weicker proposal. Senator Weicker just smiled and said he doubted it.

In point of fact, the courts have ruled again and again that a state of mind, i.e., our gayness, cannot be illegal per se, so our references to "legalization of homosexuality" meant virtually nothing. Even some of the legislators may have known what was going on, but it still offered the political cover they needed. These amendments kept coming up and we hoped to use the same second-degree amendment again (though it didn't work the next year when Weiss tried to use it), so we didn't gloat.

In coverage in the gay and lesbian media, GRNL used the McDonald amendment to admonish our constituency about the need to improve on grassroots pressure, stating, "We at Gay Rights National Lobby do not want to act just as a 'damage control' operation." But we had dodged a bullet.

Some thought this compromise was the handiwork of Dan Bradley, but I didn't even know Dan at the time. Later Dan, who was the president of the national Legal Services Corporation, and was in his own battle to save the entire legal aid for the poor program from the Reagan administration, came out to me. Eventually he became the highest-ranking openly gay official in the Carter administration and joined the Gay Rights National Lobby board of directors. Dan's coming out resulted in countless news items on this truly remarkable man. We not only worked closely on Legal Services matters and on GRNL, but Dan was there almost from the beginning on the kickoff of the Human Rights Campaign Fund. (On a personal note, Dan and I were together when I first saw Will, who became the love of my life. In fact, I remember brazenly telling Dan that Will had the most beautiful smile in the world and I was going to go over and fall in love with him. Although most of my political friends find it hard to believe, I've always been shy in the bars and it's still amazing to me that I followed up my comment. Dan's death from AIDS deprived the community of not only an effective, fearless advocate but also a dear friend.)

In addition to the amendment to the Legal Services Corporation bill, Rep. Larry McDonald (D-GA) introduced a House Concurrent Resolution stating the sense of Congress that homosexual acts and the class of individuals who advocate such conduct shall never receive special consideration or a protected status under law; to the Committee on the Judiciary.[1]

The gay and lesbian community correctly assumed that such a resolution was unlikely to pass (although it strikes me now as somewhat similar to the recently passed Colorado initiative striking down existing lesbian and gay civil rights protections and prohibiting any future protections).[2] However, the so-called Family Protection Act (FPA) seemed to strike genuine fear in many of us. The Family Protection Act, sponsored by Ronald Reagan's best friend, Senator Paul Laxault (R-NV), was an omnibus "shopping list" for the New Right and included a number of antigay provisions, as well as provisions that were antiwomen, antiblack, and antilabor.

In my letter to members of Congress I pointed out the irony of the far right's approach:

> If bills such as this, which attempt to artificially regulate and enforce a narrowly defined traditional family life, are necessary, perhaps the family is in more danger than we thought. Surely the institution of the family isn't so weak that we must deny justice and basic civil rights to groups in our society to ensure its survival.

If we had successfully ducked the McDonald assault, we got hit right between the eyes when the Washington, DC, city council revised its sexual assault laws and passed a bill decriminalizing consensual sodomy and fornication. Congress, which has never really given up the idea of the District as the last colony, has the authority to overturn such local legislation and that's exactly what the Moral Majority insisted it do.

Falwell's Moral Majority had supported the previous antigay bills but initially focused most of their energy on building a strong grassroots pressure and mail operation, with countless paid organizers as their primary expense. Now their grassroots operation went into overdrive. Despite our best efforts to generate constituent mail, these guardians of morality probably produced twenty to fifty letters for every constituent letter we were able to inspire. But one of their methods of doing so was to simply lie to their own constituents, in this case implying that the DC bill would legalize bestiality. I've always wondered how people who profess to be so moral can justify their continued lies, not only to legislators but also to their own constituents.

Also, Reagan was extremely popular and there were constant articles about how the fundamentalist mobilization had played a key role in his victory, so the Congress was scared to death and lacking even the usual minimal guts. We won when the issue came before the House District of Columbia Committee, but the procedures allowed anyone to bring the matter to the floor. Given the current context of particular political cowardice, and the avalanche of mail from misinformed fundamentalists, we got creamed.

Right after the vote, a reporter from *The Washington Post* approached me for a quote and I responded with what I still think of as the best but least politically prudent quote of my life: "Not only will two-thirds of the Members of the House who voted to overturn D.C. sodomy and fornication laws violate those laws, but half will do so by midnight tonight!" Of course, it was just inflammatory enough to make the news for a couple of days.

Since we were getting defeated regularly on such issues, sometimes by wide margins, many friends and associates wondered how I could face these losses. As I indicated earlier, we simply didn't have the political clout to force our issues onto the floor of the House and Senate. Although I'm sure it must make them crazy, the reality is that the political clout of Rev. Jerry Falwell, Gary Jarmin, Rep. Larry McDonald, and Rev. Pat Robertson helped our efforts incredibly by pressing their hate mongering and bigotry.

In general, many people during this period must have expected me to be deeply despondent most of the time. We certainly weren't winning very often, at least as they could see it. However, I remember thinking that we were making progress at the time.

What I didn't say then, probably because there was little the board could do about it, was that what really made me completely crazy were the opportunities that we were missing. In politics, timing is everything, and far too often we simply didn't have the resources or staff to take advantage of golden opportunities. I'd simply have to learn to live with that unpleasant reality or make myself even crazier than some people already perceived me to be.

Chapter 12

Bedfellows Make Strange Politics:
Of Hypocrisy and Honesty,
Coming Out and "Outing"

When I got involved in gay rights lobbying I had no desire whatsoever to know the sexual habits or inclinations of the legislators or staff I dealt with. I understood that hypocrisy was part of the political landscape, but I had no idea how pervasive the hypocrisy was or how badly I would want honesty. As it turned out, the sexual relations of the elected officials and others we were lobbying would play a key role in my lobbying and political advocacy.

Initially I failed to understand how much the legislators' hypocrisy, whether it related to being gay or to illicit heterosexual behavior, would continue to throw me on the horns of significant ethical dilemmas. On the one hand, it's very difficult—to say the least—to listen to legislators pompously pontificate against civil rights for lesbians and gay men because "we must maintain high moral standards" when I knew they were gay, cheating on their spouse, etc. Did I have an obligation to the constituency I served to protect their interests by using every weapon available, including legislators' own hypocrisy and sexual peccadilloes?

Beyond any political consequence, others' coming out helps young lesbians and gay men find their heroes, heroines, and role models. It also shows that the gay community includes some of the best-known political, business, arts and entertainment, and, yes, even sports figures. My own coming out was one of the best things I ever did, not only for myself but also for my relationships with my family, friends, and so on. Rather than erecting walls, my honesty had facilitated bridges.

Yet I've also always believed that such a disclosure must be handled on a case-by-case basis and by the individual in question alone. Activists can urge people to move forward on such a course but have an obligation to respect others' privacy. Further, I've always thought that the best way to enable people to come out is to continue to improve the overall atmosphere so it's increasingly easy for everyone to pursue an open and honest approach to their lives without retribution. Happily, as I reflect on the past twenty-some years of activism, I can see we have helped build a more tolerant, accepting society where people can more comfortably make a decision to be honest about their sexual orientation.

The issue of coming out and "outing" has been around in one form or another for as long as I can remember. When I weighed all the pluses and minuses, I've opposed revealing the sexual orientation of others or in other ways forcing people to "come out." One can rationalize outing due to the hypocrisy of those who vote against us while we privately know they are gay themselves, but in the final analysis such outing strikes me as using people's sexuality against them—which is wrong. I also do not believe in what I call "the slippery slide" of outing: saying it isn't generally okay, but we need to make an exception in case of "Senator ____" because he's such a leader against us, or "because he always votes against fairness." It quickly can become "she must be exposed because, even though she hasn't been negative and has, in fact, been a consistent supporter, she's denying the community an important role model."

My first such encounter, as I was just getting involved in gay rights, was with State Senator Allan Spear, who had just been elected in the 1972 elections. His honesty and integrity set a standard that was largely unmatched in my remaining years of advocacy. He was a leader in the anti–Vietnam War movement and a history professor, and it quickly became clear how brilliant he is. And while he is a very principled man, he also is quite practical. His support for lesbian and gay civil rights was completely consistent with his progressive political record and a good match for his University of Minnesota district. However, when Allan first ran for the state senate in 1972, he wasn't open about being gay; despite the liberal nature of his district and his own reputation as a wild-eyed radical "bomb thrower," he felt it could cost him the election in a very close race with a liberal Republican. He was probably right.

Once he had been elected, Allan got a lot of pressure from some gay activists such as Jack Baker, then University of Minnesota student body president. Baker was very savvy about securing massive publicity, but it seemed to me that Jack was more concerned about visibility than winning and was hardly oriented to practical politics. Jack was dogmatic and quite demanding about Allan coming out—now—and the more Jack pushed, the more resistant Allan became.

Even if Allan wasn't willing to come out immediately, he nonetheless demonstrated his deep commitment to enacting nondiscrimination laws for gay people. From the moment I began lobbying the state legislature, Spear let me use his office and phone when he was either in committee or full session. In short order we became fast friends. As we spent growing time together, Allan gave me extremely valuable advice on our legislative strategy and talked politics with me. Our friendship helped me enormously and made me less one-issue oriented and a better-rounded political operative. In short, both the community and I owe him more than we could ever repay.

Like Baker, I hoped Allan would eventually decide to come out. The gay movement was still very young and it was a pivotal point, when his coming out would generate substantial publicity and he could serve as a positive role model. It was hard to estimate, but it would probably have made our lobbying effort more successful as well. Still, I felt the question of coming out is a very personal one, so I didn't press him. (Only later did I realize that several other legislators I lobbied—both at the state and national levels—were also gay. Unlike Allan Spear, though, most of them never acknowledged their sexual orientation to me. I continued to make the assumption someone was straight unless I had clear evidence to the contrary.)

Over time Allan began to discuss the possibility of his coming out and how it could be done most appropriately. In the meantime, he was carefully removing barriers to such a coming out by initiating conversations with his family, political associates, and fellow legislators, including the charming, liberal, and politically courageous Senate Majority Leader Nick Coleman. Nick, who had been the chief sponsor of the gay rights legislation in 1973, was, of course, extremely supportive. In fact, it was discussions with Coleman that eventually led to Allan's decision to move forward when Coleman's girlfriend, Debbie Howell, a reporter for the *Minneapolis Star,* offered to do a sensitive story whenever Allan was ready.

When Allan's sexual orientation was announced in a front-page article in the *Minneapolis Star,* he became the second openly gay elected official in the nation, with Elaine Noble, who had been elected state representative in one of the more progressive districts of Boston. Today there are more than thirty openly gay or lesbian elected officials across the country. The night of Allan's "revelation," which took much more courage and integrity than a similar decision would take today, Allan's best friends, Lee and Marcia Greenfield, and I spent the evening with him to lend support. I recall that one very old woman in a senior citizen high-rise who'd been a Spear supporter gave him holy hell and indicated her disappointment in him. But Allan's circle of friends and associates at both the Capitol and in the broad political community were very progressive and the overwhelming response was of friendship and support.

Allan never had been a one-issue person and he felt strongly against being pigeonholed as "the gay legislator." Happily, he was concerned and informed about many issues and such a development never became a problem. Further, because of the way his friends and associates closed ranks behind him and how hard Allan himself worked in anticipation of his next reelection bid, he easily secured a second term a couple of years later. In fact, he has subsequently survived a serious redistricting which threw him into a new constituency. As I write, Allan's political star has continued to rise, first with election to the prestigious position of the chair of the Senate Judiciary Committee. More recently he was elected president of the state senate in 1993, demonstrating that openness and honesty about his gayness need not be a barrier to advancement to legislative leadership positions.

Years later, when the Campaign Fund held a retirement testimonial on my behalf, they arranged for a number of letters for a memorial book. One of the most cherished that I received that night was from Allan Spear, who wrote, "You were one of the first gay activists I ever met—even before I was 'out' and you played a major role in bringing me 'out' and into the movement." Although I'm not at all sure I can take such credit, I can think of few things that could make me prouder.

If Allan Spear represented one end of the spectrum, another state legislator came to represent the other. Through a weird quirk, the 1974 elections resulted in a state house of representatives virtually devoid of lawyers, and the Speaker of the House, Martin Sabo, decided to abolish the House Judiciary Committee. Under some pressure to protect his people from a tough political vote, Speaker Sabo, who has always been a personal advocate of gay rights, referred the state lesbian and gay civil rights bill to the Business Subcommittee of the full Commerce Committee—one of the most conservative bodies. It would make it very difficult, if not impossible, to get the bill to the floor.

It was in this context, as we dug for every possible angle to find enough votes to get the bill out of both subcommittee and full committee—including finding second cousins and former college roommates of committee members—that I came upon a major break. One evening I went out to dinner with Senator Spear and we decided to stop at the bar before calling it an evening. Sutton's, the most popular gay bar in Minneapolis, had recently moved from a small, dumpy space a few blocks away to a large, two-floor elegant bar with several distinct rooms and atmosphere, including a quiet, tasteful cocktail lounge. I had been working at the bar for a couple of years at the coat check but had the evening off.

We got into political conversation with another state senator, who wasn't out but had been firmly supportive despite a relatively conservative district, and a former high state Republican official. When I decided to take a break from these "political hack" conversations and go cruise the dance floor, I was startled. Across the dance floor, with lots of young, hot sweaty male bodies, I spotted a state representative from outstate Minnesota. A bit older and not anybody you'd quickly cruise on the dance floor, this representative had always voted against us on gay issues. He was a conservative Democrat, or what was called in Minnesota a "wood tick." More important, from my point of view, he sat on the critical Business Subcommittee of Commerce. At the precise moment I spotted him, he saw me and virtually ran for the front door. I went over to tell Allan and the others, and by then he had regained his composure and decided to try to be casual, saying hello to me before leaving the bar.

As I've mentioned, I have generally opposed activists revealing others' sexual orientations or in other ways forcing people to come out. However, all of this abstract theory—which I view as important to my approach—all seemed irrelevant as I faced the serious challenge of getting the bill out of House subcommittee. We were one vote short of getting the bill out and, if it failed here, the nondiscrimination bill was down the tubes. So I decided to pursue a course of action I never would have even considered under less severe circumstances. It feels important to me to stress that I am not bragging in retelling the story; in fact, to the contrary, I'm a bit embarrassed by what I felt I had to do.

In short, as I was roaming through the House Office Building, trying to round up votes of swing legislators, I saw the aforementioned state representative sitting in his office alone. Perhaps emboldened by running into him the other night, I walked into his office, closed the door, and asked if I could have a moment of his time. Given the circumstances, he had little choice but to say yes and I proceeded with my bluff: "Representative, I just wanted to let you know that the gay civil rights bill in going to come up in your subcommittee tomorrow. I know you're going to do the right thing (I paused for effect) because I understand you have a special sensitivity to the issue. It may cause you a little grief from constituents, although it isn't going to cost you reelection, and I just wanted to thank you in advance for your support." With that, and not really waiting for a meaningful conversation, I stood up, turned, and left. Although I wanted him to vote with us and was willing for him to be apprehensive that I might otherwise bring him out, I never would have done so. The next day, when the bill came up in the subcommittee, he voted with us and, to everyone's amazement, we got the bill out of subcommittee.

Even now, years later, when people are congratulatory or at least tell me it's an interesting story, I still feel more than a little guilt. I have even asked myself whether what I did wasn't a form of blackmail. However, I've rightly or wrongly convinced myself that it stopped short of such a harsh action. At the time, I felt I had no choice. Several years later, after I had moved to Washington, DC, this representative was arrested in an awkward cruise setting. He lied about several aspects of his situation, but it still cost him his home life and career.

I guess the first time I ran into the hypocrisy of legislators' stances on sexual issues was when the consenting adults bill repealing Minnesota's sodomy and fornication statutes came up for a floor vote in the state house of representatives. I had been brought up to be honest and was shocked when legislators candidly admitted that these sex laws violated peoples' privacy and that they were violated virtually every day, by straight people as well as gay people. However, because these legislators knew the laws were not being enforced, they felt it was appropriate to maintain them as some sort of statement against homosexuality.

One such legislator was a rather unattractive, overweight, suburban, and quite moralistic Republican. As we did our head counts, we confirmed what we suspected: he would oppose repealing the sodomy and fornication laws, which applied to both homosexuals and heterosexuals. So when I discovered, quite by accident, that this pompous bag of wind had picked up a bisexual woman friend of mine and had oral sex with her, I was shocked. Aside from being disgusted by her lack of taste, I wondered whether we could or should address it directly with the legislator. I went so far as to have my friend write a letter to the legislator, not only supporting the consenting adults legislation but also reminding him of the circumstances of their meeting. She gave it to me to deliver it to him at an opportune moment. Many things would have been implied if I delivered it to him. Although I was fairly certain he'd vote against our privacy-based position if I didn't take the letter to him, I resisted temptation and eventually ripped the letter up. It just felt too much like blackmail to me to go forward. To this day, I'm uncertain whether it was a matter of principle or simply my fear I'd be accused of blackmail.

As I mentioned previously, we stumbled on another case of complete hypocrisy with the lobbyist for the Minnesota Catholic Conference who strenuously opposed lesbian and gay civil rights and the consenting adults bill because it would cause "the destruction of the moral fabric of society." A couple years after I left Minnesota to launch the national lobby he was arrested as a "john," picking up a female prostitute; so much for his exalted "moral fabric"! Before this personal scandal hit, this lobbyist again managed to convince Archbishop John Roach to oppose the statewide lesbian and gay civil rights bill in 1975, at the end of the session. This decision broke an earlier pledge we had arranged through the Urban Affairs Commission of the Archdiocese, and again the statewide nondiscrimination legislation went down to defeat, with the Catholic Church's opposition certainly contributing to that loss.

Just a matter of days after our loss on the state civil rights bill this same archbishop was scheduled to receive the "National Brotherhood" award from the National Conference of Christians and Jews at a black-tie dinner for 2,000 people in downtown St. Paul. To say it struck us as hypocritical and inappropriate is an understatement. However, I and most of the rest of us who had worked so hard to pass the state bill didn't have the energy to mount a protest, or at least I thought so. When I watched TV the evening of the award dinner the station cut into the program to announce that Archbishop Roach had been pied. As he stood up to receive his award, he got a sloppy whipped cream pie right in the face. Realizing the potential public relations and political damage, I immediately got to all the media denouncing the pieing, thereby assuring that the public knew that most gay activists would never do anything so outrageous or childish. The truth is I thought the incident was both funny as hell and totally appropriate. I soon learned that the person who had hired the person to pie Roach was a Catholic priest who'd lobbied for us in the 1975 session. Needless to say, when the archdiocese learned who the instigator was, that priest was sent to some remote place in Outer Mongolia.

To Roach's credit, it was one of the few occasions when I saw a positive result of such a stunt. He sought to discover what caused such an incident and he grew tremendously as a result. When the repeal of St. Paul's lesbian and gay rights ordinance came up a couple of years later, Roach joined the bishops of the other denominations to oppose repeal of human rights. Years later, he allowed the Catholic Conference to support the statewide legislation, enabling the powerful Joint Religious Legislative Committee (JRLC) to support fairness. Despite the positive development on this occasion, however, such stunts as the pieing are usually just self-indulgent.

There were at least a couple of other occasions when the opponents' hypocrisy about sex drove me nuts. One was a rural state representative, who later went on to serve in Congress, who consistently and vigorously opposed the consenting adults bill decriminalizing sodomy and fornication, and was later exposed for engaging in adultery. The indiscretion—and his hypocrisy—led to his defeat for reelection to Congress.

On another occasion I was out cruising at Minneapolis's Loring Park, which was frequented by gay men. I went there hoping to meet some hot man and, on other occasions, to monitor the police's antigay behavior. I thought I recognized one of those driving the same little circle of cruising streets but initially thought I had to be wrong. It looked like one of the most vitriolic lobbyists for various veterans' groups who had testified against the state lesbian and gay civil rights measure. He had subsequently begun a run against our chief House sponsor, using Rep. John Tomlinson's support for gay rights. After going past him six or seven times, I was sure it was him and I reversed course and began following him. Although initially he did not realize he was being tailed, and I do not think he ever recognized me, he eventually figured he had been spotted and took off for the nearby freeway. I pursued, following him about halfway to St. Paul.

I took this information to Rep. Tomlinson, who was in a heated and tight race with the guy, but John was too principled to use the revelation, even privately, to get the lobbyist to stop attacking him for his leadership on lesbian and gay rights. John won reelection by a respectable margin and I continued to frequent the cruising park—for political purposes, of course. I never saw the veterans' lobbyist again.

National

When I moved to Washington, DC, I did not know what to expect in almost every respect. I viewed my job not only as one-to-one lobbying of members of Congress but, more fundamentally, as the building of a national lobbying effort from the ground up, including the development of an effective grassroots network, coalition building, and so on. It was also my job to make measurable progress on the national level if I wanted to build the enthusiasm of lesbians and gay men across the country.

So I focused much of my early lobbying, which was before the AIDS crisis, on increasing the cosponsorship of the national lesbian and gay civil rights bill. I set out to secure that cosponsorship, directing most of my early efforts on liberal representatives who hadn't previously cosponsored. As I have explained, I quickly learned that members of Congress did not usually meet directly with lobbyists but instead utilized staff members, buffering themselves from such arm twisting. So I didn't often get a chance to directly discuss either the "gut issue" of lesbian and gay rights with legislators or have any personal interaction which might suggest that a given legislator was gay. But this did mean that I dealt with a significant number of congressional staffers and, although I've never been one of those gay people who claimed they can always tell when someone else was gay, you'd have to have been completely out of it to not understand that an awful lot of congressional staffers were gay (I say "gay" rather than lesbian and gay because my sensors made it much easier to figure out which men I was lobbying were likely to be gay). Frankly, walking through a congressional office building reminded me of being in a damn gay bar; in fact, a short time later when I started going to a gay bar in Southwest Washington, the Lost and Found, my hunches were reinforced.

But if there were countless gays among Hill staff, they sure were not about to come out, nor did I find them very helpful. In fact, more often than not I found that presumably nongay women were far more cooperative. My perceptions were reinforced by discussions with the one gay staffer who had come out publicly. Gary Aldridge is a nice, down-to-earth guy who worked as an environmental expert for Senator Alan Cranston (D-CA). Gary was startled when other gay people on the Hill, with only a couple of exceptions, shunned him after it was publicly known he was gay, presumably because associating with him might lead to suspicion about themselves.

Within a year of my becoming the first gay rights lobbyist in 1978, a *New York Times* reporter contacted me about doing a major story about gay staff on Capitol Hill. At first I was excited about the opportunity, given my need to publicize our newly emerging lobbying effort. However, as I began to talk with this woman, before the actual interview, I concluded that she was likely to do a story that distorted the effects of gay staff people. It seemed to me that her angle would be McCarthyesque about the "Secret Cabal of Gay Staffers." Not only would such an article have been destructive to gay staffers, and the lesbian and gay movement in general, but it was also far from accurate. Gay staff people were like others in their interest to protect their bosses from any bill or cause they viewed as potentially damaging—including gay rights.

If I was happy to have avoided a trap by *The New York Times,* I have often looked back with regret on something I said during an interview with Ken Bode, then of NBC. Although the interview generally went well, Bode asked me how many gay people were in Congress. Instead of telling him I wasn't sure, which would have been accurate, I said I didn't know of any. That was a lie, and I could immediately tell from the way his eyebrows went up that he not only didn't believe me but that I'd shot my credibility with him.

It was also after I moved to Washington that I saw Barney Frank again for the first time in years. In 1974 I had been elected to the national board of directors of Americans for Democratic Action, the bipartisan liberal group that played such a key role in launching my Minnesota lobbying efforts, and I attended the national board meeting in Boston. That weekend I met Barney, a liberal state representative from Boston who was the chief sponsor of the statewide lesbian and gay civil rights legislation in Massachusetts. I had read about him in *The Advocate* and enthusiastically introduced myself to him. Frank was obviously both brilliant and extremely witty, and I was excited that our movement had been fortunate enough to secure the assistance of such an excellent nongay legislator. Only a good deal later did I realize I had been working under a significant misperception. I tried to follow Barney's progress on the Massachusetts lesbian and gay civil rights bill and we occasionally spoke during the next two or three years.

At the time I moved to Washington, DC, to assume the leadership of the Gay Rights National Lobby it was a young, largely unknown group and I saw one of my many tasks as beginning the long process of gaining publicity and visibility for the organization. So, when Eastern Airlines offered a discount fare for three weeks travel anywhere in their system, I jumped at the opportunity. I traveled to about fifteen cities in the twenty-one days, (spending an unbelievable number of visits to their hub in Atlanta) meeting with key activists and reporters for the gay newspapers in each city.

One of the cities on the itinerary was Boston, where I used the home and offices of noted activist Brian McNaught as a base of operations. Brian was an extremely cute and sweet individual who had played an early role in the emergence of Dignity and the gay Catholic community. Since I had grown up Catholic, I guess I felt an immediate and natural affinity for him, and he and his lover were charming, gracious hosts. During my time in Boston I made arrangements to get together with State Rep. Frank. It was an extremely challenging situation to start at ground zero building a national lobbying effort, and I wanted to pick Barney's extraordinary brains about what we were doing. When Barney arrived, Brian excused himself to let us talk while he ran a few errands.

My meeting with Barney was going quite well and he seemed to think I was on a good track for the difficult task of building a national lobbying effort. Suddenly he lowered his voice, which made it a bit difficult to understand him, because he tended to talk very, very fast and it always sounded like he had a mouth full of marbles. He said, "Come here with me" and dragged me out into the hall and down to the men's bathroom. As brilliant and delightful as Barney was, he was not long on social graces at that point and the entire exchange was one of the more bizarre I'd encountered.

As you might imagine, I was completely confused about what this terrific but nongay legislator had in mind. Once in the bathroom, Barney—who was quite overweight and smoking a truly disgusting cigar—proceeded to blurt out, "I'm one!" He repeated the statement several times. I was completely perplexed and said something like "What? You're what?" He finally explained, to my utter shock, that he was gay. Looking back, I suspect he was doing something similar to what I'd done myself in Minnesota, when I came out by telling someone who wasn't in my daily loop. He got the psychic relief of coming out yet knew I wasn't in a position to make his life difficult if somehow it wasn't cool.

He asked my advice about coming out and I tried to give him useful input. After establishing the fact that Barney had neither a boyfriend nor a circle of gay friends, I told him a bit about Allan Spear's experience, suggesting that coming out could create a lot of pressure and he might want to spend a bit more time getting socially integrated into the gay community. But I also told him that he should make conscious decisions that would continue to build toward the time when, hopefully he would feel comfortable in coming out.

I also warned him of one potential pitfall: many of the friends he made as he built a social support system would probably urge him not to come out, in part because they thought it might expose them or in other ways put pressure on them to take a similar course. I knew from my experience with Allan Spear that such a coming out by an articulate, bright legislator could have a very positive impact on both the gay and nongay communities, and provide very positive role models for young lesbians and gay men, so I warned Barney that—at the proper time—I would probably urge him to come out. After a few minutes more of the conversation in the bathroom, we went back to Brian's offices to talk about general legislative strategy, what Barney was doing to pass the Massachusetts bill, and steps I was taking to build GRNL.

It wasn't all that much later that the Vatican threw a real curve by demanding that all Catholic clergy who were serving in elective office had to step back from those positions. The congressperson from Barney's suburban district was Fr. Robert Drinian, a progressive legislator. He quickly announced that he would comply with the Vatican's demand, opening the congressional seat. Since Barney was one of the best-known and most highly regarded state legislators in the country, it was natural for him to get into the race. Although it was a period when I was just overwhelmed with the various aspects of putting a lobbying effort together, I stayed in touch with Barney and tried to be as supportive and helpful as possible, in terms of his candidacy for Congress as well as his own sexual orientation.

I recall that partway through his race, which was going very well, Barney came to Washington, DC, to meet with a number of progressive political action committees, unions, and other key liberals. He let me know he was coming and we arranged to go to dinner at one of Washington's nicer gay restaurants. That dinner was premeditated on my part, as I wanted him to get used to the gay community, but I got a lot of grief later from two friends, Alan Baron, former executive director of the Democratic National Committee and political commentator, and Bill Olwell, who as the vice president for Political Action of the United Food and Commercial Workers (UFCW), was the highest-ranking openly gay labor union official in the nation. Both Alan and Bill, who had tentatively taken me under their wings, thought I had unnecessarily endangered Barney's candidacy by taking him to the gay establishment before his election. The restaurant was in a relatively isolated part of town and I thought they were overreacting, but I acquiesced and backed off from any further ventures for Barney into the gay community until after the elections.

A few years later, after Barney had really built up solid friendship and support systems within the gay community, I urged him to move forward and come out publicly. As I predicted, it seemed to me that many of his new friends—who weren't out themselves—were trying to influence him to not take the plunge. But Barney had been increasingly candid with his colleagues. For instance, on a fact-finding trip to the Middle East, when a fellow legislator kept trying to fix him up with an attractive stewardess, he finally just said something like, "Tom, I might be much more attracted to her brother than her." Likewise, Barney had candid conversations with Senator Kennedy and a number of others.

Although he felt he could probably win reelection in his district even if he came out, Barney had already emerged as an up-and-coming shining star of the Democratic legislators and some had already talked with him about trying to move up the leadership ladder. My contention was that, whether or not he ever told another soul, his candor to that point had probably closed off the possibility of any leadership position unless society's attitudes continued to change. I'm not all that sure anything I said had much impact on him, or just what factors contributed to his final decision, but he came out a short time later.

These days, on the rare occasions when we either get together or talk on the phone, he tells me how he and his lover Herb were right there in line when all the members of Congress had pictures taken with then-President and Mrs. Bush. He survived a couple of very unpleasant bumps along the way, which I felt resulted directly from his late coming out and the challenge of getting acclimated to the gay community. My sense is that Barney is very happy and, by the way, his considerable wit and ability has allowed him to continue to be a very serious and influential player in the House.

I have deeply valued my friendship with Allan Spear, not only because of the way it advanced the movement but simply because we shared so much in terms of interest in politics, etc. Now I realize that I privately hoped Barney and I would establish a similar relationship on the national level. While we did indeed become good friends, and he was always there to provide advice and counsel on our gay rights efforts, his schedule was so busy, his temperament somewhat impatient, and his mind so quick that we seldom found the time to get together in the same fashion I had with Allan years earlier. Nonetheless, I had made a good friend as well as a political ally for years to come.

During the early years of my federal lobbying, GRNL and Campaign Fund board members, activists around the country, and some friends often asked about who was and who wasn't gay and "what the count was." I had my own rules about reaching that conclusion—namely, that I had to hear it from several sources unless there was firsthand knowledge by someone I could trust. But, because of the nature of the issue, the "game" was really little more than gossiping and guessing. One legislator I heard about from a reliable source was a far-right representative from the East Coast. While he fit the mode of the newer, aggressive Republican gut-fighter during work hours, I learned that he regularly hired hustlers to hit and beat him. This political sadist turns out to be a clear sexual masochist.

It was admittedly very frustrating to know that there were countless right-wing, homophobic members of Congress whom we strongly suspected, based on the "several sightings" rule, to be gay. I recall at least one occasion when a large portion of an entire state delegation was rumored to be gay. We had no easy way to verify the information, and no doubt we didn't hear about countless other members of Congress who were gay but were not the subject of rumors. I remember our count on one occasion was a little more than forty members of the House of Representatives—which probably shouldn't have surprised us as much since it fit the 10 percent rule applied to 435 representatives. There was no way to really know, though.

One gay person, who was not a member of Congress but who was nonetheless a key political operative on Capitol Hill, was Terry Dolan. Dolan was the director of the vicious National Conservative Political Action Committee, which savaged liberal incumbents on a range of social issues, including lesbian and gay rights. Although Dolan was a key leader of the hateful and bigoted "New Right," he regularly frequented gay bars, including the leather bar I often went to, the Eagle. A number of acquaintances have told me of several occasions when Dolan was known to "trick out." Despite that knowledge and very direct questioning by nongay reporters who suspected Dolan was gay, I never felt I had the right to out him. Some felt it was his hypocrisy that was being exposed, but I continue to believe that such explanations are little more than rationalizations for feeling compelled to use someone's sexual orientation against them. Two or three years later Dolan died of AIDS-related causes, which was not revealed initially because he had arranged with his doctor to cover up the real cause of death.

Another person who died from AIDS was Representative Stewart McKinney (R-CT). Unlike Dolan and any number of right-wing senators and representatives, however, McKinney had a long track record of support and cosponsorship of the lesbian and gay civil rights bill and opposition to the range of antigay amendments that popped up from time to time. As the ranking minority member of the House District of Columbia Committee, McKinney vigorously if unsuccessfully defended the DC Sexual Assault bill—which included repeal of the sodomy and fornication statutes. But McKinney, who was both married with children and had a male lover, initially attempted to cover up his AIDS diagnosis. (The facts of his situation eventually did come out, though that resulted in far less potentially important publicity for the funding-starved health crisis.)

Around the same time as Congress overturned the DC Sexual Assault bill, with its consenting adults provisions, right-wing John Bircher Rep. Larry McDonald (D-GA) continued to put forward amendments to the Legal Services Corporation legislation, which could cut off gay and lesbian citizens' access to that taxpayer-funded program. During one of the floor battles I was in the anteroom off the House floor talking with the Legal Services lobbyist, Mary Burdett, when she introduced me to Dan Bradley. I later learned that he was the national president of the Legal Services Corporation, a holdover from the Carter administration. As president it was his job to lead the defense of LSC from the Reagan administration, which was determined to abolish legal aid for the poor. Dan's brilliant defense of the program made him a genuine hero in progressive circles.

When I met Dan, who was from Florida and fit the image of a modern-day good ol' Southern gentleman, he said several times—meaningfully—that he knew Jack Campbell, a very affluent gay activist from Miami. However, because Jack was active in Democratic political circles and was well-known by key political operatives throughout the state, I just did not pick up on Dan's repeated clue. Maybe a couple of months later, I was coming out of a black gay bookstore in a rather seedy part of town when I ran into Dan Bradley, who recognized me. He was very warm and friendly, reminding me of where we'd initially met and explained that he'd been discreetly trying to let me know he was gay when we'd met. I probably should have picked up on it, but I'd been so absorbed in how to stop the McDonald amendment that I didn't.

We quickly figured out we were both going to the Eagle, so we walked over together, talking nonstop on the way. Dan was a warm, engaging conversationalist and a lot of fun to be with; in the brief time it took to walk to the Eagle he made me feel like we had known each other for years. It was immediately clear why he was such a terrific political operative. When we got to the Eagle, we got our beers and continued to talk nonstop for about half an hour or forty-five minutes, with each of us obviously enjoying it. After years in important but high-pressure positions which didn't allow him to be honest about significant aspects of his life, I think Dan had been privately yearning for the wonderful freedom of coming out, and he probably got (at least I hope he did) a little bit of that experience as we talked. I had missed the wonderful combination of gay movement and sheer politics I experienced with Allan Spear back in Minnesota, so my conversations with Dan were a pure joy to me as well.

After a while I happened to look across the room and saw a very attractive, masculine, and muscular black man that I immediately fell for. I remember asking Dan, "Do you see that gorgeous man over there with the beautiful smile?" When he indicated in the affirmative I said, "I'm going to go over and fall in love with him!" The reason I remember it all so vividly was that I was normally very shy in gay bars and never considered such direct approaches. Anyhow, I did go over and meet Will, we did indeed fall in love, and we were together for several years.

Dan and I began to get together with some regularity and spent quite a bit of time talking about everything from how to defeat the McDonald amendments that often came up in those days to whether he should come out publicly. Like the Allan Spear situation, I wanted Dan to come out but I felt strongly it was his decision and so I tried to be a useful sounding board and a source of encouragement. Eventually Dan decided to come out publicly by joining the board of directors of the Gay Rights National Lobby. He eventually did an interview with longtime associate Taylor Branch, the author of the wonderful history of the black civil rights movement, which resulted in a feature story in *New Yorker* magazine. Although I don't remember him doing an actual press conference, Dan met with a number of press people he knew well from his days at Legal Services.

Some time later, as we got the Human Rights Campaign Fund off the ground, Dan became the chair of HRCF's advisory committee. In that capacity, Dan signed letters to many prominent community leaders asking them to join him on the advisory committee. As a result, several mayors and seven bishops lent their names. When ABC's *Nightline* did a show focusing on the emerging political clout of the lesbian and gay movement, Dan was interviewed live. He later served as an active, committed board member of the Campaign Fund. I remained on good terms even after I left GRNL and the Campaign Fund and visited him once or twice in Florida, where he had retired with AIDS before he passed away. Dan was also very close to my successor at the Campaign Fund, Vic Basile.

For contrast, there's the case of right-wing Representative Bob Bauman from Maryland. I'd heard for a very long time that Bauman was a gay Republican, and in fact many people urged me to expose him, but it wasn't until the scandal broke that any of my friends knew for sure. The speculation was that he was exposed because he was considering running for the Senate, either against liberal Republican Senator Charles Mathias or Senator Paul Sarbanes. Whatever caused it, Bauman's indiscretions at various cruising spots and a go-go boy came out and it damaged him severely, both politically and personally. In truth, I thought the so-called scandal was totally overblown and I seriously doubt if it would have been made into such a big deal if it weren't for his New Right connections, his obnoxious behavior in the House, and his hypocritical antigay votes. Bauman initially compounded the problem—at least from gay people's perspective—by claiming that his difficulties started and stopped with alcoholism—another version of "Boy, was I drunk last night!"

I'd never met or dealt with Bauman at the time his scandal broke, but a couple of years later, in 1983, I was contacted by an intermediary who indicated that Bauman wanted to make amends for his past hypocrisy and the tacky way he'd initially handled the revelation about him. Most people were aware of his right-wing, antigay votes, yet only a few people outside of Washington knew how able and talented he was as a tactician and strategist. My thought at the time was that it was an incredible waste of talent. Because of the way he handled the exposure of his sexual orientation, however, I couldn't even consider reaching out to him and utilizing his considerable skills. All that changed when I learned that Bauman now wanted to come out as a proud gay man.

The entire period that I was being solicited to bring Bauman into the Gay Rights National Lobby was when I was under siege by David Goodstein, Larry Bush, Jim Foster, and, it seemed at the time, covertly by Ginny Apuzzo. Frankly, I was so overwhelmed that I'm not sure that my judgement was all that sound. However, when I met with Bauman I was impressed. I privately thought he was taking this step because he wanted to write a book, which ended up being pretty much on the mark. Since he could not do a book from his reliance on that "boy was I drunk last night" excuse of his, he had to be able to speak as a proud gay conservative and needed some bridge to get him there. But I didn't mind as long as he could be helpful to us in the meantime. We already had the active and public lobbying assistance of Dan Bradley as well as an agreement by former Congressman Jim Corman, whose daughter worked for the Lobby. Now, if we could enlist Bauman's help in working with Republicans and get the whole effort well coordinated, we'd have a very formidable lobbying team to address the emerging AIDS crisis.

There was some pressure within the community to not reach out or include him, though. His opposition to lesbian and gay rights was only one stance he took that repelled much of our overwhelmingly liberal movement; his opposition to the ERA and to pro-choice legislation, and his support for apartheid in South Africa were just a few of the problems that made any inclusion of Bauman a real minefield. On the other hand, the movement has long indicated a desire from its "liberal only" base to include more conservatives and Republicans. So before I decided to secure his involvement I tried to talk with every board member as well as confidants Barney Frank and a couple of our key Capitol Hill supporters. I heard some complaints from a few individuals (including those at the reception we held in Bauman's honor at the GRNL offices), but the people most directly involved in the Lobby and the Campaign Fund were all convinced of the merits of going forward.

Much of that period of my life is a bit of a blur, probably as some sort of subconscious defense mechanism relating to the Goodstein assault. I vaguely recall arranging a dinner in a Capitol Hill restaurant with Bauman, myself, and Barney Frank, who was increasingly out socially but hadn't yet come out publicly. Although the dinner was cordial and pleasant and Barney was very supportive of him, I recall that Bauman made some tacky reference to it in his book.

We arranged a second, more positive coming out for Bauman. The American Bar Association convention was meeting in Atlanta, and we thought we might be more likely to get extensive coverage from the site. GRNL board member Frank Scheuren arranged accommodations and Bauman, a rather young friend of his, and I flew to Atlanta (in fact, when I met this young kid I was quite concerned about how it would look). The next day I took Bauman to the local NBC affiliate to do the *Today* show with Jane Pauley. Afterward I drove him over to the American Bar Association convention, where Dan Bradley was fighting a valiant if initially futile effort to get the ABA to endorse lesbian and gay rights.

When Dan had come out via joining GRNL's board, we'd discussed other community endeavors he should get involved in and I had urged him to use the considerable connections he had developed with the ABA to help pass a gay rights resolution. The plan was for Bauman to hold a press conference and participate in a Bar Association panel and help in the lobbying effort of the Bar. However, if I recall our time in Atlanta correctly, Bauman begged off of a number of commitments while we were there—even though we'd had to pay for his flight and that of his young boyfriend—so he could go to AA meetings.

Almost from the beginning, Bauman continued to raise the issue of being paid on a consultant basis; although I did feel his ability warranted such a contract, GRNL's funds had been badly hurt by the attacks of *The Advocate* and other publications that printed Bush's columns. I made it clear from the very beginning that I didn't know how I was going to keep from laying off current staff, let alone retain a new consultant. We ended up agreeing that if new, "found" money could be uncovered—presumably from gay Republicans who'd want to help the movement do a better job within GOP circles— we would be able to retain Bauman. But this was all before the severity of the AIDS crisis was understood, affluent gay Republicans weren't particularly inclined to contribute, and I wasn't sure we could find such money.

I vividly recall helping a well-connected volunteer, Marvin Collins, to arrange a private dinner at the home of Robert Alfandre for Bauman. Bauman was to meet, and hopefully impress, eight to ten affluent gay Republicans who could help fund a consultant contract for him. By the day of the dinner I was already growing weary of Bauman's self-centered and selfish approach. Late in the afternoon of the Alfandre dinner, Bauman called to cancel. Although I was sick as a dog that evening, Bob Alfandre understandably insisted that I come over to explain to his guests why Bauman stood them up. There was no good excuse and I remember the evening as a disaster.

With all of the Goodstein attacks, I became preoccupied with trying to defend myself from all the lies and distortions, so I didn't have time to mess around with someone who kept failing to do what they said. For a brief time I shuttled Bauman off to deputy director Jerry Weller. I couldn't even get his assistance with fund-raising to retain him, and he was unwilling to assist on AIDS funding unless he was paid, so I gave it up. Not until a good deal later, when Bauman's book came out, did I imagine that he would represent the facts of his interaction with the Lobby and myself so badly. I concluded that Bauman totally lacked in integrity and let the matter drop.

Countless other legislators and prominent public officials, at national and state levels, I've known to be gay or been told such by an adequate number of reliable sources. There's the Western state Republican who was outed on billboards in his state; I have no direct knowledge of his sexual orientation and know of no one who does, but he's widely perceived within the gay community to be gay. Although I wouldn't have favored such billboards (I wasn't asked), it is interesting to note that this legislator's voting record on the various antigay Helms amendments did seem to improve after the outing. On another occasion a major gay publication outed a prominent Washington, DC–based official, not because he had done anything homophobic they could point to but because he worked for an institution perceived to be homophobic.

As I look back at some of instances I've cited I realize how lucky I've been to play a small part in the coming out of a number of wonderful and extremely successful public officials. But while I view those individuals' coming out as extremely positive for the broader development of role models within the gay and lesbian community, I continue to believe that outing is wrong and amounts to using a person's sexuality against him or her. This puts me at odds with much of the newer generation of activists, as well as a number of friends and associates I admire and respect. I continue to feel, however, that there's no logical way to negotiate the slippery slide of determining when it's okay to bring another person out.

Chapter 13

The Politics of Self-Indulgence?
A Self-Confessed "Insider" Assesses
His Experience with Protest Activities

This chapter is titled "The Politics of Self-Indulgence" with a question mark for good reason. While many, if not most, legislative types are almost always opposed to protest, I personally believe there are a number of occasions when strong, effective protest can strengthen the hand of those working on the inside, and sometimes can even produce direct results by themselves. In the twenty-three years in which I've worked full-time for lesbian and gay civil rights, I've been involved in more than a few protests myself. However, in the final analysis, I think each of us has to make a decision whether we are going to be "inside players" or one of the "hell-raisers" on the outside, because to try to do both consistently almost always leads to being discounted. But I didn't know that when I started—there were no "insiders" and I wanted to help shake things up and fight for fairness.

My first real opportunity came when two lesbians were thrown out of a low-life dump of a bar, The Poodle, in downtown Minneapolis for dancing together. They took their case to Gay House, which I was then running. Although Gay House was a social service agency and not a political group, I helped to organize a protest. Looking back, it all seems a little crazy, but about forty of us, twenty men and twenty women, went in to dance, each woman on a man's arm. We danced one or two dances with our original partner and then I yelled out, "Rotate." Suddenly there were twenty same-sex couples dancing together. The management didn't do anything, perhaps because they'd been tipped off by the press, and in the final analysis, the protest got us a cover story in the *Minneapolis Star* but made little long-term impact.

During this same general time period, around 1971 or 1972, we began to organize within the state Democratic Party (known as the DFL). Although I started the DFL Gay Rights Caucus, I left early on for one of my attempts to live in New York City. By the time I returned, just prior to the state convention, others, including Jack Baker, were running the effort. While I remained a Hubert Humphrey supporter and worked the convention as an usher, the DFL Gay Rights Caucus was all decked out in obnoxious lavender T-shirts and was completely aligned with McGovern. As history explains, McGovern won the Democratic nomination, with the California primary and support of the gay community playing key roles.

As I've described previously, we used the bigotry of Northwestern Bell Telephone to stage vigorous protests. Northwestern Bell had refused to hire a gay man when they discovered, from his draft records, that he was gay. After their so-called public relations person issued an outrageous statement we ran a month-long picket and blanketed as many pay phones as possible with tough-to-remove stickers over the coin slots. Although the latter action was probably a bit self-indulgent, the picket and the many press articles it inspired played a critical role in helping demonstrate the real need for amending the Minneapolis civil rights ordinance. Around that time I began to believe that we needed to move from a confrontational public relations mode to our within-the-system, establishment approach. Even though visibility at that early stage was definitely important, I thought there were other, more tangible measures of our success.

One "semi-protest" I was very proud to be involved in was the very first Gay Pride Day in Minneapolis (it must have been in 1971). I had just returned from New York City to learn that my roommate, Steve Badeau, was spearheading the plans we'd made to have the first Pride Day in the local gay park, Loring Park. Our small apartment was covered with banners, posters, etc. Having just returned from the Big Apple's Pride parade, where I marched with personal heroes Marc Rubin and Pete Fisher and hundreds of thousands of others, coming back to help lead Minneapolis's first was quite different. We had about 200 people, but the small crowd, in a town where gay people lived in the same city as their families and weren't very out, was extremely uplifting. No, it didn't change any public policy, but it was anything but self-indulgent. It built enthusiasm and spirit among the small but growing band of dedicated activists that seemed to have to do everything in those early days in the Twin Cities.

In Chapter 4 I address a major conflict within the gay and lesbian community about whether to include transvestites and transsexuals in the lesbian and gay civil rights bill in the upcoming 1975 legislative session. Those demanding inclusion, who were not transpersons themselves, were led by Tim Campbell. I didn't know much about him except he'd appeared out of nowhere and had never been part of the lobbying efforts. I argued that whether it was right or wrong or whether it was even the same issue wasn't the point. The simple reality was that we couldn't afford the political weight of such an inclusion.

Campbell, backed up by Jack Baker and a very small handful of other activists, pulled a series of outrageous antics that managed to turn an issue we'd worked hard to make serious and respectable back into a joke. More important, their actions brought significant media attention and alerted our opponents of our efforts. Obviously, I can't say objectively whether their antics brought the result they wanted, but our nondiscrimination bill did fail. At the time, I would have bet anything Tim wouldn't stick around to do any tough work. Although he never did much lobbying (thank God!), he did continue to be active in the Twin Cities for a number of years, and, on community-police relations, he was often a lone voice on the mark (I'd moved to DC by then).

Campbell had to be dealt with again a couple of years later when Anita Bryant, fresh from her successful leadership of the repeal of Dade County, Florida's lesbian and gay rights ordinance, was scheduled to come to the Twin Cities for the opening of a fruit market. Tim made it very clear that he might engage in violence. After consultation with the leaders of the Lesbian Feminist Organizing Committee (LFOC), including future state representative Karen Clark and her then-lover, Patty Shamus, we decided the best action was to bring Tim into a community-wide steering committee to plan a protest of Bryant's appearance. Tim appeared to be intimidated by the strong, assertive lesbians involved in the committee and it seemed we had him contained. In part, to try to give the protest the right flavor and lighten things up a bit, we settled on calling it the "National Fruit Days." The second, more important priority, was to draw a crowd size that would be truly newsworthy, which was easier said than done in a city not known for protest and where the most people we'd ever provided was the 200 at the first lesbian and gay Pride Day.

As one of the press spokespersons, I was stationed down at the actual entrance of the fruit market, far out of sight of the location where our protestors parked and gathered. Suddenly, it started raining cats and dogs and I just knew it would kill our protest. But I was dead wrong. I'll never forget the incredible Gunga Din–like march, as our people weren't going to let a little rain stop them—not tens, not hundreds, but well over 2,000 angry but proud protestors. Again, it didn't change any public policy, but few events in my twenty-plus years in the movement have meant more to me. Even now, as I simply retell the story, I get goose bumps.

One protest I passed up was after we got creamed in the 1978 repeal of the St. Paul lesbian and gay rights ordinance. I'd lobbied it in the first place and the ordinance had worked well, without any controversy, for more than three years. For months I'd thrown my heart and soul into the effort to retain it, working closely with dear friends Kerry Woodward and Larry Bye. But, despite polls that showed us winning right up until the vote, we got creamed. Most of the rest of the crowd went to the Baptist church of the leader of our opposition, but I was just so numb I couldn't even get myself to go. In hindsight, had I protested, I might have gotten some of the pain and rage out of my system; instead, I was burnt out and bitter for months, finding myself looking at everyone I saw in St. Paul and wondering if they'd voted against our rights. It wasn't until I finally moved to Washington, DC, to become the GRNL executive director that I finally recovered from that pain. Who knows if marching that April night would have changed anything?

Once I got to DC, I was back into the reform politics that has always felt like home. Although I'd been an early advocate of a national march on Washington when I still lived in Minneapolis, once I was in DC for a while I changed my mind. I concluded that such a march would make very little difference legislatively and would cost huge amounts of money—money that could be spent more effectively on any number of projects, including our national lobbying effort.

My opposition to the 1979 march was shared by most other established leaders and the national groups. When we all saw we couldn't stop it, though, we embraced it. GRNL justified our reversal based on antigay legislation such as the McDonald Resolution and actions such as the Washington for Jesus rally, stating, "One of our early concerns was whether it would be timely for our legislative concerns. Clearly, such reservations are no longer valid now that McDonald's antigay resolution has been introduced." Once we shifted positions, we sought to help maximize the turnout, as well as help coordinate the constituent lobbying the day after. We said, "Those that have looked at the march with a jaundiced eye because it might be 'too militant' need to look at it for what it is—an effort for citizens to seek redress from their government. It is truly in the best American tradition." After the march, I was absorbed with other aspects of my long-term plan for our legislative advancement: creating the National Convention Project to get a lesbian and gay rights plank, getting into a civil rights coalition, creating the Campaign Fund, and so on.

The shift within the lesbian and gay civil rights movement from the counterculture protest approach that dominated the earliest stages of the movement to a suit-and-tie lobbying approach for most of the 1980s was overwhelming. However, I argued with close friends that the time for protest had not passed, but that our movement just needed to use such actions more strategically and not every time we were upset or angry. Although I didn't feel I could play such a role because of my position as our lobbyist, I thought we had to maintain a diversified range of strategies and tactics.

So when we released GRNL's 1981 "Plan for Action" to new members and to every local lesbian and gay group in the country, we included not only points on the creation of a constituent network, mobilization of nongay support, opposition to the Family Protection Act, meetings with senators and representatives, and the need to demonstrate a compelling need for lesbian and gay rights. We also specifically included a section titled "Public Protest at a Member's District Office." It stated, in part:

> Although many elected officials will be the first to tell you privately how obnoxious they feel the Moral Majority to be, many are also intimidated by them and dread the grief they get from that self-righteous crew. . . . We must make it clear that amendments which would deny gay and lesbian citizens access to various government programs and services are an outrage! Properly presented, the general public will agree with us.
>
> Members of Congress must be made aware that an anti-justice vote on such an amendment will result in at least as much grief and negative publicity. . . . We recognize that, for many, public protests, pickets, etc. go against the grain. But [we advocate] well-thought-out protests which show elected officials the negative consequences of their actions and which show the public the injustice of the position taken by the Senator or Rep.

A short time after I came back to HRCF in 1985 I participated in what I call the "red carpet arrest." The orchestrated AIDS arrest, planned by the Campaign Fund's Vic Basile, was a final tribute to Dan Bradley and included blocking Pennsylvania Avenue in front of the White House. It all had been coordinated with the police, and I vividly recall my arrest and cuffing by a very hot black officer. They took pictures of each arrest, and I tried my best later to buy the picture of that attractive officer cuffing me. The whole experience had a surrealistic feel to it, as our "protest" blocking the street was complete with precut squares of red carpet so we didn't get our suits dirty. The national movement leaders participated—from Rev. Troy Perry to AIDS activist Larry Kramer—and we got out of jail with a $50 bond each. Afterward we went to the Four Seasons Hotel for drinks, which is hard to imagine under similar circumstances, such as a civil rights protest in Selma or Birmingham, but doesn't mean it wasn't valid or worthwhile.

But these were protest activities in which I've been directly involved. Before I was around legendary figures such as Jim Owles, Marc Rubin, and Marty Robinson, and groups such as Gay Activists Alliance of New York City were pulling off unbelievable "zaps" of the establishment and fighting with the only weapons available to them then in a guerilla war for fairness. What bothers me today is the tendency for many, if not most, protests to represent people acting out their rage and anger and only then trying to figure out some strategic justification for their actions. I'd be less troubled if these

protests were based on a desire to make change—or even a candid acknowledgement of the occasional real need to vent—rather than pretending it's all
strategically based. It is this type of protest, almost a form of therapy, that I
define as the "politics of self indulgence."

After all, we're not supposed to be spoiled children acting out, but instead we should be doing something important to advance fairness and human dignity for lesbian and gay Americans. But don't get me wrong—I do
think the vast majority of us do consider whether our actions are going to be
effective. Certainly, some of those involved in both ACT UP and Queer Nation are among some of the most creative, innovative, and productive activists our movement's ever known, and many, maybe most, know how to exercise the self-discipline to help keep themselves on the right track.

However, I'd be less than honest if I didn't admit that my anger at those
who engage in the politics of self-indulgence is heightened dramatically because so many of the activists who are attracted to such protest are the youn-
gest, greenest around. Too often, they tend to act as if the movement began
the day they walked in the door and are ready to dismiss many activists'
years of experience as irrelevant, ancient history. This ignorance and arrogance is incredibly galling, and therefore it is hard to see it also represents a
new wave of eager activists coming in; in fact, some have already met with
some success, in terms of the way the government handles experimental
drugs, for instance. But, having seen activists come and go through more
than twenty years, I've observed that these instant gratification freaks seldom stick around for the long haul.

Having lived through the 1979 March on Washington and seeing how futile it was to oppose it, I supported the 1987 March on Washington from the
beginning. The 1979 march hadn't brought immediate legislative impact,
but it clearly contributed to a genuine building of a sense of national community. A well-done march in 1987 could only build on this, and by then we
had my preauthorized constituent mail initiative, then known as the National Mailgram Program and subsequently as Speak Out. Unfortunately,
the Fairness Fund wasn't sufficiently developed, and we knew far too little
about the canvassing process, so we signed up a tiny number of people after
a huge amount of work. Although most of the 600,000 lesbians and gay men
who attended the march left ecstatic, we were despondent at our failure to
really capitalize on such a huge event.

Perhaps the single individual I find myself thinking of most directly
when I contemplate protest as the "politics of self-indulgence" is noted activist and playwright Larry Kramer. I first met Larry at the beginning of the
AIDS crisis and vividly remember facing at least a couple of his now–well-
known temper tantrums. It quickly became clear that he knew very little
about either politics or the legislative process. It wasn't until a good deal

later that I understood he also had no desire to learn about either, and hid behind this ignorance as his excuse to attack and assault some of our movement's most dedicated and able activists.

For instance, Kramer has often denounced the Human Rights Campaign Fund, asking why, if we could have thirty people on staff, we didn't just hire thirty lobbyists. Explaining to him that an effective lobbying effort must include adequate support staff, a political action committee able to raise funds for supportive candidates and mobilize volunteers for their campaigns, and the range of critical grassroots initiatives that are essential to an effective lobbying effort fell on deaf ears—because he doesn't want to know! In interviews in the gay press, Kramer never lets the facts get in his way when having one of his tirades. For instance, he claims no national organization has been able to build a membership of more than 20,000 people while, in fact, the Human Rights Campaign Fund actually has more than 60,000 members today [1993].

Although Kramer has obviously done some good things, including helping start both ACT UP and the Gay Men's Health Crisis (GMHC), he inevitably leaves in a huff when he doesn't get his way on some issue of real or imagined importance. Part of his attacks on current lesbian and gay leadership probably can be described as deriving from his limited view of what leadership is about. Larry Kramer, like far too many people in our community, is still waiting for a savior to rescue us. While I'm sure he wishes he could play that role, I think he knows he can't. Instead he relies on the simplistic idea that leadership is solely about someone's inspired speaking style. For instance, he attacked the Campaign's executive director, Tim McFeeley, (among many, many others) mercilessly because Kramer's only criterion for leadership seems to be whether the individual in question is a great public speaker (actually, Tim happens to be a very good speaker) and whether they share Larry's never-ending rage.

Even though Tim and I have vigorously disagreed on both major and minor issues and no doubt will again, and despite the shortcomings each of us in the movement has, Tim has overseen the dramatic growth of the Campaign Fund to a $5 million operation. He's played a key role in building on all previous efforts to the point where we are today, with President Clinton fully understanding the role the gay and lesbian community played in his election, and the nation seriously discussing and debating the antiquated policy of driving gay people from the military. And Tim is just one of many able, dedicated movement leaders at whom Kramer spouts his venom.

Obviously, I could go on and on about this man's destructive, self-indulgent behavior. Fundamentally, what makes me saddest about Kramer's rhetoric is that it represents the antithesis of "empowerment." Cutting through the venom and self-contempt, the message he sends out is that everything is horrible and that it's impossible to make things better. Who wants to be active when it's all so hopeless? And then he wonders why he always ends up disappointed and angry at the people and groups he's helped launch. Unfortunately for our community, far too many young activists hang on Kramer's every word and may carry on his hateful internal attacks. It is this self-indulgence that most deeply saddens me.

On a final note, I've continued to be deeply offended by activists who go to great lengths to point out that they are not *gay* activists but *AIDS* activists, as if there is something unrespectable about being a gay or lesbian activist. I'm no psychiatrist, but I think internalized homophobia plays a major role in their distinction. My other major irritation is the amount of resistance we've met from AIDS organizations on even the most simple requests— requests that could significantly enhance the government's response to the crisis.

Chapter 14

Wrapping Up a Movement Career:
Retiring on Disability, Acknowledgment,
and . . . Victory!

I returned to Washington, DC, the week after the Fourth of July of 1990 from a twenty-six–city speaking, canvassing, and organizing tour of the Southwest and Southeast. I was exhausted but very satisfied with a venture that went better than I could imagine. I noticed that within a very short time I had begun to lose weight, but given my historic battle of the bulge, at first I wasn't too troubled by the slimming process. However, it quickly became clear—and my doctors confirmed—that this wasn't just normal weight loss but part of the wasting syndrome that was common in AIDS. Since I had been HIV positive for seven or eight years, I wasn't shocked by the development.

By the time I prepared to return to my middle-American and middle-class Minnesota roots for the Labor Day State Fair, the weight loss was beginning to be quite pronounced. That development meant that any thoughts I had initially about withholding from my mother my new diagnosis of full-blown AIDS were unrealistic. In fact, when I came into their apartment my mom's first words were, "What's going on? Are you sick?" Indeed, as the increasing weight loss and energy drain were making very, very clear, I was getting sick, and much more quickly than I could have dreamed. I promptly reported the development to HRCF executive director Tim McFeeley, as I thought it could begin to impact my performance. By the beginning of October, it had become clear that my advancing illness would require me to retire by November 1.

I suspected that the staff would have a little going away party on my last day, but I was totally unprepared for the lavish decorations put up by my excellent administrative assistant, David Simmons. Each division had prepared a brief, comedy-laden presentation. For instance, the legislative division presented an authentic-looking bill, H.R. 10000000000, briefly summarized as "The Steve Endean Organized the World Act of 1991, to require all organizers in every organization in the United States of America, to organize as effectively as Mr. Endean." It went on to describe the bill as be-

Steve Endean, from the Steve Endean Collection. Photographer unknown.
Courtesy of HRC.

ing known more informally as the "Wee Bee Goes to Washington Act."
Some of the joke gifts focused around my political organizing, but more
centered on my active sex life. The "Public Facilities" section of the bill,
patterned on my cherished civil rights bill, included truck stops, bookstores,
and baths.

Each division strove to top the next, and their efforts meant more to me
than I could possibly ever say. Without playing favorites, the real affection
of my own field staff was probably the most important to me. We'd really
been able to build quite a formidable team, as demonstrated by their continued success after my retirement.

Late in the event, former and current HRCF executive directors Vic
Basile and Tim McFeeley asked me if they could sponsor a formal retirement event, perhaps as a fund-raiser. However, I've never sought out such
acknowledgement and was embarrassed by the idea of a testimonial. Vic
thought my sex life lent itself to a roast rather than a testimonial, but
I thought my ego was still too fragile for such an event. In point of fact, I initially hoped I could just put them off long enough that they'd forget the idea
altogether. But no such luck.

Tim, who is as persistent as a bulldog, would ask me about doing an
event every time he saw me. I finally gave in and agreed, providing that we
do it when the Campaign Fund's major donors and key players were in for
their national conference. That way, we'd have a built-in advantage in terms
of turnout, so I wouldn't run the risk of being embarrassed by a less-than-
impressive attendance. As it ended up, I didn't need to worry—more than
350 people came, even at the rather steep charge of $75 per person. It was an
evening I'll never forget.

The wonderful group of friends who organized the event for the Campaign Fund coordinated a range of individuals, both well-known and dear
friends, who spoke during the event and/or gave terrific letters of tribute. It's
funny, but as a young activist I craved such acknowledgement and recognition, but as time passed and I became more confident of my own abilities
and accomplishments, the kind words of others became less important. The
sole exception to that is the way such words and articles might impact both
of my parents, who had been incredibly supportive, even when I began very
early on a course of activism that I think they had reservations about.

Next, we had a call at the podium from recently withdrawn presidential
candidate Paul Tsongas. He was the commencement speaker at his daughter's graduation but took time out for a long-distance call to share some very
kind thoughts about me. He said that he had continually raised the lesbian
and gay civil rights issue during his campaign—which he proudly felt contributed to Bill Clinton's vigorous subsequent support—because I had convinced Paul to become our chief Senate sponsor of the gay civil rights bill

several years earlier and then continued to work very closely with him through the years. It might have been a stretch, but it was very generous, and I do think our work together was productive. He's a very genuine and nice human being whose commitment to the issue doesn't come from close friendships with gay people but from his belief in fairness in general.

The same commitment to justice and fairness had much to do with the views of former Vice President Walter Mondale, who wrote these kind words:

> Your hard work, creativity and dedication to equal rights for all people has truly made an impact. You have helped build a foundation in Minnesota and in Washington upon which gay men and lesbians can create a more just and compassionate nation. Whether you know it or not, you were a very important person in shaping my views toward the gay community in our country.

My mother sent a very sweet and loving note about her pride in me, which reminded me that many of my early fights—which took place in Minneapolis where both my parents lived and were known professionally—must have been hard on them, particularly on my mother, who grew up a devout Catholic. The *Star Tribune* marked the occasion of my testimonial with a glowing editorial praising me and, to my embarrassment, comparing me to one of my heroes, Hubert Humphrey.

Finally, the words of old friend Rep. Barney Frank, which focused on both my political and personal life, meant a great deal to me:

> Steve Endean is one of a handful of Americans who deserve the hero's mantle in the category of those who began the fight against homophobia. . . . He has also been a genuine, living, breathing human being—who jokes, swears, schemes, gets mad, gets even, enjoys himself and enjoys his friends. . . . It is precisely these human qualities that have made him one of the most effective fighters for gay and lesbian rights in the history of this country.

The entire evening, and the fact that dear friends from more than ten cities came in especially for the occasion, meant a tremendous amount to me and really helped me reach a sense of completion as a movement activist. In reality, though, I still thought I could make a few contributions.

The National Endorsement Campaign

Undertaking a national endorsement effort had been a goal since I arrived in Washington, DC, and since 1980 it had actually been among our goals and objectives. When I assumed leadership of the Gay Rights National Lobby we needed to show federal legislators that lesbian and gay civil rights was not a bizarre, outside-the-mainstream issue; just as it had in Minnesota, it seemed to call for putting together an endorsement list of prominent community leaders supporting our rights. The whole endeavor struck me as little more than as a "spine fortification" process for gutless legislators. But with too much to do and too little time and resources to get it all done, we never devoted the energy to launch it.

Then as the director of the Human Rights Campaign Fund's field division, I resurrected the project, using the same name I'd been calling it since I first conceived of the endeavor (actually, longtime activists Barbara Gittings and Kay Tobin recently reminded me that they'd advocated such a venture at a national lesbian and gay conference in Denver in the mid-1970s). I was free of direct Hill lobbying responsibility, and even from the joy/burden of building Speak Out, so finally I could focus on the project with the attention it required (at least that's what I thought until I faced the various personal onslaughts, including hospital visits, etc., resulting from my having AIDS).

We'd had a number of false starts previously, in part because of the magnitude of the venture. This time we settled on a pilot project in Minnesota, with the assistance of Bob Meek, one of the best, most savvy political operatives in the state, who agreed to direct the pilot. A longtime DFL party activist who'd only recently come out, Bob had political knowledge, eye for detail, and an intense desire to make a difference on the issue. Bob believed in the National Endorsement Campaign (NEC), both because he understood intuitively how far it could move us forward and because it helped at all three levels: local, state, and federal lesbian and gay civil rights legislation. As I came to realize on a range of initiatives, Bob really threw himself into these projects, and on this occasion he recruited his lover, John, to assist him on the Minnesota pilot project. Finally, conversations with my old friend, State Senator Allan Spear, assured me that the project could assist future state legislative efforts as well as help convince congresspeople to be more supportive. Knowing how pivotal his pilot project was to the entire national campaign only enhanced his enthusiasm.

We'd begin the process by identifying large numbers of state and local community leaders. In turn, they would be asked to return their signed endorsement statements in the postage-paid reply envelopes. Of course, there would be a cover letter, in this case signed by four very prestigious community leaders, and we made a point of restricting our campaign to nondiscrimination in jobs, housing, and public accommodations alone. No domestic partners legislation. No gay marriage or gay adoption. No ordination. Not even ending the military ban, although if we'd seen the level of controversy coming, we might have included it.

Since a key aspect of the project has been to make it safe and even popular to support fairness for gay people, a top priority was to get prominent, and perhaps even surprising, signatories. A major distinction I've always noticed between gay civil rights and rights for racial minorities or women was that people didn't pause before endorsing equal rights for minorities because someone would think they were black or Hispanic; but there was still far too much stigma surrounding gay rights, causing many to think, "Why is he or she supporting that, I wonder?"

Four key people fit the bill for the Minnesota pilot project. Alan Page had been an All-Pro Minnesota Viking, was the first defensive lineman to ever be named Most Valuable Player of the National Football League, and had, after his retirement, been named to the NFL Hall of Fame. Married with children, very secure, and an extremely bright Minnesota assistant attorney general, his signature would send a critical message that everyone could speak out for lesbian and gay civil rights. He also served on the University of Minnesota's Board of Regents. However, despite Page's initial agreement, we were never able to utilize his prestige either in Minnesota or nationally because he was elected to the Minnesota Supreme Court and therefore couldn't continue to be a signer since it would be deemed as inappropriate for a justice who might have to rule on such matters.

Our other signatories were also very prestigious, even if not quite as surprising: Joan Mondale, the wife of the former vice president and a well-regarded civic leader in her own right; Wheelock Whitney, a well-known Minneapolis businessman, former candidate for governor, and, as the key fund-raiser and donor to Minnesota's GOP Governor Arne Carlson's race, a pivotal Republican; and Beverly McKinnell, then-president of the state League of Women Voters. We sent out the endorsement requests in waves and received a great response. Among those lending their endorsements were the mayors of both Minneapolis and St. Paul, the bishops of several major denominations, the governor, lt. governor, attorney general, secretary of state, state auditor, state treasurer, several city council members and state legislators, and so on.

Before the pilot project was hardly off the ground, the *Star Tribune* editorialized and helped demonstrate clearly the impact of such an endorsement initiative. When Governor Arne Carlson, a Republican, had gotten grief from the right wingers within his party by cochairing the Human Rights

Campaign Fund's annual fund-raising dinner in Minnesota, the *Star Tribune* used the endorsement approach to help clarify the right "we/they" for Minnesota citizens looking at the battle:

> Carlson's endorsement of the Fund follows Minnesota's progressive, nonpartisan civil-rights tradition. If Independent Republicans think Carlson is out of step, they'd better look again at who is marching with him. He's keeping company with Wheelock Whitney, the IR Party's own gubernatorial candidate in 1982; Joan Mondale; Alan Page; Beverly McKinnell, president of the Minnesota League of Women Voters's, Episcopal Bishop Robert Anderson; ELCA Bishop Lowell Erdahl and Catholic Archbishop John Roach.[1]

Although experience suggested that the most effective way to go at the project was to send out waves of endorsement letters, starting with some of the easier ones first, the flip side was getting a list so slanted to the liberal side of the political spectrum that others contemplating the endorsement would think they were just joining a "progressive only" list. For instance, nationally I wanted Jane Fonda, Ed Asner, and Martin Sheen, but not as the earliest endorsers because their liberalism made their support a bit too predictable. While no doubt I am more comfortable with them personally, I'd have much preferred to start with Charlton Heston, Bob Hope, country singer Garth Brooks, and race car driver Richard Petty.

So with the Minnesota pilot project going great, my retirement on disability left me with some time to work on the national piece—at least when I was feeling well enough. I underestimated how much work it was, though, and was often a bit behind on almost every aspect of the endeavor. In hindsight, my bad health definitely slowed the effort down, and eventually I came to realize that my health difficulties made it hard to ensure the follow-through and ongoing contact with those considering endorsing. I felt it was necessary for the Campaign Fund to hire a staff person for continuity but, until the budget allowed hiring such a person, the national project necessarily depended on myself, a terrific volunteer, Bruce Milner, and Cheryl Camillo, the HRCF receptionist, who took on far more administrative support than was fair to someone already doing so much. With the exception of others within my home base of the field division, it seemed clear that the National Endorsement Campaign didn't enjoy much immediate enthusiasm—even among those on staff.

Bob Meek and I had agreed that many more local opinion leaders would lend their names if they saw a list of not only other well-known local leaders already endorsing but also prominent national leaders from all walks of life. For example, the labor leader on the Iron Range or in Duluth, Minnesota, who might have been reluctant to endorse, might think again if he saw the name of his own international union president already listed, and AFL-CIO president Lane Kirkland already on board. Ministers, priests, nuns, and rabbis might be more likely to sign if they saw that countless national religious leaders had already lent their support, and everyone might feel just a little safer if they knew that some of their own favorite entertainers had already signed on. So it wasn't really just spine fortification of elected officials but of community leaders at all levels.

So just as we had with the Minnesota pilot project, we set out to get an impressive list of signers on the letter enlisting endorsers. With the wonderful help of Coretta Scott King, we were able to secure the support of Harry Belafonte; Dr. Paul Sherry, the president of the United Church of Christ; Joan Mondale; Rabbi Alexander Shindler, president of the Union of American Hebrew Congregations; prominent GOP businessperson Justin Dart; Becky Cain, the national president of the League of Women Voters; Bishop Edmund Browning, president of the Episcopal Church of America; and former mayor and cabinet member Federico Peña.

We certainly wanted prominent entertainment leaders as well (and Lily Tomlin, Paul Newman, and Richard Dreyfuss were just three who come to mind), but I was determined not to create a situation where smart-aleck journalists could attack the list as "the Broadway-Hollywood out-of-touch with reality crowd." Therefore, it was critical that we reach a truly wide range of key national opinion leaders from the religious, labor, sports, civil rights, business, legal, entertainment, and political communities. Many people, including Vic Basile, the former HRCF executive director, offered valuable suggestions and/or directly made contacts; Vic was particularly helpful since he really had his fingers on the pulse of who knew whom and how to move them.

Reverend Ken South of the AIDS National Interfaith Network and Reverend Bill Johnson of the United Church of Christ (UCC), a friend of almost twelve years, played key roles in helping to secure religious support. Broadway Cares/Equity Fights AIDS helped the endorsement campaign with securing the help and signatures of a number of entertainers.

We've also benefited from the determined, inspired chair of our business task force, who used his extensive network of contacts to secure the endorsements of a number of prominent business leaders—a group many had previously thought would be impossible to mobilize on our side. The most notable early endorsement he secured was of prominent financier Warren Buffet, who is often on the cover of various business publications. In addition, we now have Jim Manzi, the president of the Lotus Corporation; Richard Fisher, the CEO of Morgan Stanley; Marvin Davis of Paramount Studios; Barry Diller, former CEO of Fox; and countless others. Such endorsements, and I'm convinced they are only the tip of the iceberg, will be surprising to legislators and suggest how mainstream the issue is becoming. Several state activists helped us by providing lists of names and addresses of prominent community leaders within their states who were supportive on lesbian and gay civil rights.

But I'd be less than candid if I didn't acknowledge how many other people either got busy with other things or were unwilling to even share addresses of prominent community leaders (such as entertainers) because they wanted to be the only group in the community who was in touch with them. This was despite our assurances that our purpose was to secure, centralize, and mobilize support for local, state, and federal nondiscrimination legislation, not fund-raising. I often found myself shaking my head in frustration and irritation at the way petty positional junk got in the way of advancing the national effort.

Obviously, we paid attention to which legislators are seen as pivotal as we sought to build the list of endorsers. In some cases, we were building on local or state efforts that had already gone before us (No on 9 in Oregon, No on 2 in Colorado, the Portland, Maine, effort to retain their local ordinance) as well as the lesbian and gay caucuses' efforts within religious denominations. Of course we also turned to the groups who had endorsed nondiscrimination laws for gay and lesbian citizens—groups such as the League of Women Voters, the American Bar Association, and the AFL-CIO—and we wanted to get the endorsements of the state legislators or city council members who had already voted with us at the local level. In some states or areas, the best we could hope for initially would be local human rights commissioners or directors. Depending on how our endorsement initiatives developed, it might be possible to go back to these endorsers on other emerging issues such as the military ban, but we couldn't use their endorsement on other issues, no matter how important, without their permission.

With my health varying widely from day to day and even moment to moment, our initial timelines were shot to hell. Because most people didn't yet understand the importance of the endorsement campaign (the same had been true of many of our long-term projects), we weren't really under any serious time pressure, though. In some ways, the National Endorsement Campaign is just another form of building an infrastructure, and I hope it will be useful in a range of ways, from ads in the press to getting selected endorsers to testify for the legislation or to sign op-eds in their local papers, and so on. Although we haven't dealt with this yet, there's no reason we shouldn't go after the major donors to the key members of Congress to secure their endorsements.

As this venture becomes successful, many people will loudly denounce us for failing to ask X, Y, or Z. Although it might be hard for me to hold my tongue, I guess our success will be worth the minor inconvenience and irritation. I wouldn't be candid if I didn't complain loudly about the petty, parochial approach of groups in such gay meccas as Los Angeles, San Francisco, and New York City. We had significant difficulties with gay and lesbian groups there, who already had their rights and didn't seem to give a damn if gay and lesbian citizens in Kansas or Missouri got theirs or not, or ways they could help through minimal efforts such as sharing addresses or even just doing mailings to key potential endorsers. Eventually, I hope that local and state groups will finally understand how much the National Endorsement Campaign can help them, so they will begin to help build the endorsement list in their own state or locality. I can envision the National Endorsement Campaign eventually encompassing sublists not only from each state, in fact, but each congressional district. Once we have 50 to 100 key leaders from each congressional district on board, we'll be far closer to seeing national legislation enacted that prohibits discrimination against gay and lesbian Americans.

Despite the barriers and a frustrating lack of cooperation at times, we did very well. With the help of gay labor union activists (and the fact that President Clinton had been so outspoken for fairness) we just secured the endorsements of AFL-CIO president Lane Kirkland and many International Union presidents. Nobel Peace Prize-winner Elie Wiesel lent his prestigious support, and when we didn't hear back from Reverend Jesse Jackson after several letters requesting endorsement, I personally got his signature right after he finished reading names at the October 1993 Washington AIDS Memorial Quilt display. He didn't seem too thrilled with the approach, but I knew he was a strong supporter and probably just hadn't gotten around to signing because of his campaign efforts. Ultimately we were able to build our endorsement list to over 200 bishops and "bishop-level" religious leaders as well as 300 to 400 other community leaders.

However, as the situation developed, the project momentarily stalled when I not only lost sight in my left eye to AIDS but also experienced constant nausea and was sick for more than two months. In addition, newly assigned staff became preoccupied with fighting the military ban. Finally, after significant delays, we began to get back to designing the promotional campaign and enhancing the overall National Endorsement Campaign list. My increasing weight loss and growing weakness initially didn't stop me from traveling with friends, but it did slow my drive for work-related efforts such as the NEC and this book.

When the Campaign Fund hires someone to direct the endorsement effort, I hope they'll get someone with the combination of political savvy and persistence necessary to accomplish the task. Unfortunately, they're going to have to cope with all the petty, unreasonable hassles from within the community, particularly from the AIDS organizations. But if we're able to keep building on our current efforts and the Campaign Fund hires someone in this position, the initiative should help demonstrate to members of Congress (and to local and state legislators as well) that support for basic civil rights for lesbian and gay Americans is indeed mainstream.

The 1993 March on Washington

As the winter snows melted into the spring of 1993 I began to grow excited by the upcoming March on Washington for Lesbian and Gay Rights. The highlight of the weekend for me was our third and most complete "Dinner with the Dinosaurs" for all the original Gay Rights National Lobby and Human Rights Campaign Fund board members. More than thirty-five of us, most dear friends, got together in a private room near Dupont Circle. At about that time I learned that an interview I'd given to the *Detroit Free Press* had led to fairly extensive media coverage and a major picture. I may be fooling myself, but I think all the media attention and acknowledgement I'm getting now will someday provide some minimal consolation to my family when I'm gone.

Shortly before the march and dinner I learned that the statewide nondiscrimination bill in Minnesota, a bill which had been my first and overwhelming obsession for more than twenty years, would be coming up shortly. We first began lobbying the bill in 1973, and now it appeared that—if we could stave off the onslaught of fundamentalist calls and letters—we finally had a chance. But this right-wing constituent assault meant that the vote would be coming much, much quicker than I'd expected. By convincing a friend to sell me his frequent flyer credits I was able to get a good airfare, and a reporter friend decided to follow me to document the occasion.

Upon arriving, I met with a columnist for the *Star Tribune,* who wrote a very favorable piece along the lines of "old war horse, on last legs, goes home to fight for dream." It was a good article, but I'd somehow hoped it might help the bill's chances and I doubted that it did that. On getting over to the Capitol, I connected with three other "old war horses" from my early days, met with Senator Spear and Rep. Karen Clark, chief sponsors of the bill and close friends of mine, and was invited to sit in on the daily strategy session to count votes and assess our chances.

On far more occasions than I care to think about, new-generation activists tend to disparage old-timers such as myself as a way of building themselves up. But the lobbying group "It's Time Minnesota!" could not have responded more affirmatively, and both cochairs were as inclusive and warm as they could be. I was assigned several GOP legislators, and an old association with a Republican state senator led to meeting with six Republican senators. Only one was seen as a possibility, but we had good conversations and, when the vote was counted, we'd picked up a conservative business-person from the suburbs.

By the day of the vote, it appeared too close to call. I was up all night the night before the vote, deathly ill, but I somehow managed to get over to the Capitol to sit in the gallery and watch the senate debate and vote. It was as dramatic as one could possibly imagine. When we finally prevailed 37-30 it was like a dream come true. The "It's Time" people continued in the same vein they'd begun, telling the media who interviewed them to talk to me also, as I'd started it all twenty years earlier. As fate would have it, when the House vote came up that afternoon I was sitting with some of the feminist lobbyists who'd first taught me to lobby years earlier. After several amendments, including some that were slightly obnoxious but necessary if we were to win, the final House vote came and we won by a surprisingly easy 78-55 vote. Twenty years of work, hoping, and dreaming finally were becoming a reality. The governor, Arne Carlson, was a Republican but also a lifelong supporter of lesbian and gay rights. He signed the bill on April 2, 1993. Victory at last!

Editor's Afterword

Steve Endean died in 1993 as he had lived: amid controversy. That year, in response to President Clinton's proposal to lift the ban on homosexuals serving in the U.S. military, the compromise known as "Don't Ask, Don't Tell" was adopted. Due in part to that compromise and in part to lingering divisions among GLBT groups, the Human Rights Campaign Fund came under attack that year and weathered its second period of crisis since Endean had been forced out ten years earlier. Political to the core, Steve would have understood the role of compromise; gay activist to the core, he also would have continued to fight against discrimination.

Happily, he lived to see Minnesota become the eighth state to pass legislation prohibiting discrimination based on sexual orientation. Eight additional states have adopted some form of protection since then, but Steve's central goal of a national gay and lesbian rights bill has yet to be realized. If such legislation seems in 2006 even more fanciful than it did twenty years ago, it is well to remember that the purpose of the bill—to prohibit discrimination against gay men and lesbians in employment, housing, and family issues—is being fulfilled by state, local, and private actions. Even national legislation, in the form of the Employment Nondiscrimination Act of 1996, lost in the Senate by only one vote.

A great deal has happened in the twenty-five years since Steve founded the Human Rights Campaign ("Fund" was dropped in 1995). Although it has not been a history of continual advances for GLBT people (consider present efforts to ban same-sex marriages, for example, and ongoing divisions among activists), we have definitely made "progress" in the way Steve understood the term. True, homophobia and the violence and discrimination resulting from it have not disappeared from American life and may not for decades to come, but they do seem a little less acceptable in our public life than when Steve began his career. If that is the case, we have countless activists to thank, foremost among them Steve Endean.

It has been a privilege to get to know Steve through his words in these past few years. Visionary he may have been, but his were not pipe dreams.

His basic faith in the American political system and its ability to right wrongs may seem naive, especially to the more cynical among us, but he had no illusions about how change occurs. "We can expect fairness," he told a reporter in 1990, "but we're simply not going to get it without being heard." Heard he was, and heard we need to be until his vision of full equality is a reality.

Part III:
Appendixes

Appendix A

Membership Lists of Boards of Directors

ORIGINAL BOARD OF DIRECTORS
OF THE GAY RIGHTS NATIONAL LOBBY

Pokey Anderson	Houston, TX
Virginia Apuzzo	New York City, NY
Terry Bean	Eugene, OR
Dan Bradley	Miami, FL
Larry Bye	San Francisco, CA
Jack Campbell	Miami, FL
State Rep. Karen Clark	Minneapolis, MN
Gwen Craig	San Francisco, CA
R. Adam DeBaugh	Silver Spring, MD
Karen DeCrow	Syracuse, NY
Kathy Deitsch	San Antonio, TX
Meryl Friedman	Brooklyn, NY
Barbara Gittings	Philadelphia, PA
Mary Hartman	Minneapolis, MN
Cathie Hartnett	Washington, DC
Franklin Kameny	Washington, DC
Paul Kuntzler, Treasurer	Washington, DC
Kate McQueen, Cochair	South Portland, ME
Jean O'Leary, Exec. Comm.	Los Angeles, CA
Rev. Troy D. Perry	Los Angeles, CA
Chuck Renslow	Chicago, IL
Roz Richter	New York City, NY
Rev. Jim Sandmire	San Francisco, CA
Frank Scheuren	Atlanta, GA
Leanne Seibert	Coral Gables, FL
State Senator Allan Spear	Minneapolis, MN
Bruce Voeller	New York City, NY
Jerry Weller, Cochair	Portland, OR
Claude Winfield	New York City, NY
Louise Young	Dallas, TX

Appendix B

Cosponsors of the National Lesbian and Gay Civil Rights Bill

94th Congress (1975-1976)

House of Representatives Sponsors, 1975

Bella Abzug (D-NY), chief sponsor
Ed Koch (D-NY)
Robert Nix (D-PA)
Pete McCloskey (R-CA)
John Burton (D-CA)
Don Fraser (D-MN)
Ron Dellums (D-CA)
Walter Fauntroy (D-DC)
Michael Harrington (D-MA)
Pete Stark (D-CA)
Stephen Solarz (D-NY)
Fred Richmond (D-NY)
Jonathan Bingham (D-NY)

Ben Rosenthal (D-NY)
Parren Mitchell (D-MD)
George Brown (D-CA)
Henry Waxman (D-CA)
Herman Badillo (D-NY)
Charles Rangel (D-NY)
Elizabeth Holtzman (D-NY)
Patricia Schroeder (D-CO)
Gerry Studds (D-MA)
Richard Ottinger (D-NY)
Phil Burton (D-CA)
Norman Mineta (D-CA)

House of Representatives Sponsors, 1976

Chief sponsor Rep. Bella Abzug (D-NY) for 28 cosponsors, including the following new cosponsors:

Les AuCoin (D-OR)
Yvonne Burke (D-CA)

Augustus Hawkins (D-CA)
George Miller (D-CA)

95th Congress (1977-1978)

House of Representatives Sponsors, 1977

Chief sponsor Rep. Ed Koch (D-NY) for 38 cosponsors, including the following new cosponsors:

Ted Weiss (D-NY)	Charles Diggs (D-MI)
Stewart McKinney (R-CT)	Ed Markey (D-MA)
John Conyers (D-MI)	Abner Mikva (D-IL)
Shirley Chisholm (D-NY)	Toby Moffett (D-CT)
Bill Clay (D-MO)	Jim Scheuer (D-NY)
Cardiss Collins (D-IL)	

House of Representatives Sponsors, 1978

Chief sponsor Rep. Ed Koch (D-NY) for 40 cosponsors, including the following new cosponsors:

Bill Green (R-NY)	Don Edwards (D-CA)

96th Congress (1979-1980)

House of Representatives Sponsors, 1979 (H.R. 2074)

Chief sponsor Rep. Ted Weiss (D-NY), with Rep. Henry Waxman (D-CA), for 56 cosponsors, including the following new cosponsors:

Martin Sabo (D-MN)	Bob Carr (D-MI)
Mike Barnes (D-MD)	Bob Duncan (D-OR)
Julian Dixon (D-CA)	Leon Panetta (D-CA)
Bob Edgar (D-PA)	Rick Nolan (D-MN)
Bill Lehman (D-FL)	Ed Roybal (D-CA)
Mickey Lehman (D-TX)	Jim Howard (D-NJ)
Mike Lowry (D-WA)	Robert Matsui (D-CA)
Jim Shannon (D-MA)	Robert Garcia (D-CA)
Jim Weaver (D-OR)	Vic Fazio (D-CA)
Sidney Yates (D-IL)	John Anderson (R-IL)
Louis Stokes (D-OH)	

Senate Sponsors, 1979 (S. 2081)

Paul Tsongas (D-MA), chief sponsor	Daniel Moynihan (D-NY)
Lowell Weicker (R-CT)	Bob Packwood (R-OR) [1980]

97th Congress (1981-1982)

House of Representatives Sponsors, 1981 (H.R. 1454)

Chief sponsors Rep. Ted Weiss (D-NY) and Rep. Henry Waxman (D-CA) for 59 cosponsors, including the following new cosponsors:

Barney Frank (D-MA)	John Seiberling (D-OH)
Tony Beilenson (D-CA)	Cecil Heftel (D-HI)
Mervyn Dymally (D-CA)	Daniel Akaka (D-HI)
Tom Foglietta (D-PA)	Bill Coyne (D-PA)
George Crockett (D-MI)	Harold Washington (D-IL)
William Brodhead (D-MI)	Chuck Schumer (D-NY)
Norman Dicks (D-WA)	Henry Reuss (D-WI)

Senate Sponsors, 1981 (S. 1708)

Paul Tsongas (D-MA), chief sponsor	Lowell Weicker (R-CT)
Alan Cranston (D-CA)	Ted Kennedy (D-MA)
Bob Packwood (R-OR)	Daniel Inouye (D-HI)
Daniel Patrick Moynihan (D-NY)	

98th Congress (1983-1984)

House of Representatives Sponsors, 1983 (H.R. 427)

Chief sponsor Rep. Ted Weiss (D-NY), with Rep. Henry Waxman (D-CA), for 38 cosponsors, including the following new cosponsors:

Robert Torricelli (D-NJ)	Barbara Mikulski (D-MD)
Barbara Boxer (D-CA)	Bob Borski (D-PA)
FoFo Sunia (D-Guam)	Bill Richardson (D-NM)
Wesley Watkins (D-OK)	Steny Hoyer (D-MD)
Bruce Morrison (D-CT)	Jim Moody (D-WI)
Howard Berman (D-CA)	Antonio Won Pat (D-Guam)
Jim Bates (D-CA)	Gary Ackerman (D-NY)

Mel Levine (D-CA)
Peter Kostmayer (D-PA)
Pete Stark (D-CA)
Gerry Sikorski (D-MN)
David Bonier (D-MI)
Alan Wheat (D-MO)
Jim Leach (R-IA)
Estabban Torres (D-CA)

Major Owens (D-NY)
Robert Kastenmeier (D-WI)
Sala Burton (D-CA)
Matthew Martinez (D-CA)
Doug Bosco (D-CA)
Morris Udall (D-IA)
Charlie Hayes (D-IL)

Senate Sponsors, 1983 (S. 430)

Paul Tsongas (D-MA), chief sponsor
Alan Cranston (D-CA)
Bob Packwood (R-OR)
Daniel Patrick Moynihan (D-NY)
Ted Kennedy (D-MA)

Daniel Inouye (D-HI)
Spark Matsunaga (D-HI)
Ernest Hollings (D-SC)
Gary Hart (D-CO)

99th Congress (1985-1986)

House of Representatives Sponsors (H.R. 230)

Chief sponsor Rep. Ted Weiss (D-NY) for 72 cosponsors, including the following new cosponsors:

Corinne (Lindy) Boggs (D-LA)
Joseph Kolter (D-PA)
Alton Waldon Jr. (D-NY)

Neil Abercrombie (D-HI)
Chester (Chet) Atkins (D-MA)

Senate Sponsors (S. 1432)

John Kerry (D-MA), chief sponsor
Alan Cranston (D-CA)
Ted Kennedy (D-MA)

Daniel Inouye (D-HI)
Daniel P. Moynihan (D-NY)
Lowell Weicker (R-CT)

100th Congress (1987-1988)

House of Representatives Sponsors, 1987 (H.R. 709)

Chief sponsor Rep. Ted Weiss (D-NY) for 73 cosponsors, including the following new cosponsors:

John Lewis (D-GA)
Peter DeFazio (D-OR)
Ken Gray (D-IL)
Albert Bustamante (D-TX)
Christopher Shays (R-CT)
Sam Gejdenson (D-CT)

Joseph Kennedy (D-MA)
Ben Cardin (D-MD)
Nancy Pelosi (D-CA)
Lane Evans (D-IL)
Bob Mrazek (D-NY)

Senate Sponsors, 1987 (S. 464)

Alan Cranston (D-CA), chief sponsor
Lowell Weicker (R-CT)
John Kerry (D-MA)
Daniel Patrick Moynihan (D-NY)
Ted Kennedy (D-MA)

Daniel Inouye (D-HI)
Brock Adams (D-WA)
Paul Simon (D-IL)
Barbara Mikulski (D-MD)
John Chafee (R-RI)

101st Congress (1989-1990)

House of Representatives Sponsors, 1989 (H.R. 655)

Chief sponsor Rep. Ted Weiss (D-NY) for 79 cosponsors, including the following new cosponsors:

Jolene Unsoeld (D-WA)
Elliot Engel (D-NY)
Tom Campbell (R-CA)
Kwesi Mfume (D-MD)

Mary Rose Oakar (D-OH)
Craig Washington (D-TX)
Jose Serrano (D-NY)
Claudine Schneider (R-RI)

Senate Sponsors, 1989 (S. 47)

Alan Cranston (D-CA), chief sponsor
John Kerry (D-MA)
Ted Kennedy (D-MA)
Daniel Moynihan (D-NY)
Claiborne Pell (D-RI)
Howard Metzenbaum (D-OH)

Barbara Mikulski (D-MD)
Daniel Akaka (D-HI)
Paul Simon (D-IL)
Daniel Inouye (D-HI)
John Chafee (R-RI)
Brock Adams (D-WA)

102nd Congress (1991-1992)

House of Representatives Sponsors, 1991 (H.R. 1430)

Chief sponsor Rep. Ted Weiss (D-NY) for 110 cosponsors, including the following new cosponsors:

Jim McDermott (D-WA)
Connie Morella (R-MD)
Nita Lowey (D-NY)
Barbara Kennelly (D-CT)
Rose DeLauro (D-CT)
John Miller (R-WA)
Louise Slaughter (D-NY)
Ed Feighan (D-OH)
Mike Kopetski (D-OR)
Bernie Sanders (D-VT)
Tom Lantos (D-CA)
George Hochbrueckner (D-NY)
Jim Moran (D-VA)
John Cox (D-IL)
Henry Gonzalez (D-TX)
Howard Pastor (D-IA)
Wayne Owens (D-UT)
Lucien Blackwell (D-PA)
Ben Nighthorse Campbell (D-CO)
William Jefferson (D-LA)

Harold Ford (D-TN)
Eleanor H. Norton (D-DC)
Patsy Mink (D-HI)
Neal Abercrombie (D-HI)
Maxine Waters (D-CA)
Tom Andrews (D-ME)
Donald Payne (D-NJ)
Robert Andrews (D-NJ)
Bruce Vento (D-MN)
Bernard Dwyer (D-NJ)
Ron Wyden (D-OR)
Jim Traficant (D-OH)
John Olver (D-MA)
Ben Jones (D-GA)
Harry Johnston (D-FL)
Nick Mavroules (D-MA)
Frank Pallone (D-NJ)
Ron Machtley (D-RI)
David Skaggs (D-CO)

Senate Sponsors, 1991 (S. 574)

Alan Cranston (D-CA), chief sponsor
John Kerry (D-MA)
Ted Kennedy (D-MA)
Daniel Patrick Moynihan (D-NY)
Daniel Inouye (D-HI)
Daniel Akaka (D-HI)
Claiborne Pell (D-RI)
John Chafee (R-RI)

Paul Simon (D-IL):
Brock Adams (D-WA)
Paul Wellstone (D-MN)
Bob Packwood (R-OR)
Patrick Leahy (D-VT)
Howard Metzenbaum (D-OH)
Harris Wofford (D-PA)
Barbara Mikulski (D-MD)

Appendix C

African-American Support for Lesbian and Gay Rights

Although a small but vocal number of black people have recently been quoted as opposing lesbian and gay civil rights and taking issue with comparisons between the two groups, the overwhelming majority of members of the Congressional Black Caucus (CBC), throughout time, have been coponsors and vigorous supporters of fairness and nondiscrimination for lesbian and gay Americans.

In addition, such noted African-American leaders as Coretta Scott King, Reverend Jesse Jackson, TransAfrica director Randall Robinson, journalist Roger Wilkens, the NAACP's Reverend Ben Chavez, as well as countless African-American mayors of major American cities have also lent their support.

State	Representative
California	Augustus Hawkins
	Mervyn Dymally
	Julian Dixon
	Ron Dellums
	Maxine Waters
	Yvonne B. Burke
Florida	Carrie Meek
	Alcee Hastings
	Corrine Brown
Georgia	John Lewis
Illinois	Harold Washington
	Charles Hayes
	Bobby Rush
	Cardiss Collins
	Mel Reynolds
Louisiana	William Jefferson
Maryland	Parren Mitchell
	Kweisi Mfume
	Albert Wynn

Michigan	Charles Diggs
	George Crockett
	John Conyers
	Barbara R. Collins
Mississippi	Bennie Thompson
Missouri	Bill Clay
	Alan Wheat
New Jersey	Donald Payne
New York	Shirley Chisholm
	Herman Badillo
	Ed Towns
	Charles Rangel
	Major Owens
North Carolina	Eva Clayton
	Mel Watt
Ohio	Louis Stokes
Pennsylvania	Robert Nix
	Bill Gray
	Lucian Blackwell
South Carolina	Jim Clyburn
Tennessee	Harold Ford
Texas	M. Leland
	C. Washington
	E. B. Johnson
District of Columbia	Walt Fauntroy
	E.H. Norton

Part IV:
Time Line and Remembrances

Stephen Robert Endean: Time Line

August 6, 1948   Born in Davenport, Iowa, to parents Marilyn and Robert Endean. The Endeans adopted a sister, Mary Ellen, as a two-month-old infant in 1963

1954-1959   Grew up in Rock Island, Illinois, through third grade and family then moved to Peoria, Illinois, where Steve attended fourth through sixth grade

1966   Graduated from Lincoln High School in Bloomington, Minnesota (a Minneapolis suburb)

1967   Attended College of St. Thomas in St. Paul, MN (living on campus) freshman year of college

1968-1972   Attended University of Minnesota (Minneapolis), majoring in Political Science

       Pledged Phi Gamma Delta (Fijis), serving in virtually every position (house manager, Carny chair, Greek Week chair

       Did legislative internships with State Rep. Rick Nolan and Rep. Pete Petrafeso

Fall 1970   Volunteered for Wendell Anderson for Governor campaign, Democratic-Farmer-Labor Party (DFL), but quit campaign shortly before the election because he feared his being gay could embarrass the campaign; Anderson won narrowly

Winter 1970   Volunteered full-time for Governor Anderson's Inaugural Committee

Winter 1971   Steve "decided to stop being gay" so he might pursue a political career and maybe even run for office, but discovered being gay isn't specific acts but a state of mind

Spring 1971   Served as Scheduling Coordinator for the Harry Davis for Mayor Campaign (Davis was the first black DFL Party nominee but lost to a right-wing police officer)

Late Spring 1971	Finally mustered courage to go to gay drop-in center and, only a short time later, became Board Chair of Gay House
Early Summer 1971	Founded Gay Rights Legislative Committee (GRLC), the first gay/lesbian political group in Minnesota
Summer 1971	Began gay rights lobbying with advocacy of state nondiscrimination bill and consenting adults legislation (repeal of sodomy and fornication statutes as they pertain to consenting adults in private) in presentation to the Joint Religious Legislative Committee. Although it resulted in a favorable impression, Catholic Church vetoed JRLC support of our agenda
Spring 1972	With well-known activists Jack Baker and Mike McConnell and several others, launched effort to get state's Democratic Party (DFL) to endorse lesbian and gay rights
Early Summer 1972	Volunteered at the Minnesota DFL (Democratic Party) State Convention, when the first lesbian and gay rights plank was adopted
Summer 1972	After supporting Hubert Humphrey for nomination, he organized picket of presidential candidate George McGovern at Twin Cities airport because of backtracking on support for gay rights
Winter 1973	Became the first gay rights lobbyist in Minnesota and one of first full-time gay rights lobbyists in the country. Both consenting adults and nondiscrimination bills passed out of the House and Senate committees
Winter 1973	Steve complements tiny movement "salary" through 1975 by working as coat check, "Well-Hung Coats by Wee-Bee" (Steve's nickname) at city's most popular gay bar, Sutton's
Winter 1974	Leads picketing against Northwestern Bell Telephone company's discrimination against gays and lesbians
Spring 1974	Lobbies enactment of amendment to Minneapolis Human Rights Ordinance to protect gay and lesbian citizens (the third major city to adopt such an ordinance)

Spring 1974	Helps win readoption of Minnesota DFL Party gay rights plank (despite new, tougher requirement of 60 percent delegate support)
Early Summer 1974	Gay Rights Legislative Committee (GRLC) becomes the Minnesota Committee for Gay Rights (MCGR). Steve becomes paid coordinator
Fall 1974	City of St. Paul adopts gay/lesbian rights ordinance, becoming fifth major city in nation with such non-discrimination law
Winter 1975	Despite protests by some activists demanding gay marriage and adoption and protection of transpersons, gay rights proposal makes it to floor of House of state legislature before homophobia kills the bill
Winter 1975	Rep. Bella Abzug (D-New York City) introduces first national lesbian and gay civil rights bill in response to constituents, but forgets to include "employment" in bill
1976	Steve becomes cochair of board of directors of National Gay Task Force (NGTF). Task Force unsuccessfully tries to win mention of gay rights in Democratic National Platform and lobbyists are actually locked out of platform hearings
Late Spring 1976	Attend founding, invitation-only meeting—called by *Advocate* owner David Goodstein—of Gay Rights National Lobby
1976	As in 1974, Steve organizes gay people to help with door-to-door campaigning for key MN Legislative candidates
1977	Despite extensive preparation, the third state lobbying effort loses close vote to last-minute phone and mail campaigns by right-wing, fundamentalist assault
1977	Works five weeks in Florida to defeat Anita Bryant's repeal of Dade County (Miami) ordinance, which unfortunately wins overwhelmingly
January-April 1978	Serves as one of leaders of unsuccessful effort to block repeal of St. Paul's lesbian and gay rights ordinance
September 13, 1978	Moves to Washington, DC, to become first lobbyist/director of Gay Rights National Lobby

Fall 1978	Announces "GRNL's New Beginning"—with new, attractive newsletter, extends members for six months while building fund-raising base. A top early commitment to national field operation to generate grassroots mail and other forms of constituent pressure
October 1979	GRNL co-coordinated (with March) National Constituent Lobby the day after 1979 March on Washington
Fall 1979	Launched "National Convention Project/Gay Vote '80" to secure Democratic Party Platform (later allowed NGTF to cosponsor to avoid conflict)
1979	Leaves Board of National Gay Task Force (NGTF)
December 1979	Convinces Senator Paul Tsongas (D-MA) to introduce first lesbian and gay rights bill in Senate
Summer 1980	Organized first congressional "field hearings" on West Coast, bringing in prominent witnesses as well as individuals speaking to the devastating impact of discrimination. GRNL had worked with Rep. Henry Waxman (D-CA) and Rep. Ted Weiss (D-NY) on "congressional briefings," which were unofficial in nature, a year or so earlier
Summer 1980	Founded Human Rights Campaign Fund (HRCF), first national gay rights PAC (political action committee)
Spring 1982	Campaign Fund undertakes first major election cycle. Tennessee Williams signs groundbreaking HRCF direct mail; Mike Farrell (B.J. Hunnicut of M*A*S*H) explains the importance of campaign fund efforts in a short video
Spring 1982	GRNL coordinates project to secure labor endorsement results in American Federation of State, County and Municipal Employees (AFSCME) national endorsement—laying a base for endorsement from entire labor movement
Spring 1982	Part of small delegation of lesbian and gay activists that meets with former Vice President Walter Mondale, the likely Democratic nominee for President
Fall 1982	Mondale keynotes HRCF's New York City Waldorf dinner, garnering publicity in *USA Today, New York Times,* and coverage on *Nightline*

Fall 1982	Raised over $125,000 in HRCF contributions to about 140 supportive congressional candidates, winning over 80 percent of races in November
1983	Based on AFSCME resolution, advocacy of openly-gay union vice president Bill Olwell and proposal by Service Employees International Union (SEIU) president John Sweeney, the entire AFL-CIO endorses nondiscrimination for gay and lesbian Americans in jobs, housing, and public accommodations
1983	Gay Rights National Lobby lobbies to win first federal funding of AIDS research, education, and prevention
Spring 1983	Conflict with and attacks by *Advocate* magazine owner David Goodstein, gay journalist Larry Bush, and former fund-raising consultant Jim Foster undercut funding and support for Gay Rights National Lobby and Human Rights Campaign Fund, leading Steve to resign from leadership. Despite support from both Boards, the repeated attacks undercut the growth and future progress of the groups' programs
Fall 1983	Finally secures support and cosponsorship of Senator Ted Kennedy (D-MA)
1984	Steve joins the staff of National Committee for Full Employment
Fall 1985	Endean returns to Gay Rights National Lobby as consultant for direct legislative advocacy. When contract ended, he ended work with GRNL because he didn't respect GRNL director, Nancy Roth
1985	Gay Rights National Lobby merges with Human Rights Campaign Fund (the surviving partner)
1986	Endean founded Fairness Fund to generate overnight constituent mail on AIDS and lesbian and gay rights and to develop other aspects of grassroots program
Fall 1987	After months of fund-raising to launch group, the focus becomes enrollment at the 2nd National March on Washington, although Fairness Fund didn't have adequate canvassing operation to take advantage of 600,000 people participating
Winter 1987	Fairness Fund merges into Human Rights Campaign Fund, becoming HRCF's field division

1988	Activated overnight Western Union mailgrams to Congress on a range of issues, but with particular emphasis on AIDS issues
January-March 1989	Tested system where people aren't billed on the phone but instead pre-paid mailgrams. Endean and Fairness Fund staffer Lee Bush tests petition canvassing for Speak Out at NAMES Project Quilt presentations in Ohio. Success led to extensive follow-up at local Pride events across the country
1990	Speak Out enrollment went from 15,000 in 1989, to over 25,000 in 1990 and eventually 150,000-200,000 participants, in every state and every district. And, despite criticism of "orchestrated mail," Speak Out has turned around congressional votes, eliminating what Endean calls "massive gap of good intentions" and addresses issues which come up at last minute
Spring 1991	Works with local political strategist on a Minnesota Pilot Project of the "National Endorsement Campaign," building support of opinion leaders
Fall 1991	Based on success of Pilot Project and the fact that he retired on disability with AIDS (tested positive in 1985), Steve initiates National Endorsement Campaign
1991	Honored by National Gay and Lesbian Health Foundation, as well as by HRCF nationally and in Minnesota
1993	Finishes writing *Bringing Lesbian and Gay Rights Into the Mainstream*
[August 4, 1993]	[Died in Washington, DC, two days short of his forty-fifth birthday, of complications from AIDS]

Congressional Tribute to Steve Endean

Martin Olav Sabo

HON. MARTIN OLAV SABO
IN THE HOUSE OF REPRESENTATIVES
MONDAY, NOVEMBER 4, 1991

Mr. Speaker, I wish today to honor one of the leaders in the fight for fairness for lesbian, gay, and bisexual Americans—Steve Endean. Steve Endean became a gay activist in my home State of Minnesota more than 20 years ago, when the organized movement for gay civil rights was in its infancy. Steve was the first lobbyist for lesbian, gay, and bisexual civil rights at the Minnesota State Capitol in St. Paul, when I was Speaker of the Minnesota House, and he was a leader in efforts to pass the Minneapolis city ordinance on gay rights.

In 1978, after working at the local level for several years, Steve Endean moved to Washington, DC, and founded the Gay Rights National Lobby, one of the first national political organizations in Washington working to outlaw discrimination on the basis of sexual orientation.

Steve Endean was a founder of the Human Rights Campaign Fund. Later he became the field director of the expanded Human Rights Campaign Fund and helped build its renowned grassroots network. Today, thanks largely to Steve Endean, the Human Rights Campaign Fund is the Nation's largest lesbian, gay and bisexual civil rights organization and one of the country's largest political action committees.

Steve Endean left the Human Rights Campaign Fund last Friday, but that will not stop his work for equal opportunity for all Americans regardless of their sexual orientation. "A lot of elected officials, even if they don't oppose fairness for lesbians and gay men, choose to duck the issue," said Endean recently to the Minnesota *Star Tribune*. "They are misjudging the prevailing winds." He cited a 1991 Penn and Schoen poll that showed over 75 percent of the respondents supported protection from job discrimination for lesbian, gay, and bisexual Americans.

Never one to rest, Steve Endean has embarked on a new campaign to ask prominent Minnesotans to support laws barring discrimination against gays, lesbians, and bisexuals. The first leaders to take this stand include

Joan Mondale, wife of the former vice president; Alan Page, an attorney and former Vikings football player; Wheelock Whitney, a former Republican gubernatorial candidate, and Beverly McKinnell, president of the League of Women Voters of Minnesota.

Steve Endean has been a pioneer in the movement to provide fair treatment for all people regardless of their sexual orientation. I am proud to recognize him today and thank him for all the good work he has done.

Tribute to Steve Endean

Robert R. Meek

In 1970, twenty-one-year-old Steve Endean's first job in politics was as a driver for Wendell Anderson, the Democratic-Farmer-Labor (DFL) Party's candidate for governor of Minnesota. People on Anderson's campaign did not know that Steve was gay. Remember that the Stonewall Riots of 1969 occurred in New York, not in Minnesota, and it was extremely rare for any gay people to be public about their sexuality. The few gay people in politics one heard about in those days were folks who were arrested (e.g., President Lyndon Johnson's aide Walter Jenkins in 1964). Fearing that his sexual orientation could be made an issue in the gubernatorial election, Steve quietly walked away from the Anderson campaign. His campaign colleagues were mystified at his absence, as Steve had been a good and valued worker. Anderson went on to win the election and Steve reappeared to help on the Inaugural as a volunteer.

Loving politics and considering a career as an elected official, Steve next decided that he had to "quit being gay." He gave nongay life a try for several months and concluded it would not work. He concluded that being gay was more than some physical acts that could be stopped or started at will, but the state of mind that permanently defined his personality. After a brief attempt at living in New York City, Steve returned to Minnesota and helped run Minneapolis's first Gay Pride festival. Steve then became Minnesota's first gay rights lobbyist in 1971, supporting his political activities by checking coats in one of Minneapolis's gay bars.

I met Steve in 1972 when he was a volunteer at the Minnesota DFL Party's State Convention in Rochester, Minnesota, and I was a young officer of the state's Democratic Party. Some three dozen young lesbians and gays clad in lavender T-shirts, supported by a strong DFL Feminist Caucus delegation, won the upset adoption of a gay rights plank in the party's platform. DFL officials were so convinced that support for gay rights would be political suicide (some critics said "DFL" would now stand for "Dopers, Fairies, and Lesbians") that they asked their legislative candidates to publicly disavow the platform, which also supported abortion rights and marijuana.

The great majority of DFL legislative candidates promptly rebuked the party platform, but despite the landslide defeat of our presidential candidate, George McGovern—McGovern even lost in Minnesota—the DFL Party won control of the legislature for the first time in its history. Party officials eventually concluded that the disavowed platform had helped in its legislative victories—the platform positions so frightened the candidates that they were forced to work their tails off.

Steve quickly became a respected force in Minnesota politics as a meticulously organized, highly affable State Capitol lobbyist, dressed in crisp white shirts and striped ties. His Gay Rights Legislative Committee helped Minnesota's two largest cities, Minneapolis and Saint Paul, adopt gay rights ordinances (protection for basic civil rights in jobs and housing) and Steve lobbied for such legislation at the state level.

I went to Washington, DC, to work for then-Senator Hubert Humphrey—the Democratic Party's pioneer of civil rights—and returned to DFL Party staff in 1977, the year Steve's third major legislative push in Minnesota lost by a narrow two votes following an avalanche of right-wing antigay mail. In 1978, fundamentalist religious groups in Saint Paul—inspired by an Anita Bryant–led repeal of Miami-Dade County's gay rights ordinance the previous year, launched a campaign to do the same in Saint Paul.

One day Steve walked into my office at the DFL headquarters and asked me to run the antirepeal campaign in Saint Paul. His case for me to take the job was that I was a good campaigner, had grown up in Saint Paul's largest suburb, and was straight. I thought Steve had lost his mind. Despite favorable poll numbers for retaining gay rights, it seemed clear to me that the repeal effort was sure to succeed as the case for gay rights had been made with the city council members but never with the voting public—particularly the portion of the public likely to vote in such a referendum.

In addition, I had spent my life avoiding being gay. I was quite religious. So although I had been privately attracted to men since I was six, I believed in God and had been taught the then-traditional notion that God hated gays. I prayed a lot, convinced that I could change. I got involved in politics at the ripe old age of ten in a school debate for Barry Goldwater for president in 1964; political activity was the one thing I liked that liked me back and I feared putting that first love in jeopardy. So I declined Steve's offer. The campaign against repeal was conducted brilliantly and, sadly, lost overwhelmingly.

That was the last I saw of Steve for ten years. I would later learn that he took the Saint Paul defeat very hard and moved to Washington, DC, to carry on the fight for gay rights at the national level. In a series of campaign and corporate jobs, I listened silently and in horror to slurs against gay people and was threatened with dismissal by a corporate supervisor who "thought" I was gay. She had fired the last guy who was gay and wasn't going to have another one.

I came out in mid-1980s and looked up Steve in Washington, DC, to get his advice on AIDS volunteer work I was doing. I took Steve to lunch. He looked successful and stronger and when I told him how much I admired him—and that I was gay—he cracked a big smile, said he was surprised, and that there were several ways I could be helping him.

I learned Steve had taken over the Gay Rights National Lobby in 1978 and founded the Human Rights Campaign Fund (now HRC, www.hrc.org) in 1980 only to be purged by then-*Advocate* publisher David Goodstein. Steve, the prototypical Midwesterner—born in Davenport, Iowa, childhood in Peoria, Illinois, and raised in Bloomington, Minnesota (then home of the Minnesota Twins and Vikings, at whose games Steve worked as a peanut vendor)—was not the LA-based Goodstein's vision of a national gay rights leader.

Convinced from his Minnesota defeats that grassroots organizing was the missing link in lesbian and gay politics, Steve next founded the Fairness Fund in 1986 to build an overnight mail capacity for fighting right-wing amendments in Congress and to urge sponsorship of lesbian and gay civil rights. Soon the Fairness Fund merged into the HRC as its field operation. As director of HRC's field operation, Steve built his Speak Out preauthorized overnight mail program from scratch to 150,000-plus participants by the early 1990s.

I also learned that Steve was HIV positive, which came up in the context of his anger over the insanity of some AIDS organizers in rejecting political organizers at their walks and quilt displays. Steve had come of age in the pre-AIDS era and prized his sexual freedom. He did not accept today's wisdom that sex is evil. He was active in Black and White Men Together (www.nabwmt.com). He enjoyed sex. Somewhere along the way, he had been infected. He hoped for a cure, keeping himself in great physical health (a good diet, working out, taking whatever medicines and vitamins that were available).

Steve's family lived in Minnesota and he visited the Twin Cities often. I was in Washington, DC, for business on a regular basis. I became Steve's outside (volunteer) consultant. We'd sit down for coffee and in four or five hours, Steve would outline the key issues he was fighting internally—PR, marketing, management—and externally, the right wing's superb grassroots organizing, closeted athletes, politicians and Hollywood stars who refused to come out, and increasing difficultly in telephone solicitation because of answering machines and hang-ups (Steve wanted organizers to break through by going door-to-door in neighborhoods with large gay and lesbian populations). His first lesson for me came when I casually referred to *gay* as a person's sexual *preference*. "Bob," he interrupted, "just when did you *choose* to be gay? The word is *orientation* and the only choice you make is whether to acknowledge it."

As his health declined, Steve came to me with two special projects. One was to do a pilot project in Minnesota of a National Endorsement Campaign in which prominent community leaders would be signed up in advance in support of gay and lesbian rights. He was convinced that advance recruitment of leading supporters could help nip right wing efforts in the bud. The second task was to help him with his memoirs, which he thought of as a cookbook of lessons from his movement career that lesbians and gays could study for examples, both the successes and the defeats. He fought with every ounce of his strength, through the retching and diarrhea of a wasting disease and hospital stays, to record his experiences for future generations of lesbian and gay activists.

Steve's happiest moment in his final year was when he returned to Minnesota in 1993 to be part of the successful lobbying push for adoption of Minnesota's Human Rights Act. He was extremely honored to be welcomed by the young organizers who led to victory the effort he had begun twenty years earlier. The last time I saw Steve was at his home in Washington, DC. We sat on his bed and talked about how difficult it was for him—as a self-proclaimed control freak—to let go of his life to the God in which he had such great faith. Steve died on August 4, 1993, at his home surrounded by family and friends. Memorial services—one in DC, one in Minneapolis—were held following Steve's death. His ashes are interred at the Metropolitan Community Church (www.mcchurch.org) in Washington, DC.

Following his death several publishers turned down Steve's memoirs. In 1999, a gifted professor of history, Vicki Eaklor of Alfred University, came to me wanting to make another effort to find a publisher. Vicki's dedication, expertise, and hard work are the reasons why Steve's memoir is now in your hands.

For me, Steve was the Hubert Humphrey and Dr. Martin Luther King of gay and lesbian rights. Like Humphrey and King, Steve was a trailblazer of the first order who could imagine and pursue a world of freedom and fairness when one did not exist. A bulldog of perseverance, Steve never quit, no matter the hurdles. Early in his Washington career, ill from overwork and at rest in his bed over his office, he was resurrected (true story) by a bell rung by an assistant every time a check arrived in response to his latest fund-raising appeal. Talk about a Wonderful Life!

Steve strongly believed that coming out is the best thing a gay person can do. Not just the best thing for the person's well-being, but for society's well-being. He loved to tell the story of a cab ride from O'Hare. The driver heard something he didn't like on the radio news, and a sports conversation with a Chicago cabbie suddenly turned into a diatribe against gay people.

Steve said, "Look, I'm your passenger and I'm gay. If you really feel this way about gay people, just stop the cab and I'll pay you here and get out on the freeway." Steve didn't know how the cab driver would react. But Steve did know three very important things. First, people often express biased views out of habit without serious thought—they hear something evil and accept it as gospel. Second, many folks have never been challenged to think about gays and lesbians as actual people—their sisters and brothers, their friends and neighbors. And third, most Americans would reject irrational prejudices and the hurtful discrimination if given the opportunity to do so, perhaps not immediately but over time. Steve believed that unconsidered opinions (you hear it, you think it) are all too common and subject to change if you can engage the person in a discussion. Such discussions would often require the courage to speak up and then listen—two qualities Steve admired greatly.

The driver paused, thought about what Steve had said, and replied that being gay was "no big deal." The enlightened cab driver then returned to a conversation about sports with Steve Endean, the football-watching, hamburger-eating, dog-owning, Georgetown Hoya's season ticket holder, team bowler, Democrat, Christian, son who loved his parents, brother who adored his sister, and gay rights leader who knew what would play in Peoria because he had lived there and shared their values.

People's choices come to define their lives and, in Steve Endean's case, for the greater good. At a young age, Steve Endean chose to work honestly and openly within the political system to change it step-by-step from one that denied and oppressed gay and lesbian citizens to one that would extend to them the civil rights promised to every American. Steve had the courage to set out to make an enormous difference in American life—and he succeeded.

Steve Endean: A Remembrance

Allan H. Spear

I first met Steve Endean in the spring of 1972 at Sutton's, a gay bar on the seedy fringe of downtown Minneapolis. He was short, squarely built, with close-cropped brown hair. Although most gay men might not consider him handsome, he had a pleasant, open face, only slightly marred by an accident that had almost killed him as a teenager. Sutton's was Steve's favorite hangout. During Minnesota's long winter season, he staffed Sutton's coat check. When he wasn't working, he was often there anyway, never drinking much, but making the rounds, checking on the latest community gossip, and, most important, letting everyone know what he was up to at city hall or the legislature and what they needed to do to help.

I was at a critical point in my life when I met Steve. I was thirty-five years old and just coming out. I had recently ended an affair with a woman and was finally ready to admit to myself and to close friends that I was gay. The usual difficulties of the coming-out process were complicated, in my case, by my political activism. I was deeply involved in Democratic Party politics (or, as we call it in Minnesota, the DFL Party) and had political ambitions. I had little idea how to reconcile this with my sexual orientation. The appearance of a cadre of openly gay activists within the DFL that spring had led me to finally emerge from the closet, but I still needed a lot of help in making the transition.

Steve said many times later on that he considered me to be his mentor. In some ways, I suppose that was true. I was eleven years older than Steve and more politically experienced; when he started lobbying the legislature, I helped him navigate the system. But I think that in even more important ways, Steve was my mentor. He taught me how to be both openly gay and successful in politics. At a time when there were precious few role models for an aspiring gay politician, Steve gently showed me how to balance my political ambitions with my sexual orientation.

Shortly after meeting Steve, I became a candidate for the Minnesota state senate and was elected in a liberal district centering on the University of Minnesota, where I taught in the history department. I did not run as an openly gay man in that first election, and when I arrived in St. Paul as a freshman legislator in January 1973, gay rights was not my top priority. But many people in the gay and lesbian community knew that I was gay and I came under increasing pressure to come out. Steve never joined in this. As a gay activist, he certainly hoped that I would come out. (I would have been the first openly gay legislator in the country if I had come out then; as it turned out, I was the second.) But he also understood that coming out is an intensely personal process, even for a public official, and that I needed to do so at my own pace. He always made me feel that he was first of all my friend and his first concern was about me; what was best for the gay movement came second.

Steve's approach is best illustrated in an incident that occurred in the summer of 1974. Even though I was not yet publicly out, I had worked with Steve and our mutual friend Larry Bye in the spring of that year to establish Minnesota's first ongoing gay political action group—the Minnesota Committee for Gay Rights—and I was becoming increasingly outspoken on gay issues. In light of that, I was asked to speak at Minnesota's fledgling Gay Pride celebration. A week before the event, I received a call from Ron Gold, the public relations director for the newly formed National Gay Task Force. Gold had heard about me and told me that if I would agree to come out at Gay Pride, NBC would cover the event for its national news program. I asked Steve what I should do. He immediately asked me what I wanted to do. I told him that I wasn't comfortable coming out that way. Without hesitation, he told me that if that was the case I shouldn't do it. Gold was unhappy with my decision and shared his disappointment with several local gay activists who upbraided me for my lack of courage. Steve was completely supportive and told me to simply wait until I was ready. Six months later I was—and I came out in my own way and on my own schedule.

For several years in the early 1970s, Steve embodied gay political activism in Minnesota. He alone was responsible for the passage of a gay and lesbian human rights ordinance in Minneapolis in the spring of 1974 and a similar ordinance in St. Paul a few months later; neither would have happened without him. A few of his friends helped, but he did most of the lobbying himself. Steve finally realized that he couldn't do it all himself, and the organization of Minnesota Committee for Gay Rights was an attempt to give him some institutional support. But he immediately became the coordinator of MCGR and continued to be the dominant figure in the movement. He had unflagging energy and indomitable determination. It is hard to realize today how difficult it was thirty years ago to give over your entire life to the struggle for gay and lesbian rights. The issue then was considered marginal and slightly silly, even by most liberals. Yet Steve never had doubt about our ultimate success, and his example converted countless people to his cause.

My friendship with Steve was closest between 1974, when I came out, and 1978, when he left Minnesota. It was during these years that Steve's energies focused in the Minnesota legislature and our efforts to pass a gay and lesbian rights bill. I was the chief Senate author of the bill in 1975 and again in 1977, and Steve was the lead lobbyist. We both thought that Minnesota would become the first state in the nation to enact gay and lesbian rights. The DFL had big majorities in both Houses of the legislature (especially in 1977) and friendly governors who would sign the bill. In 1977 we came close, but we both underestimated the strength of the religious right which was then just emerging as a force in American politics. In the end, they demonstrated their superior ability to mount a grassroots effort to influence the legislature.

Steve and I were more than political allies. We became good friends, celebrating the victories together and supporting each other after the painful defeats. Our friendship was a somewhat odd one as we were different in many ways. I was much more "highbrow" in my tastes—in food, movies, books. Going out to dinner together usually resulted in an argument as Steve inevitably wanted to go to a hamburger joint and I wanted something more elegant. Our personal lives were also very different. Steve was famously promiscuous and loved to regale me with stories of his weekend adventures at the Lawson YMCA in Chicago. I was far more reticent sexually and finally settled into a long-term monogamous relationship that is still going strong after twenty-two years. Steve was also far more focused on gay and lesbian issues than I was. As a legislator, representing a diverse constituency, I involved myself in a wide range of issues. Steve took the proper liberal positions on other issues but had trouble really getting excited about anything other than gay rights. When he decided to move to Washington, he first considered a position working on labor issues with an agency of the AFL-CIO. He ultimately realized, though, that he could not really make a full commitment to any cause outside of the gay and lesbian movement.

But what we shared transcended our differences. We were both political junkies, who simply could never get enough of politics, and we shared a common approach to politics. There are two sides to political life. The first is the process, the game of politics, which to a true addict can be every bit as exciting as the best-played football or baseball game. The second is the substance, the issues, which give politics its meaning and purpose. A politician who masters only the process is simply a hack; an idealist who cares only about the issues can never be effective. Steve and I shared the view that both the process and the issues were important and that if we were ever to succeed in making gay rights part of the political mainstream we needed to augment our commitment to the issue with a mastery of the political process.

This may seem like conventional wisdom today, but for many gay people a generation ago it was controversial. The gay rights movement grew out of both the political radicalism and the counterculture of the 1960s. For many early gay activists, efforts to understand the system and work within it smacked of selling out to the establishment. Steve was one of the pioneers who shifted the focus of the gay rights movement from radical protest to patient and painstaking efforts to achieve incremental change. He carefully learned how to lobby legislators and worked ceaselessly to gain their trust and respect. He knew that change would not come quickly or all at once, and when it didn't, he was often the subject of criticism. The more militant element within the Minnesota gay community was always ready to pounce on him. I remember when he put out a flyer asking people to come to the legislature to help lobby, but cautioning anyone that came not to dress "flamboyantly." The militants were outraged. Dressing flamboyantly, they maintained, was part and parcel of being gay; Steve was asking people to deny their identity. But Steve held his ground. If we want to be effective at the legislature, he insisted, we had to play by its ground rules.

Despite his understanding that this was going to be a long struggle, Steve became disillusioned after the repeal of the St. Paul ordinance in 1978. We knew that change would take time, but we had not been prepared for rollbacks and we had never anticipated the intensity of the backlash that would grow out of Anita Bryant's successful efforts in Florida. Steve had several reasons to leave Minnesota. Already, his sexual attraction to black men made white-bread Minnesota slim pickings for him, despite his frequent forays to Chicago, and he was burned out and needed a change of scenery. The St. Paul defeat devastated him, though: not only had one of his early achievements been undone, but the loss in St. Paul meant effectively that passage of a statewide gay and lesbian rights bill was years away. Having seen gay rights defeated by an almost two-to-one margin in one of Minnesota's most liberal cities, legislators were not likely to risk a vote for gay rights on a statewide basis. With the outlook in Minnesota grim, Steve eagerly embraced the opportunity to revive and lead the Gay Rights National Lobby.

After Steve moved to Washington, I saw less of him, but we remained good friends. He called me frequently for advice and consolation and we got together when he visited Minnesota or I went to Washington. He was always full of ideas for new approaches to what was, on the national level, even a more long-term struggle than we had once thought it would be in Minnesota. I remember most vividly the time he called to tell me about his idea to start a political action committee to endorse and finance candidates running for Congress. He told me that he was going to call it the Human Rights Campaign Fund. I asked him, "Why not the Gay Rights Campaign

Fund?" Because, he said, then the candidates that we most need to support won't take our contributions. His sense of the practical, which he had developed in Minnesota, never deserted him.

I had told Steve on many occasions that, while I admired what he was doing, I had no desire to become involved with any of the national gay organizations. I saw too much internal bickering and backbiting and wanted no part of it. But when Steve came under attack from David Goodstein, he begged me to come on the board of Gay Rights National Lobby and even, for a brief time, to serve as cochair. He insisted that he needed someone whom he trusted absolutely. I did it out of loyalty to Steve, but I hated it and was no good at it. I remember particularly one terrible weekend in Chicago where the board met at the height of Goodstein's battle to oust Steve from his positions with both GRNL and HRCF. He was constantly under siege from Goodstein's man Larry Bush, who insisted that the board meeting be open to the press. We obviously needed some privacy to consider how to handle the crisis that confronted us, but Bush was literally banging on our door all weekend. Steve survived temporarily but shortly after that decided that he needed to resign.

Coming four years after the defeat in St. Paul, Steve's loss of his positions at GRNL and HRCF was another devastating blow to him. He had after all brought GRNL back from the dead and had almost single-handedly founded HRCF. Now he was forced out for reasons that he could never fully understand. I couldn't either. Goodstein did have one legitimate point: Steve was overextended and probably should not have continued to chair both organizations, especially as HRCF evolved into a major lobbying group. Steve did have difficulty delegating responsibility and he took on too much himself, but this was no reason to force him out of both organizations. I think that there was a class component to Goodstein's hostility toward Steve. Goodstein wanted someone with more formal education and more polished style, preferably with a business background, to head the national gay organizations. Steve, with all of his organizing skills, was too rough-hewn, too plain-spoken for him. He didn't fit Goodstein's image.

Once again, Steve recovered. He came back to HRCF, he continued to be a player in the movement, and he came up with more and more creative ideas: the Fairness Fund, Speak Out, the National Endorsement Project. Steve and I came to disagree more about gay politics in the 1980s than we had earlier. I objected to Steve's exclusive focus on the Congress. I had come to believe that the best opportunity to make progress on gay and lesbian issues was at the state and local level, and I often complained to Steve that HRCF raised money at the local level but didn't contribute to state and local campaigns. Steve insisted that HRCF had to focus its resources on where it was most effective and let other organizations take on the other struggles. I also taunted Steve by telling him that I would never attend a black-tie dinner, which had become a signature fund-raising strategy for HRCF. I had never worn a tuxedo in my life, I told him, and was not about to do so now. I eventually relented, in part. I went to one of the dinners—but wore a business suit.

Still, we continued to trust and respect each other, and Steve continued to inspire me. I had been amazed by his ability to bounce back after defeat. Now I was awed by the courage he showed in the face of his struggle with AIDS. As soon as the AIDS epidemic began, Steve told me that he was almost certain that he was infected. Even without being tested, he said, he was sure that his sexual history made him the perfect candidate. Yet he never panicked. In fact, he continued to insist that the gay civil rights agenda not be totally set aside in order to concentrate exclusively on AIDS issues. "You know," he told me once while he was still healthy, "I'm probably going to die of AIDS some day, but my heart is still with the civil rights struggle. I can't just think about AIDS all of the time." After he became sick, he continued to work for the movement as much as his health would permit. He never felt sorry for himself. He told me shortly before he died: "I think that I've lived a full life. Maybe not in years, but in accomplishments. I've done most of the things I've wanted to do."

The one thing Steve most wanted to do before he died was to see the Minnesota gay rights bill pass. In early 1993, I called him and told him he should come to Minnesota if he possibly could because I thought that we could finally pass the bill and I wanted him to see it. The St. Paul ordinance had been reenacted in 1991 and this time it survived a referendum. Clearly the climate had changed since the late 1970s and it looked like we had the votes in both Houses to finally win the struggle that Steve had begun twenty years earlier. Steve never hesitated. "If that bill passes," he told me, "I can die happy." He arrived a few days before the bill was to come up for a vote and despite being seriously ill, he insisted on helping with the lobbying effort. He came to the legislature and went back to see several legislators that he had first lobbied two decades before. On the day of the vote he was deathly sick, but he sat in the gallery, first in the Senate, then in the House, to watch the bill pass. Later in the month, when the governor signed the bill, I asked for the pen that he had used and I sent it to Steve. No one deserved it more. I recently learned that when Steve died, he left the pen, in his will, to the man who now lobbies for gay rights at the Minnesota legislature. It was only a cheap ballpoint, but it had clearly been one of Steve's proudest possessions.

Steve returned to Minnesota one last time in the summer of 1993 to be grand marshal of the Minnesota Gay Pride parade. He told me then that he wouldn't live much longer and that he was making his funeral plans. There would be a service in Washington, but he also wanted one in Minnesota. Did I think anyone would come? Did anyone remember him? I assured him that many people would come, but he wasn't so sure. He told me that he had already asked Barney Frank and Troy Perry to come to Minnesota to speak at his service and that they had agreed. That way, he told me, even if people didn't know who he was they would come to hear Barney and Troy and that would ensure a big crowd. When the time came, Barney and Troy came to Minnesota and they spoke movingly about Steve, and the Metropolitan Community Church, where the service was held, was full. As I spoke to people in the crowd, I learned what I already knew. They had come for Steve. He hadn't been forgotten. With all of his achievements, he was still, until the very end, underestimating himself. He was, in retrospect, one of the giants of the gay and lesbian rights movement.

Notes

Chapter 1

1. The Stonewall riots occurred June 27-28, 1969, at the Stonewall Inn, a gay bar in Greenwich Village. That night patrons resisted and fought back when police raided the bar. Although there is disagreement over the significance of Stonewall, it remains for many an important marker, after which visibility, activism, and gay and lesbian liberation became more prominent in the ongoing movement.

2. No *Life* cover was found, but Baker and McConnell appeared in *Look* magazine on January 26, 1971.

3. The Equal Rights Amendment, prohibiting discrimination on the basis of sex, was passed by Congress and sent to the states for ratification in 1972. Despite a three-year extension beyond the 1979 deadline, only thirty-five of the required thirty-eight states had ratified it by 1982, so it never became law. It has come before Congress repeatedly since but has yet to be passed again.

4. By 2003, only thirteen states had sodomy laws. In that year, the U.S. Supreme Court decision in *Lawrence v. Texas* effectively invalidated those remaining laws.

5. The St. Paul ordinance was repealed April 25, 1978.

6. Matlovich appeared on the cover of *Time* on September 8, 1975.

Chapter 5

1. Hedrick Smith, *The Power Game* (New York: Random House, 1988), p. 251.

2. *The Washington Lobby*, Fifth Edition (Washington, DC: Congressional Quarterly, Inc., 1987), pp. 7-9.

Chapter 6

1. CLEC refers to a competitive local exchange carrier, or telephone company.

Chapter 7

1. In 1992, voters in Colorado approved Amendment 2, which prohibited protection based on sexual orientation. The U.S. Supreme Court, in *Romer v. Evans*, declared Amendment 2 unconstitutional in 1996.

2. *Minneapolis Star*, June 19, 1973.

3. Ross Perot expressed these views in an interview on ABC's *20/20*, May 29, 1992. See http://www.qrd.org/qrd/orgs/NGLTF/1992/perot.meet-6.10.92 and http://

www.issues2002.org/Celeb/Ross_Perot_Families_+_Children.htm.

4. In 1992, Cracker Barrel added sexual orientation to its written nondiscrimination policy.

5. Michael Hardwick was arrested under Georgia's sodomy law in 1982. Although charges against him were dropped, Hardwick participated in a suit to test the legality of the law. When Hardwick won that suit Georgia appealed the ruling to the Supreme Court in the case *Bowers v. Hardwick*, and in 1986 the Court upheld Georgia's sodomy law as applied to homosexuals.

Chapter 8

1. *The Washington Post*, December 8, 1992, p. A11.

2. Bill S. 157, mentioned with no text included, in *Congressional Record*, Vol. 127, Part 1 (January 19, 1981), p. 464.

3. *Congressional Record*, July 29, 1982, p. E3576.

4. "Letter from the Dutch Parliament to the American Congress," January 1980.

Chapter 11

1. *Congressional Record*, Vol. 127, Part 1 (January 20, 1981), p. 538.

2. See Note 1 in Chapter 7.

Chapter 14

1. "Protecting against IR extremism," *Minneapolis Star Tribune*, October 1, 1991, p. 12A.

Index

Page numbers followed by the letter "i" indicate illustrations.